English Language Arts

Lesson Guide

5

Book Staff and Contributors

Kristen Kinney-Haines   *Director, English Language Arts*
Amy Rauen   *Director, Instructional Design*
Mary Beck Desmond   *Senior Text Editor*
Allyson Jacob   *Text Editor*
Tricia Battipede   *Senior Creative Manager*
Julie Jankowski   *Senior Visual Designer*
Caitlin Gildrien   *Visual Designer*
Sheila Smith   *Print Designer*
Tricia Battipede, Mike Bohman, Shannon Palmer   *Cover Designers*
Robyn Campbell, Heather Evans, Alane Gernon-Paulsen, Tara Gleason, Tim Mansfield, Melisa Rice,
     Tisha Ruibal   *Writers*
Amy Eward   *Content Specialist; Senior Manager, Writers and Editors*
Dan Smith   *Senior Project Manager*

Doug McCollum   *Senior Vice President, Product Development*
Kristin Morrison   *Vice President, Design, Creative, and User Experience*
Rohit Lakhani   *Vice President, Program Management and Operations*
Kelly Engel   *Senior Director, Curriculum*
Christopher Frescholtz   *Senior Director, Program Management*
Erica Castle   *Director, Creative Services*
Lisa Dimaio Iekel   *Senior Production Manager*

Illustrations Credits

All illustrations © K12 unless otherwise noted
Characters: Tommy DiGiovanni, Matt Fedor, Ben Gamache, Shannon Palmer
Cover: Spiral © Silmen/iStock; Polygon © LPETTET/iStock
Program Overview: Courtesy of ABDO Publishing

About K12 Inc.
K12 Inc. (NYSE: LRN) drives innovation and advances the quality of education by delivering state-of-the-art digital learning platforms and technology to students and school districts around the world. K12 is a company of educators offering its online and blended curriculum to charter schools, public school districts, private schools, and directly to families. More information can be found at K12.com.

ISBN: 978-1-60153-576-4

Printed by Walsworth, Marceline, MO, USA, April 2019

Table of Contents

A Wonder of the World

A Wrinkle in Time

Finding Their Way

Moments in History

Persuasion and Opinion

Get to Know a Supreme Court Justice

Inside Out and Back Again

Choice Reading Project

Money

The Adventures of Sherlock Holmes

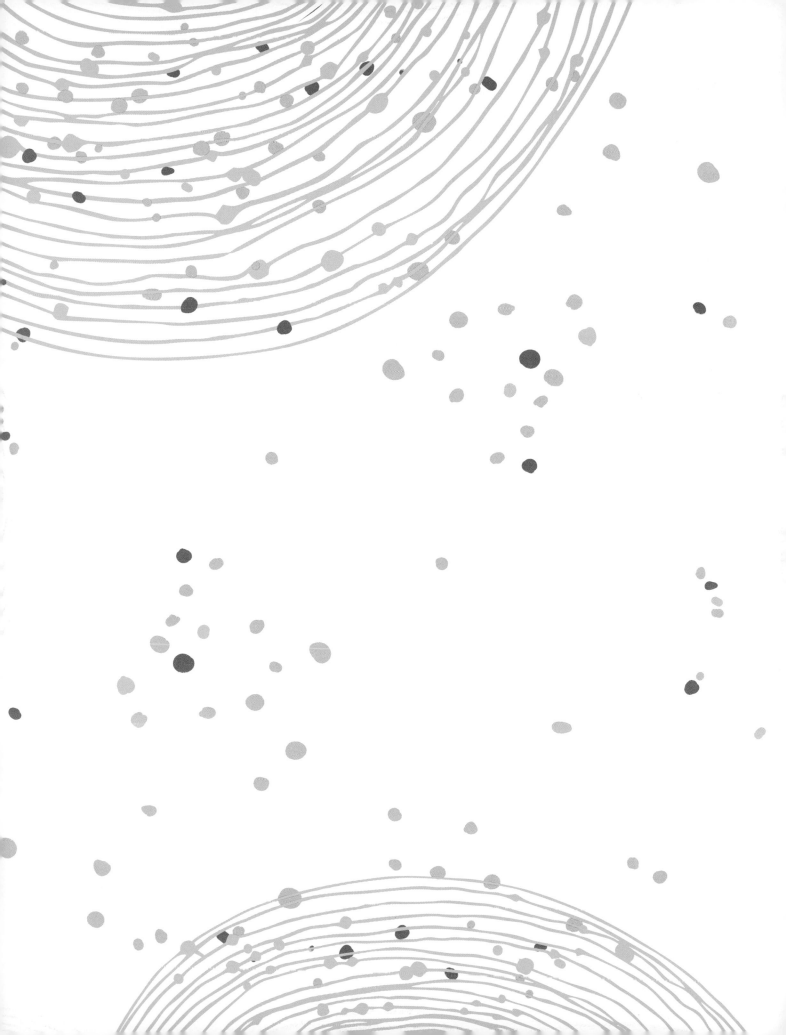

K12 Summit English Language Arts 5 Overview

Welcome to Summit English Language Arts 5. We are grateful for this opportunity to play a role in the English language arts education of your students. We offer this overview of the content and structure of the course as part of our effort to help you best support them. At any time, if you have questions or would like further clarification, please reach out to us. Let's begin.

Summit English Language Arts 5 encourages students to learn independently. As a Learning Coach, your role is to support and enhance the learning experience. Each lesson includes rich interactivity to ensure that students build the depth of understanding they need to succeed on state assessments. Online interactions provide a wealth of data, so teachers know exactly where students are struggling. Offline practice, during which students write directly in an activity book, offers variety. With rich content that engages and motivates students, and enough practice to reinforce each concept, this course includes the tools and technology that students need to succeed.

Course Components

Online Lessons

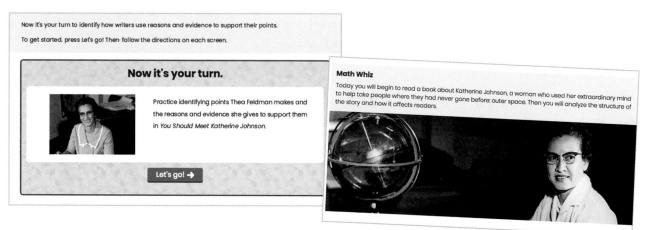

The online lessons make up the core instruction and multiple opportunities for practice in Summit ELA 5. These lessons include

- Instruction in reading, writing, word study, and spelling in a predictable lesson structure

- Interactive activities and assessments that challenge students to use higher-order thinking skills

- A carefully thought-out progression from guided to independent practice

- Computer-scored practice with instant and meaningful feedback

- Learning experiences that support struggling students

- Independent practice using Stride, an adaptive tool that offers individualized practice based on specific need

- Student-friendly learning goals

- Engaging games to review and practice skills

- Access to Big Universe, a digital library of thousands of fiction and nonfiction texts

Rich offline print materials support learning with ample opportunity for students to demonstrate mastery of concepts taught online. Contemporary literature, timely and engaging nonfiction, and a digital library give readers a variety of reading experiences.

Lesson Guide

The lesson guide that accompanies the course makes it quick and easy for Learning Coaches to understand each lesson at a glance—without logging in. The lesson guide provides an overview of a lesson's content, activities, and materials; answer keys for activity book pages; alerts when special Learning Coach attention is needed; and other features to aid the Learning Coach in supporting students.

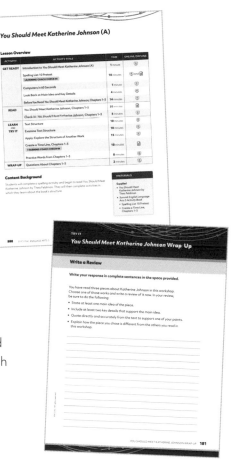

Activity Book

Summit ELA 5 includes an activity book where students can put pencil to paper every instructional day. Key activity book features:

- Full color pages with sufficient space for students' answers

- Activities that require students to write explanations, analyze and reflect on readings through extended responses, and work through the writing process from brainstorming to publishing

- Custom drafting paper with built-in space for revising

- Spelling Pretest pages that double as study aids

- Spelling Activity Bank pages that offer students choice in how to practice their Spelling words

- A glossary of keywords from the course

Reading Materials

Summit ELA 5 offers students diverse perspectives through both classic and contemporary fiction and nonfiction texts. Print and digital formats are offered. The following materials are included.

Expeditions in Reading: Fiction and nonfiction readings are brought to life through full-color illustrations and photographs. Select words and phrases are defined to support comprehension. While this collection is provided in both print and digital formats, K12 recommends that students read the print format whenever possible and use the digital format on those occasions when learning may need to take place on the go. Research continues to show that students are better able to comprehend their reading when holding a book in their hands.

Trade books: Students receive printed copies of contemporary, high-quality trade books that span genres from traditional chapter books to graphic novels.

Nonfiction magazines: A full-color magazine, in both print and digital formats, is included with the course and focuses on high-interest topics while teaching students important skills for comprehending a wide variety of text features.

Big Universe: Access to Big Universe, a leveled e-book library, is built into the course. In Big Universe students have at their fingertips over 14,000 fiction and nonfiction texts from more than forty publishers on countless topics.

Course Structure

Summit ELA 5 uses a well-balanced approach to literacy that connects reading, writing, grammar, vocabulary, and spelling into one integrated course. Dedicated time for keyboarding practice is also included. The course is designed to lead students through concepts based on current state and national academic standards. The material is structured to fit a typical 180-day school year, but it can also be easily adapted to fit individual needs.

Summit ELA 5 is divided into **units**. Units are divided into a series of **workshops**, which are in turn divided into **daily lessons**. Each unit contains workshops, and a workshop centers on a major focus (reading, writing, or word study) and also includes spelling practice. Each workshop ends with time dedicated to review and a quiz or graded writing assignment. A separate **Big Ideas** lesson synthesizes the course content and occurs at the end of each unit.

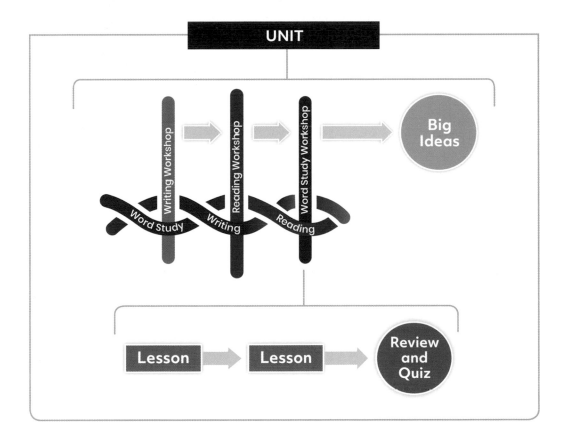

Lesson Model Overview

Reading and writing workshops in Summit ELA 5 follow a multiday learning cycle, consisting of an initial lesson, one or more middle lessons, and a final lesson. Word study workshops, however, are each made up of one lesson only. Regardless of length, each workshop follows a consistent, predictable instructional formula.

GET READY

Get Ready activities introduce and orient students to the lesson content. Spelling activities are also located in the Get Ready section.

LEARN AND TRY IT

Learn and Try It activities include one or more cycles of bite-size instruction coupled with guided practice, followed by opportunities to apply new skills. Reading workshops also contain a Read section, in which students read from the workshop text and answer comprehension questions.

WRAP-UP

Wrap-Up activities include one or two ungraded questions that serve to gauge students' understanding as they exit the lesson. These activities may also include independent practice in Stride, independent reading, and keyboarding practice. On the final day of each workshop, the Wrap-Up section is preceded by a graded quiz or graded written assignment.

Initial and Middle Days   During the initial and middle days, students learn, practice, and apply the core content.

As students work through these lessons, they are asked to work more and more independently. They progress from explicit instruction, through guided practice, to independent practice and application.

Final Day   In reading, word study, and writing skills workshops, the final day of the workshop includes a computer-graded quiz based on the workshop's key objectives. Activities in those lessons prepare students for the quiz. In Planning and Drafting, and Revising and Publishing writing workshops, the final day includes a submitted writing assignment—either students' written drafts or their final published writing pieces.

		INITIAL DAY	MIDDLE DAYS	FINAL DAY
READING WORKSHOP	**GET READY**	Lesson Introduction	Lesson Introduction	Lesson Introduction
		Spelling	Spelling	
		60-Second English	Recall	
		Look Back	Before You Read	
		Before You Read		
	READ	Read	Read	
		Check-In	Check-In	
	LEARN AND TRY IT	**LEARN**	**LEARN**	**TRY IT** Activity Book
		TRY IT Guided	**TRY IT** Guided	Read and Record
		TRY IT Apply	**TRY IT** Apply	Review
		TRY IT Activity Book	**TRY IT** Activity Book	
		TRY IT Vocabulary	**TRY IT** Vocabulary	
	QUIZ			Reading Quiz
				Spelling Quiz
	WRAP-UP	Formative Assessment	Formative Assessment	Keyboarding
				Stride
WRITING SKILLS WORKSHOP	**GET READY**	Lesson Introduction	Lesson Introduction	Lesson Introduction
		Spelling	Spelling	
		Look Back		
	LEARN AND TRY IT	**LEARN** Grammar, Usage, and Mechanics	**LEARN** Grammar, Usage, and Mechanics	**TRY IT** Activity Book
		TRY IT Grammar, Usage, and Mechanics	**TRY IT** Grammar, Usage, and Mechanics	**Review:** Grammar, Usage, and Mechanics
		LEARN Writing Skills	**LEARN** Writing Skills	
		TRY IT Writing Skills	**TRY IT** Writing Skills	
		TRY IT Activity Book	**TRY IT** Activity Book	
	QUIZ			Writing & Grammar, Usage, and Mechanics Quiz
				Spelling Quiz
	WRAP-UP	Formative Assessment	Formative Assessment	Keyboarding
		Go Read!	Go Read!	Stride

		INITIAL DAY	MIDDLE DAYS	FINAL DAY
PLANNING AND DRAFTING WORKSHOP	**GET READY**	Lesson Introduction	Lesson Introduction	Lesson Introduction
		Spelling	Spelling	
		Look Back		
	LEARN AND TRY IT	**LEARN** Grammar, Usage, and Mechanics	**LEARN** Grammar, Usage, and Mechanics	**Review:** Grammar, Usage, and Mechanics
		TRY IT Grammar, Usage, and Mechanics	**TRY IT** Grammar, Usage, and Mechanics	
		LEARN Writing Skills	**LEARN** Writing Skills	
		TRY IT Writing Skills	**TRY IT** Activity Book	
		TRY IT Activity Book		
	QUIZ			Grammar, Usage, and Mechanics Quiz
				Spelling Quiz
				Submit Draft
	WRAP-UP	Formative Assessment	Formative Assessment	Keyboarding
			Go Read!	Stride
REVISING AND PUBLISHING WORKSHOP	**GET READY**	Lesson Introduction	Lesson Introduction	Lesson Introduction
		Look Back	Look Back	
	LEARN AND TRY IT	**LEARN** Writing Skills	**LEARN** Writing Skills	**LEARN** Writing Skills
		TRY IT Activity Book	**TRY IT** Activity Book	**TRY IT** Writing Skills
	QUIZ			Submit Published Writing
	WRAP-UP	Formative Assessment	Formative Assessment	Keyboarding
		Go Read!	Go Read!	Stride

WORD STUDY WORKSHOP		SINGLE LESSON DAY
	GET READY	Lesson Introduction
		Look Back
	LEARN AND **TRY IT**	**LEARN**
		TRY IT Guided
		TRY IT Activity Book
		Go Write!
		Review
	QUIZ	Word Study Quiz
	WRAP-UP	Keyboarding
		Stride
		Go Read!

Activity Descriptions

This table describes each activity type in Summit ELA 5.

GET READY	Description
Unit Overview	The Unit Overview briefly introduces students to the content that will be covered in the unit.
Lesson Introduction	The Lesson Introduction introduces the content of each lesson within an engaging context. It also presents the objectives as student-friendly goals, defines new keywords that students will encounter in the lesson, and lists the key state standards covered in the lesson.
Spelling	Spelling activities include pretests, offline practice in the activity book, online practice activities or games, and graded quizzes.
60-Second English	The 60-Second English activities get students excited about upcoming content and prompt curiosity.
Before You Read	Before You Read activities introduce vocabulary from the reading by way of online flashcards, provide background information to set context for the upcoming reading, and ask guiding questions to help students set a purpose for reading.
Recall	Recall activities prepare students to continue reading by refreshing their knowledge of what they read in the previous lesson.
Look Back	Look Back activities provide a quick review of the prerequisite skills that are essential to understanding the new content. Students who struggle with the Look Back should seek additional help before proceeding.

LEARN AND TRY IT	Description
Read	Read activities direct students to complete an independent reading assignment.
Check-In	Check-In activities evaluate students' basic comprehension of what they just read. These activities are not graded, but results are visible to the teacher.
Learn	Learn activities are direct instruction. The format of this instruction varies, including guided exploration of a text or writing sample with narrated animation, or video featuring an expert teacher and interactive questions.
Try It	Learn activities are followed by a series of Try It activities. Try It activities differ depending on topic and specific purpose, but all share the purpose of allowing students to practice and apply what they've learned.
Read and Record	Read and Record activities allow students to practice reading fluently. Students record themselves reading text aloud, listen to their recording, and evaluate their reading using a fluency checklist.
Review	Students review the workshop content either by answering questions or playing a game, after which they take a graded quiz.
Go Write!	Go Write! activities provide dedicated time for freewriting.

WRAP-UP	Description
Formative Assessment	Formative assessments are those activities with "Questions About" in the activity title. These include 1–2 ungraded questions that gauge students' understanding at the end of the lesson. Although the questions are ungraded, the results are available to teachers.
Quiz	Final days of workshops include graded online quizzes, and/or graded writing assignments that students must submit.
Keyboarding	A Keyboarding activity at the end of each workshop provides dedicated time for keyboarding practice using a keyboarding program of choice.
Stride	Additional independent practice with ELA concepts is provided in Stride.
Go Read!	Go Read! activities allow for free reading time at the end of Writing and Word Study workshops.

A Balance of Online and Offline Time

Summit ELA 5 online activities make up about 60 percent of core lesson time. Equally critical to learning is that students spend time reading (for both instruction and pleasure), and put pencil to paper. Summit ELA 5 incorporates daily reading, and offline activities in a predictable place in each lesson sequence. After completing online practice in which instant feedback can help to address any misunderstandings, students complete an activity in their activity book or continue to work on a longer writing assignment.

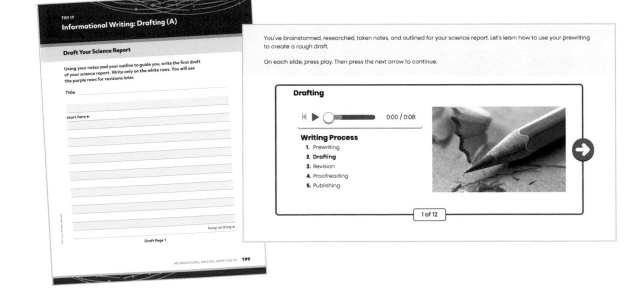

Special Features

In addition to the standard units and lessons, Summit ELA 5 has these special features.

Big Ideas Lessons

A Big Ideas lesson occurs at the end of each unit. In these lessons, students keep their skills fresh by reviewing prior content, practice answering the types of questions they will encounter on state assessments, and complete an assignment that allows them to connect and apply what they have learned. Note that some of these assignments are graded assessments.

Choice Reading Projects

Summit ELA 5 contains one Choice Reading Project unit. In this unit, students encounter a unique reading workshop designed to build their comprehension and critical-thinking skills as they read a work or works of their choice and complete a related project. Research indicates that opportunities for choice enhance student performance and motivate readers.

Students will select a project and corresponding book or books from a bank of options. All but one of the projects will require you to acquire a book on your own. The remaining project option will use a book or books available in Big Universe. To help students make a choice, the online lessons include synopses of the books and descriptions of the related projects. Review the options with students well enough in advance so that, if selecting a project whose related reading is not in Big Universe, you can acquire the necessary book in time for students to begin the unit.

Embedded Keyboarding Practice

On Your Choice days and on the final day of each workshop, students will practice their keyboarding skills using an external website or program. You will need to work with students to select an appropriate keyboarding practice website or program; K12 does not specify which resource to use. A few suggestions are provided in the online activity, including a program that is navigable by keyboard and screen-reader accessible. Depending on which program is chosen, students may need to set up an account to save their progress. You should assist with this, if needed.

Assessment Overview

To ensure that students can show what they have learned and to support high academic outcomes, students need exposure to the types of questions they will see on state assessments.

Online Interactive Questions

Online interactive questions, similar in style and format to today's digital state assessments, provide powerful opportunities for students to demonstrate deep understanding. For this reason, a variety of online question types, including drag-and-drop and fill-in-the-blank, are used throughout Summit ELA 5.

Correctly fill in the blank.

I wouldn't have believed that a dog could surf, but I was at the beach this summer and I saw a collie catch a wave _____. It was one of the most incredible things I've ever witnessed.

| dedicated | segregation | firsthand |

Check Answer

← 1 2 3 →

Which word or phrase **best** completes the passage?

I was just waking up when I heard the [Choose...] of little feet outside in the hallway. Then came the gentle taps on my door and more so [shuffling] behind it, and I knew my youngest cousins had arrived.

Choose...
whoosh
slurp
squelch
pitter patter

Check Answer

← 1 2 3 4 5 6 7 8 9 →

Graded Assessments

Summit ELA 5 includes both online computer-scored quizzes and teacher-graded assignments.

Assessment Type	How Many?
Workshop Quizzes	45
Spelling Quizzes	28
Writing Assignments - Drafts	4
Writing Assignments - Published	4
Big-Ideas: Mini-Projects	4
Big Ideas: Critical Skills Assignments	4
Big Ideas: Responses to Prompts	4
Choice Reading Project	1
Mid-Year Assessment	1
End-of-Year Assessment	1

Instructional Approach: Reading Workshops

Close Reading and Textual Analysis

Summit ELA 5 uses a close-reading approach: students read first for comprehension and then reread to support further study of texts. Research shows that students who participate in repeated readings of instructional-level texts demonstrate better outcomes.

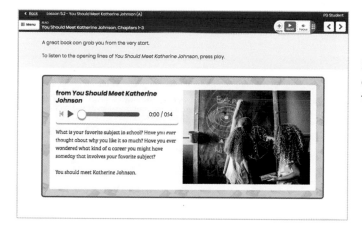

Students are first introduced to a reading selection by listening to a brief reading from it.

Students then spend dedicated time reading independently.

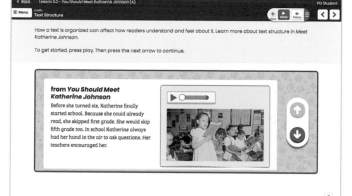

In the Learn activity, students engage in guided analysis of the text.

A Mix of Contemporary and Classic Literature and Engaging Informational Texts

The reading workshops engage students in works of literature and nonfiction texts from various genres. Fiction selections range from the classic to the contemporary, with slight twists to keep the reader's interest piqued: well-loved classics from Arthur Conan Doyle are given new life in the shape of a graphic novel and drama, and contemporary award-winning novels—including a novel-length narrative poem—provide fifth grade students with a solid foundation in fiction. Biographies, narrative nonfiction, magazine articles, interviews, government documents, and opinion pieces make up a well-rounded nonfiction experience for the student reader.

Reading List

TITLE	AUTHOR	DELIVERY	GENRE
A Ride in the Night	from *Will Clark, Boy Adventurer* by Katharine E. Wilkie	*Expeditions in Reading*	narrative nonfiction
A Wrinkle in Time	Madeleine L'Engle	trade book	fiction, novel
Caleb's Story	Patricia McLachlan	trade book	fiction, novel
The Most Famous Woman in the World	from *Clara Barton: Founder of the American Red Cross* by Augustus Stevenson	*Expeditions in Reading*	narrative nonfiction
Hidden Figures	Margot Lee Shetterly	trade book	nonfiction
Katherine Johnson Biography	Margot Lee Shetterly	*Expeditions in Reading*	nonfiction, biography
Mathematician Katherine Johnson at Work	Sarah Loff	*Expeditions in Reading*	nonfiction, biography
Mary Jackson Biography	Margot Lee Shetterly	*Expeditions in Reading*	nonfiction, biography
Dorothy Vaughan Biography	Margot Lee Shetterly	*Expeditions in Reading*	nonfiction, biography
NASA Langley's Modern Figures Reflect on *Hidden Figures*	Eric Gillard	*Expeditions in Reading*	nonfiction
Inside Out and Back Again	Thanhha Lai	trade book	narrative poetry
Make Your Own Microscope	K12	*Expeditions in Reading*	nonfiction, biography
The Adventure of the Blue Carbuncle	Sir Arthur Conan Doyle	*Expeditions in Reading*	fiction, mystery
The Adventure of the Red-Headed League	Sir Arthur Conan Doyle	*Expeditions in Reading*	fiction, mystery
Mesmerized: How Ben Franklin Solved a Mystery that Baffled all of France	Mara Rockliff	trade book	narrative nonfiction
Queen of the Falls	Chris Van Allsburg	trade book	narrative nonfiction
Run, Kate Shelley, Run	Julia Pferdehirt	*Expeditions in Reading*	narrative nonfiction

Reading List (continued)

TITLE	AUTHOR	DELIVERY	GENRE
Sarah, Plain and Tall	Patricia McLachlan	tradebook	fiction, novel
The Adventure of the Three Students	K12	*Expeditions in Reading*	drama
Solar Power for Public Buildings	K12	*Expeditions in Reading*	nonfiction, opinion
Solar Powered Public Buildings? Not So Fast, California!	K12	*Expeditions in Reading*	nonfiction, opinion
Opening Statement to the Senate Judiciary Committee	Sonia Sotomayor	*Expeditions in Reading*	nonfiction
Stick to Real Microscopes	K12	*Expeditions in Reading*	nonfiction, opinion
The Adventure of the Six Napoleons	Vincent Goodwin	trade book	graphic novel
The Mary Celeste: An Unsolved Mystery from History	Jane Yolen	trade book	narrative nonfiction
Where Is Niagara Falls?	Megan Stine	trade book	nonfiction
Who Is Sonia Sotomayor?	Megan Stine	trade book	nonfiction, biography
You Should Meet Katherine Johnson	Thea Feldman	trade book	nonfiction, biography
Young Frederick Douglass: The Slave Who Learned to Read	Linda Walvoord Girard	*Expeditions in Reading*	nonfiction
From Barter to Bitcoin: A History of Money	K12	nonfiction magazine	nonfiction
Making Money	K12	nonfiction magazine	nonfiction
The Future of Money	K12	nonfiction magazine	nonfiction
The Value of Money	K12	nonfiction magazine	nonfiction

Instructional Approach: Writing Workshops

A Balance of Explicit Instruction and Authentic Writing Experiences

Summit ELA 5 writing workshops prepare students to express themselves as educated people in the twenty-first century. Students analyze model writing samples and then work through the writing process to develop original compositions of their own. An emphasis on thoughtful planning takes the fear out of writing as students learn tangible strategies to make the process manageable. Grammar, usage, and mechanics activities focus on grammatical terms, sentence construction, recognizing and fixing errors, punctuation, and using precise language. Students practice these skills in editing activities and apply them to their own writing assignments.

An Organized Approach to Teaching Process

Students will complete four major assignments by following the writing process: prewriting, drafting, revising, proofreading, and publishing. Assignments include a personal narrative, a science report, an editorial, and a history presentation. Each assignment is completed over a series of two workshops, with both the rough draft and the final work submitted to the teacher. Additional writing skills workshops break down the skills needed using model writing samples and short writing assignments.

Research skills, including how to do research online ethically and effectively, are an integral part of the writing workshops. Students will conduct and incorporate research into their informational, opinion, and presentation writing.

UNITS 1-3	UNITS 4-6	UNITS 7-9	UNITS 10-12
NARRATIVE	**INFORMATIONAL**	**OPINION**	**PRESENTATION**
Writing Skills	Writing Skills	Writing Skills	Writing Skills
Plan and Draft	Plan and Draft	Plan and Draft	Plan and Draft
Revise and Publish	Revise and Publish	Revise and Publish	Revise and Publish

Instructional Approach: Word Study Workshops

A Focus on Words and Strategies

Word study workshops expose students to a wide variety of vocabulary words, which in turn helps them with reading comprehension and writing. In each word study workshop, students are taught a set of vocabulary words and definitions while also learning about word relationships and using context clues to figure out unfamiliar words. Students look at synonyms, antonyms, and etymology to expand on the core word set. Workshop topics run from understanding nuance and shades of meaning to using Greek and Latin roots and affixes to determine word meanings. Several workshops are dedicated to figurative language and homonyms, providing a thorough word study experience that helps grow students' speaking, reading, listening, and writing vocabularies.

Instructional Approach: Spelling

A Focus on Patterns

In Summit ELA 5 students learn to spell words quickly by studying spelling patterns that are common to many words. Throughout the word lists, students develop an understanding of sound-symbol relationships and spelling patterns, identify affixes and how they affect the meaning of words, and recognize base words and roots in related words.

However, some words do not follow conventional spelling patterns. Spelling lists in Summit ELA 5 include words that follow the spelling pattern being studied, as well as "Heart Words" (words we must learn to spell by heart).

Repetition, Variety, and Choice

In nearly all lessons, students are given opportunities to practice and master the spelling words. Each spelling list begins with a pretest, showing which words the student may already know and which require more practice. Pretests are followed by offline practice in which students complete an activity of their choice from a supplied bank. From there, students continue with online practice and a review game before wrapping up the spelling cycle with a graded quiz.

Individualized Learning

Summit ELA 5 is designed to help all students succeed.

Branching Pathways Particularly difficult concepts include practice with branching pathways for struggling students. These interactions are designed to uncover misconceptions and common errors to create a "tighter net" that catches struggling students at the point of instruction. Students receive feedback targeted to their individual responses and are then led through a reteaching activity that corrects the misconception or common error, if they need it.

Stride An engaging teaching tool that motivates students toward mastery and rewards learning with games, Stride offers students individualized practice. Following each workshop's quiz, students will practice related concepts based on their specific needs. Time to use Stride is integrated right into the course to ensure sufficient independent practice time.

Stride's adaptive technology guides students to practice where they need it most—and then serves up a variety of content that is lively and engaging. Stride's vast database of questions, video lessons, and printable resources delivers grade-level appropriate content aligned to the rigor of the Common Core and individual state standards. Stride's assessments identify where students are performing on specific grade-level standards throughout the year and help identify critical foundational gaps missed in prior grade levels. Test prep capabilities pinpoint student strengths and weaknesses for improved student outcomes on end-of-year assessments.

The Help Me Button Located on the lesson menu, this is an additional personalization feature that lets students opt into activities that are dynamically chosen based on the concept they are studying. Recommendations are powered by a sophisticated engine designed to serve up the activities most likely to be effective for the individual student.

How to Use This Guide

This lesson guide contains information that will be helpful to you as you begin Summit English Language Arts 5 and daily as you work through the program. Here is what the lesson guide contains and how to use it.

Lesson Title

The lesson title indicates the lesson topic and matches the title you will see in the online course.

Learning Coach Check-In

This label indicates that your participation is particularly important for the activity it appears in. A description of how to support your student is included with the specific activity in the Activities section of the lesson guide.

Content Background

This information will help you better understand the content students will be learning.

Synopsis

In reading lessons, this section gives a brief summary of the reading selection.

Lesson Goals

The goals indicate what students will do in the lesson.

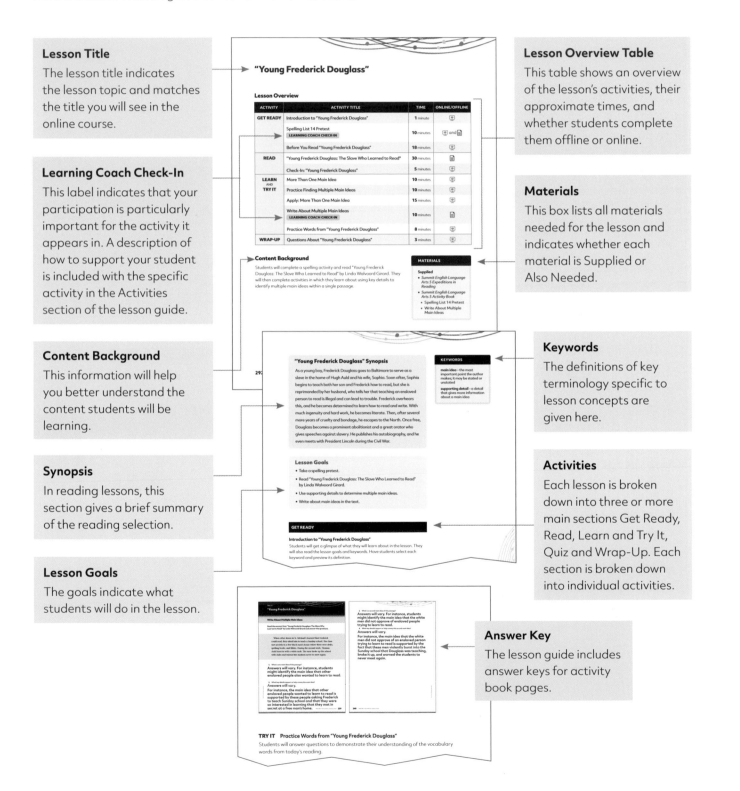

Lesson Overview Table

This table shows an overview of the lesson's activities, their approximate times, and whether students complete them offline or online.

Materials

This box lists all materials needed for the lesson and indicates whether each material is Supplied or Also Needed.

Keywords

The definitions of key terminology specific to lesson concepts are given here.

Activities

Each lesson is broken down into three or more main sections Get Ready, Read, Learn and Try It, Quiz and Wrap-Up. Each section is broken down into individual activities.

Answer Key

The lesson guide includes answer keys for activity book pages.

Lessons with Graded Assessments

Check in with students when a lesson has a graded assessment.

- The final lesson of every workshop has a computer-scored quiz. Check to make sure students have completed and submitted this quiz.

- Teacher-graded assignments appear throughout the course. You may need to help students submit these assignments to their teacher. Discuss with the teacher the best method of turning in students' work.

Remember

Academic support at home is critical to student success. While Summit ELA 5 empowers students to work independently, this guide is designed help you support your students each day to help them maximize their learning.

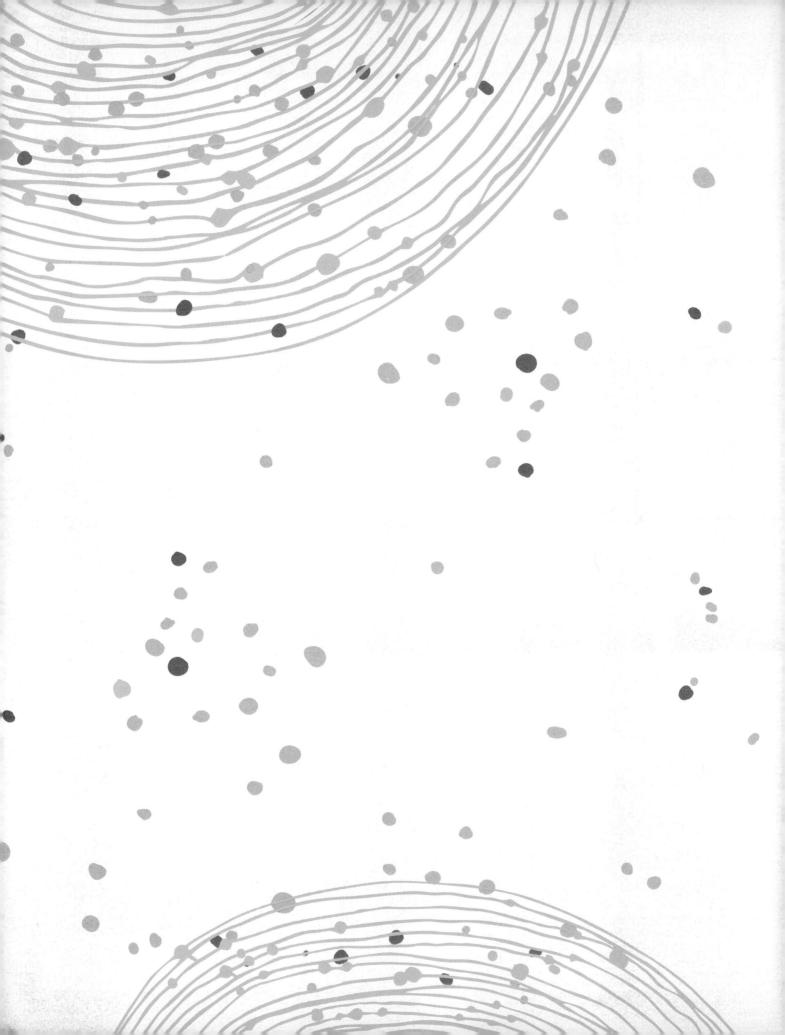

Author Study

Author Study (A)

Lesson Overview

ACTIVITY	ACTIVITY TITLE	TIME	ONLINE/OFFLINE
GET READY	Author Study Unit Overview	**1** minute	🖥
	Introduction to Author Study (A)	**1** minute	🖥
	Spelling List 1 Pretest **LEARNING COACH CHECK-IN**	**10** minutes	🖥 and 📄
	Patricia MacLachlan's Stories in 60 Seconds	**1** minute	🖥
	Look Back at Reading Strategies	**5** minutes	🖥
	Before You Read *Sarah, Plain and Tall*, Chapters 1–3	**14** minutes	🖥
READ	*Sarah, Plain and Tall*, Chapters 1–3	**30** minutes	📄
	Check-In: *Sarah, Plain and Tall*, Chapters 1–3	**5** minutes	🖥
LEARN AND **TRY IT**	Narrator's Point of View in *Sarah, Plain and Tall*	**10** minutes	🖥
	Anna's Point of View	**10** minutes	🖥
	Apply: Point of View	**15** minutes	🖥
	Write About Point of View and Theme **LEARNING COACH CHECK-IN**	**10** minutes	📄
	Practice Words from *Sarah, Plain and Tall*, Chapters 1–3	**6** minutes	🖥
WRAP-UP	Questions About *Sarah, Plain and Tall*, Chapters 1–3	**2** minutes	🖥

Content Background

Students will begin reading *Sarah, Plain and Tall*, a novel by Patricia MacLachlan. They will learn about themes, making inferences , and the effect of narrative point of view on a text.

Themes, the big ideas that authors convey in a text, emerge and develop over the course of a story. To identify and interpret a theme, good readers pay attention to what the characters in a story say and do. Themes are not single words; they are complete thoughts or statements.

Theme: Love is more important than money.

Not a theme: love

> ### MATERIALS
>
> **Supplied**
> - *Sarah, Plain and Tall* by Patricia MacLachlan
> - *Summit English Language Arts 5 Activity Book*
>   - Spelling List 1 Pretest
>   - Write About Point of View and Theme

Making inferences, or drawing conclusions from a text, is a crucial reading skill. Not everything in a story is directly stated or spelled out. Instead, readers must notice and make sense of textual evidence.

> **Textual evidence:** A character eats more than his share of pizza and refuses to let others play with his toys.

> **Inference:** The character is selfish.

Narrative point of view refers to the perspective from which a story is told. Stories told from the first-person point of view have narrators who are characters in the text. They reveal their own private thoughts and feelings, but they do not know what other characters privately think or feel.

So, like readers, first-person narrators must make inferences about other characters and about events.

KEYWORDS

narrator – the teller of a story

point of view – the perspective a story is told from

theme – the author's message or big idea

Sarah, Plain and Tall, Chapters 1–3 Synopsis

Twelve-year-old Anna Witting lives with her younger brother Caleb and their widowed father on the American prairie in the early 1900s. The children miss their mother and worry about Papa, who is not as happy as he once was. Papa tells them that he has placed an ad for a wife, and a woman named Sarah has replied. The excited children write letters back and forth with Sarah, who lives in Maine. Sarah decides to come visit the Wittings to see if she would like to marry Papa. While she is clearly glad to meet the children, Sarah seems lonely and homesick. Anna and Caleb worry that she will decide to return home.

Lesson Goals

- Take a spelling pretest.
- Begin reading *Sarah, Plain and Tall* by Patricia MacLachlan.
- Examine the narrator's point of view, big ideas, and vocabulary in *Sarah, Plain and Tall*.

GET READY

Introduction to Author Study (A)

Students will get a glimpse of what they will learn about in the lesson. They will also read the lesson goals and keywords. Have students select each keyword and preview its definition.

Spelling List 1 Pretest

Students will take a spelling pretest.

LEARNING COACH CHECK-IN   Have students turn to Spelling List 1 Pretest in *Summit English Language Arts 5 Activity Book* and open the online Spelling Pretest activity. Online, students will listen to the spelling word, type the word in the space indicated, and then check their answer. In the activity book, students will write the correct spelling of the word in the tables provided and indicate with a ✓ or an ✗ if they spelled the word correctly or incorrectly online. Students will repeat this process with the remaining words.

As needed, help students with the interaction between the online activity and the activity book page until they become comfortable with what they need to do. As students practice their spelling words throughout the workshop, they should pay special attention to words they spelled incorrectly on the pretest.

This is the complete list of words students will be tested on.

Two Vowels Together	Base *grace*	Prefix *uni–*	Heart Words
area	grace	unicorn	cemetery
diagonal	graceful	unicycle	coyote
diary	gracious	universal	symbol
duet	disgraceful	universe	
fluency			
nucleus			
patio			
pioneer			
poetry			
rodeo			
ruin			
stereo			
triumph			
variety			

Spelling List 1 Pretest

1. Open the Spelling Pretest activity online. Listen to the first spelling word. Type the word. Check your answer.

2. Write the correct spelling of the word in the Word column of the Spelling Pretest table on the next page.

Word	✓	✗
1 blindfold		

3. Put a check mark in the ✓ column if you spelled the word correctly online.

Word	✓	✗
1 blindfold	✓	

Put an X in the ✗ column if you spelled the word incorrectly online.

Word	✓	✗
1 blindfold		✗

4. Repeat Steps 1–3 for the remaining words in the Spelling Pretest.

Spelling List 1 Pretest

Write each spelling word in the Word column, making sure to spell it correctly.

Word	✓	✗	Word	✓	✗
1 area			14 variety		
2 diagonal			15 gracious		
3 diary			16 grace		
4 duet			17 graceful		
5 fluency			18 disgraceful		
6 nucleus			19 cemetery		
7 patio			20 coyote		
8 pioneer			21 symbol		
9 poetry			22 unicorn		
10 rodeo			23 unicycle		
11 ruin			24 universal		
12 stereo			25 universe		
13 triumph					

Students should use the ✓ and X columns to indicate whether they spelled each word correctly or incorrectly online.

Patricia MacLachlan's Stories in 60 Seconds

Students will watch a short video designed to spark their interest in the author Patricia MacLachlan.

Look Back at Reading Strategies

Students will review some key strategies that good readers employ to help them engage with and understand the texts they read.

Before You Read *Sarah, Plain and Tall*, Chapters 1–3

Students will be introduced to some key vocabulary words that they will encounter in the upcoming reading, learn some important historical background related to the reading, and answer questions to help them set a purpose for their reading.

READ

Sarah, Plain and Tall, Chapters 1–3

Students will read the first three chapters of *Sarah, Plain and Tall* by Patricia MacLachlan.

Check-In: *Sarah, Plain and Tall*, Chapters 1–3

Students will answer several questions to demonstrate their comprehension of the first three chapters of *Sarah, Plain and Tall*.

LEARN AND TRY IT

LEARN   Narrator's Point of View in *Sarah, Plain and Tall*

Students will complete an online activity to learn about the importance and influence of narrative point of view in the story.

TRY IT Anna's Point of View

Students will complete an online activity in which they analyze several passages and answer several questions related to the story's narrative point of view.

TRY IT Apply: Point of View

Students will apply to a new work what they've learned about analyzing narrative point of view.

TRY IT Write About Point of View and Theme

Students will answer questions about the story's point of view and themes. They will complete Write About Point of View and Theme from *Summit English Language Arts 5 Activity Book*.

LEARNING COACH CHECK-IN   This activity page contains open-ended questions, so it's important that you review students' responses. Give students feedback, using the sample answers provided to guide you.

TRY IT
Author Study (A)

Write About Point of View and Theme

Read the passage from from *Sarah, Plain and Tall* by Patricia MacLachlan. Then answer the questions in complete sentences.

Caleb read and read the letter so many times that the ink began to run and the folds tore. He read the book about sea birds over and over.

"Do you think she'll come?" asked Caleb. "And will she stay? What if she thinks we are loud and pesky?"

"You are loud and pesky," I told him. But I was worried, too. Sarah loved the sea, I could tell. Maybe she wouldn't leave there after all to come where there were fields and grass and sky and not much else.

"What if she comes and doesn't like our house?" Caleb asked. "I told her it was small. Maybe I shouldn't have told her it was small."

"Hush, Caleb. Hush."

AUTHOR STUDY (A)   **3**

---

1. In *Sarah, Plain and Tall*, Anna is the story's first-person narrator. The narrator's point of view influences our understanding of the story's characters and events.
Answers will vary.
   a. Based on the passage, what is one thing readers only know because Anna is a first-person narrator? Identify the specific sentence in the passage that reveals it.

Students' answer should demonstrate an understanding that readers know Anna's private feelings about the possibility of Sarah coming west because Anna is a first-person narrator. Anna reveals those private feelings to readers with the sentence, "But I was worried, too."

   b. Name at least one thing that readers do not know because Anna is a first-person narrator.

Readers do not know how Caleb feels about the way Anna speaks to him. They do not know, for instance, whether Caleb is insulted or hurt by Anna's words or if he understands them as playful and good-natured.

4   AUTHOR STUDY (A)

---

2. A theme is a big idea that a writer conveys.
Answers will vary.
   a. What is one of the themes in the first three chapters of *Sarah, Plain and Tall*?

_____
            See below.
_____

   b. What evidence from the text led you to notice this theme?
Theme: New experiences can be frightening; **Evidence:** Sarah, when she first arrives, looks lonely and sad and immediately misses the sea.
Theme: Change can be exciting; **Evidence:** Anna and Caleb are thrilled when they receive letters from Sarah and eagerly await her arrival when she comes west.
Theme: Strong relationships between people take time to develop; **Evidence:** While Sarah is kind to the children when she first arrives, she does not immediately sing with them, she does not smile when she comments that there is no sea on the prairie, and she initially feels quite lonely.
Theme: Children long for stable, secure, and complete families; **Evidence:** Both Anna and Caleb are eager for Sarah to arrive, hopeful that she will stay with them, and want her to marry their father and be their stepmother.

AUTHOR STUDY (A)   **5**

2a. One theme conveyed in the opening chapters of the book is that new experiences can be frightening. Other themes in these chapters are that change can be exciting; that strong relationships between people take time to develop; and that children long for stable, secure, and complete families.

TRY IT Practice Words from *Sarah, Plain and Tall*, Chapters 1–3

Students will complete an online activity in which they answer questions to demonstrate their understanding of the vocabulary words from the reading.

WRAP UP

Questions About *Sarah, Plain and Tall*, Chapters 1–3

Students will answer questions to show that they understand the first three chapters of *Sarah, Plain and Tall*, including its narrative point of view and emerging themes.

Author Study (B)

Lesson Overview

ACTIVITY	ACTIVITY TITLE	TIME	ONLINE/OFFLINE
GET READY	Introduction to Author Study (B)	**1** minute	🖥️
	Spelling List 1 Activity Bank	**10** minutes	📄
	Recall *Sarah, Plain and Tall*, Chapters 1–3	**4** minutes	🖥️
	Before You Read *Sarah, Plain and Tall*, Chapters 4–6	**10** minutes	📄
READ	*Sarah, Plain and Tall*, Chapters 4–6	**30** minutes	🖥️
	Check-In: *Sarah, Plain and Tall*, Chapters 4–6	**5** minutes	🖥️
LEARN AND **TRY IT**	Characters Develop Themes in *Sarah, Plain and Tall*	**10** minutes	🖥️
	Sarah, Anna, and Caleb's Actions	**10** minutes	🖥️
	Apply: Character's Action and Influence on Theme	**15** minutes	🖥️
	Write a "What If?" **LEARNING COACH CHECK-IN**	**15** minutes	📄
	Practice Words from *Sarah, Plain and Tall*, Chapters 4–6	**8** minutes	🖥️
WRAP-UP	Questions About *Sarah, Plain and Tall*, Chapters 4–6	**2** minutes	🖥️

Content Background

Students will continue to read *Sarah, Plain and Tall* by Patricia MacLachlan. In this lesson, they will focus on how characters' actions reveal themes.

Themes are the big ideas that authors convey in a text. One way authors reveal theme is through their characters' actions. Specifically, authors connect a character's actions to consequences.

Action: A girl who is afraid of heights climbs a tree to rescue her elderly neighbor's beloved cat.

Consequence: The cat is saved, and the neighbor is grateful. Others admire the girl for her bravery.

Theme: It's noble to face one's fears in order to help others.

> ### MATERIALS
>
> **Supplied**
> - *Sarah, Plain and Tall* by Patricia MacLachlan
> - *Summit English Language Arts 5 Activity Book*
>   - Spelling List 1 Activity Bank
>   - Write a "What If?"
>
> **Also Needed**
> - completed Spelling List 1 Pretest activity page from Author Study (A)

To understand the link between character actions and theme, it's helpful to ask questions:

- Why is the character acting that way?

- How does the character feel about his or her action?

- What happens as a result of the character's action?

- What idea or message does the author suggest by showing the action and the consequences?

KEYWORDS

point of view – the perspective a story is told from

theme – the author's message or big idea

Advance Preparation

Gather students' completed Spelling List 1 Pretest activity page from Author Study (A). Students will refer to this page during Get Ready: Spelling List 1 Activity Bank.

Sarah, Plain and Tall, Chapters 4–6 Synopsis

Sarah and the family begin getting acquainted. Sarah shares stories about her life in Maine, and the Wittings introduce her to life on the prairie. Papa and Anna are at first shy around Sarah, while Caleb is enthusiastic and affectionate. Though everyone gets along, it is clear that Sarah is a bit homesick, and both Caleb and Anna remain concerned that she will decide to return to Maine rather than marry Papa. They listen closely to what Sarah says, hoping for hints that she is settling in on the farm and will stay. One night, Papa lets everyone slide down a large hay mound, the closest thing to a sand dune at the sea that the farm has. On another day, Sarah takes on teaching Caleb and Anna how to swim, choosing the cow pond for the lesson.

Lesson Goals

- Practice all spelling words offline.

- Continue reading *Sarah, Plain and Tall*.

- Explore how character actions help reveal themes.

- Learn how a narrator's point of view affects a story.

- Understand the vocabulary in *Sarah, Plain and Tall*.

Introduction to Author Study (B)

Students will get a glimpse of what they will learn about in the lesson. They will also read the lesson goals and keywords. Have students select each keyword and preview its definition.

Spelling List 1 Activity Bank

Students will practice all spelling words from the workshop by completing Spelling List 1 Activity Bank from *Summit English Language Arts 5 Activity Book*. Make sure students have their completed Spelling List 1 Pretest activity page from Author Study (A) to refer to during this activity.

Remind students to pay special attention to words they spelled incorrectly on the Spelling Pretest.

Recall *Sarah, Plain and Tall*, Chapters 1–3

Students will answer some questions to review the reading that they have already completed.

Before You Read *Sarah, Plain and Tall*, Chapters 4–6

Students will be introduced to some key vocabulary words that they will encounter in the upcoming reading.

Sarah, Plain and Tall, Chapters 4–6

Students will read Chapters 4–6 of *Sarah, Plain and Tall* by Patricia MacLachlan.

Check-In: *Sarah, Plain and Tall*, Chapters 4–6

Students will answer several questions to demonstrate their comprehension of Chapters 4–6 of *Sarah, Plain and Tall*.

LEARN AND TRY IT

LEARN   Characters Develop Themes in *Sarah, Plain and Tall*

Students will complete an online activity to learn about how character actions and behavior help develop themes in the story.

TRY IT   Sarah, Anna, and Caleb's Actions

Students will complete an online activity in which they analyze several passages and answer several questions about how character actions develop and convey theme.

TRY IT   Apply: Character's Action and Influence on Theme

Students will apply to a new work what they've learned about how the actions of a story's characters influence its themes.

TRY IT   Write a "What If?"

Students will answer questions about character actions and theme in *Sarah, Plain and Tall*. They will complete Write a "What If?" from *Summit English Language Arts 5 Activity Book*.

LEARNING COACH CHECK-IN   This activity page contains open-ended questions, so it's important that you review students' responses. Give students feedback, using the sample answers provided to guide you.

Additional answers

1b. Answers will vary. Without this event, Sarah might not have felt as comfortable and happy with the Wittings but instead may have grown even more homesick. Had Papa behaved differently, the story's themes may have been different. For example, if the idea that it is worthwhile to make others feel comfortable and welcome in a new place had not been conveyed here, the theme shown to readers, if Papa had done nothing, is that one can't do much to make others feel comfortable in a new place.

TRY IT   Practice Words from *Sarah, Plain and Tall*, Chapters 4–6

Students will complete an online activity in which they answer questions to demonstrate their understanding of the vocabulary words from the reading.

WRAP-UP

Questions About *Sarah, Plain and Tall*, Chapters 4–6

Students will answer questions to show that they understand Chapters 4–6 of *Sarah, Plain and Tall*, including how the actions of the story's characters influence its themes.

Author Study (C)

Lesson Overview

ACTIVITY	ACTIVITY TITLE	TIME	ONLINE/OFFLINE
GET READY	Introduction to Author Study (C)	**1** minute	🛜
	Spelling List 1 Practice	**10** minutes	🛜
	Recall *Sarah, Plain and Tall*, Chapters 4–6	**4** minutes	🛜
	Before You Read *Sarah, Plain and Tall*, Chapters 7–9	**10** minutes	🛜
READ	*Sarah, Plain and Tall*, Chapters 7–9	**30** minutes	📄
	Check-In: *Sarah, Plain and Tall*, Chapters 7–9	**5** minutes	🛜
LEARN AND **TRY IT**	How to Summarize	**10** minutes	🛜
	Practice Summarizing	**10** minutes	🛜
	Apply: Summarizing	**15** minutes	🛜
	Write a Summary of *Sarah, Plain and Tall* **LEARNING COACH CHECK-IN**	**15** minutes	📄
	Practice Words from *Sarah, Plain and Tall*, Chapters 7–9	**8** minutes	🛜
WRAP-UP	Questions About *Sarah, Plain and Tall*, Chapters 7–9	**2** minutes	🛜

Content Background

Students will finish reading *Sarah, Plain and Tall* by Patricia MacLachlan. Then they will learn what belongs and what doesn't belong in an effective summary.

An effective summary

• Is significantly shorter than the text it is summarizing

• Focuses on major characters, key details, and crucial events

• Leaves out minor characters, details, and events

• Paraphrases the text's plot

• Follows the same order as the text being summarized

MATERIALS

Supplied
• *Sarah, Plain and Tall* by Patricia MacLachlan
• *Summit English Language Arts 5 Activity Book*s
• Write a Summary of *Sarah, Plain and Tall*

KEYWORDS

summary – a short retelling that includes only the most important ideas or events of a text

Sarah, Plain and Tall, Chapters 7–9 Synopsis

Neighbors Matthew and Maggie come to visit and help Papa plow. Maggie comforts Sarah and suggests she learn to ride a horse and drive a wagon on her own. Later, Sarah demands that Papa teach her both of those skills, and Papa agrees. But then a storm approaches, and Sarah and Papa work together to repair the roof before the storm hits. Everyone must stay in the barn overnight for safety during the storm. Anna notices that Sarah and Papa are growing closer, and after the storm, they all emerge to see the fields covered in hail, which makes the fields look like the sea. Sarah does learn to ride a horse and drive the wagon and one day goes into town alone. Caleb and Anna spend an anxious day waiting for her to return, afraid that she won't. Sarah does return and assures the children that she will stay with them. The story ends with the family eating dinner together and Anna thinking about the future—about the wedding between Sarah and Papa and what lies ahead for them all.

Lesson Goals

- Practice all spelling words online.
- Continue reading *Sarah, Plain and Tall*.
- Explore how important events and key details help reveal big ideas in a story.
- Write a summary of *Sarah, Plain and Tall*.
- Understand the vocabulary in *Sarah, Plain and Tall*.

GET READY

Introduction to Author Study (C)

Students will get a glimpse of what they will learn about in the lesson. They will also read the lesson goals and keywords. Have students select each keyword and preview its definition.

Spelling List 1 Practice

Students will practice all spelling words from the workshop.

Recall *Sarah, Plain and Tall*, Chapters 4–6

Students will answer some questions to review the reading that they have already completed.

Before You Read *Sarah, Plain and Tall*, **Chapters 7–9**

Students will be introduced to some key vocabulary words that they will encounter in the upcoming reading. They will also review what a summary is and what belongs in one.

READ

Sarah, Plain and Tall, **Chapters 7–9**

Students will read Chapters 7–9 of *Sarah, Plain and Tall* by Patricia MacLachlan.

Check-In: *Sarah, Plain and Tall*, **Chapters 7–9**

Students will answer several questions to demonstrate their comprehension of Chapters 7–9 of *Sarah, Plain and Tall*.

LEARN AND **TRY IT**

LEARN How to Summarize

Students will complete an online activity to learn about how to create an effective summary.

TRY IT Practice Summarizing

Students will complete an online activity in which they analyze several passages from Chapter 8 of *Sarah, Plain and Tall* and answer several questions about how to effectively summarize them.

TRY IT Apply: Summarizing

Students will apply to a new work what they've learned about summarizing effectively.

TRY IT Write a Summary of *Sarah, Plain and Tall*

Students will summarize Patricia MacLachlan's book. They will complete the Write a Summary of *Sarah, Plain and Tall* activity page from *Summit English Language Arts 5 Activity book*.

LEARNING COACH CHECK-IN This activity page contains open-ended questions, so it's important that you review students' responses. Give students feedback, using the sample answers provided to guide you.

TRY IT Practice Words from *Sarah, Plain and Tall*, Chapters 7–9

Students will complete an online activity in which they answer questions to demonstrate their understanding of the vocabulary words from the reading.

WRAP-UP

Questions About *Sarah, Plain and Tall*, Chapters 7–9

Students will answer questions to show that they understand Chapters 7–9 of *Sarah, Plain and Tall*, including what does and does not belong in a summary of a passage from that section of the book.

Author Study (D)

Lesson Overview

ACTIVITY	ACTIVITY TITLE	TIME	ONLINE/OFFLINE
GET READY	Introduction to Author Study (D)	**1** minute	🖥️
	Spelling List 1 More Practice	**10** minutes	🖥️
	Recall *Sarah, Plain and Tall*, Chapters 7–9	**4** minutes	🖥️
	Before You Read *Caleb's Story*, Chapters 1–2	**10** minutes	🖥️
READ	*Caleb's Story*, Chapters 1–2	**30** minutes	📄
	Check-In: *Caleb's Story*, Chapters 1–2	**5** minutes	🖥️
LEARN AND **TRY IT**	Compare and Contrast Characters Across Texts	**10** minutes	🖥️
	Caleb Then and Now	**10** minutes	🖥️
	Apply: Compare and Contrast Characters	**15** minutes	🖥️
	Compare and Contrast a Character **LEARNING COACH CHECK-IN**	**15** minutes	📄
	Practice Words from *Caleb's Story*, Chapters 1–2	**8** minutes	🖥️
WRAP-UP	Questions About *Caleb's Story*, Chapters 1–2	**2** minutes	🖥️

Content Background

Students will begin reading another novel by Patricia MacLachlan. This novel, *Caleb's Story*, continues the story of the Witting family but is told from the perspective of a different character. Note that students will not complete *Caleb's Story* during this workshop. They will read the first four chapters of the book. Students can choose to use Go Read! time in other lessons to finish the book on their own.

In this lesson, students will learn about how to effectively compare and contrast characters based on textual details. To compare and contrast characters in a text, readers must examine what characters say, do, think, and feel. When two characters face the same (or similar) problems or situations, it's possible to explore their reactions and uncover how they are alike and how they differ.

Situation: Fred and Sue find a diamond ring on the street.
Reactions: Fred wants to keep the ring; Sue wants to find its owner.
Compare/contrast: Fred doesn't care about others' feelings; Sue does.

MATERIALS

Supplied
- *Caleb's Story* by Patricia MacLachlan
- *Sarah, Plain and Tall* by Patricia MacLachlan
- *Summit English Language Arts 5 Activity Book*
  - Compare and Contrast a Character

Caleb's Story, Chapters 1–2 Synopsis

It is several years after *Sarah, Plain and Tall* takes place. Jacob and Sarah are married and have a daughter, Cassie. Anna, now a young woman, will be living in town, finishing school, and working for a doctor. Anna gives her journals to Caleb and instructs him to write in them in her absence. Caleb, now about 12 or 13 years of age, doubts he can do that, thinking himself not much of a writer. But Anna insists. After a game of hide and seek, Cassie reports seeing a man behind the barn. Caleb thinks she is imagining things but learns later that her story is true. Caleb, Sarah, and Cassie meet the man, who states he's there to see Jacob. They eventually invite him inside and he falls asleep upstairs. Much about him remains a mystery.

Lesson Goals

- Practice all spelling words online.
- Begin reading *Caleb's Story* by Patricia MacLachlan.
- Examine narrative point of view.
- Recognize the big ideas in *Caleb's Story* and how characters shape them.
- Explore how characters change and grow across Patricia MacLachlan's texts.
- Understand the vocabulary in *Caleb's Story*.

GET READY

Introduction to Author Study (D)

Students will get a glimpse of what they will learn about in the lesson. They will also read the lesson goals.

Spelling List 1 More Practice

Students will practice all spelling words from the workshop.

Recall *Sarah, Plain and Tall*, Chapters 7–9

Students will answer some questions to review the reading that they have already completed.

Before You Read *Caleb's Story*, Chapters 1–2

Students will be introduced to some key vocabulary words that they will encounter in the upcoming reading. They will also learn some background information about *Caleb's Story* and answer questions to prepare for the reading.

Caleb's Story, Chapters 1–2

Students will read Chapters 1–2 of *Caleb's Story* by Patricia MacLachlan.

Check-In: *Caleb's Story*, Chapters 1–2

Students will answer several questions to demonstrate their comprehension of Chapters 1–2 of *Caleb's Story*.

LEARN AND TRY IT

LEARN   Compare and Contrast Characters Across Texts

Students will complete an online activity to learn about how to use textual details to better understand the ways in which characters change and the ways in which they stay the same.

TRY IT   Caleb Then and Now

Students will complete an online activity in which they analyze several passages from *Sarah, Plain and Tall* and *Caleb's Story*, answering several questions to explore what the textual details show about how Caleb changes and remains the same across the stories.

TRY IT   Apply: Compare and Contrast Characters

Students will apply to a new work what they've learned about comparing and contrasting characters.

TRY IT   Compare and Contrast a Character

Students will choose a character who appears in both *Sarah, Plain and Tall* and *Caleb's Story* and then compare and contrast that character across texts. Have students complete the Compare and Contrast a Character activity page from *Summit English Language Arts 5 Activity Book*.

LEARNING COACH CHECK-IN   This activity page contains open-ended questions, so it's important that you review students' responses. Give students feedback, using the sample answers provided to guide you.

TRY IT   Practice Words from *Caleb's Story*, Chapters 1–2

Students will complete an online activity in which they answer questions to demonstrate their understanding of the vocabulary words from this lesson's reading.

WRAP-UP

Questions About *Caleb's Story*, Chapters 1–2

Students will answer questions to show that they understand Chapters 1–2 of *Caleb's Story*, including the ways in which the characters have changed or stayed the same and how we know.

Author Study (E)

Lesson Overview

ACTIVITY	ACTIVITY TITLE	TIME	ONLINE/OFFLINE
GET READY	Introduction to Author Study (E)	**1** minute	🖥️
	Spelling List 1 Review Game	**10** minutes	🖥️
	Recall *Caleb's Story*, Chapters 1–2	**4** minutes	🖥️
	Before You Read *Caleb's Story*, Chapters 3–4	**10** minutes	🖥️
READ	*Caleb's Story*, Chapters 3–4	**30** minutes	📄
	Check-In: *Caleb's Story*, Chapters 3–4	**5** minutes	🖥️
LEARN AND **TRY IT**	Compare and Contrast Settings and Events	**10** minutes	🖥️
	Practice Comparing and Contrasting Settings and Events	**10** minutes	🖥️
	Apply: Compare and Contrast Events	**15** minutes	🖥️
	Compare and Contrast Settings and Events in Two Stories **LEARNING COACH CHECK-IN**	**15** minutes	📄
	Practice Words from *Caleb's Story*, Chapters 3–4	**8** minutes	🖥️
WRAP-UP	Questions About *Caleb's Story*, Chapters 3–4	**2** minutes	🖥️

Content Background

Students will continue reading *Caleb's Story* by Patricia MacLachlan. They will then learn how to effectively compare and contrast settings and events based on details from the text.

A story's setting can have a major effect on its characters and its events. For instance, a story set in the winter might have its characters face a blizzard, while a story set in the summer might be about the effect of a brutal heat wave. Comparing and contrasting settings and their influence can deepen one's understanding of the texts being examined.

Note that students will not complete *Caleb's Story* during this workshop. They will read the first four chapters of the book. Students can choose to use Go Read! time in other lessons to finish the book on their own.

MATERIALS

Supplied
- *Caleb's Story* by Patricia MacLachan
- *Sarah, Plain and Tall* by Patricia MacLachlan
- *Summit English Language Arts 5 Activity Book*
  - Compare and Contrast Settings and Events in Two Stories

Caleb's Story, Chapters 3–4 Synopsis

Caleb goes about his chores while privately wondering who John is and why he's come to the family farm. Caleb tells John that he is writing about him in his journal, but John is not interested. Cassie, for her part, is eager to turn John into her playmate, even though John is reluctant. John joins them for family dinner, but he does not reveal anything about himself, and Sarah tells him that Jacob will surely spend the night in town because the weather is so bad. Caleb then spots John taking a pill from a medicine bottle. The next day, John does Caleb's chores for him and teases Cassie good-naturedly. Jacob returns and meets John. Jacob soon realizes that John is his father, whom Jacob believed to be dead. Caleb and Sarah are stunned.

Lesson Goals

- Practice all spelling words online.
- Continue reading *Caleb's Story*.
- Compare and contrast settings and events both within *Caleb's Story* and between *Caleb's Story* and *Sarah, Plain and Tall*.
- Recognize the big ideas in *Caleb's Story*.
- Understand the vocabulary in *Caleb's Story*.

GET READY

Introduction to Author Study (E)
Students will get a glimpse of what they will learn about in the lesson. They will also read the lesson goals.

Spelling List 1 Review Game
Students will practice all spelling words from the workshop.

Recall *Caleb's Story*, Chapters 1–2
Students will answer some questions to review the reading that they have already completed.

Before You Read *Caleb's Story*, Chapters 3–4
Students will be introduced to some key vocabulary words that they will encounter in the upcoming reading.

Caleb's Story, **Chapters 3–4**

Students will read Chapters 3–4 of *Caleb's Story* by Patricia MacLachlan.

Check In: *Caleb's Story*, **Chapters 3–4**

Students will answer several questions to demonstrate their comprehension of Chapters 3–4 of *Caleb's Story*.

LEARN AND TRY IT

LEARN   Compare and Contrast Settings and Events

Students will complete an online activity to learn how to effectively compare and contrast settings and events by focusing on textual details.

TRY IT   Practice Comparing and Contrasting Settings and Events

Students will complete an online activity in which they analyze several passages from *Sarah, Plain and Tall* and *Caleb's Story*, answering several questions to explore what the textual details show about how the settings and events of the stories are similar and how they are different.

TRY IT   Apply: Compare and Contrast Events

Students will apply to a new work what they've learned about comparing and contrasting events and settings.

TRY IT   Compare and Contrast Settings and Events in Two Stories

Students will compare and contrast the settings and events of *Sarah, Plain and Tall* with those of *Caleb's Story*. They will complete the Compare and Contrast Settings and Events in Two Stories activity page from *Summit English Language Arts 5 Activity Book*.

LEARNING COACH CHECK-IN   This activity page contains open-ended questions, so it's important that you review students' responses. Give students feedback, using the sample answers provided to guide you.

TRY IT   Practice Words from *Caleb's Story*, Chapters 3–4

Students will complete an online activity in which they answer questions to demonstrate their understanding of the vocabulary words from the reading.

WRAP-UP

Questions About *Caleb's Story*, Chapters 3–4

Students will answer questions to show that they understand Chapters 3–4 of *Caleb's Story*, including how this book's settings and events are similar to and different from the settings and events of *Sarah, Plain and Tall*.

Author Study Wrap-Up

Lesson Overview

ACTIVITY	ACTIVITY TITLE	TIME	ONLINE/OFFLINE
GET READY	Introduction to Author Study Wrap-Up	**1** minute	📶
TRY IT	Write About Texts by Patricia MacLachlan **LEARNING COACH CHECK-IN**	**24** minutes	📄
	Read and Record	**10** minutes	📶
	Review *Sarah, Plain and Tall* and *Caleb's Story*	**15** minutes	📶
QUIZ	Author Study	**40** minutes	📶
	Spelling List 1	**10** minutes	📶
WRAP-UP	Keyboarding	**10** minutes	📶
	More Language Arts Practice	**10** minutes	📶

Advance Preparation

During the Keyboarding activity, students will practice their keyboarding skills using an external website or program. **You will need to work with students to select an appropriate keyboarding practice website or program; K12 does not specify which resource to use.** A few suggestions are provided in the online activity.

Depending on which program you choose, students may need to set up an account to save their progress. If needed, assist students in setting up and running their chosen keyboarding practice program.

> ### MATERIALS
>
> **Supplied**
> - *Sarah, Plain and Tall* by Patricia MacLachlan
> - *Caleb's Story* by Patricia MacLachlan
> - *Summit English Language Arts 5 Activity Book*
>   - Write About Texts by Patricia MacLachlan

> ### Lesson Goals
> - Review *Sarah, Plain and Tall* and *Caleb's Story*.
> - Take a spelling quiz.
> - Take a quiz on *Sarah, Plain and Tall* and *Caleb's Story*.

Introduction to Author Study Wrap-Up

Students will read the lesson goals.

TRY IT

Write About Texts by Patricia MacLachlan

Students will complete Write About Texts by Patricia MacLachlan from *Summit English Language Arts 5 Activity Book*.

LEARNING COACH CHECK-IN   This activity page contains open-ended questions, so it's important that you review students' responses. Give students feedback, using the sample answers provided to guide you.

Read and Record

Good readers read quickly, smoothly, and with expression. This is called *fluency*. Students will record themselves reading aloud. They will listen to their recording and think about how quick, smooth, and expressive they sound.

Review *Sarah, Plain and Tall* and *Caleb's Story*

Students will answer questions to review what they have learned about *Sarah, Plain and Tall* and *Caleb's Story*.

Author Study

Students will complete the Author Study quiz.

Spelling List 1

Students will complete the Spelling List 1 quiz.

Keyboarding

Students will practice their keyboarding skills using an external website or program.

More Language Arts Practice

Students will practice skills according to their individual needs.

Context Clues and Word Relationships

Lesson Overview

ACTIVITY	ACTIVITY TITLE	TIME	ONLINE/OFFLINE
GET READY	Introduction to Context Clues and Word Relationships	**1** minute	🖥️
LEARN AND **TRY IT**	Look Back at Synonyms and Antonyms	**9** minutes	🖥️
	Context Clues and Word Relationships	**10** minutes	🖥️
	Practice Using Context Clues and Word Relationships	**10** minutes	🖥️
	Apply: Context Clues and Word Relationships LEARNING COACH CHECK-IN	**15** minutes	📄
	Review Context Clues and Word Relationships	**15** minutes	🖥️
QUIZ	Context Clues and Word Relationships	**15** minutes	🖥️
WRAP-UP	Keyboarding	**10** minutes	🖥️
	More Language Arts Practice	**10** minutes	🖥️
	Go Read!	**25** minutes	🖥️ or 📄

Content Background

Students will revisit using context clues and word relationships to help them define unknown words. The word list for this workshop contains words that students will typically encounter during standardized tests.

Advance Preparation

During the Keyboarding activity, students will practice their keyboarding skills using an external website or program. **You will need to work with students to select an appropriate keyboarding practice website or program; K12 does not specify which resource to use.** A few suggestions are provided in the online activity.

Depending on which program you choose, students may need to set up an account to save their progress. If needed, assist students in setting up and running their chosen keyboarding practice program.

During the Go Read! activity, students will have the option of using the digital library. Allow extra time for students to make their reading selection, or have students make a selection before beginning the lesson.

MATERIALS

Supplied
- *Summit English Language Arts 5 Activity Book*
  - Apply: Context Clues and Word Relationships

Also Needed
- reading material for Go Read!

Lesson Goals

- Use context clues to help determine meaning of unknown words.

- Use synonyms and antonyms to better understand the meaning of words.

- Use words commonly associated with grade-level assessments.

GET READY

Introduction to Context Clues and Word Relationships

Students will get a glimpse of what they will learn about in the lesson. They will also read the lesson goals.

LEARN AND TRY IT

LEARN   Look Back at Synonyms and Antonyms

Students will revisit synonyms and antonyms to prepare them for Word Relationships.

LEARN   Context Clues and Word Relationships

Students will learn that word relationships, such as synonyms and antonyms, can help them figure out the meaning of words. Students will then learn that context clues can help them figure out the meaning of words.

TRY IT   Practice Using Context Clues and Word Relationships

Students will answer questions about context clues and word relationships.

TRY IT   Apply: Context Clues and Word Relationships

Students will complete Apply: Context Clues and Word Relationships from *Summit English Language Arts 5 Activity Book*.

LEARNING COACH CHECK-IN   This activity page contains open-ended questions, so it's important that you review students' responses. Give students feedback, using the sample answers provided to guide you.

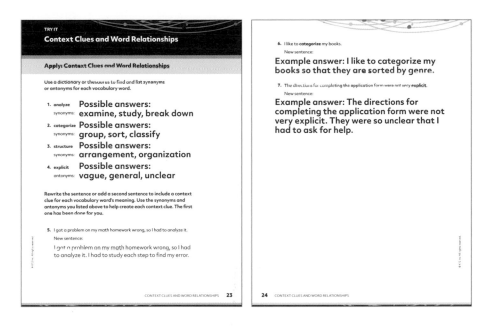

TRY IT   Review Context Clues and Word Relationships

Students will answer questions to review what they have learned about word relationships and context clues.

QUIZ

Context Clues and Word Relationships

Students will complete the Context Clues and Word Relationships quiz.

WRAP-UP

Keyboarding

Students will practice their keyboarding skills using an external website or program.

More Language Arts Practice

Students will practice skills according to their individual needs.

Go Read!

Students will read for pleasure. They should choose a book or a magazine that interests them, or they may choose a selection from the digital library, linked in the online lesson.

Students should read for the entire time. Have students select something to read ahead of time to help them stay focused.

Narrative Writing Skills (A)

Lesson Overview

ACTIVITY	ACTIVITY TITLE	TIME	ONLINE/OFFLINE
GET READY	Introduction to Narrative Writing Skills (A)	**1** minute	🖥️
	Spelling List 2 Pretest **LEARNING COACH CHECK-IN**	**10** minutes	🖥️ and 📄
	Look Back at Verb Tense	**5** minutes	🖥️
LEARN AND **TRY IT**	Use Past Perfect Tense	**10** minutes	🖥️
	Practice Using Past Perfect Tense	**15** minutes	🖥️
	Explore the Writing in *Sarah, Plain and Tall*	**10** minutes	🖥️
	Explore the Writing in *Caleb's Story*	**15** minutes	🖥️
	Write What Happens Next **LEARNING COACH CHECK-IN**	**30** minutes	📄
WRAP-UP	Questions About Introductions and Past Perfect	**4** minutes	🖥️
	Go Read!	**20** minutes	🖥️ or 📄

Content Background

A *narrative* is a story—it can be either fiction or nonfiction. Students will analyze how authors write narratives and then apply those skills to their own narrative writing. In this lesson, students will focus on the introduction and organization of a narrative.

Grammar, Usage, and Mechanics   Students will also begin learning about the perfect tense of verbs, beginning with the past perfect tense. The past perfect tense shows action that was completed in the past before another action happened.

> **Example:** The cat **had eaten** the entire cake before we arrived.

Advance Preparation

During the Go Read! activity, students will have the option of using the digital library. Allow extra time for students to make their reading selection, or have students make a selection before beginning the lesson.

MATERIALS

Supplied
- *Summit English Language Arts 5 Activity Book*
  - Spelling List 2 Pretest
  - Write What Happens Next

Also Needed
- reading material for Go Read!

Lesson Goals

- Take a spelling pretest.
- Form and use the past perfect tense.
- Analyze how an author of a narrative introduces the narrator, characters, and setting.
- Analyze how an author organizes a narrative.
- Write an introduction to and organize your own narrative.
- Read for pleasure.

GET READY

Introduction to Narrative Writing Skills (A)

Students will get a glimpse of what they will learn about in the lesson. They will also read the lesson goals and keywords. Have students select each keyword and preview its definition.

Spelling List 2 Pretest

Students will take a spelling pretest.

LEARNING COACH CHECK-IN   Have students turn to Spelling List 2 Pretest in the activity book and open the online Spelling Pretest activity. Online, students will listen to the spelling word, type the word in the space indicated, and then check their answer. In the activity book, students will write the correct spelling of the word in the tables provided and indicate with a ✓ or an ✗ if they spelled the word correctly or incorrectly online. Students will repeat this process with the remaining words.

This is the complete list of words students will be tested on.

/k/ Spelled *ch*	/f/ Spelled *ph*	Base Word *scholar*
anchor	atmosphere	scholar
chemical	microphone	scholarship
architect	phantom	scholastic
chord	symphony	
schedule		
chrome		
headache		
monarch		
orchestra		
scheme		

Look Back at Verb Tense

Students will practice forming and using the simple verb tenses.

LEARN AND TRY IT

LEARN   Use Past Perfect Tense

Students will learn how to form and use the past perfect tense of a verb.

TRY IT   Practice Using Past Perfect Tense

Students will answer questions about forming and using the past perfect tense. They will receive feedback on their answers.

LEARN   Explore the Writing in *Sarah, Plain and Tall*

Students will learn how a writer introduces a narrator and characters and establishes a situation in a narrative. They will also explore how a narrative is organized.

NOTE   Review the term *narrator* with students. Discuss how pronouns can reveal a narrator's point of view.

TRY IT   Explore the Writing in *Caleb's Story*

Students will answer questions about how a writer introduces a narrator and characters, establishes a situation, and organizes a narrative. They will receive feedback on their answers.

TRY IT Write What Happens Next

Students will complete Write What Happens Next in *Summit English Language Arts 5 Activity Book*.

LEARNING COACH CHECK-IN This activity page contains open-ended questions, so it's important that you review students' responses. Give students feedback, using the sample answers provided to guide you.

NOTE Have students keep their completed activity page in a safe place so they can refer to it later.

TRY IT
Narrative Writing Skills (A)

Write What Happens Next

Use the story prompt to answer the questions.
Answers will vary.
Story prompt: You open the door and find a sealed envelope.
What happens next?

1. Think about your story.

  a. Who will narrate the story?
  Possible answer: I will narrate the story.

  b. What other characters will be in the story? Describe at least one character.
  Possible answer: My brother, Elijah, will be in the story, and my dog, Maggie, will be in the story.

  c. Where is your story set? Describe the door in more detail.
  Possible answer: The door is to my tent. I was camping in my backyard.

2. Write an introduction to your story that introduces the narrator and the setting. If you choose, introduce other characters. Use your answers to Question 1 to help.
Possible answer: I slowly unzipped the door to my tent. My dog, Maggie, and I camped in my backyard last night. Maggie ran out ahead of me and began sniffing something. I looked closer. It was an envelope! I picked it up and noticed that it was addressed to me. NARRATIVE WRITING SKILLS (A) **27**

3. What happens next? Complete the diagram to describe how your story will be organized. (Do not write the whole story now. Just briefly describe what will happen.)

Beginning
Possible answer: I find the envelope. I read the letter. It contains a riddle that I try to solve.

Middle
Possible answer: I ask my brother for help. Together, we figure out the answer to the riddle. The answer leads us to a surprise.

End
Possible answer: Maggie, Elijah, and I enjoy the surprise.

28 NARRATIVE WRITING SKILLS (A)

WRAP-UP

Questions About Introductions and Past Perfect

Students will answer questions to show that they understand the elements of an introduction to a narrative and how to form a verb in the past perfect tense.

Go Read!

Students will read for pleasure. They should choose a book or a magazine that interests them, or they may choose a selection from the digital library, linked in the online lesson.

Students should read for the entire time. Have students select something to read ahead of time to help them stay focused.

Narrative Writing Skills (B)

Lesson Overview

ACTIVITY	ACTIVITY TITLE	TIME	ONLINE/OFFLINE
GET READY	Introduction to Narrative Writing Skills (B)	**1** minute	
	Spelling List 2 Activity Bank	**10** minutes	📄
LEARN AND **TRY IT**	Use Present Perfect Tense	**15** minutes	🖥
	Practice Using Present Perfect Tense	**15** minutes	🖥
	Writing About Characters and Events in *Sarah, Plain and Tall*	**15** minutes	🖥
	Writing About Characters and Events in *Caleb's Story*	**10** minutes	🖥
	Write About Characters and Events **LEARNING COACH CHECK-IN**	**30** minutes	📄
WRAP-UP	Questions About Pacing and Present Perfect	**4** minutes	🖥
	Go Read!	**20** minutes	🖥 or 📄

Content Background

Students will continue learning about narrative writing by analyzing how authors write narratives and then applying those skills to their own writing. In this lesson, students will focus on using dialogue, description, and pacing to develop characters and events in a narrative.

Grammar, Usage, and Mechanics Students will also continue learning about the perfect tense of verbs. They will learn that the present perfect tense has two uses:

1. To show an action that happened at a vague time in the past
   Example: Emma **has gone** to that restaurant before.

2. To show an action that started in the past and has continued into the present
   Example: I **have loved** this poem since I was very young.

Advance Preparation

Gather students' completed Spelling List 2 Pretest activity page from Narrative Writing Skills (A). Students will refer to this page during Get Ready: Spelling List 2 Activity Bank.

Gather students' completed Write What Happens Next activity page from Narrative Writing Skills (A). Students will refer to this page during Write About Characters and Events.

During the Go Read! activity, students will have the option of using the digital library. Allow extra time for students to make their reading selection, or have students make a selection before beginning the lesson.

Lesson Goals

- Practice spelling words offline.

- Form and use the present perfect tense.

- Analyze how an author of a narrative uses dialogue, description, and pacing.

- Use dialogue, description, and pacing in your own narrative.

- Read for pleasure.

KEYWORDS

description – writing that uses words that show how something looks, sounds, feels, tastes, or smells

dialogue – the words that characters say in a written work

narrative – a kind of writing that tells a story

pacing – the speed at which events unfold or information is revealed in a narrative

present perfect tense – verb tense that shows an action that either (1) happened at a vague time in the past or (2) started in the past and has continued into the present

---

GET READY

Introduction to Narrative Writing Skills (B)

Students will get a glimpse of what they will learn about in the lesson. They will also read the lesson goals and keywords. Have students select each keyword and preview its definition.

Spelling List 2 Activity Bank

Students will practice all spelling words from the workshop by completing Spelling List 2 Activity Bank from *Summit English Language Arts 5 Activity Book*. Make sure students have their completed Spelling List 2 Pretest activity page from Narrative Writing Skills (A) to refer to during this activity.

Remind students to pay special attention to words they spelled incorrectly on the Spelling Pretest.

Spelling List 2 Activity Bank

Circle any words in the box that you did not spell correctly on the pretest. Using your circled words, complete one activity of your choice. Complete as much of the activity as you can in the time given.

If you spelled all words correctly on the pretest, complete your chosen activity with as many spelling words as you can.

anchor	schedule	orchestra	microphone	scholar
chemical	chrome	scheme	phantom	scholarship
architect	headache	atmosphere	symphony	scholastic
chord	monarch			

Spelling Activity Choices

Silly Sentences

1. Write a silly sentence using your words from the spelling word list.
2. Underline the spelling word in each sentence.
   Example: The dog was driving a car.
3. Correct any spelling errors.

NARRATIVE WRITING SKILLS (B) 29

Spelling Story

1. Write a very short story using your words from the spelling word list.
2. Underline the spelling words in the story.
3. Correct any spelling errors.

Riddle Me This

1. Write a riddle for your words from the spelling word list.
   Example: "I have a trunk, but it's not on my car."
2. Write the answer, which is your word, for each riddle.
   Example: Answer: elephant
3. Correct any spelling errors.

RunOnWord

1. Gather some crayons, colored pencils, or markers. Write each of your words, using a different color for each word, end to end as one long word.
   Example: dogcatbirdfishturtle
2. Rewrite the words correctly and with proper spacing.

30 NARRATIVE WRITING SKILLS (B)

Complete the activity that you chose.

My chosen activity:

Students should use this page to complete all steps in their chosen activity.

NARRATIVE WRITING SKILLS (B) 31

LEARN AND TRY IT

LEARN   Use Present Perfect Tense

Students will learn how to form and use the present perfect tense of a verb.

TRY IT   Practice Using Present Perfect Tense

Students will answer questions about forming and using the present perfect tense. They will receive feedback on their answers.

LEARN   Writing About Characters and Events in *Sarah, Plain and Tall*

Students will learn how a writer uses dialogue and description to develop characters and events in a narrative. Students will also explore how writers use pacing (make the writing move along more quickly or more slowly) to better tell a story.

SUPPORT   Students may understand how to form dialogue, but they might struggle with how to use dialogue to serve a purpose in writing. Give an example of something students said recently. Ask, "What do those words show about what was happening? What do those words show about you?" If students struggle, think aloud. For example, "This morning I said, 'I can finally wear a short-sleeved shirt!' Those words show that the weather is warm and that it hasn't been warm for a while. They also reveal that I like the warm weather."

TRY IT   Writing About Characters and Events in *Caleb's Story*

Students will answer questions about how a writer uses dialogue, description, and pacing in a narrative.

TRY IT   Write About Characters and Events

Students will complete Write About Characters and Events in *Summit English Language Arts 5 Activity Book*. Make sure students have their completed Write What Happens Next activity page from Narrative Writing Skills (A) to refer to during this activity.

LEARNING COACH CHECK-IN   This activity page contains open-ended questions, so it's important that you review students' responses. Give students feedback, using the sample answers provided to guide you.

NOTE   Have students keep their completed activity page in a safe place so they can refer to it later.

Questions About Pacing and Present Perfect

Students will answer questions to show that they understand how a writer uses pacing in a narrative and how to form a verb in the present perfect tense.

Go Read!

Students will read for pleasure. They should choose a book or a magazine that interests them, or they may choose a selection from the digital library, linked in the online lesson.

Students should read for the entire time. Have students select something to read ahead of time to help them stay focused.

Narrative Writing Skills (C)

Lesson Overview

ACTIVITY	ACTIVITY TITLE	TIME	ONLINE/OFFLINE
GET READY	Introduction to Narrative Writing Skills (C)	**1** minute	🖥️
	Spelling List 2 Review Game	**10** minutes	🖥️
LEARN AND **TRY IT**	Use Future Perfect Tense	**10** minutes	🖥️
	Practice Using Future Perfect Tense	**10** minutes	🖥️
	Word Choice and Conclusions in *Sarah, Plain and Tall*	**15** minutes	🖥️
	Word Choice and Conclusions in *Caleb's Story*	**15** minutes	🖥️
	Write a Conclusion and Revise Your Word Choice **LEARNING COACH CHECK-IN**	**35** minutes	📄
WRAP-UP	Questions About Word Choice and Future Perfect	**4** minutes	🖥️
	Go Read!	**20** minutes	🖥️ or 📄

Content Background

Students will learn about word choice in narratives, including transitions, concrete language, and sensory language, and about how to conclude a narrative.

Grammar, Usage, and Mechanics Students will also learn about the remaining perfect tense, the future perfect. The future perfect tense shows an action that will be completed in the future before another action happens.

> **Example:** The dog **will have sniffed** every inch of the yard by the time I finish my chores.

Advance Preparation

Gather students' completed Write What Happens Next activity page from Narrative Writing Skills (A) and Write About Characters and Events activity page from Narrative Writing Skills (B). Students will refer to these pages during Write a Conclusion and Revise Your Word Choice.

During the Go Read! activity, students will have the option of using the digital library. Allow extra time for students to make their reading selection, or have students make a selection before beginning the lesson.

MATERIALS

Supplied
- *Summit English Language Arts 5 Activity Book*
  - Write a Conclusion and Revise Your Word Choice

Also Needed
- completed Write What Happens Next activity page from Narrative Writing Skills (A)
- completed Write About Characters and Events activity page from Narrative Writing Skills (B)
- reading material for Go Read!

Lesson Goals

- Practice all spelling words online.
- Form and use the future perfect tense.
- Analyze how an author of a narrative uses concrete and sensory language, and transitions.
- Analyze how an author of a narrative writes a conclusion.
- Use sensory language and transitions in your own narrative.
- Write the conclusion to your own narrative.
- Read for pleasure.

KEYWORDS

conclusion – the final paragraph of a written work

concrete – real or physical; able to be perceived by the senses

future perfect tense – verb tense that shows an action that will be completed in the future before another action happens

narrative – a kind of writing that tells a story

sensory language – language that appeals to the five senses

transition – a word, phrase, or clause that connects ideas

GET READY

Introduction to Narrative Writing Skills (C)

Students will get a glimpse of what they will learn about in the lesson. They will also read the lesson goals and keywords. Have students select each keyword and preview its definition.

Spelling List 2 Review Game

Students will practice all spelling words from the workshop.

LEARN AND TRY IT

LEARN   Use Future Perfect Tense

Students will learn how to form and use the future perfect tense of a verb.

TRY IT   Practice Using Future Perfect Tense

Students will answer questions about forming and using the future perfect tense. They will receive feedback on their answers.

LEARN   Word Choice and Conclusions in *Sarah, Plain and Tall*

Students will look closer at the words writers use in narratives. They will learn how a writer uses transitional words, phrases, and clauses to show the order of events. They will also examine concrete and sensory language.

In addition, students will learn how the conclusion of a narrative should follow logically from the events in the story. That is, even if the conclusion contains a surprise, it has to make sense.

TRY IT   Word Choice and Conclusions in *Caleb's Story*

Students will answer questions about how a writer uses transitional, concrete, and sensory language. They will also answer a question about the conclusion of a narrative.

> **TIP**   In this activity, students read excerpts from *Caleb's Story* that they were not required to read in the Author Study workshop. If students are inspired, encourage them to complete *Caleb's Story* during the Go Read! activity.

TRY IT   Write a Conclusion and Revise Your Word Choice

Students will complete Write a Conclusion and Revise Your Word Choice in *Summit English Language Arts 5 Activity Book*. Make sure students have their completed Write What Happens Next activity page from Narrative Writing Skills (A) and Write About Characters and Events activity page from Narrative Writing Skills (B) to refer to during this activity.

> **LEARNING COACH CHECK-IN**   This activity page contains open-ended questions, so it's important that you review students' responses. Give students feedback, using the sample answers provided to guide you.

TRY IT

Narrative Writing Skills (C)

Write a Conclusion and Revise Your Word Choice

Use the story prompt to answer the questions.

Story prompt: **You open the door and find a sealed envelope. What happens next?**

1. Choose a sentence from your response to the prompt. Rewrite the sentence to make it more concrete.

   a. Original sentence:
   Possible answer: **I went inside to find my brother.**

   b. Revised sentence:
   Possible answer: **I sprinted inside to find my brother.**

2. Choose a sentence from your response to the prompt. Rewrite the sentence so that it includes a transition.

   a. Original sentence:
   Possible answer: **He looked up.**

   b. Revised sentence:
   Possible answer: **Finally, he looked up.**

NARRATIVE WRITING SKILLS (C)   **37**

38   NARRATIVE WRITING SKILLS (C)

3. Write the conclusion to your story.
Possible answer: **When I saw the skipping stones, I couldn't believe my eyes. The stones were arranged in a message, "Congrats Eve!" I looked at Elijah. He smiled.**

"You made it through your first night camping," he said. I laughed and gave him a thankful hug.

May I please read your story?

WRAP-UP

Questions About Word Choice and Future Perfect

Students will answer questions to show that they understand how to use concrete language and how to form a verb in the future perfect tense.

Go Read!

Students will read for pleasure. They should choose a book or a magazine that interests them, or they may choose a selection from the digital library, linked in the online lesson.

Students should read for the entire time. Have students select something to read ahead of time to help them stay focused.

Narrative Writing Skills Wrap-Up

Lesson Overview

ACTIVITY	ACTIVITY TITLE	TIME	ONLINE/OFFLINE
GET READY	Introduction to Narrative Writing Skills Wrap-Up	**1** minute	🛜
TRY IT	Use Narrative Writing Skills **LEARNING COACH CHECK-IN**	**30** minutes	📄
	Review Perfect Tenses	**20** minutes	🛜
QUIZ	Perfect Tenses and Narrative Writing Skills	**30** minutes	🖥
	Spelling List 2	**10** minutes	🖥
WRAP-UP	Keyboarding	**10** minutes	🛜
	More Language Arts Practice	**19** minutes	🖥

Advance Preparation

During the Keyboarding activity, students will practice their keyboarding skills using an external website or program. **You will need to work with students to select an appropriate keyboarding practice website or program; K12 does not specify which resource to use.** A few suggestions are provided in the online activity.

Depending on which program you choose, students may need to set up an account to save their progress. If needed, assist students in setting up and running their chosen keyboarding practice program

Lesson Goals

- Review perfect tenses and narrative writing skills.
- Take a spelling quiz.
- Take a quiz on perfect tenses and narrative writing skills.

GET READY

Introduction to Narrative Writing Skills Wrap-Up

Students will read the lesson goals.

Use Narrative Writing Skills

Students will complete Use Narrative Writing Skills in *Summit English Language Arts 5 Activity Book* to review the writing objectives that will be assessed on the quiz.

LEARNING COACH CHECK-IN This activity page contains open-ended questions, so it's important that you review students' responses. Give students feedback, using the sample answers provided to guide you.

Use Narrative Writing Skills

Choose a prompt from the list, or write your own prompt.

Story prompts:

- You are having dinner with your favorite athlete. What happens?
- You travel back in time to when your grandparents were children. What happens?
- You suddenly have the ability to talk to animals. What happens?

Use your prompt to answer the questions.

1. Who will narrate your story?

Possible answer: I will narrate my story.

2. Where will the setting of your story be? Be more specific than the prompt. For example, write where and when your story takes place.

Possible answer: The setting will be my grandfather's family's apartment in the Bronx, New York, in the 1950s.

---

3. Write a short introduction. Use description to give information about your narrator and setting. You can use dialogue, if you choose. Remember, show, don't tell.

Possible answer: I looked at the small television with two tall antennas, which played a black-and-white show. Out the window I saw tall buildings. The newspaper on the table had a date of 1952. "Where are we?" I asked a familiar-looking boy. "Home," he said, "in the Bronx."

4. Briefly describe what would happen in the middle of your story.

Possible answer: I learn the boy's name and realize he's my grandfather. He tells me his dog is missing, and we go on an adventure to find it.

5. Write a sentence (or sentences) that could be in your story. In these sentences, use sensory detail to show what's happening.

Sentences should include words that can be perceived through the five senses. For example, *The magenta clouds glowed behind the skyscrapers. The cold wind made me shiver.*

---

6. Write dialogue that could be in your story.

Possible answers:

Character's name
Narrator

Character's name
Grandpa

What's the matter?

My dog, Ralphie. He's missing!

Well, just post something online about it. Does your school have a website?

a. What is one detail this dialogue reveals about the characters?

Possible answer: The narrator does not realize that there were no websites in the 1950s!

b. What is one detail this dialogue reveals about what is happening?

Possible answer: Grandpa's dog is missing. The narrator needs help to solve this problem.

---

7. Briefly describe what would happen in the conclusion to your story. Explain how your conclusion makes sense with the rest of your story.

Possible answer: We find the dog. I close my eyes to rest, and I wake up in the present day. My conclusion makes sense because we will work together to find the dog. It also makes sense that the whole story was a dream—you can't really travel back in time!

8. Which part of your story would have a slow pace? Explain.

Students should choose a part of the story that they believe is important and that they want to show in a lot of detail.

Review Perfect Tenses

Students will answer questions to review what they have learned about the past perfect, present perfect, and future perfect verb tenses.

Perfect Tenses and Narrative Writing Skills

Students will complete the Perfect Tenses and Narrative Writing Skills quiz.

Spelling List 2

Students will complete the Spelling List 2 quiz.

Keyboarding

Students will practice their keyboarding skills using an external website or program.

More Language Arts Practice

Students will practice skills according to their individual needs.

Big Ideas: Mini-Project

Lesson Overview

Big Ideas lessons provide students the opportunity to further apply the knowledge acquired and skills learned throughout the unit workshops. Each Big Ideas lesson consists of these parts:

1. **Cumulative Review:** Students keep their skills fresh by reviewing prior content.

2. **Preview:** Students practice answering the types of questions they will commonly find on standardized tests.

3. **Synthesis:** Students complete an assignment that allows them to connect and apply what they have learned. Synthesis assignments vary throughout the course.

   In the Synthesis portion of this Big Ideas lesson, students will complete a small creative project that ties together concepts and skills they have encountered across workshops. These small projects are designed to deepen students' understanding of those concepts and skills.

   LEARNING COACH CHECK-IN   Make sure students complete, review, and submit the assignment to their teacher.

All materials needed for this lesson are linked online and not provided in the Activity Book.

MATERIALS

Supplied
- Mini-Project Instructions (printout)

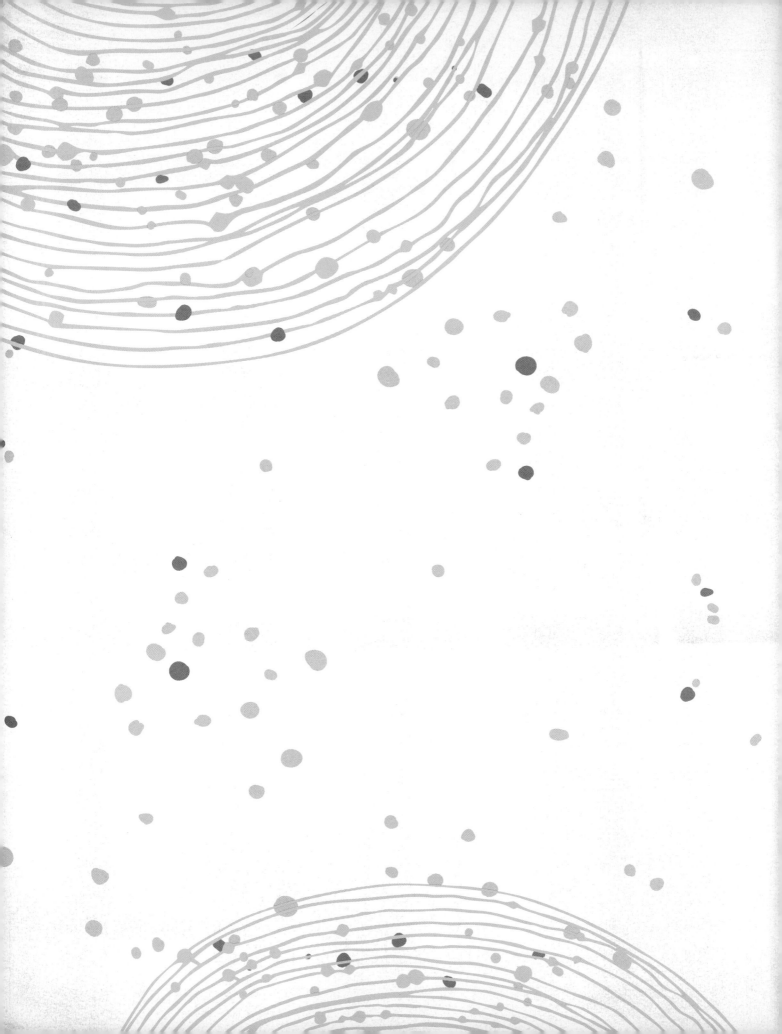

Fascinating Tales
from History

The Mary Celeste (A)

Lesson Overview

ACTIVITY	ACTIVITY TITLE	TIME	ONLINE/OFFLINE
GET READY	Fascinating Tales from History Unit Overview	**1** minute	🖥️
	Introduction to *The Mary Celeste* (A)	**1** minute	🖥️
	Spelling List 3 Pretest **LEARNING COACH CHECK-IN**	**10** minutes	🖥️ and 📄
	Mystery at Sea in 60 Seconds	**1** minute	🖥️
	Look Back at Main Idea	**4** minutes	🖥️
	Before You Read *The Mary Celeste*, Part 1	**13** minutes	🖥️
READ	*The Mary Celeste*, Part 1	**30** minutes	📄
	Check-In: *The Mary Celeste*, Part1	**5** minutes	🖥️
LEARN AND **TRY IT**	What's the Main Idea?	**10** minutes	🖥️
	The Main Idea of *The Mary Celeste*, Part 1	**10** minutes	🖥️
	Apply: Main Idea	**15** minutes	🖥️
	Write About the Main Idea and Make Predictions **LEARNING COACH CHECK-IN**	**10** minutes	📄
	Practice Words from *The Mary Celeste*, Part 1	**8** minutes	🖥️
WRAP-UP	Questions About Main Idea	**2** minutes	🖥️

Content Background

Students will complete a spelling activity and begin to read *The Mary Celeste: An Unsolved Mystery from History* by Jane Yolen. They will then complete activities in which they learn how to determine the main idea in a nonfiction text by using supporting details.

MATERIALS

Supplied
- *The Mary Celeste: An Unsolved Mystery from History* by Jane Yolen
- *Summit English Language Arts 5 Activity Book*
  - Spelling List 3 Pretest
  - Write About the Main Idea and Make Predictions

The Mary Celeste, Part 1 Synopsis

The *Dei Gratia* had sailed across the Atlantic from New York in 1872. Several weeks into the journey, the crew of the *Dei Gratia* spotted a ship on the horizon. They were about 600 miles west of Portugal at the time, and they were surprised to come across this other ship. The ship, the *Mary Celeste*, had left from New York about a month earlier but was now moving oddly—as if no one was steering the ship—and only a few of its sails were set. The captain of the *Dei Gratia*, David Morehouse, tried to contact the *Mary Celeste* by raising signal flags and calling out to it. There was no reply. Sensing that something was wrong, Morehouse ordered three of his men into a small boat and told them to row across to the *Mary Celeste* to investigate.

Lesson Goals

- Take a spelling pretest.

- Begin reading *The Mary Celeste: An Unsolved Mystery from History* by Jane Yolen.

- Examine the key details, main idea, and vocabulary in the reading.

GET READY

Fascinating Tales from History Unit Overview

Students will read a summary of what they will learn in the Fascinating Tales from History unit.

Introduction to *The Mary Celeste* (A)

Students will get a glimpse of what they will learn about in the lesson. They will also read the lesson goals and keywords. Have students select each keyword and preview its definition.

Spelling List 3 Pretest

Students will take a spelling pretest.

Have students turn to Spelling List 3 Pretest in the activity book and open the online Spelling Pretest activity. Online, students will listen to the spelling word, type the word in the space indicated, and then check their answer. In the activity book, students will write the correct spelling of the word in the tables provided and indicate with a ✓ or an ✗ if they spelled the word correctly or incorrectly online. Students will repeat this process with the remaining words.

As needed, help students with the interaction between the online activity and the activity book page until they become comfortable with what they need to do. As students practice their spelling words throughout the workshop, they should pay special attention to words they spelled incorrectly on the pretest.

This is the complete list of words students will be tested on.

Words That Begin with *schwa* Spelled *a*	Words That End with *schwa* Spelled *a*	Base *deficit*
ability	data	deficiency
adobe	drama	deficient
algebra	fauna	deficit
allowance	flora	
amend	pasta	
aware	pizza	
	plasma	
	scuba	

NOTE Have students keep their completed activity page in a safe place so they can refer to it later.

GET READY
The Mary Celeste (A)

Spelling List 3 Pretest

1. Open the Spelling Pretest activity online. Listen to the first spelling word. Type the word. Check your answer.

2. Write the correct spelling of the word in the Word column of the Spelling Pretest table on the next page.

	Word	✓	✗
1	blindfold		

3. Put a check mark in the ✓ column if you spelled the word correctly online.

	Word	✓	✗
1	blindfold	✓	

Put an X in the ✗ column if you spelled the word incorrectly online.

	Word	✓	✗
1	blindfold		X

4. Repeat Steps 1–3 for the remaining words in the Spelling Pretest.

THE MARY CELESTE (A) **43**

44 THE MARY CELESTE (A)

The Mary Celeste (A)

Spelling List 3 Pretest

Write each spelling word in the Word column, making sure to spell it correctly.

	Word	✓	✗		Word	✓	✗
1	ability			10	flora		
2	adobe			11	pasta		
3	algebra			12	pizza		
4	allowance			13	plasma		
5	amend			14	scuba		
6	aware			15	deficiency		
7	data			16	deficient		
8	drama			17	deficit		
9	fauna						

Students should use the ✓ and X columns to indicate whether they spelled each word correctly or incorrectly online.

Mystery at Sea in 60 Seconds

Students will watch a short video designed to spark their interest in *The Mary Celeste: An Unsolved Mystery from History*.

Look Back at Main Idea

Students will review what a main idea is in a nonfiction text, how to identify main ideas, and the fact that main ideas may be stated or unstated.

Before You Read *The Mary Celeste*, Part 1

Students will be introduced to some key vocabulary words that they will encounter in the upcoming reading and learn some important historical background related to the reading.

READ

The Mary Celeste: An Unsolved Mystery from History, Part 1

Students will read the first 10 pages of *The Mary Celeste: An Unsolved Mystery from History* by Jane Yolen, stopping when they complete the page that ends with this sentence: "From the *Mary Celeste* there was silence."

Check-In: *The Mary Celeste*, Part 1

Students will answer questions to demonstrate their comprehension of the first section of *The Mary Celeste: An Unsolved Mystery from History*.

LEARN AND TRY IT

LEARN   What's the Main Idea?

Students will complete an online activity to learn about using supporting details to identify the main idea of a nonfiction passage.

TRY IT   The Main Idea of *The Mary Celeste*, Part 1

Students will complete an online activity in which they analyze several passages and answer several questions related to main ideas and supporting details.

TRY IT   Apply: Main Idea

Students will apply to a new work what they've learned about supporting details and main idea.

TRY IT Write About the Main Idea and Make Predictions

Students will answer questions about the main idea of the text to this point and what they think will happen next based on key details they have encountered. Have students complete the Write About the Main Idea and Make Predictions activity page from *Summit English Language Arts 5 Activity Book*.

LEARNING COACH CHECK-IN This activity page contains open-ended questions, so it's important that you review students' responses. Give students feedback, using the sample answers provided to guide you.

TRY IT Practice Words from *The Mary Celeste*, Part 1

Students will complete an online activity in which they answer questions to demonstrate their understanding of the vocabulary words from the reading.

WRAP-UP

Questions About Main Idea

Students will answer questions to show that they understand how to identify the main idea in a passage, and they will demonstrate their ability by identifying the main idea and supporting details in a passage from *The Mary Celeste: An Unsolved Mystery from History*.

The Mary Celeste (B)

Lesson Overview

ACTIVITY	ACTIVITY TITLE	TIME	ONLINE/OFFLINE
GET READY	Introduction to *The Mary Celeste* (B)	**1** minute	🖥️
	Spelling List 3 Activity Bank	**10** minutes	📄
	Recall *The Mary Celeste*, Part 1	**5** minutes	🖥️
	Before You Read *The Mary Celeste*, Part 2	**10** minutes	🖥️
READ	*The Mary Celeste*, Part 2	**30** minutes	📄
	Check-In: *The Mary Celeste*, Part 2	**5** minutes	🖥️
LEARN AND **TRY IT**	The Key Is in the Details	**10** minutes	🖥️
	Key Details in *The Mary Celeste*, Part 2	**10** minutes	🖥️
	Apply: Key Details	**15** minutes	🖥️
	Write About the Ship's Log **LEARNING COACH CHECK-IN**	**15** minutes	📄
	Practice Words from *The Mary Celeste*, Part 2	**7** minutes	🖥️
WRAP-UP	Questions About Key Details	**2** minutes	🖥️

Content Background

Students will complete a spelling activity and continue to read *The Mary Celeste: An Unsolved Mystery from History* by Jane Yolen. They will then complete activities in which they learn how to differentiate between key (more important) details and minor (less important details) in the text.

Advance Preparation

Gather students' completed Spelling List 3 Pretest activity page from *The Mary Celeste* (A). Students will refer to this page during Get Ready: Spelling List 3 Activity Bank.

MATERIALS

Supplied
- *The Mary Celeste: An Unsolved Mystery from History* by Jane Yolen
- *Summit English Language Arts 5 Activity Book*
  - Spelling List 3 Activity Bank
  - Write About the Ship's Log

Also Needed
- completed Spelling List 3 Pretest activity page from *The Mary Celeste* (A)

The Mary Celeste, Part 2 Synopsis

Two crew members from the *Dei Gratia*—Deveau and Wright—boarded the *Mary Celeste* and searched around. They found that, apart from a missing life boat and a few key navigational tools that were gone, everything was in place. The captain's wife had left her valuables on board. There was fresh water and uncooked food in the galley. The ship's cargo was undisturbed. Yet the *Mary Celeste* was definitely deserted. When the crew members of the *Dei Gratia* returned to their own ship, they told Captain Morehouse what they had discovered. Deveau said he suspected that the people on board the *Mary Celeste* had left quickly but expected to return. Captain Morehouse, who knew the captain of the *Mary Celeste*—Captain Briggs—to be a responsible and capable leader, feared the worst.

Lesson Goals

- Practice all spelling words offline.

- Continue reading *The Mary Celeste: An Unsolved Mystery from History* by Jane Yolen.

- Determine main ideas and distinguish between key supporting details and minor supporting details.

GET READY

Introduction to *The Mary Celeste* (B)

Students will get a glimpse of what they will learn about in the lesson. They will also read the lesson goals and keywords. Have students select each keyword and preview its definition.

Spelling List 3 Activity Bank

Students will practice all spelling words from the workshop by completing Spelling List 3 Activity Bank from *Summit English Language Arts 5 Activity Book*. Make sure students have their completed Spelling List 3 Pretest activity page from *The Mary Celeste* (A) to refer to during this activity.

Remind students to pay special attention to words they spelled incorrectly on the Spelling Pretest.

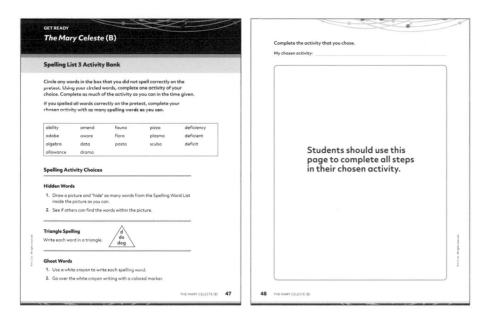

Recall *The Mary Celeste*, Part 1

Students will answer questions to review the reading that they have already completed.

Before You Read *The Mary Celeste*, Part 2

Students will be introduced to some key vocabulary words that they will encounter in the upcoming reading.

READ

The Mary Celeste, Part 2

Students will read the next several pages of *The Mary Celeste: An Unsolved Mystery from History* by Jane Yolen, stopping when they complete the page that ends with this sentence: "Now, by the laws of the sea, she belongs to us."

Check-In: *The Mary Celeste*, Part 2

Students will answer several questions to demonstrate their comprehension of the second section of *The Mary Celeste: An Unsolved Mystery from History*.

LEARN AND TRY IT

LEARN   The Key Is in the Details

Students will complete an online activity to learn about recognizing the difference between key details and minor details in nonfiction texts.

TRY IT   Key Details in *The Mary Celeste*, Part 2

Students will complete an online activity in which they analyze several passages and distinguish between key details and minor details in them.

TRY IT   Apply: Key Details

Students will apply to a new work what they've learned about key and minor details.

TRY IT   Write About the Ship's Log

Students will answer a question to demonstrate their understanding of the difference between key details and minor details in a text. Have students complete Write About the Ship's Log from *Summit English Language Arts 5 Activity Book*.

LEARNING COACH CHECK-IN   This activity page contains an open-ended question, so it's important that you review students' responses. Give students feedback, using the sample answers provided to guide you.

TRY IT   Practice Words from *The Mary Celeste*, Part 2

Students will complete an online activity in which they answer questions to demonstrate their understanding of the vocabulary words from the reading.

WRAP-UP

Questions About Key Details

Students will answer questions to show that they understand the difference between key details and minor details, and they will demonstrate their ability to identify a main idea from this section of *The Mary Celeste: An Unsolved Mystery from History*.

The Mary Celeste (C)

Lesson Overview

ACTIVITY	ACTIVITY TITLE	TIME	ONLINE/OFFLINE
GET READY	Introduction to *The Mary Celeste* (C)	**1** minute	
	Spelling List 3 Review Game	**10** minutes	
	Recall *The Mary Celeste*, Part 2	**5** minutes	
	Before You Read *The Mary Celeste*, Part 3	**10** minutes	
READ	*The Mary Celeste*, Part 3	**30** minutes	
	Check-In: *The Mary Celeste*, Part 3	**5** minutes	
LEARN AND **TRY IT**	*The Mary Celeste* Says	**10** minutes	
	Show What You Know About *The Mary Celeste*	**10** minutes	
	Apply: Summarizing	**15** minutes	
	Write a Summary **LEARNING COACH CHECK-IN**	**15** minutes	
	Practice Words from *The Mary Celeste*, Part 3	**7** minutes	
WRAP-UP	Questions About Summarizing	**2** minutes	

Content Background

Students will complete a spelling activity and finish reading *The Mary Celeste: An Unsolved Mystery from History* by Jane Yolen. They will then complete activities in which they learn about writing a summary, quoting accurately from the text, and paraphrasing.

MATERIALS

Supplied
- *The Mary Celeste: An Unsolved Mystery from History* by Jane Yolen
- *Summit English Language Arts 5 Activity Book*
  - Write a Summary

The Mary Celeste, Part 3 Synopsis

Captain Morehouse of the *Dei Gratia* decided to salvage the *Mary Celeste*, and three members of his crew repaired the ship and sailed it to Gibraltar. The crew of the *Dei Gratia* was eventually awarded one-fifth of the insured value of the *Mary Celeste*. The disappearance of those on board *Mary Celeste* became a major news story, though gossip and rumors often overshadowed the facts of the incident. In the end, it was never established what happened to the people who were on the *Mary Celeste*, and several different theories about their fate remain even today.

Lesson Goals

- Practice all spelling words online.

- Finish reading *The Mary Celeste: An Unsolved Mystery from History* by Jane Yolen.

- Determine the key supporting details and main ideas of the reading.

- Summarize the text, quoting accurately and paraphrasing effectively.

GET READY

Introduction to *The Mary Celeste* (C)

Students will get a glimpse of what they will learn about in the lesson. They will also read the lesson goals and keywords. Have students select each keyword and preview its definition.

Spelling List 3 Review Game

Students will practice all spelling words from the workshop.

Recall *The Mary Celeste,* Part 2

Students will answer questions to review the reading that they have already completed.

Before You Read *The Mary Celeste*, Part 3

Students will be introduced to some key vocabulary words that they will encounter in the upcoming reading.

READ

The Mary Celeste, Part 3

Students will finish reading *The Mary Celeste: An Unsolved Mystery from History* by Jane Yolen.

Check-In: *The Mary Celeste*, Part 3

Students will answer several questions to demonstrate their comprehension of the final section of *The Mary Celeste: An Unsolved Mystery from History*.

LEARN AND TRY IT

LEARN   *The Mary Celeste* Says

Students will complete an online activity to learn about writing summaries that include main ideas and key details and that quote accurately from the text, but that are mostly paraphrased.

TRY IT   Show What You Know About *The Mary Celeste*

Students will complete an online activity in which they answer several questions about summarizing with main ideas and key details, using direct quotations, and paraphrasing.

TRY IT   Apply: Summarizing

Students will apply to a new work what they've learned about finding main ideas and key details, quoting accurately from the text, and paraphrasing.

TRY IT   Write a Summary

Students will demonstrate their ability to effectively summarize *The Mary Celeste: An Unsolved Mystery from History*. Have students complete Write a Summary from *Summit English Language Arts 5 Activity Book*.

LEARNING COACH CHECK-IN   This activity page contains an open-ended question, so it's important that you review students' responses. Give students feedback, using the sample answers provided to guide you.

The Mary Celeste (C)

Write a Summary

Write your responses in complete sentences.

Write a summary of the last section of *The Mary Celeste: An Unsolved Mystery from History*. In your summary, be sure to state the main ideas from this part of the book and several key details. Your summary should be mostly paraphrased. You should retell events in your own words, but it is acceptable to include one direct quotation from the text. If you include a direct quotation, remember to quote accurately and use quotation marks.

Answers will vary. Students' summary should cover Captain Morehouse's decision to salvage the *Mary Celeste*, the salvage trial, and the newspaper coverage of the mystery surrounding the *Mary Celeste*. Finally, the summary should state that there are many theories about what happened to the people on board the ship, but that the truth of what happened remains unknown. Most of the summary should be paraphrased rather than a direct reproduction of author Jane Yolen's language, but properly formatted and accurate direct quotations can be included.

TRY IT   Practice Words from *The Mary Celeste*, Part 3

Students will complete an online activity in which they answer questions to demonstrate their understanding of the vocabulary words from the reading.

WRAP-UP

Questions About Summarizing

Students will answer questions to show that they understand the main ideas and key details from *The Mary Celeste: An Unsolved Mystery from History*, as well as how to summarize effectively and use direct quotations correctly.

The Mary Celeste Wrap-Up

Lesson Overview

ACTIVITY	ACTIVITY TITLE	TIME	ONLINE/OFFLINE
GET READY	Introduction to *The Mary Celeste* Wrap-Up	**1** minute	
TRY IT	Write About *The Mary Celeste* **LEARNING COACH CHECK-IN**	**30** minutes	
	Read and Record	**10** minutes	
	Review Main Idea and Key Details from *The Mary Celeste*	**20** minutes	
QUIZ	Main Ideas and Key Details in *The Mary Celeste*	**30** minutes	
	Spelling List 3	**10** minutes	
WRAP-UP	Keyboarding	**10** minutes	
	More Language Arts Practice	**9** minutes	

Advance Preparation

During the Keyboarding activity, students will practice their keyboarding skills using an external website or program. **You will need to work with students to select an appropriate keyboarding practice website or program; K12 does not specify which resource to use.** A few suggestions are provided in the online activity.

Depending on which program you choose, students may need to set up an account to save their progress. If needed, assist students in setting up and running their chosen keyboarding practice program.

MATERIALS

Supplied
- *The Mary Celeste: An Unsolved Mystery from History* by Jane Yolen
- *Summit English Language Arts 5 Activity Book*
  - Write About *The Mary Celeste*

Lesson Goals

- Review *The Mary Celeste: An Unsolved Mystery from History*.
- Take a quiz on *The Mary Celeste: An Unsolved Mystery from History*.
- Take a spelling quiz.

Introduction to *The Mary Celeste* Wrap-Up

Students will read the lesson goals.

TRY IT

Write About *The Mary Celeste*

Students will complete Write About *The Mary Celeste* from *Summit English Language Arts 5 Activity Book*.

LEARNING COACH CHECK-IN This activity page contains open-ended questions, so it's important that you review students' responses. Give students feedback, using the sample answers provided to guide you.

TRY IT

***The Mary Celeste* Wrap-Up**

Write About *The Mary Celeste*

Write your response in complete sentences.

The final pages of *The Mary Celeste: An Unsolved Mystery from History* offer several theories about what happened to the people on board the ship, and the narrator says she has her own theory.

- Based on what you read in the book, what do you think took place? Why have you taken this position?
- Describe your theory about the events that led to the abandonment of the *Mary Celeste* and provide several details from the text that support it.
- Be sure to also include at least one direct quotation that helps support your theory.

Answers will vary.

- **Students' theory may appear in the book or may be one they come up with on their own, but the response must include multiple key details from the text to support whatever theory is offered.**
- **The response should also quote directly and accurately from the text in a way that helps support whatever position students take.**

THE MARY CELESTE WRAP-UP **53**

54 THE MARY CELESTE WRAP-UP

Read and Record

Good readers read quickly, smoothly, and with expression. This is called *fluency*. Students will record themselves reading aloud. They will listen to their recording and think about how quick, smooth, and expressive they sound.

TIP Encourage students to rerecord as needed.

Review Main Idea and Key Details from *The Mary Celeste*

Students will answer questions to review what they have learned about *The Mary Celeste: An Unsolved Mystery from History*.

Main Ideas and Key Details in *The Mary Celeste*

Students will complete the *The Mary Celeste* quiz.

Spelling List 3

Students will complete the Spelling List 3 quiz.

Keyboarding

Students will practice their keyboarding skills using an external website or program.

More Language Arts Practice

Students will practice skills according to their individual needs.

Narrative Writing: Prewriting (A)

Lesson Overview

ACTIVITY	ACTIVITY TITLE	TIME	ONLINE/OFFLINE
GET READY	Introduction to Narrative Writing: Prewriting (A)	**1** minute	🖥️
	Spelling List 4 Pretest **LEARNING COACH CHECK-IN**	**10** minutes	🖥️ and 📄
	Look Back at Perfect Tenses	**5** minutes	🖥️
LEARN AND **TRY IT**	Find Shifts in Verb Tense	**10** minutes	🖥️
	Practice Finding Shifts in Verb Tense	**15** minutes	🖥️
	Explore a Student's Personal Narrative	**15** minutes	🖥️
	Brainstorming for a Personal Narrative	**15** minutes	🖥️
	Brainstorm for Your Personal Narrative **LEARNING COACH CHECK-IN**	**47** minutes	📄
WRAP-UP	Questions About Brainstorming and Tense Shifts	**2** minutes	🖥️

Content Background

Students will begin working on a **personal narrative** about a meaningful moment in their lives. They will complete this assignment over the course of several lessons by following the writing process. Students will begin by prewriting.

Writing Process

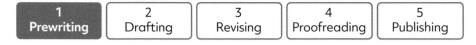

| 1 Prewriting | 2 Drafting | 3 Revising | 4 Proofreading | 5 Publishing |

During **prewriting**, writers choose a topic and create a plan for their writing assignment. In this lesson, students will complete the first part of prewriting, choosing a topic. To do that, they'll **brainstorm** by listing and evaluating several different topics.

Grammar, Usage, and Mechanics   Students will learn how to recognize a shift in verb tense and determine whether that shift is appropriate. A shift in verb tense occurs when the verbs in a sentence are in different tenses. It is incorrect for verbs to shift tense within a clause:

MATERIALS

Supplied
- *Summit English Language Arts 5 Activity Book*
  - Spelling List 4 Pretest
  - Brainstorm for Your Personal Narrative
- Personal Narrative Instructions (printout)

Also Needed
- folder for organizing personal narrative writing assignment pages

Incorrect shift: My eyes **grew** wide and **gleam**.

Verbs in different clauses may shift in tense if the shift is logical:

Correct shift: I **shrieked** because I **had wished** many times for a pet frog.

Advance Preparation

Gather a folder that students can use to keep all notes and activity pages related to their personal narrative.

KEYWORDS

brainstorming – before writing, a way for the writer to come up with ideas

personal narrative – an essay about a personal experience of the writer

prewriting – the stage or step of writing in which a writer chooses a topic, gathers ideas, and plans what to write

Lesson Goals

- Take a spelling pretest.
- Determine if a shift in verb tense is correct.
- Identify the steps in the writing process.
- Analyze how an author brainstorms.
- Brainstorm topics for your personal narrative.

GET READY

Introduction to Narrative Writing: Prewriting (A)

Students will get a glimpse of what they will learn about in the lesson. They will also read the lesson goals and keywords. Have students select each keyword and preview its definition.

Spelling List 4 Pretest

Students will take a spelling pretest.

LEARNING COACH CHECK-IN   Have students turn to Spelling List 4 Pretest in *Summit English Language Arts 5 Activity Book* and open the online Spelling Pretest activity. Online, students will listen to the spelling word, type the word in the space indicated, and then check their answer. In the activity book, students will write the correct spelling of the word in the tables provided and indicate with a ✓ or an ✗ if they spelled the word correctly or incorrectly online. Students will repeat this process with the remaining words.

As needed, help students with the interaction between the online activity and the activity book page until they become comfortable with what they need to do. As students practice their spelling words throughout the workshop, they should pay special attention to words they spelled incorrectly on the pretest.

This is the complete list of words students will be tested on.

Spelling Words	Abbreviations	Heart Words
ounce	oz	amateur
pint	pt	colonel
pound	lb	maneuver
quart	qt	
square	sq	
volume	vol.	
versus	vs.	

Look Back at Perfect Tenses
Students will practice forming and using the perfect verb tenses.

LEARN AND TRY IT

LEARN   Find Shifts in Verb Tense
Students will learn how to recognize a shift in verb tense and determine whether that shift is appropriate.

NOTE   In the next lesson, students will learn how to fix a shift in verb tense. For now, students will focus on recognizing a shift in tense and deciding whether it's correct.

TRY IT   Practice Finding Shifts in Verb Tense

Students will answer questions about recognizing shifts in verb tense and determining whether those shifts are appropriate. They will receive feedback on their answers.

LEARN   Explore a Student's Personal Narrative

To help them better understand their writing assignment, students will read a model personal narrative and explore the elements that make it successful.

LEARN   Brainstorming for a Personal Narrative

Students will learn about the writing process in general. Then they will closely investigate brainstorming, which is the first part of the prewriting step.

There are many ways to brainstorm. This activity introduces students to one effective brainstorming technique: making a list of ideas and systematically evaluating those ideas.

TRY IT   Brainstorm for Your Personal Narrative

Students will complete Brainstorm for Your Personal Narrative in *Summit English Language Arts 5 Activity Book*.

LEARNING COACH CHECK-IN   Review students' responses. Ensure that students have selected a topic for their personal narrative that meets the criteria listed in Question 3 of the activity page. When students have completed the page, they should store it in a folder so that they can refer to it throughout the writing process.

NOTE   In addition to the brainstorming activity, this activity page contains the instructions for the personal narrative. Students should read the instructions carefully, but in this lesson, they should complete the brainstorming activity only (not the entire assignment). If you or students wish, you can download and print another copy of the Personal Narrative Instructions online.

Questions About Brainstorming and Tense Shifts

Students will answer questions to show that they understand how to brainstorm a topic for a narrative and how to recognize a shift in verb tense.

Narrative Writing: Prewriting (B)

Lesson Overview

ACTIVITY	ACTIVITY TITLE	TIME	ONLINE/OFFLINE
GET READY	Introduction to Narrative Writing: Prewriting (B)	**1** minute	🛜
	Spelling List 4 Activity Bank	**10** minutes	📄
LEARN AND **TRY IT**	Fix Shifts in Verb Tense	**10** minutes	🛜
	Practice Fixing Shifts in Verb Tense	**10** minutes	🛜
	Prewriting for a Personal Narrative	**20** minutes	🛜
	Prewrite for Your Personal Narrative LEARNING COACH CHECK-IN	**42** minutes	📄
WRAP-UP	Questions About Prewriting and Tense Shifts	**2** minutes	🛜
	Go Read!	**25** minutes	🛜 or 📄

Content Background

Students will continue working on their **personal narrative** about a meaningful moment in their lives. They will complete this assignment over the course of several lessons by following the writing process. In this lesson, students will complete the prewriting step.

Writing Process

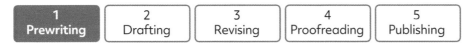

In this part of **prewriting**, students will use a graphic organizer to plan their narrative's beginning, middle, and end. They will also plan the **setting** and the way they will use **description** and **dialogue** to convey the **narrator's** feelings.

Grammar, Usage, and Mechanics   Students will learn how to fix an inappropriate shift in verb tense. In general, to fix an inappropriate shift in verb tense in a sentence, choose a single tense and use it throughout the sentence. Additionally, the tense must make sense with surrounding text.

In the following example, the second sentence has an incorrect shift. To fix the shift, put both verbs in the past tense because that is consistent with the tense in the first sentence.

MATERIALS

Supplied
- *Summit English Language Arts 5 Activity Book*
  - Spelling List 4 Activity Bank
  - Prewrite for Your Personal Narrative
- Personal Narrative Instructions (printout)

Also Needed
- completed Spelling List 4 Pretest activity page from Narrative Writing: Prewriting (A)
- folder in which students are storing personal narrative writing assignment pages
- reading material for Go Read!

Incorrect shift: I shrieked because I had wished many times for a pet frog. Whenever I **tell** a joke, the frog **croaked**.

Revised shift: I shrieked because I had wished many times for a pet frog. Whenever I **told** a joke, the frog **croaked**.

Students will also learn how to revise incorrect shifts that involve the perfect tenses.

Advance Preparation

Gather students' completed Spelling List 4 Pretest activity page from Narrative Writing: Prewriting (A). Students will refer to this page during Get Ready: Spelling List 4 Activity Bank.

Gather the folder that students are using to store the activity pages related to their personal narrative. The folder should contain the following:

- Students' completed Brainstorm for Your Personal Narrative activity page from Narrative Writing: Prewriting (A)

During the Go Read! activity, students will have the option of using the digital library. Allow extra time for students to make their reading selection, or have students make a selection before beginning the lesson.

Lesson Goals

- Practice spelling words offline.
- Fix an incorrect shift in verb tense.
- Analyze how an author plans a personal narrative.
- Plan the sequence, narrator, characters, and setting of your personal narrative.
- Read for pleasure.

KEYWORDS

character – a person or animal in a story

description – writing that uses words that show how something looks, sounds, feels, tastes, or smells

dialogue – the words that characters say in a written work

narrator – the teller of a story

personal narrative – an essay about a personal experience of the writer

prewriting – the stage or step of writing in which a writer chooses a topic, gathers ideas, and plans what to write

setting – where or when a literary work takes place

GET READY

Introduction to Narrative Writing: Prewriting (B)

Students will get a glimpse of what they will learn about in the lesson. They will also read the lesson goals and keywords. Have students select each keyword and preview its definition.

Spelling List 4 Activity Bank

Students will practice all spelling words from the workshop by completing Spelling List 4 Activity Bank from *Summit English Language Arts 5 Activity*

Book. Make sure students have their completed Spelling List 4 Pretest activity page from Narrative Writing: Prewriting (A) to refer to during this activity.

Remind students to pay special attention to words they spelled incorrectly on the Spelling Pretest.

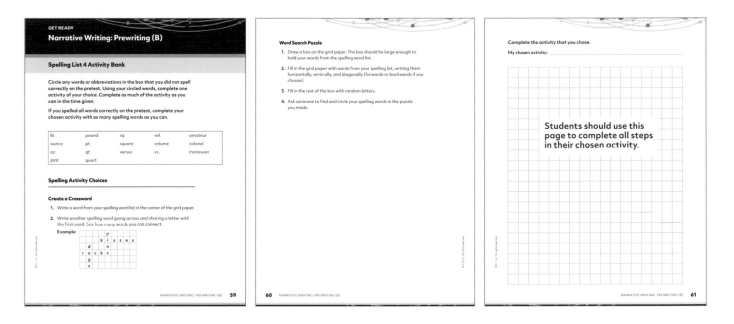

LEARN AND TRY IT

LEARN   Fix Shifts in Verb Tense

Students will learn how to revise an inappropriate shift in verb tense.

TRY IT   Practice Fixing Shifts in Verb Tense

Students will answer questions about revising shifts in verb tense. They will receive feedback on their answers.

LEARN   Prewriting for a Personal Narrative

Students will investigate how a student prewrites for her personal narrative.

> **TIP**   Students may wish to jot notes on their Prewrite for Your Personal Narrative activity page as they work through this activity.

TRY IT   Prewrite for Your Personal Narrative

Students will complete Prewrite for Your Personal Narrative in *Summit English Language Arts 5 Activity Book*. Make sure students have their completed Brainstorm for Your Personal Narrative activity page from Narrative Writing: Prewriting (A) to refer to during this activity.

Review students' responses. Ensure that the narrative students are planning is in line with the assignment criteria outlined on the Brainstorm for Your Personal Narrative activity page. It's especially important to ensure that students have not planned too broad a time line to cover in two pages. When students have completed the page, they should store it in the folder they are using to organize their writing assignment pages.

SUPPORT To help students shorten the time line of their narrative, have them choose a new beginning from the Middle box of their graphic organizer.

NOTE If you or students wish, you can download and print another copy of the Personal Narrative Instructions online.

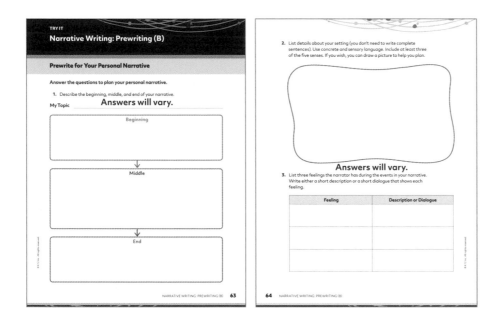

Questions About Prewriting and Tense Shifts

Students will answer questions to show that they understand how to prewrite for a narrative and how to fix a shift in verb tense.

Go Read!

Students will read for pleasure. They should choose a book or a magazine that interests them, or they may choose a selection from the digital library, linked in the online lesson.

Students should read for the entire time. Have students select something to read ahead of time to help them stay focused.

Narrative Writing: Drafting (A)

Lesson Overview

ACTIVITY	ACTIVITY TITLE	TIME	ONLINE/OFFLINE
GET READY	Introduction to Narrative Writing: Drafting (A)	**1** minute	🖥️
	Spelling List 4 Review Game	**10** minutes	🖥️
	Checkmate	**10** minutes	🖥️
LEARN AND **TRY IT**	Drafting a Personal Narrative	**15** minutes	🖥️
	Draft Your Personal Narrative LEARNING COACH CHECK-IN	**62** minutes	📄
WRAP-UP	Question About Drafting	**2** minutes	🖥️
	Go Read!	**20** minutes	🖥️ or 📄

Content Background

Students will continue working on their personal narrative about a meaningful moment in their lives. They will complete this assignment over the course of several lessons by following the writing process. In this lesson, students will begin drafting their narrative.

Writing Process

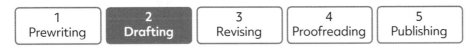

| 1 Prewriting | 2 Drafting | 3 Revising | 4 Proofreading | 5 Publishing |

During **drafting**, students will use their prewriting as a guide as they write a rough draft of their personal narrative. A rough draft is a complete first version of a piece of writing. Writers create rough drafts to get all of their ideas fleshed out and in order from beginning to end. In other words, a rough draft is a starting point, or a first attempt at a complete narrative. During revision and proofreading, writers refine their ideas and fix any errors.

Students are expected to write about half of their rough draft in this lesson (although they may write more if they wish). They will have time to finish and submit their draft in Narrative Writing: Drafting (B).

MATERIALS

Supplied
- *Summit English Language Arts 5 Activity Book*
  - Draft Your Personal Narrative
- Personal Narrative Instructions (printout)
- Drafting Paper (printout)

Also Needed
- folder in which students are storing personal narrative writing assignment pages
- reading material for Go Read!

Advance Preparation

Gather the folder that students are using to store the activity pages related to their personal narrative. The folder should contain the following:

- Students' completed Brainstorm for Your Personal Narrative activity page from Narrative Writing: Prewriting (A)

- Students' completed Prewrite for Your Personal Narrative activity page from Narrative Writing: Prewriting (B)

During the Go Read! activity, students will have the option of using the digital library. Allow extra time for students to make their reading selection, or have students make a selection before beginning the lesson.

Lesson Goals

- Practice spelling words online.
- Practice grammar skills by editing a passage.
- Analyze how an author writes a rough draft.
- Start the rough draft of your personal narrative.
- Read for pleasure.

GET READY

Introduction to Narrative Writing: Drafting (A)

Students will get a glimpse of what they will learn about in the lesson. They will also read the lesson goals and keywords. Have students select each keyword and preview its definition.

Spelling List 4 Review Game

Students will practice all spelling words from the workshop.

Checkmate

Students will edit a short passage to practice applying grammer skills. This passage contains errors and questions related to subject-verb agreement and shifts in verb tense.

LEARN Drafting a Personal Narrative

Students will investigate how a student drafts a personal narrative.

TIP Emphasize that rough drafts are not perfect. Even expert writers make many revisions to their rough drafts.

TRY IT Draft Your Personal Narrative

Students will complete half of their rough draft using Draft Your Personal Narrative in *Summit English Language Arts 5 Activity Book*. If students wish, they may complete more than half of their draft.

Make sure students have their completed Brainstorm for Your Personal Narrative activity page from Narrative Writing: Prewriting (A) and Prewrite for Your Personal Narrative activity page from Narrative Writing: Prewriting (B) to refer to during this activity.

LEARNING COACH CHECK-IN Review students' responses. Ensure that students' draft is in line with the assignment criteria outlined on the Brainstorm for Your Personal Narrative activity page. Students should store their draft in the folder they are using to organize their writing assignment pages.

NOTE If you or students wish, you can download and print another copy of the Personal Narrative Instructions online. Additional sheets of Drafting Paper are also available online.

TRY IT
Narrative Writing: Drafting (A)

Draft Your Personal Narrative

Write the first draft of your personal narrative. Write only on the white rows. You will use the purple rows for revisions later.

Title

start here ▶

Students should write their draft in the white rows only.

keep writing ▶

Draft Page 1

NARRATIVE WRITING: DRAFTING (A) 65

66 NARRATIVE WRITING: DRAFTING (A)

keep writing ▶

Draft Page 2

keep writing ▶

Draft Page 3

Draft Page 4

keep writing ▶

Draft Page 5

keep writing ▶

Draft Page 6

Draft Page 7

keep writing ▶

Draft Page 8

WRAP-UP

Question About Drafting

Students will answer a question to show that they understand how to draft a narrative.

Go Read!

Students will read for pleasure. They should choose a book or a magazine that interests them, or they may choose a selection from the digital library, linked in the online lesson.

Students should read for the entire time. Have students select something to read ahead of time to help them stay focused.

Narrative Writing: Drafting (B)

Lesson Overview

ACTIVITY	ACTIVITY TITLE	TIME	ONLINE/OFFLINE
GET READY	Introduction to Narrative Writing: Drafting (B)	**1** minute	🖥️
TRY IT	Review Shifts in Verb Tense	**10** minutes	🖥️
QUIZ	Shifts in Verb Tense	**20** minutes	🖥️
	Spelling List 4	**10** minutes	🖥️
TRY IT	Finish Drafting Your Personal Narrative **LEARNING COACH CHECK-IN**	**59** minutes	📄
WRAP-UP	Turn In Your Personal Narrative	**1** minute	🖥️
	Keyboarding	**10** minutes	🖥️
	More Language Arts Practice	**9** minutes	🖥️

Content Background

Students will continue working on their **personal narrative** about a meaningful moment in their lives. In this lesson, students will finish and submit their rough draft. Later, they will revise, proofread, and publish their personal narrative.

Writing Process

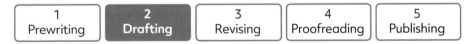

| 1 Prewriting | 2 Drafting | 3 Revising | 4 Proofreading | 5 Publishing |

Advance Preparation

Gather the folder that students are using to store the activity pages related to their personal narrative. The folder should contain the following:

- Students' completed Brainstorm for Your Personal Narrative activity page from Narrative Writing: Prewriting (A)

- Students' completed Prewrite for Your Personal Narrative activity page from Narrative Writing: Prewriting (B)

- Students' in-progress Draft Your Personal Narrative activity page from Narrative Writing: Drafting (A)

> ### MATERIALS
>
> **Supplied**
> - *Summit English Language Arts 5 Activity Book*
>   - Draft Your Personal Narrative
> - Personal Narrative Instructions (printout)
> - Drafting Paper (printout)
>
> **Also Needed**
> - folder in which students are storing personal narrative writing assignment pages

During the Keyboarding activity, students will practice their keyboarding skills using an external website or program. **You will need to work with students to select an appropriate keyboarding practice website or program; K12 does not specify which resource to use.** A few suggestions are provided in the online activity.

Depending on which program you choose, students may need to set up an account to save their progress. If needed, assist students in setting up and running their chosen keyboarding practice program.

Lesson Goals

- Review how to find and fix shifts in verb tense.
- Take a quiz on shifts in verb tense.
- Take a spelling quiz.
- Finish and submit the rough draft of your personal narrative.

GET READY

Introduction to Narrative Writing: Drafting (B)

Students will read the lesson goals.

TRY IT

Review Shifts in Verb Tense

Students will answer questions to review what they have learned about shifts in verb tense.

QUIZ

Shifts in Verb Tense

Students will complete the Shifts in Verb Tense quiz.

Spelling List 4

Students will complete the Spelling List 4 quiz.

TRY IT

Finish Drafting Your Personal Narrative

Students will complete the rough draft of their personal narrative. Students should gather the Draft Your Personal Narrative activity page that they started in Narrative Writing: Drafting (A) and complete it.

Make sure students also have their completed Brainstorm for Your Personal Narrative activity page from Narrative Writing: Prewriting (A), and Prewrite for Your Personal Narrative activity page from Narrative Writing: Prewriting (B) to refer to during this activity.

LEARNING COACH CHECK-IN Review students' draft. Ensure that students' draft is in line with the assignment criteria outlined on the Brainstorm for Your Personal Narrative activity page. If necessary, remind students not to focus on perfection at this stage of the writing process.

NOTE If you or students wish, you can download and print another copy of the Personal Narrative Instructions online. Additional sheets of Drafting Paper are also available online.

WRAP-UP

Turn In Your Personal Narrative Draft

Students will submit their writing assignment to their teacher.

Keyboarding

Students will practice their keyboarding skills using an external website or program.

More Language Arts Practice

Students will practice skills according to their individual needs.

Nuance

Lesson Overview

ACTIVITY	ACTIVITY TITLE	TIME	ONLINE/OFFLINE
GET READY	Introduction to Nuance	**1** minute	🖥️
	Look Back at Shades of Meaning	**4** minutes	🖥️
LEARN AND **TRY IT**	Small Differences Matter	**10** minutes	🖥️
	Practice Recognizing Nuances in Words	**10** minutes	🖥️
	Apply: Nuance **LEARNING COACH CHECK-IN**	**15** minutes	📄
	Go Write!	**15** minutes	📄
	Review Nuance	**15** minutes	🖥️
QUIZ	Nuance	**15** minutes	🖥️
WRAP-UP	Keyboarding	**10** minutes	🖥️
	More Language Arts Practice	**10** minutes	🖥️
	Go Read!	**15** minutes	🖥️ or 📄

Content Background

Students will learn several words whose meanings are similar but subtly different, and they will practice using those words appropriately and effectively.

Advance Preparation

During the Keyboarding activity, students will practice their keyboarding skills using an external website or program. **You will need to work with students to select an appropriate keyboarding practice website or program; K12 does not specify which resource to use.** A few suggestions are provided in the

Depending on which program you choose, students may need to set up an account to save their progress. If needed, assist students in setting up and running their chosen keyboarding practice program.

MATERIALS

Supplied
- *Summit English Language Arts 5 Activity Book*
  - Apply: Nuance

Also Needed
- reading material for Go Read!

During the Go Read! activity, students will have the option of using the digital library. Allow extra time for students to make their reading selection, or have students make a selection before beginning the lesson.

Lesson Goals

- Recognize subtle differences in the meanings of words.
- Use context clues to help determine meaning of unknown words.
- Use synonyms and antonyms to better understand the meaning of words.

GET READY

Introduction to Nuance

Students will get a glimpse of what they will learn about in the lesson. They will also read the lesson goals and keywords. Have students select each keyword and preview its definition.

Look Back at Shades of Meaning

Students will revisit content related to the idea that words can have similar, but not identical, meanings.

LEARN AND TRY IT

LEARN   Small Differences Matter

Students will learn that words with subtle differences in meaning give writers choices in how to convey their messages.

Students will also learn that context clues, synonyms, and antonyms can help them determine which word best completes a sentence.

TRY IT   Practice Recognizing Nuances in Words

Students will answer questions to practice recognizing nuance and choosing between words with subtly different meanings.

TRY IT   Apply: Nuance

Students will complete Apply: Nuance from *Summit English Language Arts 5 Activity Book*.

LEARNING COACH CHECK-IN   This activity page contains open-ended questions, so it's important that you review students' responses. Give students feedback, using the sample answers provided to guide you.

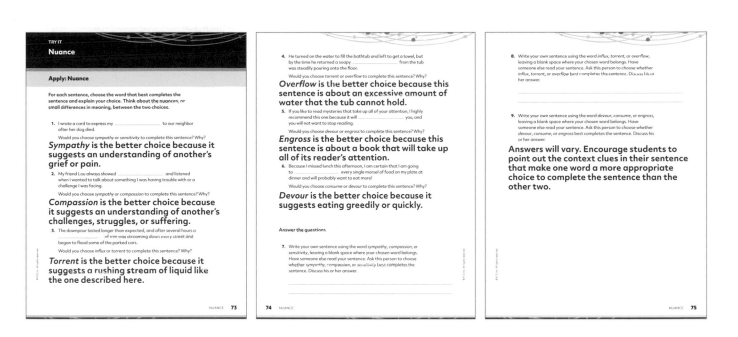

TRY IT   Go Write!

Students will write independently for pleasure. As they write, they should think about the nuances of words so that they choose words that are exactly right for the message they want their writing to convey.

TRY IT   Review Nuance

Sstudents will answer questions to review what they have learned about nuance.

Nuance

Students will complete the Nuance quiz.

Keyboarding

Students will practice their keyboarding skills using an external website or program.

More Language Arts Practice

Students will practice skills according to their individual needs.

Go Read!

Students will read for pleasure. They should choose a book or a magazine that interests them, or they may choose a selection from the digital library, linked in the online lesson.

Students should read for the entire time. Have students select something to read ahead of time to help them stay focused.

Mesmerized (A)

Lesson Overview

ACTIVITY	ACTIVITY TITLE	TIME	ONLINE/OFFLINE
GET READY	Introduction to *Mesmerized* (A)	**1** minute	📶
	Spelling List 5 Pretest **LEARNING COACH CHECK-IN**	**10** minutes	📶 and 📄
	Look Back at Using Context Clues	**4** minutes	📶
	Before You Read *Mesmerized*, Part 1	**15** minutes	📶
READ	*Mesmerized*, Part 1	**30** minutes	📄
	Check-In: *Mesmerized*, Part 1	**5** minutes	📶
LEARN AND **TRY IT**	Main Idea and Making Inferences	**10** minutes	📶
	Details, Inferences, and Main Ideas in *Mesmerized*	**10** minutes	📶
	Apply: Make Inferences to Find Main Ideas	**15** minutes	📶
	Write About Franklin and Mesmer **LEARNING COACH CHECK-IN**	**10** minutes	📄
	Practice Words from *Mesmerized*, Part 1	**8** minutes	📶
WRAP-UP	Questions About *Mesmerized*, Part 1	**2** minutes	📶

Content Background

Students will complete a spelling activity and begin to read *Mesmerized* by Mara Rockliff. They will then complete activities in which they learn about using details to make inferences (conclusions drawn from evidence in the text) and finding main ideas.

MATERIALS

Supplied
- *Mesmerized: How Ben Franklin Solved a Mystery that Baffled All of France* by Mara Rockliff
- *Summit English Language Arts 5 Activity Book*
  - Spelling List 5 Pretest
  - Write About Franklin and Mesmer

Mesmerized, Part 1 Synopsis

During the American Revolution, Benjamin Franklin goes to France to seek French aid for the American cause. He arrives in Paris to find that the city is enthralled by recent scientific advances, and he is a celebrity because of his own scientific achievements. One person who is particularly popular in Paris at this time is an Austrian doctor named Anton Mesmer. Dr. Mesmer claims to have discovered a mysterious force that can cure people of all manner of ills. People flock to Dr. Mesmer for treatment, but some French doctors question whether his mysterious force is real. They bring their concerns to the king, and he turns to Ben Franklin for help.

KEYWORDS

inference – a guess that readers make using the clues that authors give them in a piece of writing

main idea – the most important point the author makes; it may be stated or unstated

scientific method – a way to find answers by experimenting, observing, and drawing conclusions

supporting detail – a detail that gives more information about a main idea

Lesson Goals

- Take a spelling pretest.

- Begin reading *Mesmerized* by Mara Rockliff.

- Make inferences and use key details to determine main ideas in the reading.

- Explore vocabulary in the reading.

GET READY

Introduction to *Mesmerized* (A)

Students will get a glimpse of what they will learn about in the lesson. They will also read the lesson goals and keywords. Have students select each keyword and preview its definition.

Spelling List 5 Pretest

Students will take a spelling pretest.

LEARNING COACH CHECK-IN   Have students turn to Spelling List 5 Pretest in the activity book and open the online Spelling Pretest activity. Online, students will listen to the spelling word, type the word in the space indicated, and then check their answer. In the activity book, students will write the correct spelling of the word in the tables provided and indicate with a ✓ or an ✗ if they spelled the word correctly or incorrectly online. Students will repeat this process with the remaining words.

As needed, help students with the interaction between the online activity and the activity book page until they become comfortable with what they need

to do. As students practice their spelling words throughout the workshop, they should pay special attention to words they spelled incorrectly on the pretest.

This is the complete list of words students will be tested on.

Related Words	Related Words	Root *prehend*
comparable	resign	apprehend
compare	resignation	comprehend
janitor	restoration	comprehensive
janitorial	restore	
major		
majority		
perspiration		
perspire		
preside		
president		

NOTE Have students keep their completed activity page in a safe place so they can refer to it later.

Spelling List 5 Pretest

1. Open the Spelling Pretest activity online. Listen to the first spelling word. Type the word. Check your answer.

2. Write the correct spelling of the word in the Word column of the Spelling Pretest table on the next page.

Word	⊘	⊗
1 blindfold		

3. Put a check mark in the ⊘ column if you spelled the word correctly online.

Word	⊘	⊗
1 blindfold	✓	

   Put an X in the ⊗ column if you spelled the word incorrectly online.

Word	⊘	⊗
1 blindfold		X

4. Repeat Steps 1–3 for the remaining words in the Spelling Pretest.

MESMERIZED (A) **77**

Mesmerized (A)

Spelling List 5 Pretest

Write each spelling word in the Word column, making sure to spell it correctly.

Word	⊘	⊗	Word	⊘	⊗
1 comparable			10 president		
2 compare			11 resign		
3 janitor			12 resignation		
4 janitorial			13 restoration		
5 major			14 restore		
6 majority			15 apprehend		
7 perspiration			16 comprehend		
8 perspire			17 comprehensive		
9 preside					

Students should use the ✓ and X columns to indicate whether they spelled each word correctly or incorrectly online.

78 MESMERIZED (A)

Look Back at Using Context Clues

Students will review some key strategies that good readers employ to understand the meanings of unfamiliar words in texts.

Before You Read *Mesmerized*, Part 1

Students will be introduced to some key vocabulary words that they will encounter in the upcoming reading. They will learn how to handle the foreign language words they will find in the text, and they will answer questions to help them set a purpose for their reading.

READ

Mesmerized, Part 1

Students will read pages 6–18 of *Mesmerized* by Mara Rockliff.

Check-In: *Mesmerized*, Part 1

Students will answer several questions to demonstrate their comprehension of pages 6–18 of *Mesmerized*.

LEARN AND TRY IT

LEARN   Main Idea and Making Inferences

Students will complete an online activity to learn about using details to make inferences and arrive at main ideas.

TRY IT   Details, Inferences, and Main Ideas in *Mesmerized*

Students will answer several questions in which they find details that support inferences made from passages. They will then identify main ideas.

TRY IT   Apply: Make Inferences to Find Main Ideas

Students will apply to a new work what they've learned about using details to make inferences and identify main ideas.

TRY IT   Write About Franklin and Mesmer

Students will complete Write About Franklin and Mesmer from *Summit English Language Arts 5 Activity Book*.

LEARNING COACH CHECK-IN   This activity page contains open-ended questions, so it's important that you review students' responses. Give students feedback, using the sample answers provided to guide you.

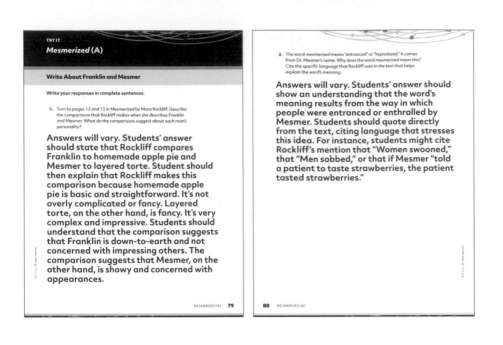

TRY IT
Mesmerized (A)

Write About Franklin and Mesmer

Write your responses in complete sentences.

1. Turn to pages 12 and 13 in *Mesmerized* by Mara Rockliff. Describe the comparisons that Rockliff makes when she describes Franklin and Mesmer. What do the comparisons suggest about each man's personality?

Answers will vary. Students' answer should state that Rockliff compares Franklin to homemade apple pie and Mesmer to layered torte. Student should then explain that Rockliff makes this comparison because homemade apple pie is basic and straightforward. It's not overly complicated or fancy. Layered torte, on the other hand, is fancy. It's very complex and impressive. Students should understand that the comparison suggests that Franklin is down-to-earth and not concerned with impressing others. The comparison suggests that Mesmer, on the other hand, is showy and concerned with appearances.

MESMERIZED (A)   **79**

2. The word *mesmerized* means "entranced" or "hypnotized." It comes from Dr. Mesmer's name. Why does the word *mesmerized* mean this? Cite the specific language that Rockliff uses in the text that helps explain the word's meaning.

Answers will vary. Students' answer should show an understanding that the word's meaning results from the way in which people were entranced or enthralled by Mesmer. Students should quote directly from the text, citing language that stresses this idea. For instance, students might cite Rockliff's mention that "Women swooned," that "Men sobbed," or that if Mesmer "told a patient to taste strawberries, the patient tasted strawberries."

80   MESMERIZED (A)

TRY IT   Practice Words from *Mesmerized*, Part 1

Students will complete an online activity in which they answer questions to demonstrate their understanding of the vocabulary words from the reading.

WRAP-UP

Questions About *Mesmerized*, Part 1

Students will answer questions to show that they understand identifying key details, making inferences, and finding main ideas.

Mesmerized (B)

Lesson Overview

ACTIVITY	ACTIVITY TITLE	TIME	ONLINE/OFFLINE
GET READY	Introduction to *Mesmerized* (B)	**1** minute	
	Spelling List 5 Activity Bank	**10** minutes	
	Recall *Mesmerized*, Part 1	**5** minutes	
	Before You Read *Mesmerized*, Part 2	**10** minutes	
READ	*Mesmerized*, Part 2	**30** minutes	
	Check-In: *Mesmerized*, Part 2	**5** minutes	
LEARN AND **TRY IT**	More Than One Main Idea	**10** minutes	
	More Main Ideas	**10** minutes	
	Apply: More Main Ideas	**15** minutes	
	Write About Multiple Main Ideas **LEARNING COACH CHECK-IN**	**15** minutes	
	Practice Words from *Mesmerized*, Part 2	**7** minutes	
WRAP-UP	Questions About *Mesmerized*, Part 2	**2** minutes	

Content Background

Students will complete a spelling activity and continue to read *Mesmerized* by Mara Rockliff. They will then complete activities in which they learn about finding multiple main ideas within a single passage by using key details and making inferences.

Advance Preparation

Gather students' completed Spelling List 5 Pretest activity page from *Mesmerized* (A). Students will refer to this page during Get Ready: Spelling List 5 Activity Bank.

MATERIALS

Supplied
- *Mesmerized: How Ben Franklin Solved a Mystery that Baffled All of France* by Mara Rockliff
- *Summit English Language Arts 5 Activity Book*
  - Spelling List 5 Activity Bank
  - Write About Multiple Main Ideas

Also Needed
- completed Spelling List 5 Pretest activity page from *Mesmerized* (A)

Mesmerized, Part 2 Synopsis

Franklin agrees to be mesmerized by Mesmer's assistant, Charles, but the treatment has no effect on him. Franklin believes that the force only exists in the minds of Mesmer's patients. He conducts experiments to prove his hypothesis. These experiments make it clear that there really is no mysterious force at work; the patients are imagining everything they feel. If the force cures them of any illness or ailment, it is only because they expect it to do so. Franklin tells the king about the results of his experiment, and Mesmer flees Paris. Soon after, Franklin returns to America. But his methods for testing medical treatments are still in use today, and today Mesmer's force could be categorized as a placebo effect.

Lesson Goals

- Practice all spelling words offline.

- Continue reading *Mesmerized* by Mara Rockliff.

- Make inferences and determine multiple main ideas within single sections of text.

- Explore vocabulary in the reading.

GET READY

Introduction to *Mesmerized* (B)

Students will get a glimpse of what they will learn about in the lesson. They will also read the lesson goals and keywords. Have students select each keyword and preview its definition.

Spelling List 5 Activity Bank

Students will practice all spelling words from the workshop by completing Spelling List 5 Activity Bank from *Summit English Language Arts 5 Activity Book*. Make sure students have their completed Spelling List 5 Pretest activity page from *Mesmerized* (A) to refer to during this activity.

Remind students to pay special attention to the words they spelled incorrectly on their Spelling Pretest.

Mesmerized (B)

Spelling List 5 Activity Bank

Circle any words in the box that you did not spell correctly on the pretest. Using your circled words, complete one activity of your choice. Complete as much of the activity as you can in the time given.

If you spelled all words correctly on the pretest, complete your chosen activity with as many spelling words as you can.

comparable	major	preside	resignation	apprehend
compare	majority	president	restoration	comprehend
janitor	perspiration	resign	restore	comprehensive
janitorial	perspire			

Spelling Activity Choices

Vowel-Free Words

1. In the left column, write only the consonants in each word and put a dot where each vowel should be.
2. Spell each word out loud, stating which vowels should be in the places you wrote dots.
3. In the right column, rewrite the entire spelling word.
4. Correct any spelling errors.

Alphabetizing

1. In the left column, write your words from the spelling word list in alphabetical order.
2. Correct any spelling errors.

Parts of Speech

1. In the left column, write the words from your spelling list that are nouns.
2. In the right column, write all the other words from your spelling list and label each word's part of speech.
3. Correct any spelling errors.

Uppercase and Lowercase

1. In the left column, write each of your words in all capital letters, or all uppercase.
2. In the right column, write each of your words in all lowercase letters.
3. Correct any spelling errors.

Complete the activity that you chose.

My chosen activity: _____

1.
2.
3.
4.
5.
6.
7.
8.
9.
10.
11.
12.
13.
14.
15.
16.
17.
18.
19.
20.
21.
22.
23.
24.

Students should use this page to complete all steps in their chosen activity.

Recall *Mesmerized*, Part 1

Students will answer questions to review the reading that they have already completed.

Before You Read *Mesmerized*, Part 2

Students will be introduced to some key vocabulary words that they will encounter in the upcoming reading. Then they will learn about the scientific method, which plays an important part in the upcoming reading.

READ

Mesmerized, Part 2

Students will read pages 19–41 of *Mesmerized* by Mara Rockliff.

Check-In: *Mesmerized*, Part 2

Students will answer several questions to demonstrate their comprehension of pages 19–41 of *Mesmerized*.

LEARN AND TRY IT

LEARN   More Than One Main Idea

Students will complete an online activity to learn about using details and inferences to arrive at more than one main idea within a single passage.

TRY IT   More Main Ideas

Students will complete an online activity in which they practice identifying multiple main ideas within single passages from *Mesmerized*.

TRY IT   Apply: More Main Ideas

Students will apply to a new work what they've learned about identifying multiple main ideas.

TRY IT   Write About Multiple Main Ideas

Students will complete Write About Multiple Main Ideas from *Summit English Language Arts 5 Activity Book*.

LEARNING COACH CHECK-IN   This activity page contains open-ended questions, so it's important that you review students' responses. Give students feedback, using the sample answers provided to guide you.

TRY IT   Practice Words from *Mesmerized*, Part 2

Students will complete an online activity in which they answer questions to demonstrate their understanding of the vocabulary words from the reading.

WRAP-UP

Questions About *Mesmerized*, Part 2

Students will answer questions to show that they understand that a single passage can have multiple main ideas, how to make inferences based on key details, and identifying more than one main idea in a passage.

Mesmerized (C)

Lesson Overview

ACTIVITY	ACTIVITY TITLE	TIME	ONLINE/OFFLINE
GET READY	Introduction to *Mesmerized* (C)	**1** minute	🖥️
	Spelling List 5 Review Game	**10** minutes	🖥️
	Recall *Mesmerized*, Part 2	**5** minutes	🖥️
	Before You Read *Mesmerized*, Part 3	**10** minutes	🖥️
READ	*Mesmerized*, Part 3	**30** minutes	📄
	Check-In: *Mesmerized*, Part 3	**5** minutes	🖥️
LEARN AND TRY IT	Effective Summaries	**10** minutes	🖥️
	More Summaries	**10** minutes	🖥️
	Apply: Summarize Another Work	**15** minutes	🖥️
	Summarize *Mesmerized* **LEARNING COACH CHECK-IN**	**15** minutes	📄
	Practice Words from *Mesmerized*, Part 3	**7** minutes	🖥️
WRAP-UP	Questions About *Mesmerized*, Part 3	**2** minutes	🖥️

Content Background

Students will complete a spelling activity and finish reading *Mesmerized* by Mara Rockliff. They will then complete activities in which they learn about writing effective summaries.

MATERIALS

Supplied
- *Mesmerized: How Ben Franklin Solved a Mystery that Baffled All of France* by Mara Rockliff
- *Summit English Language Arts 5 Activity Book*
  - Summarize *Mesmerized*

Mesmerized, Part 3 Synopsis

Today's reading is a more detailed and academic account of the events of the text. This section of the book provides readers with more information about Franklin's life and background, the scientific advances that captured the imaginations of the French during the time that Franklin was in Paris, and additional facts about Dr. Anton Mesmer's life, his practices, and his exceptional popularity in the late 1770s and early 1780s. The reading describes how Franklin and others came to question Mesmer's methods. It relates what they did to confirm their suspicions about animal magnetism. And it covers the consequences of their actions.

Lesson Goals

- Practice all spelling words online.

- Finish reading *Mesmerized*.

- Make inferences to determine supporting details and main ideas of *Mesmerized*.

- Summarize *Mesmerized*.

GET READY

Introduction to *Mesmerized* (C)

Students will get a glimpse of what they will learn about in the lesson. They will also read the lesson goals and keywords. Have students select each keyword and preview its definition.

Spelling List 5 Review Game

Students will practice all spelling words from the workshop.

Recall *Mesmerized, Part 2*

Students will answer questions to review the reading that they have already completed.

Before You Read *Mesmerized*, Part 3

Students will be introduced to some key vocabulary words that they will encounter in the upcoming reading. Then they will learn about how words enter the English language in a variety of ways.

Mesmerized, Part 3

Students will read pages 42–45 of *Mesmerized* by Mara Rockliff.

Check-In: *Mesmerized*, Part 3

Students will answer several questions to demonstrate their comprehension of pages 42–45 of *Mesmerized*.

LEARN AND TRY IT

LEARN   Effective Summaries

Students will complete an online activity to learn about what does and does not belong in an effective summary and the role that inferences play in creating an effective summary.

TRY IT   More Summaries

Students will complete an online activity in which they practice effectively summarizing passages from *Mesmerized*.

TRY IT   Apply: Summarize Another Work

Students will apply to a new work what they've learned about summarizing.

TRY IT   Summarize *Mesmerized*

Students will complete Summarize *Mesmerized* from *Summit English Language Arts 5 Activity Book*.

LEARNING COACH CHECK-IN   This activity page contains an open-ended question, so it's important that you review students' responses. Give students feedback, using the sample answers provided to guide you.

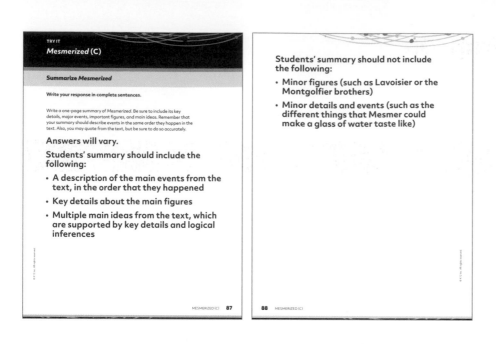

TRY IT   Practice Words from *Mesmerized*, Part 3

Students will complete an online activity in which they answer questions to demonstrate their understanding of the vocabulary words from the reading.

WRAP-UP

Questions About *Mesmerized*, Part 3

Students will answer questions to show that they understand how to write an effective summary.

Mesmerized Wrap-Up

Lesson Overview

ACTIVITY	ACTIVITY TITLE	TIME	ONLINE/OFFLINE
GET READY	Introduction to *Mesmerized* Wrap-Up	**1** minute	🖥️
TRY IT	Write About Ben Franklin **LEARNING COACH CHECK-IN**	**30** minutes	📄
	Read and Record	**10** minutes	🖥️
	Review Main Ideas, Details, and Summaries from *Mesmerized*	**20** minutes	🖥️
QUIZ	Main Ideas, Details, and Summaries from *Mesmerized*	**30** minutes	🖥️
	Spelling List 5	**10** minutes	🖥️
WRAP-UP	Keyboarding	**10** minutes	🖥️
	More Language Arts Practice	**9** minutes	🖥️

Advance Preparation

During the Keyboarding activity, students will practice their keyboarding skills using an external website or program. **You will need to work with students to select an appropriate keyboarding practice website or program; K12 does not specify which resource to use.** A few suggestions are provided in the online activity.

Depending on which program you choose, students may need to set up an account to save their progress. If needed, assist students in setting up and running their chosen keyboarding practice program.

MATERIALS

Supplied
- *Mesmerized: How Ben Franklin Solved a Mystery that Baffled All of France* by Mara Rockliff
- *Summit English Language Arts 5 Activity Book*
  - Write About Ben Franklin

Lesson Goals

- Write about Ben Franklin and the relationship he had with the people of France.
- Review *Mesmerized*.
- Take a quiz on *Mesmerized*.
- Take a spelling quiz.

Introduction to *Mesmerized* Wrap-Up
Students will read the lesson goals.

TRY IT

Write About Ben Franklin
Students will complete Write About Ben Franklin from *Summit English Language Arts 5 Activity Book*.

LEARNING COACH CHECK-IN   This activity page contains open-ended questions, so it's important that you review students' responses. Give students feedback, using the sample answers provided to guide you.

TRY IT
Mesmerized Wrap-Up

Write About Ben Franklin

Write your responses in complete sentences.

1. Think about how how Mara Rockliff depicts Ben Franklin and the time he spent in Paris in *Mesmerized*.
   Answers will vary.
   a. Describe Ben Franklin. Include details from the text and at least one direct quotation from the text that supports your description.

   Students should provide an accurate description of Franklin. Effective descriptions will likely address his scientific achievements and his logical and rational way of trying to understand things through the scientific method, including specific details from the text. The direct quotation included in this part of the response should accurately reproduce Rockliff's words, avoid altering the intended meaning of those words, and support the description of Franklin.

   b. Explain how the people of France felt about Franklin. Why did they feel as they did? Again, provide details from the text and a direct quotation that supports your explanation.

   Effective explanations should stress that Franklin was beloved in France and celebrated by the French because they admired his scientific achievements (as well as his wit and humor). The details from the text should relate to the way the French viewed Franklin, as should the direct quotation. As above, the quotation should be accurate and appropriate to the ideas being expressed in the explanation.

2. Based on what you read in *Mesmerized*, what can you infer about the way Franklin felt about Paris and the French people when he was there? Which details from the text led you to this inference?

   See below.

MESMERIZED WRAP-UP **89**

90 MESMERIZED WRAP-UP

Additional answers

2. Answers will vary. Students should make an inference about the way Franklin felt about Paris and the French people. Appropriate inferences will likely express the idea that Franklin enjoyed Paris and liked the French people. Several details from the text support and point to this inference. For instance, Paris was a hub of scientific activity and the French were highly interested in scientific achievement. As a scientist, this would have been appealing to Franklin. He would have felt as though the city and its people shared his interest in and passion for science. Further, the text states that the French loved Franklin and treated him like a celebrity; it's reasonable to assume that Franklin enjoyed the respect he received from the French people and was grateful to them for it.

Read and Record

Good readers read quickly, smoothly, and with expression. This is called *fluency*. Students will record themselves reading aloud. They will listen to their recording and think about how quick, smooth, and expressive they sound.

TIP Encourage students to rerecord as needed.

Review Main Ideas, Details, and Summaries from *Mesmerized*

Students will answer questions to review what they have learned about *Mesmerized*.

QUIZ

Main Ideas, Details, and Summaries from *Mesmerized*

Students will complete the Main Ideas, Details, and Summaries from *Mesmerized* quiz.

Spelling List 5

Students will complete the Spelling List 5 quiz.

WRAP-UP

Keyboarding

Students will practice their keyboarding skills using an external website or program.

More Language Arts Practice

Students will practice skills according to their individual needs.

Big Ideas: Critical Skills Assignment

Lesson Overview

Big Ideas lessons provide students the opportunity to further apply the knowledge acquired and skills learned throughout the unit workshops. Each Big Ideas lesson consists of these parts:

1. **Cumulative Review:** Students keep their skills fresh by reviewing prior content.

2. **Preview:** Students practice answering the types of questions they will commonly find on standardized tests.

3. **Synthesis:** Students complete an assignment that allows them to connect and apply what they have learned. Synthesis assignments vary throughout the course.

   In the Synthesis portion of this Big Ideas lesson, students will read new selections. They will answer literal and inferential comprehension questions and complete writing questions that ask for short responses about the reading selections. Students should refer to the selections while answering the questions, because the questions emphasize using textual evidence. The questions call for students to demonstrate critical thinking, reading, and writing skills.

   LEARNING COACH CHECK-IN This is a graded assessment. Make sure students complete, review, and submit the assignment to their teacher.

All materials needed for this lesson are linked online and not provided in the Activity Book.

A Wonder
of the World

Narrative Writing: Revising

Lesson Overview

ACTIVITY	ACTIVITY TITLE	TIME	ONLINE/OFFLINE
GET READY	A Wonder of the World Unit Overview	**3** minute	🖥️
	Introduction to Narrative Writing: Revising	**2** minute	🖥️
	Look Back at Narrative Writing Skills	**10** minutes	🖥️
LEARN AND **TRY IT**	Revising a Personal Narrative	**20** minutes	🖥️
	Revise Your Personal Narrative **LEARNING COACH CHECK-IN**	**60** minutes	📄
WRAP-UP	Question About Revising	**5** minutes	🖥️
	Go Read!	**20** minutes	🖥️ or 📄

Content Background

Students will continue working on their **personal narrative** about a meaningful moment in their lives. In this lesson, students will **revise** their rough draft.

Writing Process

To revise their narrative, students will use a checklist. The checklist focuses on organization (*Are any ideas in the wrong place?*) and content (*Are there details I can show instead of tell?*). At the end of this lesson, students will be ready to proofread their narrative for grammar, usage, and mechanics.

Students may not understand the difference between revising and proofreading. When revising, writers focus on large issues, such as the order and the pacing of events. When proofreading, writers fix errors in grammar, usage, and mechanics. Encourage students to focus on revision during this lesson. In the next lesson, students will proofread their narrative.

Advance Preparation

Gather the folder that students are using to store the activity pages related to their personal narrative. The folder should contain the following:

- Students' completed Brainstorm for Your Personal Narrative activity page from Narrative Writing: Prewriting (A)

- Students' completed Prewrite for Your Personal Narrative activity page from Narrative Writing: Prewriting (B)

- Students' completed rough draft from Narrative Writing: Drafting (B)

Prior to the Revise Your Personal Narrative activity in this lesson, read students' rough draft and complete Personal Narrative: Revision Feedback Sheet.

During the Go Read! activity, students will have the option of using the digital library. Allow extra time for students to make their reading selection, or have students make a selection before beginning the lesson.

Lesson Goals

- Use a checklist to revise your personal narrative.

- Read for pleasure.

GET READY

A Wonder of the World Unit Overview
Students will read a summary of what they will learn in the A Wonder of the World unit.

Introduction to Narrative Writing: Revising
Students will get a glimpse of what they will learn about in the lesson. They will also read the lesson goals and keywords. Have students select each keyword and preview its definition.

Look Back at Narrative Writing Skills
Students will review how to organize events in a narrative as well as how to introduce the narrator, characters, and situation.

LEARN   Revising a Personal Narrative

Students will learn about revising, including how to use a revision checklist. Through a guided activity, they will explore how to revise a sample student narrative.

NOTE   The activity begins with a general video on revision. This video gives some tips related to revising in a word-processing program. Students are not expected to have typed their rough drafts, but they may do so (and then revise in a word-processing program) if they wish.

TRY IT   Revise Your Personal Narrative

Students will complete Revise Your Personal Narrative in *Summit English Language Arts 5 Activity Book*. They will need their completed rough draft from Narrative Writing: Drafting (B).

LEARNING COACH CHECK-IN   Guide students through the revision process.

Gather and use the Personal Narrative: Revision Feedback Sheet that you filled out to guide a discussion with students.

1. Tell students the strengths of their narrative. Provide positive comments about the ideas, language, detail, or other elements of the narrative that you enjoyed.

2. Share your constructive feedback with students.

3. As you discuss your feedback, encourage students to actively revise their draft in response. Reassure students that it's okay to remove or move around ideas and sentences. Students should make revisions directly on their draft, using the lines they left blank.

4. Have students review their draft once more, using the Revise Your Personal Narrative activity page. Students should store their revised draft in the folder they are using to organize their writing assisgnment pages.

TIP   Remind students to focus on the checklist questions. Emphasize that they should not worry about spelling, punctuation, grammar, and so on.

NOTE   If you need a copy of the Personal Narrative Instructions, you can download and print one online.

WRAP-UP

Question About Revising

Students will answer a question to show that they understand a key revision skill.

Go Read!

Students will read for pleasure. They should choose a book or a magazine that interests them, or they may choose a selection from the digital library, linked in the online lesson.

Students should read for the entire time. Have students select something to read ahead of time to help them stay focused.

Narrative Writing: Proofreading

Lesson Overview

ACTIVITY	ACTIVITY TITLE	TIME	ONLINE/OFFLINE
GET READY	Introduction to Narrative Writing: Proofreading	**2** minutes	🖥️
	Look Back at Perfect Tenses and Shifts in Tense	**10** minutes	🖥️
LEARN AND TRY IT	Proofreading a Personal Narrative	**20** minutes	🖥️
	Proofread Your Personal Narrative **LEARNING COACH CHECK-IN**	**60** minutes	📄
WRAP-UP	Question About Proofreading	**5** minutes	🖥️
	Go Read!	**23** minutes	🖥️ or 📄

Content Background

Students will continue working on their **personal narrative** about a meaningful moment in their lives. In this lesson, students will **proofread** their revised rough draft.

Writing Process

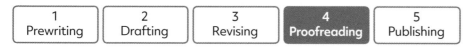

| 1 Prewriting | 2 Drafting | 3 Revising | **4 Proofreading** | 5 Publishing |

To proofread their narrative, students will use a checklist. The checklist focuses on grammar, usage, and mechanics (*Are there inappropriate shifts in verb tense? Are all words spelled correctly?*). After completing this lesson, students will be ready to prepare a clean copy of their narrative.

Proofreading is sometimes called *editing*.

Advance Preparation

Gather the folder that students are using to store the activity pages related to their personal narrative. The folder should contain the following:

- Students' completed Brainstorm for Your Personal Narrative activity page from Narrative Writing: Prewriting (A)

- Students' completed Prewrite for Your Personal Narrative activity page from Narrative Writing: Prewriting (B)

MATERIALS

Supplied

- *Summit English Language Arts 5 Activity Book*
  - Proofread Your Personal Narrative
- Personal Narrative: Proofreading Feedback Sheet (printout)
- Personal Narrative Instructions (printout)

Also Needed

- folder in which students are storing personal narrative writing assignment pages
- reading material for Go Read!

- Students' revised rough draft from Narrative Writing: Revising

Prior to the Proofread Your Personal Narrative activity in this lesson, read students' revised draft and complete Personal Narrative: Proofreading Feedback Sheet.

During the Go Read! activity, students will have the option of using the digital library. Allow extra time for students to make their reading selection, or have students make a selection before beginning the lesson.

Lesson Goals

- Use a checklist to proofread your personal narrative.

- Read for pleasure.

GET READY

Introduction to Narrative Writing: Proofreading

Students will get a glimpse of what they will learn about in the lesson. They will also read the lesson goals and keywords. Have students select each keyword and preview its definition.

Look Back at Perfect Tenses and Shifts in Tense

Students will review some of the skills that they will use to proofread their personal narrative.

LEARN AND TRY IT

LEARN   Proofreading a Personal Narrative

Students will learn about proofreading, including how to use a proofreading checklist. Through a guided activity, they will explore how to proofread a student narrative.

NOTE   The activity begins with a general video on proofreading. This video gives some tips related to proofreading in a word-processing program. Students are not expected to have typed their revised drafts, but they may do so (and then proofread in a word-processing program) if they wish.

TRY IT Proofread Your Personal Narrative

Students will complete Proofread Your Personal Narrative in *Summit English Language Arts 5 Activity Book*. They will need their revised rough draft from Narrative Writing: Revising.

LEARNING COACH CHECK-IN Guide students through the proofreading process.

1. Have students read their draft aloud, listening for errors such as missing words, incomplete sentences, and agreement errors. As students catch errors, have them fix the errors.

2. Have students review their draft once more, using the Proofread Your Personal Narrative activity page. Students should fix any additional errors that they find.

3. Review with students your comments on the Personal Narrative: Proofreading Feedback Sheet. Praise students for the errors that they caught, and guide students to recognize any errors that they have not yet fixed.

4. Have students store their edited draft in the folder they are using to organize their writing assignment pages.

OPTIONAL Have students exchange revised narratives with a peer and use the Proofread Your Personal Narrative activity page to proofread each other's narratives.

NOTE If you need a copy of the Personal Narrative Instructions, you can download and print one online.

TRY IT

Narrative Writing: Proofreading

Proofread Your Personal Narrative

Use the checklist as you proofread your personal narrative draft.

Grammar and Usage

☑ Are all sentences complete and correct?

☑ Are there any missing or extra words?

☑ Are all verbs in the appropriate tense?

☑ Are there any inappropriate shifts in verb tense?

☑ Are there any agreement errors?

☑ Are there other grammatical or usage errors?

Students should check off each item after they make any necessary changes in their personal narrative draft.

Mechanics

☑ Is the title capitalized correctly and enclosed in quotation marks?

☑ Is every word spelled correctly, including frequently confused words?

☑ Does every sentence begin with a capital letter and end with the appropriate punctuation?

☑ Is dialogue punctuated correctly?

☑ Are there other punctuation or capitalization errors?

NARRATIVE WRITING: PROOFREADING **93**

Question About Proofreading

Students will answer a question to show that they understand a key proofreading skill.

Go Read!

Students will read for pleasure. They should choose a book or a magazine that interests them, or they may choose a selection from the digital library, linked in the online lesson.

Students should read for the entire time. Have students select something to read ahead of time to help them stay focused.

Narrative Writing: Publishing

Lesson Overview

ACTIVITY	ACTIVITY TITLE	TIME	ONLINE/OFFLINE
GET READY	Introduction to Narrative Writing: Publishing	**2** minutes	🖥️
LEARN AND **TRY IT**	Publish a Personal Narrative	**15** minutes	📶
	Publish Your Personal Narrative	**60** minutes	📶
WRAP-UP	Turn In Your Personal Narrative	**1** minute	🖥️
	Keyboarding	**10** minutes	📶
	More Language Arts Practice	**17** minutes	📶
	Go Read!	**15** minutes	🖥️ or 📄

Content Background

Students will continue working on their **personal narrative** about a meaningful moment in their lives. In this lesson, students will **publish** their narrative. Then they will submit their completed narrative to their teacher.

Writing Process

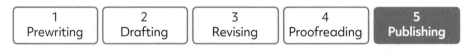

| 1 Prewriting | 2 Drafting | 3 Revising | 4 Proofreading | 5 Publishing |

Students will need to type their narrative using a word-processing program. They will complete an activity to review basic word-processing skills, such as using a keyboard and saving a document.

Advance Preparation

Gather the folder that students are using to store the activity pages related to their personal narrative. The folder should contain the following:

- Students' completed Brainstorm for Your Personal Narrative activity page from Narrative Writing: Prewriting (A)

- Students' completed Prewrite for Your Personal Narrative activity page from Narrative Writing: Prewriting (B)

- Students' revised and edited rough draft from Narrative Writing: Proofreading

MATERIALS

Supplied
- Personal Narrative Instructions (printout)

Also Needed
- folder in which students are storing personal narrative writing assignment pages
- reading material for Go Read!

KEYWORDS

personal narrative – an essay about a personal experience of the writer

publishing – the stage or step of the writing process in which the writer makes a clean copy of the piece and shares it

During the Keyboarding activity, students will practice their keyboarding skills using an external website or program. **You will need to work with students to select an appropriate keyboarding practice website or program; K12 does not specify which resource to use.** A few suggestions are provided in the online activity.

Depending on which program you choose, students may need to set up an account to save their progress. If needed, assist students in setting up and running their chosen keyboarding practice program.

During the Go Read! activity, students will have the option of using the digital library. Allow extra time for students to make their reading selection, or have students make a selection before beginning the lesson.

Lesson Goals

- Type your personal narrative.
- Submit your personal narrative.

GET READY

Introduction to Narrative Writing: Publishing

Students will get a glimpse of what they will learn about in the lesson. They will also read the lesson goals and keywords. Have students select each keyword and preview its definition.

LEARN AND TRY IT

LEARN   Publish a Personal Narrative

Students will learn about word-processing skills in preparation for typing their personal narrative.

TRY IT   Publish Your Personal Narrative

Students will type a final copy of their personal narrative. Students should gather their revised and proofread draft, and they should type it using a word-processing program.

NOTE   If you need a copy of the Personal Narrative Instructions, you can download and print one online.

Turn In Your Personal Narrative

Students will submit their writing assignment to their teacher.

Keyboarding

Students will practice their keyboarding skills using an external website or program.

More Language Arts Practice

Students will practice skills according to their individual needs.

Go Read!

Students will read for pleasure. They should choose a book or a magazine that interests them, or they may choose a selection from the digital library, linked in the online lesson.

Students should read for the entire time. Have students select something to read ahead of time to help them stay focused.

Queen of the Falls

Lesson Overview

ACTIVITY	ACTIVITY TITLE	TIME	ONLINE/OFFLINE
GET READY	Introduction to *Queen of the Falls*	**1** minute	📶
	Spelling List 6 Pretest **LEARNING COACH CHECK-IN**	**10** minutes	📶 and 📄
	Daredevils in 60 Seconds	**1** minute	📶
	Look Back at Key Details	**4** minutes	📶
	Before You Read *Queen of the Falls*	**14** minutes	📶
READ	*Queen of the Falls*	**30** minutes	📄
	Check-In: *Queen of the Falls*	**5** minutes	📶
LEARN AND **TRY IT**	Know the Details	**10** minutes	📶
	Key Details, Main Ideas, and Summaries	**10** minutes	📶
	Apply: Main Idea and Details	**15** minutes	📶
	Write About Annie Taylor **LEARNING COACH CHECK-IN**	**10** minutes	📄
	Practice Words from *Queen of the Falls*	**8** minutes	📶
WRAP-UP	Questions About *Queen of the Falls*	**2** minutes	📶

Content Background

Students will complete a spelling activity and read *Queen of the Falls* by Chris Van Allsburg. They will then complete activities in which they learn about distinguishing key details from minor ones, finding main ideas, and summarizing effectively.

MATERIALS

Supplied
- *Queen of the Falls* by Chris Van Allsburg
- *Summit English Language Arts 5 Activity Book*
  - Spelling List 6 Pretest
  - Write About Annie Taylor

Queen of the Falls Synopsis

Annie Taylor, a widow living in Bay City, Michigan, has little money. When she must close the charm school she runs, she fears living out her life in the poorhouse. So Annie has an idea: go over Niagara Falls in a barrel and garner fame and fortune. After much preparation, she successfully completes the stunt. But when she goes on tour to cash in on her achievement, she finds that audiences are not terribly interested in her or her story. A pair of shady managers steal her barrel, and Annie ultimately decides to return to Niagara Falls. There she sells postcards and souvenirs and tells anyone who is interested about her life and accomplishments. In the end, Annie Taylor comes to appreciate that, even though her stunt did not make her rich, it did teach her the value of testing her own limits and doing something that others thought impossible.

KEYWORDS

inference – a guess that readers make using the clues that authors give them in a piece of writing

main idea – the most important point the author makes; it may be stated or unstated

summary – a short retelling that includes only the most important ideas or events of a text

supporting detail – a detail that gives more information about a main idea

Lesson Goals

- Take a spelling pretest.
- Read *Queen of the Falls*, focusing on its key details and main ideas.
- Make inferences about the figures and events in *Queen of the Falls*.
- Determine the meanings of unfamiliar words in *Queen of the Falls*.

GET READY

Introduction to *Queen of the Falls*

Students will get a glimpse of what they will learn about in the lesson. They will also read the lesson goals and keywords. Have students select each keyword and preview its definition.

Spelling List 6 Pretest

Students will take a spelling pretest.

LEARNING COACH CHECK-IN   Have students turn to Spelling List 6 Pretest in the activity book and open the online Spelling Pretest activity. Online, students will listen to the spelling word, type the word in the space indicated, and then check their answer. In the activity book, students will write the correct spelling of the word in the tables provided and indicate with indicate with a ✓ or an ✗ if they spelled the word correctly or incorrectly online. Students will repeat this process with the remaining words.

As needed, help students with the interaction between the online activity and the activity book page until they become comfortable with what they need to do. As students practice their spelling words throughout the workshop, they should pay special attention to words they spelled incorrectly on the pretest.

This is the complete list of words students will be tested on.

Hard or Soft c	Hard or Soft g	Root tox
accent	budget	toxic
accept	gadget	detoxify
cyclone	hedgehog	toxin
concept	trudge	
scarce	gorgeous	
success	suggest	
vaccination	dungeon	
	gauge	
	geyser	
	sergeant	
	gigantic	

NOTE Have students keep their completed activity page in a safe place so they can refer to it later.

Daredevils in 60 Seconds

Students will watch a short video designed to spark their interest in upcoming topics.

Look Back at Key Details

Students will review how key details support the main idea.

Before You Read _Queen of the Falls_

Students will be introduced to some key vocabulary words that they will encounter in the reading, they will learn more about Niagara Falls, and they will answer questions to help them set a purpose for their reading.

READ

Queen of the Falls

Students will read _Queen of the Falls_ by Chris Van Allsburg.

Check-In: _Queen of the Falls_

Students will answer several questions to demonstrate their comprehension of _Queen of the Falls_.

LEARN AND TRY IT

LEARN   Know the Details

Students will complete an online activity to learn about distinguishing between key details and minor details, determining main ideas, and summarizing effectively.

TRY IT   Key Details, Main Ideas, and Summaries

Students will answer several questions in which they identify key details, determine a main idea, and recognize an effective summary of a passage from _Queen of the Falls_.

TRY IT   Apply: Main Idea and Details

Students will apply to a new work what they've learned about identifying key details, determining a main idea, and recognizing an effective summary.

TRY IT   Write About Annie Taylor

Students will complete Write About Annie Taylor from _Summit English Language Arts 5 Activity Book_.

LEARNING COACH CHECK-IN   This activity page contains open-ended questions, so it's important that you review students' responses.. Give students feedback, using the sample answers provided to guide you.

Write About Annie Taylor

Write your responses in complete sentences.

1. What were Annie Taylor's stated reasons for wanting to go over Niagara Falls in a barrel? Include at least one direct quotation from *Queen of the Falls* to support your answer.

Answers will vary.

Students' answer should relate Annie Taylor's stated reasons for going over Niagara Falls in a barrel: get famous and get rich. These reasons are given at several points in the book. One direct quotation that supports this answer is this sentence: "Annie went back to her room and continued to dream of the fame and fortune that would be hers once she'd conquered the falls." There are other sentences in the book that offer similar support and express similar sentiments.

QUEEN OF THE FALLS   97

---

98   QUEEN OF THE FALLS

2. Annie's stunt was successful, but it did not make her rich. In the years after 1901, she returned to Niagara Falls to sell souvenirs and to tell those who would listen about her life and her death-defying ride. Based on what it says in the text, what can you infer about Annie and how she came to view her stunt during these years? Include at least one direct quotation from *Queen of the Falls* that supports your inference.

Answers will vary.

Students' answer should show an understanding that Annie came to view her stunt as more than just a way of getting rich and famous. That is, she came to recognize that her stunt was more about doing something incredible—something that most people would never be able to do—than it was about making money. One direct quotation that supports this answer is the description of Annie's talk with a reporter. She said, "You ask any person who's stood here, looking out at those falls, what they thought of someone going over them in a barrel. Why, every last one would agree, it was the greatest feat ever performed." She then continued, "And I am content when I can say, 'I am the one who did it.'"

TRY IT   Practice Words from *Queen of the Falls*

Students will complete an online activity in which they answer questions to demonstrate their understanding of the vocabulary words from the reading.

WRAP UP

Questions About *Queen of the Falls*

Students will answer questions to show that they can distinguish between key details and minor details, identify a main idea, and comprehend the text.

Queen of the Falls Wrap-Up

Lesson Overview

ACTIVITY	ACTIVITY TITLE	TIME	ONLINE/OFFLINE
GET READY	Introduction to *Queen of the Falls* Wrap-Up	**1** minute	📶
	Spelling List 6 Activity Bank	**10** minutes	📄
TRY IT	Write About *Queen of the Falls* **LEARNING COACH CHECK-IN**	**30** minutes	📄
	Read and Record	**10** minutes	📶
	Review *Queen of the Falls*	**20** minutes	📶
QUIZ	*Queen of the Falls*	**30** minutes	📶
WRAP-UP	Keyboarding	**10** minutes	📶
	More Language Arts Practice	**9** minutes	📶

Advance Preparation

Gather students' completed Spelling List 6 Pretest activity page from *Queen of the Falls*. Students will refer to this page during Get Ready: Spelling List 6 Activity Bank.

During the Keyboarding activity, students will practice their keyboarding skills using an external website or program. **You will need to work with students to select an appropriate keyboarding practice website or program; K12 does not specify which resource to use.** A few suggestions are provided in the online activity.

Depending on which program you choose, students may need to set up an account to save their progress. If needed, assist students in setting up and running their chosen keyboarding practice program.

Lesson Goals

- Practice all spelling words offline.
- Review *Queen of the Falls*.
- Take a quiz on *Queen of the Falls*.

Introduction to *Queen of the Falls* Wrap-Up

Students will read the lesson goals.

Spelling List 6 Activity Bank

Students will practice all spelling words from the workshop by completing Spelling List 6 Activity Bank from *Summit English Language Arts 5 Activity Book*. Make sure students have their completed Spelling List 6 Pretest activity page from *Queen of the Falls* lesson to refer to during this activity.

Remind students to pay special attention to words they spelled incorrectly on the Spelling Pretest.

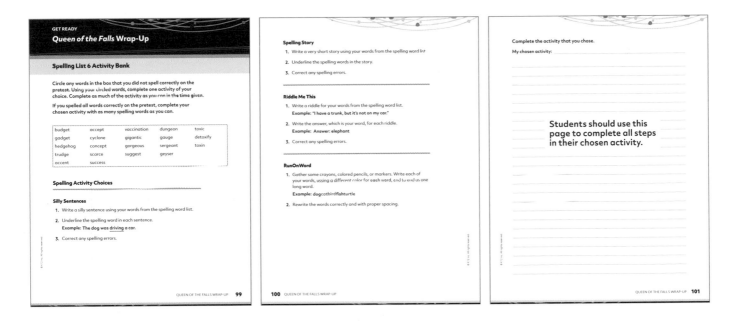

TRY IT

Write About *Queen of the Falls*

Students will complete Write About *Queen of the Falls* from *Summit English Language Arts 5 Activity Book*.

LEARNING COACH CHECK-IN   This activity page contains open-ended questions, so it's important that you review students' responses. Give students feedback, using the sample answers provided to guide you.

Read and Record

Good readers read quickly, smoothly, and with expression. This is called *fluency*. Students will record themselves reading aloud. They will listen to their recording and think about how quick, smooth, and expressive they sound.

TIP Encourage students to rerecord as needed.

Review *Queen of the Falls*

Students will answer questions to review what they have learned about *Queen of the Falls*.

QUIZ

Queen of the Falls

Students will complete the *Queen of the Falls* quiz.

WRAP-UP

Keyboarding

Students will practice their keyboarding skills using an external website or program.

More Language Arts Practice

Students will practice skills according to their individual needs.

Where Is Niagara Falls? (A)

Lesson Overview

ACTIVITY	ACTIVITY TITLE	TIME	ONLINE/OFFLINE
GET READY	Introduction to *Where Is Niagara Falls?* (A)	**1** minute	🖥️
	Spelling List 6 Practice	**10** minutes	🖥️
	Look Back at Details and Examples	**5** minutes	🖥️
	Before You Read *Where Is Niagara Falls?* Chapters 1–4	**14** minutes	🖥️
READ	*Where Is Niagara Falls?* Chapters 1–4	**30** minutes	📄
	Check-In: *Where Is Niagara Falls?* Chapters 1–4	**5** minutes	🖥️
LEARN AND **TRY IT**	Finding a Chapter's Main Idea	**10** minutes	🖥️
	Find the Main Idea of Chapter 2	**10** minutes	🖥️
	Apply: Find Main Ideas with Key Details	**15** minutes	🖥️
	Write About the Main Ideas of Chapters 3 and 4 **LEARNING COACH CHECK-IN**	**10** minutes	📄
	Practice Words from *Where Is Niagara Falls?*	**8** minutes	🖥️
WRAP-UP	Questions About *Where Is Niagara Falls?*	**2** minutes	🖥️

Content Background

Students will complete a spelling activity and read the introduction and the first four chapters of *Where Is Niagara Falls?* by Megan Stine. They will then complete activities in which they learn about using key details from several different passages to determine the main ideas of several chapters.

MATERIALS

Supplied
- *Where Is Niagara Falls?* by Megan Stine
- *Summit English Language Arts 5 Activity Book*
  - Write About the Main Ideas of Chapters 3 and 4

Where Is Niagara Falls? Chapters 1–4 Synopsis

Niagara Falls is an incredible natural wonder, and the first person to go over the falls without protection and survive was Roger Woodward, a seven-year-old boy who went over the falls after a boating accident in 1960. Of course, Woodward was not the first person to experience the awesome power of Niagara Falls or witness its great beauty. Native Americans knew about the place for centuries, and the first European saw it in 1678. People have been drawn to Niagara Falls ever since, and they often try to get as close as possible to experience the falls from every angle. In the 1800s, Augustus Porter bought land around Niagara Falls and began to build businesses there. However, he kept Goat Island natural and wild so that people could continue to enjoy its untouched beauty. Hotels soon sprang up, and, with ingenuity, a suspension bridge was built across the gorge. As tourists flocked to Niagara Falls in the nineteenth century, several daredevils came to the falls and did amazing stunts. One man dove from a platform high above the falls. Others walked across the falls on high wires, doing increasingly incredible tasks while balanced on the wire.

<table>
<tr><td>KEYWORDS</td></tr>
</table>

main idea – the most important point the author makes; it may be stated or unstated

supporting detail – a detail that gives more information about a main idea

Lesson Goals

- Practice all spelling words online.
- Read *Where Is Niagara Falls?* by Megan Stine.
- Make inferences and determine key details and main idea.
- Understand the vocabulary in *Where Is Niagara Falls?*

GET READY

Introduction to *Where Is Niagara Falls?* (A)

Students will get a glimpse of what they will learn about in the lesson. They will also read the lesson goals and keywords. Have students select each keyword and preview its definition.

Spelling List 6 Practice

Students will practice all spelling words from the workshop.

Look Back at Details and Examples

Students will review how details or examples can be used to create accurate explanations.

Before You Read *Where Is Niagara Falls?* Chapters 1–4

Students will be introduced to some key vocabulary words that they will encounter in the upcoming reading, they will learn more about Niagara Falls, and they will answer questions to help them set a purpose for their reading.

READ

Where Is Niagara Falls? Chapters 1–4

Students will read the introduction and Chapters 1–4 of *Where Is Niagara Falls?* by Megan Stine.

Check-In: *Where Is Niagara Falls?* Chapters 1–4

Students will answer several questions to demonstrate their comprehension of the introduction and Chapters 1–4 of *Where Is Niagara Falls?*

LEARN AND TRY IT

LEARN   Finding a Chapter's Main Idea

Students will complete an online activity to learn about using key details from several different passages within a chapter to help them determine that chapter's main idea or ideas.

TRY IT   Find the Main Idea of Chapter 2

Students will analyze several passages in order to identify key details and ultimately determine a main idea in Chapter 2 of *Where Is Niagara Falls?*

TRY IT   Apply: Find Main Ideas with Key Details

Students will apply to a new work what they've learned about identifying key details from multiple passages to determine one or more main ideas.

TRY IT   Write About the Main Ideas of Chapters 3 and 4

Students will complete Write About the Main Ideas of Chapters 3 and 4 from *Summit English Language Arts 5 Activity Book*.

LEARNING COACH CHECK-IN   This activity page contains open-ended questions, so it's important that you review students' responses. Give students feedback, using the sample answers provided to guide you.

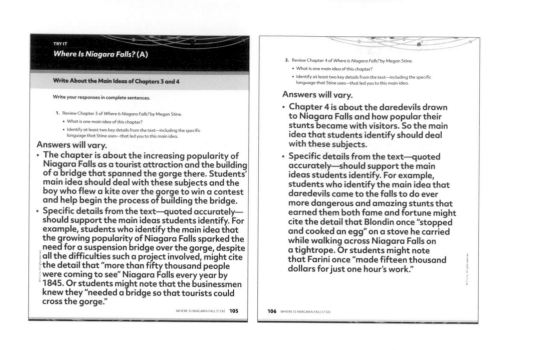

TRY IT

Where Is Niagara Falls? (A)

Write About the Main Ideas of Chapters 3 and 4

Write your responses in complete sentences.

1. Review Chapter 3 of *Where Is Niagara Falls?* by Megan Stine.
   • What is one main idea of this chapter?
   • Identify at least two key details from the text—including the specific language that Stine uses—that led you to this main idea.

Answers will vary.
• The chapter is about the increasing popularity of Niagara Falls as a tourist attraction and the building of a bridge that spanned the gorge there. Students' main idea should deal with these subjects and the boy who flew a kite over the gorge to win a contest and help begin the process of building the bridge.
• Specific details from the text—quoted accurately—should support the main ideas students identify. For example, students who identify the main idea that the growing popularity of Niagara Falls sparked the need for a suspension bridge over the gorge, despite all the difficulties such a project involved, might cite the detail that "more than fifty thousand people were coming to see" Niagara Falls every year by 1845. Or students might note that the businessmen knew they "needed a bridge so that tourists could cross the gorge."

WHERE IS NIAGARA FALLS? (A) **105**

2. Review Chapter 4 of *Where Is Niagara Falls?* by Megan Stine.
   • What is one main idea of this chapter?
   • Identify at least two key details from the text—including the specific language that Stine uses—that led you to this main idea.

Answers will vary.
• Chapter 4 is about the daredevils drawn to Niagara Falls and how popular their stunts became with visitors. So the main idea that students identify should deal with these subjects.
• Specific details from the text—quoted accurately—should support the main ideas students identify. For example, students who identify the main idea that daredevils came to the falls to do ever more dangerous and amazing stunts that earned them both fame and fortune might cite the detail that Blondin once "stopped and cooked an egg" on a stove he carried while walking across Niagara Falls on a tightrope. Or students might note that Farini once "made fifteen thousand dollars for just one hour's work."

106 WHERE IS NIAGARA FALLS? (A)

TRY IT   Practice Words from *Where Is Niagara Falls?* Chapters 1–4

Students will complete an online activity in which they answer questions to demonstrate their understanding of the vocabulary words from the reading.

WRAP UP

Questions About *Where Is Niagara Falls?* Chapters 1–4

Students will answer questions to show that they can identify key details and main ideas.

Where Is Niagara Falls? (B)

Lesson Overview

ACTIVITY	ACTIVITY TITLE	TIME	ONLINE/OFFLINE
GET READY	Introduction to *Where Is Niagara Falls?* (B)	**1** minute	
	Spelling List 6 Review Game	**10** minutes	
	Recall *Where Is Niagara Falls?* Chapters 1–4	**4** minutes	
	Before You Read *Where Is Niagara Falls?* Chapters 5–8	**10** minutes	
READ	*Where Is Niagara Falls?* Chapters 5–8	**30** minutes	
	Check-In: *Where Is Niagara Falls?* Chapters 5–8	**5** minutes	
LEARN AND **TRY IT**	Relationships and Viewpoints	**10** minutes	
	Connections and Perspectives	**10** minutes	
	Apply: Understand Events and Viewpoints	**15** minutes	
	Write About Viewpoints and Write a Summary **LEARNING COACH CHECK-IN**	**15** minutes	
	Practice Words from *Where Is Niagara Falls?* Chapters 5–8	**8** minutes	
WRAP-UP	Questions About *Where Is Niagara Falls?* Chapters 5–8	**2** minutes	

Content Background

Students will complete a spelling activity and read the remaining chapters of *Where Is Niagara Falls?* by Megan Stine. They will then complete activities in which they learn about determining an author's viewpoint, comparing and contrasting texts about the same topic, and recognizing connections between people, events, and ideas in a text.

MATERIALS

Supplied
- *Where Is Niagara Falls?* by Megan Stine
- *Summit English Language Arts 5 Activity Book*
  - Write About Viewpoints and Write a Summary

Where Is Niagara Falls? Chapters 5–8 Synopsis

The reading begins with Annie Taylor. Taylor was an older woman who had little money in 1901. Worried about her future, she got an idea to go over Niagara Falls in a barrel, hoping that it would bring her both fame and fortune. She survived the trip over the falls, but fortune eluded her as people were not very interested in hearing her talk about her stunt. Around that same time, Niagara Falls was becoming a major source of electric power because massive generators were built there to take advantage of the force generated by its falling water. Indeed, Nikola Tesla helped Westinghouse use alternating current to be first to make it possible to transmit electricity over long distances. Finally, Chapter 8 focuses on several reasons to come to Niagara Falls, describing historical attractions, such as an ice castle that once stood near the falls, tour boats and observation decks, and other things that have helped Niagara Falls remain a popular destination for tourists.

KEYWORDS

viewpoint – the perspective of a person or group

Lesson Goals

- Practice all spelling words online.
- Continue reading and explore connections in *Where Is Niagara Falls?*
- Compare viewpoints in *Where Is Niagara Falls?* and *Queen of the Falls.*
- Understand vocabulary in *Where Is Niagara Falls?*

GET READY

Introduction to *Where Is Niagara Falls?* (B)

Students will get a glimpse of what they will learn about in the lesson. They will also read the lesson goals and keywords. Have students select each keyword and preview its definition.

Spelling List 6 Review Game

Students will practice all spelling words from the workshop.

Recall *Where Is Niagara Falls?* Chapters 1–4

Students will answer questions to review the reading that they have already completed.

Before You Read *Where Is Niagara Falls?* **Chapters 5–8**

Students will be introduced to some key vocabulary words that they will encounter in the upcoming reading.

READ

Where Is Niagara Falls? Chapters 5–8

Students will read Chapters 5–8 of *Where Is Niagara Falls?* by Megan Stine.

Check-In: *Where Is Niagara Falls?* Chapters 5–8

Students will answer several questions to demonstrate their comprehension of Chapters 5–8 of *Where Is Niagara Falls?*

LEARN AND TRY IT

LEARN   Relationships and Viewpoints

Students will complete an online activity to learn about identifying connections between people, events, and ideas in a text, determining an author's viewpoint, and comparing and contrasting texts on the same subject.

TRY IT   Connections and Perspectives

Students will answer several questions to practice identifying connections between people, events, and ideas in a text, determining an author's viewpoint, and comparing and contrasting texts on the same subject.

TRY IT   Apply: Understand Events and Views

Students will apply to a new work what they've learned about identifying connections between people, events, and ideas, determining the author's viewpoint, and comparing and contrasting texts on the same subject.

TRY IT   Write About Viewpoints and Write a Summary

Students will complete Write About Viewpoints and Write a Summary from *Summit English Language Arts 5 Activity Book*.

LEARNING COACH CHECK-IN   This activity page contains open-ended questions, so it's important that you review students' responses. Give students feedback, using the sample answers provided to guide you.

Write About Viewpoints and Write a Summary

Write your responses in complete sentences.

1. Reread page 64 of *Where Is Niagara Falls?* Then answer these questions:
   - What is Megan Stine's view of William A. Banks? Why?
   - How does Stine's view of Banks compare to Chris Van Allsburg's view of Annie Taylor's second manager?
   - How did the behavior of Frank Russell and William A. (Billy) Banks affect Annie Taylor?

Answers will vary.

- Students' response should demonstrate an understanding that Stine holds a negative view of William A. Banks because he stole Annie Taylor's barrel and had a young woman "pretend to be Annie."
- Students should recognize that Chris Van Allsburg also has a negative view of Annie's second manager for the same reasons as Stine.
- Students should explain that the behavior of her managers disheartened Annie and made it harder for her to earn money based on her achievements. Their actions also forced her to make another copy of her barrel.

2. Write a one-page summary of *Where Is Niagara Falls?* Be sure to include the text's key details, major events, important figures, and main ideas. Remember that your summary should describe events in the same order they happen in the text. Also, you may quote from the text, but be sure to do so accurately.

Answers will vary.

Elements that students' summary should include:

- A description of the most important events from the text, in the order that they happened
- Key details about the way the first people reacted to seeing Niagara Falls, the development of the falls in the

nineteenth century, the daredevils that did stunts there, the role of the falls in generating electricity, and the falls today
- Multiple main ideas from the text, which are supported by key details and logical inferences

Elements that students' summary should not include:

- Descriptions of relatively minor figures (such as the wife of a Canadian governor who wanted to climb into the gorge in the 1790s, Carlisle Graham, Frank Russell, or Jacob Schoellkopf)
- Minor details and events (such as how sawmills work, where Annie Edson Taylor is buried, that there is an electric car named after Nikola Tesla, etc.)

In 50,000 years, Niagara Falls may be gone because of erosion.

TRY IT   Practice Words from *Where Is Niagara Falls?* Chapters 5–8

Students will complete an online activity in which they answer questions to demonstrate their understanding of the vocabulary words from the reading.

WRAP UP

Questions About *Where Is Niagara Falls?* Chapters 5–8

Students will answer questions to show that they can identify connections between people, events, and ideas in a text, determine an author's viewpoint, and compare and contrast texts on the same subject.

Where Is Niagara Falls? Wrap-Up

Lesson Overview

ACTIVITY	ACTIVITY TITLE	TIME	ONLINE/OFFLINE
GET READY	Introduction to *Where Is Niagara Falls?* Wrap-Up	**1** minute	🖥️
TRY IT	Write About *Where Is Niagara Falls?* **LEARNING COACH CHECK-IN**	**30** minutes	📄
	Read and Record	**10** minutes	🖥️
	Review *Where Is Niagara Falls?*	**20** minutes	🖥️
QUIZ	*Where Is Niagara Falls?*	**30** minutes	🖥️
	Spelling List 6	**10** minutes	🖥️
WRAP-UP	Keyboarding	**10** minutes	🖥️
	More Language Arts Practice	**9** minutes	🖥️

Advance Preparation

During the Keyboarding activity, students will practice their keyboarding skills using an external website or program. **You will need to work with students to select an appropriate keyboarding practice website or program; K12 does not specify which resource to use.** A few suggestions are provided in the online activity.

Depending on which program you choose, students may need to set up an account to save their progress. If needed, assist students in setting up and running their chosen keyboarding practice program.

MATERIALS

Supplied
- *Where Is Niagara Falls?* by Megan Stine
- *Summit English Language Arts 5 Activity Book*
  - Write About *Where Is Niagara Falls?*

Lesson Goals

- Review *Where Is Niagara Falls?*
- Take a spelling quiz.
- Take a quiz on *Where Is Niagara Falls?*

Introduction to *Where Is Niagara Falls?* Wrap-Up

Students will read the lesson goals.

Write About *Where Is Niagara Falls?*

Students will complete Write About *Where Is Niagara Falls?* from *Summit English Language Arts 5 Activity Book*.

LEARNING COACH CHECK-IN   This activity page contains open-ended questions, so it's important that you review students' responses. Give students feedback, using the sample answers provided to guide you.

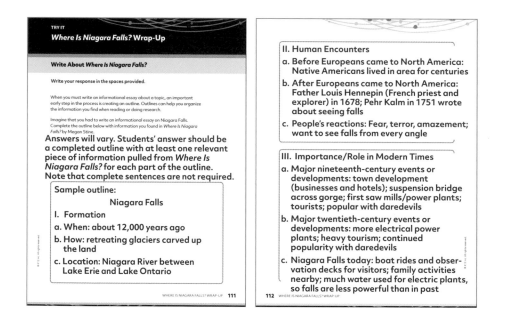

Read and Record

Good readers read quickly, smoothly, and with expression. This is called *fluency*. Students will record themselves reading aloud. They will listen to their recording and think about how quick, smooth, and expressive they sound.

TIP   Encourage students to rerecord as needed.

Review *Where Is Niagara Falls?*

Students will answer questions to review what they have learned about *Where Is Niagara Falls?*

QUIZ

Where Is Niagara Falls?

Students will complete the *Where Is Niagara Falls?* quiz.

Spelling List 6

Students will complete the Spelling List 6 quiz.

WRAP-UP

Keyboarding

Students will practice their keyboarding skills using an external website or program.

More Language Arts Practice

Students will practice skills according to their individual needs.

Dictionary Skills

Lesson Overview

ACTIVITY	ACTIVITY TITLE	TIME	ONLINE/OFFLINE
GET READY	Introduction to Dictionary Skills	**1** minute	🖥
LEARN AND **TRY IT**	Look Back at Basic Dictionary Skills	**4** minutes	🖥
	Using a Dictionary	**10** minutes	🖥
	Practice Your Dictionary Skills	**10** minutes	🖥
	Apply: More Dictionary Skills Practice **LEARNING COACH CHECK-IN**	**15** minutes	📄
	Go Write!	**15** minutes	📄
	Review Dictionary Skills	**15** minutes	🖥
QUIZ	Dictionary Skills	**15** minutes	🖥
WRAP-UP	Keyboarding	**10** minutes	🖥
	More Language Arts Practice	**10** minutes	🖥
	Go Read!	**15** minutes	🖥 or 📄

Content Background

Students will learn about using dictionaries to determine or clarify word meaning, pronunciation, and usage, and they will practice their dictionary skills. The word list for this workshop contains words that students will typically encounter during standardized tests.

Advance Preparation

During the Keyboarding activity, students will practice their keyboarding skills using an external website or program. **You will need to work with students to select an appropriate keyboarding practice website or program; K12 does not specify which resource to use.** A few suggestions are provided in the online activity.

Depending on which program you choose, students may need to set up an account to save their progress. If needed, assist students in setting up and running their chosen keyboarding practice program.

MATERIALS

Supplied
- *Summit English Language Arts 5 Activity Book*
  - Apply: More Dictionary Skills Practice

Also Needed
- reading material for Go Read!

During the Go Read! activity, students will have the option of using the digital library. Allow extra time for students to make their reading selection, or have students make a selection before beginning the lesson.

Lesson Goals

- Use various sources to determine how to pronounce words.

- Recognize small differences in the meanings of words.

- Use various sources, context clues, and synonyms and antonyms to determine and then recall the meaning of unknown words.

GET READY

Introduction to Dictionary Skills

Students will get a glimpse of what they will learn about in the lesson. They will also read the lesson goals.

LEARN AND TRY IT

LEARN   Look Back at Basic Dictionary Skills

Students will revisit content related to dictionary skills taught in previous grades to prepare them for this workshop.

LEARN   Using a Dictionary

Students will learn about ways in which dictionaries can help them find and clarify the meanings of words, figure out how to pronounce words, and understand a word's usage and part of speech.

TRY IT   Practice Your Dictionary Skills

Students will answer questions to practice their ability to read and understand dictionary entries, as well as determine which definition of a word is appropriate in a given passage or sentence.

TRY IT   Apply: More Dictionary Skills Practice

Students will use a dictionary to help them complete Apply: More Dictionary Skills Practice from *Summit English Language Arts 5 Activity Book*.

LEARNING COACH CHECK-IN   Make sure students use a dictionary, either a print or online reference, to complete this activity. If necessary, help students find the appropriate resource. Review students' responses. Give students feedback, using the sample answers provided to guide you.

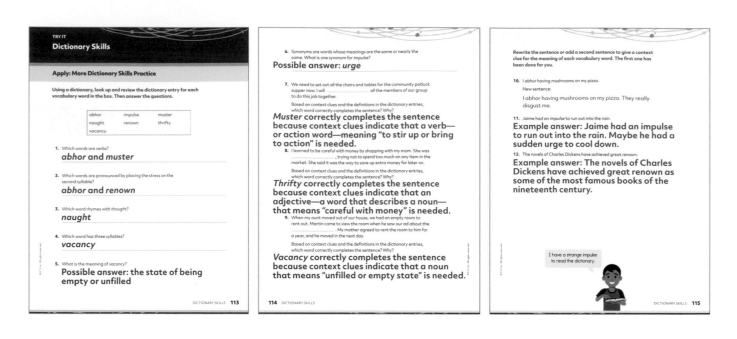

TRY IT   Go Write!

Students will write independently for pleasure. As they write, they should consider the definitions and parts of speech of the words they use, and they should consult a dictionary if they feel uncertain about any of their chosen vocabulary.

TRY IT   Review Dictionary Skills

Students will answer questions to review what they have learned about dictionary skills.

QUIZ

Dictionary Skills

Students will complete the Dictionary Skills quiz.

WRAP-UP

Keyboarding

Students will practice their keyboarding skills using an external website or program.

More Language Arts Practice

Students will practice skills according to their individual needs.

Go Read!

Students will read for pleasure. They should choose a book or a magazine that interests them, or they may choose a selection from the digital library, linked in the online lesson.

Students should read for the entire time. Have students select something to read ahead of time to help them stay focused.

Big Ideas: Respond to a Prompt

Lesson Overview

Big Ideas lessons provide students the opportunity to further apply the knowledge acquired and skills learned throughout the unit workshops. Each Big Ideas lesson consists of these parts:

1. **Cumulative Review:** Students keep their skills fresh by reviewing prior content.

2. **Preview:** Students practice answering the types of questions they will commonly find on standardized tests.

3. **Synthesis:** Students complete an assignment that allows them to connect and apply what they have learned. Synthesis assignments vary throughout the course.

   In the Synthesis portion of this Big Ideas lesson, students will respond to an essay prompt based on reading selections. To respond meaningfully, students will need to use their own ideas as well as examples from the readings. Students' writing will be assessed in four categories: purpose and content; structure and organization; language and word choice; and grammar, usage, and mechanics.

   LEARNING COACH CHECK-IN This is a graded assessment. Make sure students complete, review, and submit the assignment to their teacher.

All materials needed for this lesson are linked online and not provided in the Activity Book.

MATERIALS

Supplied
- Respond to a Prompt (printout)

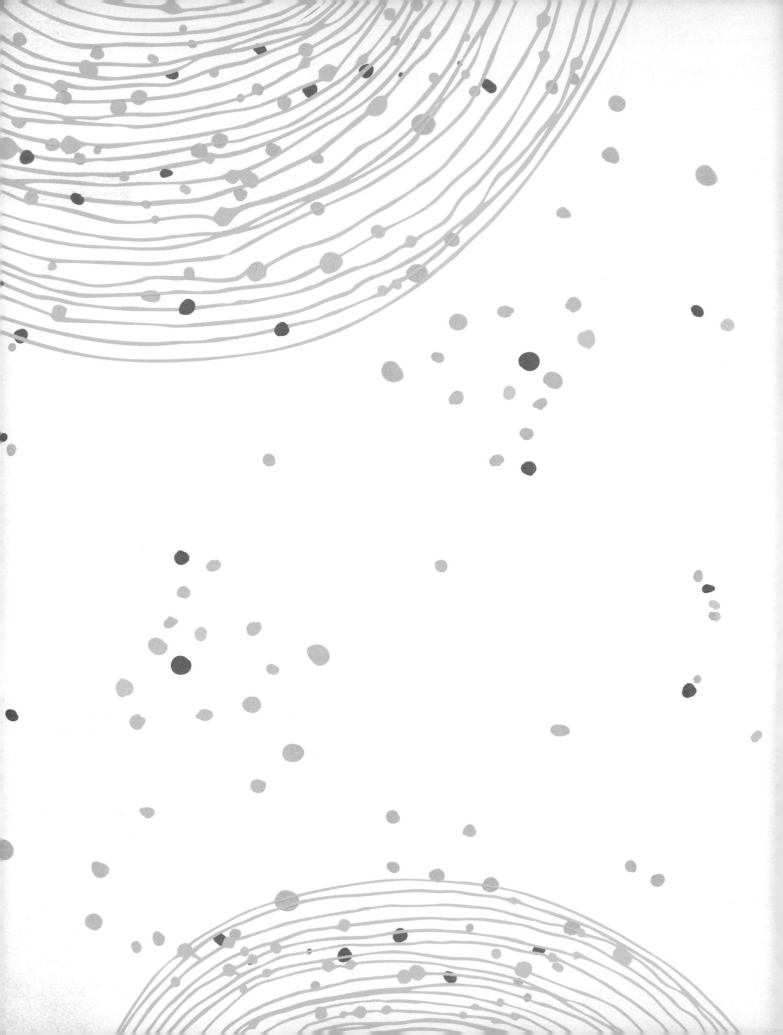

A Wrinkle in Time

Government Words

Lesson Overview

ACTIVITY	ACTIVITY TITLE	TIME	ONLINE/OFFLINE
GET READY	*A Wrinkle in Time* Unit Overview	**1** minute	🖥️
	Introduction to Government Words	**1** minute	🖥️
LEARN AND **TRY IT**	Government Words	**10** minutes	🖥️
	More Government Words	**10** minutes	🖥️
	Apply: Government Words **LEARNING COACH CHECK-IN**	**15** minutes	📄
	Go Write!	**15** minutes	📄
	Review Government Words	**10** minutes	🖥️
QUIZ	Government Words	**15** minutes	🖥️
WRAP-UP	Keyboarding	**10** minutes	🖥️
	More Language Arts Practice	**13** minutes	🖥️
	Go Read!	**20** minutes	🖥️ or 📄

Content Background

Students will learn about recognizing and understanding the meanings of words commonly used in works by and about governments. They will practice using context clues, synonyms and antonyms, and logic to help them determine the meanings of unfamiliar words.

Advance Preparation

During the Keyboarding activity, students will practice their keyboarding skills using an external website or program. **You will need to work with students to select an appropriate keyboarding practice website or program; K12 does not specify which resource to use.** A few suggestions are provided in the online activity.

Depending on which program you choose, students may need to set up an account to save their progress. If needed, assist students in setting up and running their chosen keyboarding practice program.

MATERIALS

Supplied
- *Summit English Language Arts 5 Activity Book*
  - Apply: Government Words

Also Needed
- reading material for Go Read!

During the Go Read! activity, students will have the option of using the digital library. Allow extra time for students to make their reading selection, or have students make a selection before beginning the lesson.

KEYWORDS

antonym – a word that means the opposite of another word

context clue – a word or phrase in a text that helps you figure out the meaning of an unknown word

synonym – a word that means the same, or almost the same, as another word

Lesson Goals

- Determine the meanings of words related to government.

- Use synonyms and antonyms to unlock the meanings of unfamiliar words.

- Use context clues to help determine meaning of unknown words.

- Read for pleasure.

GET READY

A Wrinkle in Time Unit Overview

Students will read a summary of what they will learn in the *A Wrinkle in Time* unit.

Introduction to Government Words

Students will get a glimpse of what they will learn about in the lesson. They will also read the lesson goals and keywords. Have students select each keyword and preview its definition.

LEARN AND TRY IT

LEARN   Government Words

Students will learn about domain-specific language and some strategies for unlocking the meanings of unfamiliar words related to government.

TRY IT   More Government Words

Students will answer questions to develop their ability to recognize and determine the meanings of words related to government.

TRY IT   Apply: Government Words

Students will complete Apply: Government Words from *Summit English Language Arts 5 Activity Book*.

LEARNING COACH CHECK-IN   This activity page contains open-ended questions, so it's important that you review students' responses. Give students feedback, using the sample answers provided to guide you.

Government Words

Apply: Government Words

Read the paragraph. Think about any context clues, antonyms, or synonyms and what they suggest about the missing word.

1. My grandfather was always very interested in government, so he decided on a career in _____ service. He began as a researcher for the federal government. He helped create policies that improved the working conditions for his fellow citizens. Later, he worked for the agency that sets the guidelines for food safety.

   a. Which word correctly fills in the blank? (civil) or democracy
   b. Explanation:

   See below.

2. Rita became a lawyer because she wanted to fight the unfairness she saw in society. Each day, she worked to help those who were not treated equally. She tried to make sure that they always received _____ in court.

   a. Which word correctly fills in the blank? liberty or (justice)
   b. Explanation:

   See below.

---

3. Religious freedom has deep roots in Maryland. In the 1600s, the colonial government passed an act that protected the rights of people to worship as they pleased. This decision to _____ many different religious views and allow people to attend whatever church they wanted to attend was extremely important. It was one of the ways in which the American colonies were different from many countries in Europe at the time.

   a. Which word correctly fills in the blank? emancipate or (tolerate)
   b. Explanation:

   See below.

4. People have power in a _____, but they also have responsibilities. They must make decisions about how their government will work and what laws it will have. One way that people exercise their power in this form of government is by voting.

   a. Which word correctly fills in the blank? (democracy) or constitution
   b. Explanation:
   Democracy is the better choice. The passage uses the phrase "form of government." It also describes a type of government in which people hold power. A **constitution** is a plan for government. It is a type of government.

Write a sentence using the given government word.
- Have someone else read your sentence.
- Explain to this person how the meaning of the given government word can be understood based on context clues, synonyms, antonyms, or reasoning.

5. constitution
   Sentence:

   See below.

6. liberty
   Sentence:

   See below.

7. emancipate
   Sentence:
   Answers will vary.
   Emancipate means "to set free." Students' sentence should show clear knowledge of this meaning.

Additional answers

1b. *Civil* is the better choice. It is a word that deals with the relationship between citizens and their government. The other details in the passage support this choice. A *democracy* is a type of government. In a democracy, power rests with the people.

2b. *Justice* is the better choice. The passage includes an antonym for justice: "unfairness." Also, there are context clues about the needs of people "who were not treated equally" when they are "in court." *Liberty* means "freedom." This passage is about laws being applied evenly to all people. It is not about granting them freedom.

3b. *Tolerate* is the better choice. The passage uses a synonym for tolerate: "allow." Its context clues also show that the state accepted people's religious views. Remember, *emancipate* means "to set free." The passage does not suggest that anyone is imprisoned or enslaved. So no one is being set free.

5. Answers will vary.
Constitution means "a plan for government." Students' sentence should show clear knowledge of this meaning.

6. Answers will vary.
Liberty means "freedom." Students' sentence should show clear knowledge of this meaning.

TRY IT   Go Write!

Students will write independently for pleasure. As they write, they should consider opportunities to use words related to government.

TRY IT   Review Government Words

Students will answer questions to review what they have learned about government words.

QUIZ

Government Words

Students will complete the Government Words quiz.

WRAP-UP

Keyboarding

Students will practice their keyboarding skills using an external website or program.

More Language Arts Practice

Students will practice skills according to their individual needs.

Go Read!

Students will read for pleasure. They should choose a book or a magazine that interests them, or they may choose a selection from the digital library, linked in the online lesson.

Students should read for the entire time. Have students select something to read ahead of time to help them stay focused.

A Wrinkle in Time (A)

Lesson Overview

ACTIVITY	ACTIVITY TITLE	TIME	ONLINE/OFFLINE
GET READY	Introduction to *A Wrinkle in Time* (A)	**1** minute	🖥️
	Spelling List 7 Pretest **LEARNING COACH CHECK-IN**	**10** minutes	🖥️ and 📄
	A Wrinkle in Time in 60 Seconds	**1** minute	🖥️
	Before You Read *A Wrinkle in Time*, Chapter 1	**15** minutes	🖥️
READ	*A Wrinkle in Time*, Chapter 1	**30** minutes	📄
	Check-In: *A Wrinkle in Time*, Chapter 1	**5** minutes	🖥️
LEARN AND **TRY IT**	Use Active Reading Strategies	**10** minutes	🖥️
	Practice Active Reading Strategies	**10** minutes	🖥️
	Apply: Active Reading Strategies	**15** minutes	🖥️
	Write About Chapter 1 and Visualize the Text **LEARNING COACH CHECK-IN**	**10** minutes	📄
	Practice Words from *A Wrinkle in Time*, Chapter 1	**8** minutes	🖥️
WRAP-UP	Questions About *A Wrinkle in Time*, Chapter 1	**5** minutes	🖥️

Content Background

Students will complete a spelling activity and read the first chapter of Madeleine L'Engle's *A Wrinkle in Time*. They will then complete activities in which they learn about using active reading strategies to engage with the text and make reading more rewarding and enjoyable.

MATERIALS

Supplied

- *A Wrinkle in Time* by Madeleine L'Engle
- *Summit English Language Arts 5 Activity Book*
  - Spelling List 7 Pretest
  - Write About Chapter 1 and Visualize the Text

A Wrinkle in Time, Chapter 1 Synopsis

Meg Murry is a young girl whose father has gone missing and who feels as though she can do nothing right. She is getting in trouble at school, and she feels very lonely at home. One dark and stormy night, Meg goes downstairs to find her brother, Charles Wallace, expecting her. Charles is a little boy, but he has remarkable intelligence and he's very sensitive. He speaks and thinks in ways that are far beyond his years. The two siblings are soon joined by their mother, a beautiful scientist. Charles Wallace tells Meg and Mrs. Murry about a new friend he's made: an old woman named Mrs. Whatsit. Almost immediately after that, Mrs. Whatsit knocks on the Murrys' door and comes in from the storm. The Murrys are kind to Mrs. Whatsit, offering her food and helping her out of her wet clothes. At first, she strikes Meg and her mother as a harmless, quirky woman. But then she tells Mrs. Murry that there is such a thing as a tesseract. Hearing that word—*tesseract*—stuns Mrs. Murry.

Lesson Goals

- Take a spelling pretest.
- Begin reading *A Wrinkle in Time* by Madeleine L'Engle.
- Use active reading strategies to understand *A Wrinkle in Time*.

GET READY

Introduction to *A Wrinkle in Time* (A)

Students will get a glimpse of what they will learn about in the lesson. They will also read the lesson goals and keywords. Have students select each keyword and preview its definition.

Spelling List 7 Pretest

Students will take a spelling pretest.

LEARNING COACH CHECK-IN   Have students turn to Spelling List 7 Pretest in *Summit English Language Arts 5 Activity Book* and open the online Spelling Pretest activity. Online, students will listen to the spelling word, type the word in the space indicated, and then check their answer. In the activity book, students will write the correct spelling of the word in the tables provided and indicate with a ✓ or an ✗ if they spelled the word correctly or incorrectly online. Students will repeat this process with the remaining words.

As needed, help students with the interaction between the online activity and the activity book page until they become comfortable with what they need to do. As students practice their spelling words throughout the workshop, they should pay special attention to words they spelled incorrectly on the pretest.

This is the complete list of words students will be tested on.

More Related Words	More Related Words	Heart Words
advantage	physical	coupon
advantageous	physician	souvenir
angel	sense	tournament
angelic	sentiment	
atom	rhyme	
atomic	rhythm	
bomb		
bombard		

NOTE Have students keep their completed activity page in a safe place so they can refer to it later.

GET READY
A Wrinkle in Time (A)

Spelling List 7 Pretest

1. Open the Spelling Pretest activity online. Listen to the first spelling word. Type the word. Check your answer.

2. Write the correct spelling of the word in the Word column of the Spelling Pretest table on the next page.

Word		
1 blindfold		

3. Put a check mark in the ⊘ column if you spelled the word correctly online.

Word		
1 blindfold	✓	

Put an X in the ⊗ column if you spelled the word incorrectly online.

Word		
1 blindfold		X

4. Repeat Steps 1–3 for the remaining words in the Spelling Pretest.

A WRINKLE IN TIME (A) **121**

A Wrinkle in Time (A)

Spelling List 7 Pretest

Write each spelling word in the Word column, making sure to spell it correctly.

Word			Word		
1 advantage			10 physician		
2 advantageous			11 sense		
3 angel			12 sentiment		
4 angelic			13 rhyme		
5 atom			14 rhythm		
6 atomic			15 coupon		
7 bomb			16 souvenir		
8 bombard			17 tournament		
9 physical					

Students should use the ✓ and X columns to indicate whether they spelled each word correctly or incorrectly online.

122 A WRINKLE IN TIME (A)

A Wrinkle in Time in 60 Seconds

Students will watch a short video designed to spark their interest in upcoming topics.

Before You Read *A Wrinkle in Time*, Chapter 1

Students will be introduced to some key vocabulary words that they will encounter in the upcoming reading, learn about reading for pleasure and how to preview a text, and answer a question to help them set a purpose for their reading.

READ

A Wrinkle in Time, Chapter 1

Students will read the first chapter of *A Wrinkle in Time* by Madeleine L'Engle.

Check-In: *A Wrinkle in Time*, Chapter 1

Students will answer several questions to demonstrate their comprehension of the first chapter of *A Wrinkle in Time*.

LEARN AND TRY IT

LEARN   Use Active Reading Strategies

Students will learn how to employ several methods that good readers use to help them engage with a text and get the most out of their reading.

TRY IT   Practice Active Reading Strategies

Students will answer several questions online to develop their understanding of the strategies that they should use to be active readers.

TRY IT   Apply: Active Reading Strategies

Students will apply to a new work what they've learned about using active reading strategies.

TRY IT   Write About Chapter 1 and Visualize the Text

Students will complete Write About Chapter 1 and Visualize the Text from *Summit English Language Arts 5 Activity Book*. Here, students will make a prediction about the story based on the reading they have completed before drawing a character or scene from the text based on their own visualization.

This activity page contains open-ended questions, so it's important that you review students' responses. Give students feedback, using the sample answers provided to guide you.

TRY IT
A Wrinkle in Time (A)

Write About Chapter 1 and Visualize the Text

Answer the question in complete sentences.

1. Chapter 1 ends with Mrs. Whatsit saying a word—tesseract—that stuns Mrs. Murry. This leaves the Murrys and readers eager to know more about Mrs. Whatsit and the role she will play. What do you think will happen next? Make a prediction about the upcoming chapters.

See right.

2. Active readers use visualizing as an important strategy to bring texts to life. Choose a character or moment from the first chapter of the novel and draw how you imagine that person or event.

A WRINKLE IN TIME (A) **123**

Additional answers

Answers will vary.

Based on the events of Chapter 1, students may predict that Mrs. Whatsit will help Meg find her father or become close friends with the Murry family.

TRY IT Practice Words from *A Wrinkle in Time*, Chapter 1

Students will answer questions to demonstrate their understanding of the vocabulary words from the reading.

WRAP-UP

Questions About *A Wrinkle in Time*, Chapter 1

Students will answer questions to show that they understand the reading.

A Wrinkle in Time (B)

Lesson Overview

ACTIVITY	ACTIVITY TITLE	TIME	ONLINE/OFFLINE
GET READY	Introduction to *A Wrinkle in Time* (B)	**1** minute	🖥️
	Spelling List 7 Activity Bank	**10** minutes	📄
	Recall *A Wrinkle in Time*, Chapter 1	**5** minutes	🖥️
	Before You Read *A Wrinkle in Time*, Chapters 2–3	**10** minutes	🖥️
READ	*A Wrinkle in Time*, Chapters 2–3	**30** minutes	📄
	Check-In: *A Wrinkle in Time*, Chapters 2–3	**5** minutes	🖥️
LEARN AND **TRY IT**	Structure and Support	**10** minutes	🖥️
	Examine Structure and Support	**7** minutes	🖥️
	Apply: Structure and Support	**15** minutes	🖥️
	Write a Summary of Chapters 1–3 **LEARNING COACH CHECK-IN**	**15** minutes	📄
	Practice Words from *A Wrinkle in Time*, Chapters 2–3	**7** minutes	🖥️
WRAP-UP	Questions About *A Wrinkle in Time*, Chapters 2–3	**5** minutes	🖥️

Content Background

Students will complete a spelling activity and continue to read *A Wrinkle in Time* by Madeleine L'Engle. They will then complete activities in which they learn more about the structure of novels and using direct quotations before applying what they learned to the reading.

Advance Preparation

Gather students' completed Spelling List 7 Pretest activity page from *A Wrinkle in Time* (A). Students will refer to this page during Get Ready: Spelling List 7 Activity Bank.

MATERIALS

Supplied
- *A Wrinkle in Time* by Madeleine L'Engle
- *Summit English Language Arts 5 Activity Book*
  - Spelling List 7 Activity Bank
  - Write a Summary of Chapters 2–3

Also Needed
- completed Spelling List 7 Pretest activity page from *A Wrinkle in Time* (A)

A Wrinkle in Time, Chapers 2–3 Synopsis

Meg gets in trouble for talking back to a teacher at school, and she speaks briefly about her father's disappearance with the principal. When she gets home, she and Charles Wallace go for a walk to the house where Mrs. Whatsit is staying. Charles Wallace makes Meg feel better. At the house, they meet Calvin O'Keefe, a boy a bit older than Meg. He says he felt as though he had to come there, and the three children go inside. There they see Mrs. Whatsit and meet Mrs. Who, who often quotes famous thinkers and writers. The kids are told to go home and eat something, so Calvin comes over to the Murry home. He feels very comfortable there right away. He and Meg grow closer, and Meg tells Calvin more about her father, who disappeared while doing some top-secret work for the government. Charles Wallace interrupts Meg and Calvin to tell them that they will be going soon. He's not sure where, but he thinks it is to find Mr. Murry. Mrs. Whatsit and Mrs. Who arrive, and then the children hear the disembodied, magical voice of Mrs. Which.

KEYWORDS

direct quotation – the exact words of a speaker or writer

Lesson Goals

- Practice all spelling words offline.

- Continue reading *A Wrinkle in Time* by Madeleine L'Engle.

- Explore the structure of *A Wrinkle in Time*.

- Use direct quotations to explain a text.

GET READY

Introduction to *A Wrinkle in Time* (B)

Students will get a glimpse of what they will learn about in the lesson. They will also read the lesson goals and keywords. Have students select each keyword and preview its definition.

Spelling List 7 Activity Bank

Students will practice spelling words by completing Spelling List 7 Activity Bank from *Summit English Language Arts 5 Activity Book*. Make sure students have their completed Spelling List 7 Pretest activity page from *A Wrinkle in Time* (A) to refer to during this activity.

Remind students to pay special attention to words they spelled incorrectly on the Spelling Pretest.

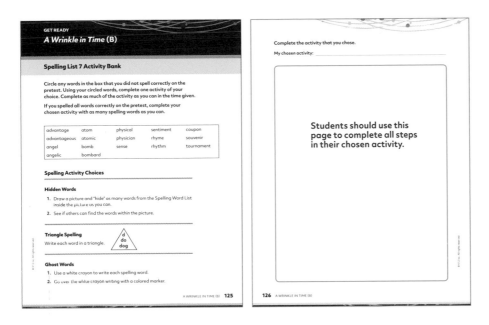

Recall *A Wrinkle in Time,* Chapter 1

Students will answer some questions to review the reading that they have already completed.

Before You Read *A Wrinkle in Time,* Chapters 2–3

Students will be introduced to some key vocabulary words that they will encounter in the upcoming reading and learn some important historical background related to the reading.

READ

A Wrinkle in Time, Chapters 2–3

Students will read Chapters 2–3 of *A Wrinkle in Time* by Madeleine L'Engle.

Check-In: *A Wrinkle in Time,* Chapters 2–3

Students will answer several questions to demonstrate their comprehension of Chapters 2–3 of *A Wrinkle in Time.*

LEARN   Structure and Support

Students will learn about the structure of longer works of fiction and the purpose of introductory chapters before focusing on direct quotations and how they can be used to support a reader's understanding of a text.

TRY IT   Examine Structure and Support

Students will answer several questions online to develop their understanding of the structure of *A Wrinkle in Time* and how to support ideas in the text by citing direct quotations from it.

TRY IT   Apply: Structure and Support

Students will apply to a new work what they've learned about examining structure and using direct quotations.

TRY IT   Write a Summary of Chapters 1–3

Students will complete Write a Summary of Chapters 1–3 from *Summit English Language Arts 5 Activity Book*. In their summary, which should briefly recount the most important events from the opening chapters in order, students should include at least one direct quotation from the book. The direct quotation should appear within quotation marks and should be an accurate representation of the text's exact words.

LEARNING COACH CHECK-IN   This activity page contains an open-ended question, so it's important that you review students' responses. Give students feedback, using the sample answers provided to guide you.

TRY IT
A Wrinkle in Time (B)

Write a Summary of Chapters 1–3

Write your response in complete sentences.

In 1–2 paragraphs, summarize the first three chapters of *A Wrinkle in Time*. In your summary, use at least one direct quotation from the text that supports an important idea or point or that helps reveal something about a character.

Answers will vary.

A good summary will mention that Meg is unhappy because she misses her father, who has disappeared, and that she feels very close to Charles Wallace. The summary will also describe Charles Wallace and his unusual maturity and intelligence, as well as the meeting with Calvin and the rather strange Mrs. Whatsit. The summary should cover events in the same order as the novel. Students should include at least one direct quotation, word for word from the text and placed inside quotation marks.

A WRINKLE IN TIME (B)   **127**

TRY IT Practice Words from *A Wrinkle in Time*, Chapters 2–3

Students will answer questions to demonstrate their understanding of the vocabulary words from the reading.

Questions About *A Wrinkle in Time*, Chapters 2–3

Students will answer questions to show that they understand the reading.

A Wrinkle in Time (C)

Lesson Overview

ACTIVITY	ACTIVITY TITLE	TIME	ONLINE/OFFLINE
GET READY	Introduction to *A Wrinkle in Time* (C)	**1** minute	🖥️
	Spelling List 7 Review Game	**10** minutes	🖥️
	Recall *A Wrinkle in Time*, Chapters 2–3	**5** minutes	🖥️
	Before You Read *A Wrinkle in Time*, Chapter 4	**10** minutes	🖥️
READ	*A Wrinkle in Time*, Chapter 4	**25** minutes	📄
	Check-In: *A Wrinkle in Time*, Chapter 4	**5** minutes	🖥️
LEARN AND TRY IT	Consider the Narrator	**10** minutes	🖥️
	Examine the Novel's Narrator	**10** minutes	🖥️
	Apply: Narrative Point of View	**15** minutes	🖥️
	Write About the Text **LEARNING COACH CHECK-IN**	**15** minutes	📄
	Practice Words from *A Wrinkle in Time*, Chapter 4	**9** minutes	🖥️
WRAP-UP	Questions About *A Wrinkle in Time*, Chapter 4	**5** minutes	🖥️

Content Background

Students will complete a spelling activity and continue to read *A Wrinkle in Time* by Madeleine L'Engle. They will then complete activities in which they learn more about the novel's third-person narrator and the effect this narrator has on their understanding of characters and events in the story.

MATERIALS

Supplied
- *A Wrinkle in Time* by Madeleine L'Engle
- *Summit English Language Arts 5 Activity Book*
  - Write About the Text

A Wrinkle in Time, Chapter 4 Synopsis

Meg, Charles Wallace, and Calvin are swept up by a mysterious force and transported to the planet of Uriel. It's beautiful and Meg, who was terrified and alone on the journey to Uriel, feels very happy once there. Mrs. Whatsit takes on a different form—that of a winged centaur-like creature—and the kids climb on her back so she can show them the planet. They hear the song that the creatures of Uriel sing, but only Charles Wallace can really begin to understand it. For Meg and Calvin, it simply makes them feel joyful. They fly high into the atmosphere and look out into the night sky. There, in the distance, they observe a "dark Thing" that upsets them. Calvin describes it as evil. When they return to the surface of Uriel, Meg asks whether the "dark Thing" is what her father was fighting.

KEYWORDS

first-person point of view – the telling of a story by a character in that story, using pronouns such as *I*, *me*, and *we*

narrator – the teller of a story

third-person point of view – the telling of a story by someone outside of the action, using the third-person pronouns *he*, *she*, and *they*

Lesson Goals

- Practice all spelling words online.

- Continue to read *A Wrinkle in Time*.

- Examine how the novel's narrator affects *A Wrinkle in Time*.

GET READY

Introduction to *A Wrinkle in Time* (C)

Students will get a glimpse of what they will learn about in the lesson. They will also read the lesson goals and keywords. Have students select each keyword and preview its definition.

Spelling List 7 Review Game

Students will practice all spelling words from the workshop.

Recall *A Wrinkle in Time*, Chapters 2–3

Students will answer some questions to review the reading that they have already completed.

Before You Read *A Wrinkle in Time*, Chapter 4

Students will be introduced to some key vocabulary words that they will encounter in the upcoming reading and learn about different types of narrators common in works of fiction.

A Wrinkle in Time, Chapter 4

Students will read Chapter 4 of *A Wrinkle in Time* by Madeleine L'Engle.

Check-In: *A Wrinkle in Time*, Chapter 4

Students will answer several questions to demonstrate their comprehension of Chapter 4 of *A Wrinkle in Time*.

LEARN AND TRY IT

LEARN   Consider the Narrator

Students will learn about the effect that a third-person narrator can have on reader understanding of a story's characters and events.

TRY IT   Examine the Novel's Narrator

Students will complete an activity to explore several passages in *A Wrinkle in Time* to better understand the influence that the novel's third-person narrator has on their understanding of characters and events in the story.

TRY IT   Apply: Narrative Point of View

Students will apply to a new work what they've learned about the effect of narrative point of view on a story.

TRY IT   Write About the Text

Students will complete Write About the Text from *Summit English Language Arts 5 Activity Book*. They are to write how the novel would be different if the third-person narrator was focused on Mrs. Whatsit rather than Meg.

LEARNING COACH CHECK-IN   This activity page contains an open-ended question, so it's important that you review students' responses. Give students feedback, using the sample answer provided to guide you.

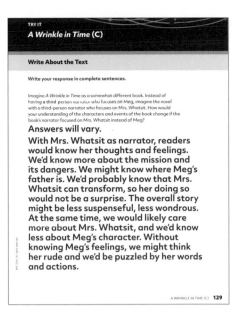

TRY IT   Practice Words from *A Wrinkle in Time*, Chapter 4

Students will answer questions to demonstrate their understanding of the vocabulary words from the reading.

WRAP-UP

Questions About *A Wrinkle in Time*, Chapter 4

Students will answer questions to show that they understand the reading.

A Wrinkle in Time (D)

Lesson Overview

ACTIVITY	ACTIVITY TITLE	TIME	ONLINE/OFFLINE
GET READY	Introduction to *A Wrinkle in Time* (D)	**1** minute	🖥️
QUIZ	Spelling List 7	**10** minutes	🖥️
GET READY	Recall *A Wrinkle in Time*, Chapter 4	**5** minutes	🖥️
	Before You Read *A Wrinkle in Time*, Chapter 5	**10** minutes	🖥️
READ	*A Wrinkle in Time*, Chapter 5	**20** minutes	📄
	Check-In: *A Wrinkle in Time*, Chapter 5	**5** minutes	🖥️
LEARN AND **TRY IT**	Character Differences and Similarities	**10** minutes	🖥️
	Compare and Contrast Characters	**7** minutes	🖥️
	Apply: Compare and Contrast	**15** minutes	🖥️
	Write About Characters **LEARNING COACH CHECK-IN**	**25** minutes	📄
	Practice Words from *A Wrinkle in Time*, Chapter 5	**7** minutes	🖥️
WRAP-UP	Questions About *A Wrinkle in Time*, Chapter 5	**5** minutes	🖥️

Content Background

Students will take a spelling quiz and continue to read *A Wrinkle in Time* by Madeleine L'Engle. They will then complete activities in which they learn about comparing and contrasting characters and using direct quotations from the text to support their ideas.

MATERIALS

Supplied

- *A Wrinkle in Time* by Madeleine L'Engle
- *Summit English Language Arts 5 Activity Book*
  - Write About Characters

A Wrinkle in Time, Chapter 5 Synopsis

Meg, Charles Wallace, and Calvin are tessered away from Uriel. After Mrs. Which mistakenly tries to stop on a two-dimensional planet, which nearly crushes the children, they arrive on a planet in Orion's Belt. The planet is very drab and gray, and nothing grows there. The children go to see the Happy Medium, a woman who has a crystal ball. When they look into the crystal ball, they see Earth, but it is partially obscured by the Dark Thing they saw earlier. This means that Earth is in danger of being overcome by the evil darkness. The children, the Mrs. Ws tell them, will help in the fight against the darkness. They also tell the children of others who have fought the darkness: religious leaders and artists and writers and musicians and scientists through history. Finally, Meg and Charles Wallace learn that their father is on a planet that has already fallen to the evil darkness.

Lesson Goals

- Take a spelling quiz.
- Continue to read *A Wrinkle in Time*.
- Compare and contrast characters in *A Wrinkle in Time*.

GET READY

Introduction to *A Wrinkle in Time* (D)

Students will get a glimpse of what they will learn about in the lesson. They will also read the lesson goals.

QUIZ

Spelling List 7

Students will complete the Spelling List 7 quiz.

GET READY

Recall *A Wrinkle in Time*, Chapter 4

Students will answer some questions to review the reading that they have already completed.

Before You Read *A Wrinkle in Time*, Chapter 5

Students will be introduced to some key vocabulary words that they will encounter in the upcoming reading and learn about the size of the universe to better appreciate the incredible journey taken by the characters in the novel.

READ

A Wrinkle in Time, Chapter 5

Students will read Chapter 5 of *A Wrinkle in Time* by Madeleine L'Engle.

Check-In: *A Wrinkle in Time*, Chapter 5

Students will answer several questions to demonstrate their comprehension of Chapter 5 of *A Wrinkle in Time*.

LEARN AND TRY IT

LEARN   Character Differences and Similarities

Students will learn how to compare and contrast characters by drawing on evidence in the text and using direct quotations to support their ideas.

TRY IT   Compare and Contrast Characters

Students will answer several questions online to develop their understanding of how to compare and contrast characters in the novel. They will use evidence from the text and direct quotations to support their ideas.

TRY IT   Apply: Compare and Contrast

Students will apply to a new work what they've learned about comparing and contrasting characters.

TRY IT   Write About Characters

Students will complete Write About Characters *Summit English Language Arts 5 Activity Book*. They are to describe how two characters of their choice are alike and how they are different. Students should use evidence from the text and at least one direct quotation to support their ideas.

LEARNING COACH CHECK-IN   This activity page contains an open-ended question, so it's important that you review students' responses. Give students feedback, using the sample answer provided to guide you.

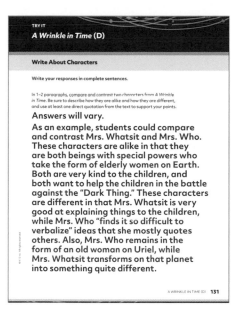

TRY IT
A Wrinkle in Time (D)

Write About Characters

Write your responses in complete sentences.

In 1–2 paragraphs, compare and contrast two characters from *A Wrinkle in Time*. Be sure to describe how they are alike and how they are different, and use at least one direct quotation from the text to support your points.

Answers will vary.

As an example, students could compare and contrast Mrs. Whatsit and Mrs. Who. These characters are alike in that they are both beings with special powers who take the form of elderly women on Earth. Both are very kind to the children, and both want to help the children in the battle against the "Dark Thing." These characters are different in that Mrs. Whatsit is very good at explaining things to the children, while Mrs. Who "finds it so difficult to verbalize" ideas that she mostly quotes others. Also, Mrs. Who remains in the form of an old woman on Uriel, while Mrs. Whatsit transforms on that planet into something quite different.

A WRINKLE IN TIME (D) **131**

TRY IT   Practice Words from *A Wrinkle in Time*, Chapter 5

Students will answer questions to demonstrate their understanding of the vocabulary words from the reading.

WRAP-UP

Questions About *A Wrinkle in Time*, Chapter 5

Students will answer questions to show that they understand the reading.

A Wrinkle in Time (E)

Lesson Overview

ACTIVITY	ACTIVITY TITLE	TIME	ONLINE/OFFLINE
GET READY	Introduction to *A Wrinkle in Time* (E)	**1** minute	🖥
	Spelling List 8 Pretest **LEARNING COACH CHECK-IN**	**10** minutes	🖥 and 📄
	Recall *A Wrinkle in Time*, Chapter 5	**5** minutes	🖥
	Before You Read *A Wrinkle in Time*, Chapter 6	**10** minutes	🖥
READ	*A Wrinkle in Time*, Chapter 6	**25** minutes	📄
	Check-In: *A Wrinkle in Time*, Chapter 6	**5** minutes	🖥
LEARN AND **TRY IT**	Examine Developing Themes	**10** minutes	🖥
	Challenges and Themes	**10** minutes	🖥
	Apply: Explore Themes	**15** minutes	🖥
	Write About Challenges and Themes **LEARNING COACH CHECK-IN**	**15** minutes	📄
	Practice Words from *A Wrinkle in Time*, Chapter 6	**9** minutes	🖥
WRAP-UP	Questions About *A Wrinkle in Time*, Chapter 6	**5** minutes	🖥

Content Background

Students will complete a spelling activity and continue to read Madeleine L'Engle's *A Wrinkle in Time*. They will then complete activities in which they learn how focusing on the challenges or problems that characters face in a story and exploring how characters react to those problems and challenges can help them uncover the themes of a work.

MATERIALS

Supplied
- *A Wrinkle in Time* by Madeleine L'Engle
- *Summit English Language Arts 5 Activity Book*
  - Spelling List 8 Pretest
  - Write About Challenges and Themes

KEYWORDS

theme – the author's message or big idea

A Wrinkle in Time, Chapter 6 Synopsis

Before they leave the Happy Medium, Meg asks to see her mother and asks that Calvin get to see his mother, as well. But when the Medium shows the children Mrs. O'Keefe in her crystal ball, Meg is saddened to find that Calvin's mother is a nasty woman who yells at her young children and threatens to hit them with a wooden spoon. Meg comforts Calvin before the children tesser again, this time arriving on a planet called Camazotz that is behind the Dark Thing. Camazotz looks much like Earth, but its people behave strangely: moving in unison, like automatons. Mr. Murry is on Camazotz, but no one knows where. The children, who are now alone and unable to rely on the guidance or help of the Mrs. Ws, walk into a town. They try to speak to a few people, but learn little. Charles Wallace is unable to read anyone's minds, but they feel as though perhaps they must go to the CENTRAL Central Intelligence building in order to find Mr. Murry. The chapter ends as the children are about to enter the building and Calvin says that he feels as if they are heading toward great danger.

Lesson Goals

- Take a spelling pretest.
- Continue to read *A Wrinkle in Time*.
- Explore the themes of *A Wrinkle in Time*.

GET READY

Introduction to *A Wrinkle in Time* (E)

Students will get a glimpse of what they will learn about in the lesson. They will also read the lesson goals and keywords. Have students select each keyword and preview its definition.

Spelling List 8 Pretest

Students will take a spelling pretest.

LEARNING COACH CHECK-IN   Have students turn to Spelling List 8 Pretest in *Summit English Language Arts 5 Activity Book* and open the online Spelling Pretest activity. Online, students will listen to the spelling word, type the word in the space indicated, and then check their answer. In the activity book, students will write the correct spelling of the word in the tables provided and indicate with a ✓ or an ✗ if they spelled the word correctly or incorrectly online. Students will repeat this process with the remaining words.

As needed, help students with the interaction between the online activity and the activity book page until they become comfortable with what they need to do. As students practice their spelling words throughout the workshop, they should pay special attention to words they spelled incorrectly on the pretest.

This is the complete list of words students will be tested on.

Contractions	Root *meter*	Prefix *multi–*	Heart Words
could've	diameter	multicolored	adjourn
we're	perimeter	multinational	flourish
should've	speedometer	multimedia	nourish
that's		multiple	
hasn't			
they'd			
they'll			
they've			
weren't			
what's			
who'd			
who'll			
haven't			
you've			
we'll			

NOTE Have students keep their completed activity page in a safe place so they can refer to it later.

GET READY
A Wrinkle in Time (E)

Spelling List 8 Pretest

1. Open the Spelling Pretest activity online. Listen to the first spelling word. Type the word. Check your answer.

2. Write the correct spelling of the word in the Word column of the Spelling Pretest table on the next page.

Word	✓	✗
1 blindfold		

3. Put a check mark in the ✓ column if you spelled the word correctly online.

Word	✓	✗
1 blindfold	✓	

Put an X in the ✗ column if you spelled the word incorrectly online.

Word	✓	✗
1 blindfold		X

4. Repeat Steps 1–3 for the remaining words in the Spelling Pretest.

A WRINKLE IN TIME (E) **133**

A Wrinkle in Time (E)

Spelling List 8 Pretest

Write each spelling word in the Word column, making sure to spell it correctly.

Word	✓	✗	Word	✓	✗
1 could've			14 you've		
2 we're			15 we'll		
3 should've			16 diameter		
4 that's			17 perimeter		
5 hasn't			18 speedometer		
6 they'd			19 adjourn		
7 they'll			20 flourish		
8 they've			21 nourish		
9 weren't			22 multicolored		
10 what's			23 multinational		
11 who'd			24 multimedia		
12 who'll			25 multiple		
13 haven't					

Students should use the ✓ and X columns to indicate whether they spelled each word correctly or incorrectly online.

134 A WRINKLE IN TIME (E)

Recall *A Wrinkle in Time*, Chapter 5

Students will answer some questions to review the reading that they have already completed.

Before You Read *A Wrinkle in Time*, Chapter 6

Students will be introduced to some key vocabulary words that they will encounter in the upcoming reading, review how writers convey big ideas to readers, and learn the meaning of the phrase "happy medium."

READ

A Wrinkle in Time, Chapter 6

Students will read Chapter 6 of *A Wrinkle in Time* by Madeleine L'Engle.

Check-In: *A Wrinkle in Time*, Chapter 6

Students will answer several questions to demonstrate their comprehension of Chapter 6 of *A Wrinkle in Time*.

LEARN AND TRY IT

LEARN   Examine Developing Themes

Students will learn how to explore the themes in a novel by focusing on the problems and challenges that characters face and examining how they react or respond to those problems and challenges.

TRY IT   Challenges and Themes

Students will complete an activity to explore several passages in *A Wrinkle in Time* to better understand the way the passages depict challenges and problems and the way in which characters react or respond to them. This will allow students to practice determining which themes the writer develops in the text.

TRY IT   Apply: Explore Themes

Students will apply to a new work what they've learned about determining themes by focusing on the challenges and problems that characters face and how the characters react or respond to those issues.

TRY IT   Write About Challenges and Themes

Students will complete Write About Challenges and Themes from *Summit English Language Arts 5 Activity Book*. Students will identify a problem or challenge that the characters in the novel face in Chapter 6. Then they will examine the characters' reactions and responses to that problem or challenge to determine a theme that this part of the novel conveys.

This activity page contains open-ended questions, so it's important that you review students' responses. Give students feedback, using the sample answers provided to guide you.

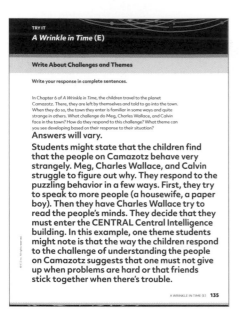

TRY IT
A Wrinkle in Time (E)

Write About Challenges and Themes

Write your response in complete sentences.

In Chapter 6 of *A Wrinkle in Time*, the children travel to the planet Camazotz. There, they are left by themselves and told to go into the town. When they do so, the town they enter is familiar in some ways and quite strange in others. What challenge do Meg, Charles Wallace, and Calvin face in the town? How do they respond to this challenge? What theme can you see developing based on their response to their situation?

Answers will vary.

Students might state that the children find that the people on Camazotz behave very strangely. Meg, Charles Wallace, and Calvin struggle to figure out why. They respond to the puzzling behavior in a few ways. First, they try to speak to more people (a housewife, a paper boy). Then they have Charles Wallace try to read the people's minds. They decide that they must enter the CENTRAL Central Intelligence building. In this example, one theme students might note is that the way the children respond to the challenge of understanding the people on Camazotz suggests that one must not give up when problems are hard or that friends stick together when there's trouble.

A WRINKLE IN TIME (E) **135**

TRY IT   Practice Words from *A Wrinkle in Time*, Chapter 6

Students will answer questions to demonstrate their understanding of the vocabulary words from the reading.

WRAP-UP

Questions About *A Wrinkle in Time*, Chapter 6

Students will answer questions to show that they understand the reading.

A Wrinkle in Time (F)

Lesson Overview

ACTIVITY	ACTIVITY TITLE	TIME	ONLINE/OFFLINE
GET READY	Introduction to *A Wrinkle in Time* (F)	**1** minute	
	Spelling List 8 Activity Bank	**10** minutes	
	Recall *A Wrinkle in Time*, Chapter 6	**5** minutes	
	Before You Read *A Wrinkle in Time*, Chapters 7–8	**10** minutes	
READ	*A Wrinkle in Time*, Chapters 7–8	**30** minutes	
	Check-In: *A Wrinkle in Time*, Chapters 7–8	**5** minutes	
LEARN AND **TRY IT**	Making Inferences	**10** minutes	
	Practice Making Inferences	**7** minutes	
	Apply: Inferences	**15** minutes	
	Write About Charles Wallace **LEARNING COACH CHECK-IN**	**15** minutes	
	Practice Words from *A Wrinkle in Time*, Chapters 7–8	**7** minutes	
WRAP-UP	Questions About *A Wrinkle in Time*, Chapters 7–8	**5** minutes	

Content Background

Students will complete a spelling activity and continue to read *A Wrinkle in Time* by Madeleine L'Engle. They will then complete activities in which they learn more about making inferences and using textual evidence, including direct quotations from the text, to support those inferences.

Advance Preparation

Gather students' completed Spelling List 8 Pretest activity page from *A Wrinkle In Time* (E). Students will refer to this page during Get Ready: Spelling List 8 Activity Bank

---

MATERIALS

Supplied
- *A Wrinkle in Time* by Madeleine L'Engle
- *Summit English Language Arts 5 Activity Book*
  - Spelling List 8 Activity Bank
  - Write About Charles Wallace

Also Needed
- completed Spelling List 8 Pretest activity page from *A Wrinkle in Time* (E)

A Wrinkle in Time, Chapters 7–8 Synopsis

Meg, Charles Wallace, and Calvin enter the CENTRAL Central Intelligence Building. They speak to a man who says he will have to turn them in, and they walk down a long hallway to find an odd-looking man with red eyes. The man communicates with them without speaking, and he's rather scary. He makes some efforts to hypnotize the children and control their minds, but they resist. The man insists that the people on Camazotz are happy because they have surrendered to the same power that controls him. Charles Wallace, whose mind is the strongest of the three, makes a decision to allow the man to control his mind. He reasons that it is the only way they will be able to figure out who or what is speaking through the man, and it is the only chance they have of finding their father. When Charles Wallace does submit to the man, he becomes an eerie and off-putting version of himself. Meg can't stand it. Her brother calls Mrs. Ws "witches" and tells Meg and Calvin that they will be much happier if they submit to IT. Meg and Calvin don't know exactly what IT is, but they are frightened because of how IT is making Charles Wallace behave. Nevertheless, they follow Charles Wallace because he says he will lead them to Mr. Murry. Chapter 8 ends with Meg at last seeing her father, who is imprisoned within some kind of transparent column. She shouts his name.

KEYWORDS

inference – a guess that readers make using the clues that authors give them in a piece of writing

Lesson Goals

- Practice all spelling words offline.
- Continue reading *A Wrinkle in Time*.
- Make inferences about the text and use direct quotations to support them.

GET READY

Introduction to *A Wrinkle in Time* (F)

Students will get a glimpse of what they will learn about in the lesson. They will also read the lesson goals and keywords. Have students select each keyword and preview its definition.

Spelling List 8 Activity Bank

Students will practice all spelling words by completing Spelling List 8 Activity Bank from *Summit English Language Arts 5 Activity Book*. Make sure students have their completed Spelling List 8 Pretest activity page from *A Wrinkle in Time* (E) to refer to during this activity.

Remind students to pay special attention to words they spelled incorrectly on the Spelling Pretest.

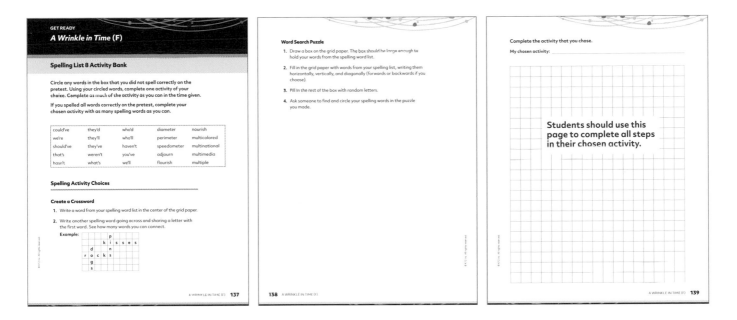

Recall *A Wrinkle in Time*, Chapter 6

Students will answer some questions to review the reading that they have already completed.

Before You Read *A Wrinkle in Time*, Chapters 7–8

Students will be introduced to some key vocabulary words that they will encounter in the upcoming reading and learn a bit about conformity.

READ

A Wrinkle in Time, Chapters 7–8

Students will read Chapters 7–8 of *A Wrinkle in Time* by Madeleine L'Engle.

Check-In: *A Wrinkle in Time*, Chapters 7–8

Students will answer several questions to demonstrate their comprehension of Chapters 7 and 8 of *A Wrinkle in Time*.

LEARN Making Inferences

Students will learn about making inferences based on details in the text and using direct quotations to support those inferences.

TRY IT Practice Making Inferences

Students will answer several questions online to develop their understanding of how to make inferences based on details and how to cite direct quotations from the text to support inferences.

TRY IT Apply: Inferences

Students will apply to a new work what they've learned about making inferences based on details in the text and using direct quotations from the text to support their inferences.

TRY IT Write About Charles Wallace

Students will complete Write About Charles Wallace from *Summit English Language Arts 5 Activity Book*. In their response, which should focus on inferences they make about Charles Wallace, students should cite details from the story and include at least one direct quotation that supports an inference they make.

LEARNING COACH CHECK-IN This activity page contains an open-ended question, so it's important that you review students' responses. Give students feedback, using the sample answers provided to guide you.

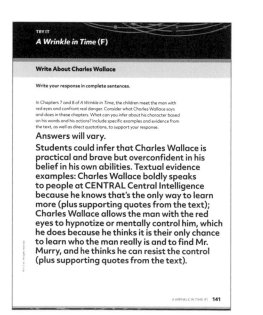

TRY IT Practice Words from *A Wrinkle in Time*, Chapters 7–8

Students will answer questions to demonstrate their understanding of the vocabulary words from the reading.

Questions About *A Wrinkle in Time*, Chapters 7–8

Students will answer questions to show that they understand the reading.

A Wrinkle in Time (G)

Lesson Overview

ACTIVITY	ACTIVITY TITLE	TIME	ONLINE/OFFLINE
GET READY	Introduction to *A Wrinkle in Time* (G)	**1** minute	🖥️
	Spelling List 8 Practice	**10** minutes	🖥️
	Recall *A Wrinkle in Time*, Chapters 7–8	**5** minutes	🖥️
	Before You Read *A Wrinkle in Time*, Chapters 9–10	**7** minutes	🖥️
READ	*A Wrinkle in Time*, Chapters 9–10	**30** minutes	📄
	Check-In: *A Wrinkle in Time*, Chapters 9–10	**5** minutes	🖥️
LEARN AND **TRY IT**	Visualize, Compare, and Contrast	**10** minutes	🖥️
	Compare and Contrast Settings	**10** minutes	🖥️
	Apply: Similarities and Differences in Settings	**15** minutes	🖥️
	Write About Two Settings LEARNING COACH CHECK-IN	**15** minutes	📄
	Practice Words from *A Wrinkle in Time*, Chapters 9–10	**7** minutes	🖥️
WRAP-UP	Questions About *A Wrinkle in Time*, Chapters 9–10	**5** minutes	🖥️

Content Background

Students will complete a spelling activity and continue to read *A Wrinkle in Time* by Madeleine L'Engle. They will then complete activities in which they learn more about visualizing the various settings of the novel and comparing and contrasting those settings.

MATERIALS

Supplied
- *A Wrinkle in Time* by Madeleine L'Engle
- *Summit English Language Arts 5 Activity Book*
  - Write About Two Settings

A Wrinkle in Time, Chapters 9–10 Synopsis

Meg frees Mr. Murry from his prison, but Charles Wallace remains under the power of IT. Mr. Murry tries to reach his son, but he cannot. Charles Wallace brings Meg, Calvin, and Mr. Murry to IT. IT is a disembodied brain with great power to invade the minds of people and get them to submit. Meg, Calvin, and Mr. Murry resist, but it's very difficult. Finally, just as they are about to fall under IT's control, Mr. Murry tessers away from Camazotz. The three land on an unfamiliar planet, and Meg is temporarily paralyzed from the journey. Not only can she not move, she cannot speak, at first, either. Further, she's very angry at her father. She feels as though he abandoned Charles Wallace. Calvin and Mr. Murry try to help Meg, encouraging her so that gradually she can speak and move slightly. But she accuses them of betraying Charles Wallace. She feels extremely cold and unhappy, but soon she, Calvin, and Mr. Murry realize they are not alone on this planet. Several strange beasts arrive. And though they look a bit frightening, they do not hurt or threaten Meg, Calvin, and Mr. Murry. Mr, Murry explains that Meg needs help, and one of the beasts picks her up.

KEYWORDS

inference – a guess that readers make using the clues that authors give them in a piece of writing

setting – where and when a literary work takes place

Lesson Goals

- Practice all spelling words online.

- Continue to read *A Wrinkle in Time*.

- Compare and contrast different settings in *A Wrinkle in Time*.

GET READY

Introduction to *A Wrinkle in Time* (G)
Students will get a glimpse of what they will learn about in the lesson. They will also read the lesson goals and keywords. Have students select each keyword and preview its definition.

Spelling List 8 Practice
Students will practice all spelling words from the workshop.

Recall *A Wrinkle in Time*, Chapters 7–8
Students will answer some questions to review the reading that they have already completed.

Before You Read *A Wrinkle in Time*, Chapters 9–10

Students will be introduced to some key vocabulary words that they will encounter in the upcoming reading.

READ

A Wrinkle in Time, Chapters 9–10

Students will read Chapters 9 and 10 of *A Wrinkle in Time* by Madeleine L'Engle.

Check-In: *A Wrinkle in Time*, Chapters 9–10

Students will answer several questions to demonstrate their comprehension of Chapters 9 and 10 of *A Wrinkle in Time*.

LEARN AND TRY IT

LEARN   Visualize, Compare, and Contrast

Students will learn about the importance of visualizing settings and how to compare and contrast settings from the novel. They will also learn about using direct quotations to support their assertions or descriptions.

TRY IT   Compare and Contrast Settings

Students will answer several questions online to develop their understanding of how to compare and contrast settings from the novel.

TRY IT   Apply: Similarities and Differences in Settings

Students will apply to a new work what they've learned about visualizing settings before comparing and contrasting them.

TRY IT   Write About Two Settings

Students will complete Write About Two Settings from *Summit English Language Arts 5 Activity Book*. They are to compare and contrast Earth and Camazotz based on the details and descriptions provided in the novel. They should include direct quotations from the text to support their answer.

LEARNING COACH CHECK-IN   This activity page contains an open-ended question, so it's important that you review students' responses. Give students feedback, using the sample answer provided to guide you.

Additional answer

Answers will vary.

Similarities: The two planets look alike. When Meg, Charles Wallace, and Calvin first arrive on Camazotz, L'Engle writes about a hill that "could easily be a hill on earth." There are "familiar trees" nearby. Down the hill, "the smokestacks of a town, and it might have been one of any number of familiar towns" on Earth. Also, there are people who live on Camazotz, and they look like human beings. They live in homes that look like houses on Earth. They work in a city that looks like cities on Earth, too.

Differences: On Camazotz, the houses are "all exactly alike." Meg senses that if she counted the flowers in each home's front yard, she would find that "there would be exactly the same number for each house." Camazotz is also different from Earth because it is a "dark planet." Its residents have surrendered to IT; everyone thinks the same. Earth is still fighting the darkness; people are still creative, independent individuals.

TRY IT   Practice Words from *A Wrinkle in Time*, Chapters 9–10

Students will answer questions to demonstrate their understanding of the vocabulary words from the reading.

WRAP-UP

Questions About *A Wrinkle in Time*, Chapters 9–10

Students will answer questions to show that they understand the reading.

A Wrinkle in Time (H)

Lesson Overview

ACTIVITY	ACTIVITY TITLE	TIME	ONLINE/OFFLINE
GET READY	Introduction to *A Wrinkle in Time* (H)	**1** minute	🖥
	Spelling List 8 More Practice	**10** minutes	🖥
	Recall *A Wrinkle in Time*, Chapters 9–10	**5** minutes	🖥
	Before You Read *A Wrinkle in Time*, Chapter 11	**10** minutes	🖥
READ	*A Wrinkle in Time*, Chapter 11	**25** minutes	📄
	Check-In: *A Wrinkle in Time*, Chapter 11	**5** minutes	🖥
LEARN AND **TRY IT**	More Themes in *A Wrinkle in Time*	**10** minutes	🖥
	Find More Themes in *A Wrinkle in Time*	**10** minutes	🖥
	Apply: Get the Message	**15** minutes	🖥
	Write About Another Theme **LEARNING COACH CHECK-IN**	**15** minutes	📄
	Practice Words from *A Wrinkle in Time*, Chapter 11	**9** minutes	🖥
WRAP-UP	Questions About *A Wrinkle in Time*, Chapter 11	**5** minutes	🖥

Content Background

Students will complete a spelling activity and continue to read *A Wrinkle in Time* by Madeleine L'Engle. They will then complete activities in which they learn more about determining themes and using evidence and direct quotations from the text to support them.

MATERIALS

Supplied
- *A Wrinkle in Time* by Madeleine L'Engle
- *Summit English Language Arts 5 Activity Book*
  - Write About Another Theme

KEYWORDS

theme – the author's message or big idea

A Wrinkle in Time, Chapter 11 Synopsis

Meg is nursed back to health by one of the creatures on Ixchel, whom she names Aunt Beast. Aunt Beast is very kind, and Meg feels safe and protected with her. She tries to explain the concept of light to Aunt Beast, who does not understand because she has no eyes and uses her other senses to experience and understand the world. Meg realizes that her own senses are limited and her own understanding of the universe is, too. When she is strong enough, Meg goes to join her father and Calvin for breakfast. She is still bitter about leaving Charles Wallace, but Aunt Beast tries to help her see that her father had no choice and that she should not blame him. She asks whether Calvin and Mr. Murry have told the beasts on Ixchel about the Mrs. Ws. She then tries to do so, but struggles to explain just what they are. Calvin suggests that they are guardian angels, and, as the chapter closes, Mrs. Which announces that they have arrived.

Lesson Goals

- Practice all spelling words online.
- Continue to read *A Wrinkle in Time*.
- Explore the themes of *A Wrinkle in Time*.

GET READY

Introduction to *A Wrinkle in Time* (H)

Students will get a glimpse of what they will learn about in the lesson. They will also read the lesson goals and keywords. Have students select each keyword and preview its definition.

Spelling List 8 More Practice

Students will practice all spelling words from the workshop.

Recall *A Wrinkle in Time*, Chapters 9–10

Students will answer some questions to review the reading that they have already completed.

Before You Read *A Wrinkle in Time*, Chapter 11

Students will be introduced to some key vocabulary words that they will encounter in the upcoming reading. They will also answer a question to review what they know about finding the theme in a work of literature.

A Wrinkle in Time, Chapter 11

Students will read Chapter 11 of *A Wrinkle in Time* by Madeleine L'Engle.

Check-In: A Wrinkle in Time, Chapter 11

Students will answer several questions to demonstrate their comprehension of Chapter 11 of *A Wrinkle in Time*.

LEARN More Themes in *A Wrinkle in Time*

Students will learn more about determining themes in a story. They will also learn about using direct quotations to support themes.

TRY IT Find More Themes in *A Wrinkle in Time*

Students will answer several questions online to develop their ability to recognize themes and find textual evidence that supports them.

TRY IT Apply: Get the Message

Students will apply to a new work what they've learned about determining themes.

TRY IT Write About Another Theme

Students will complete Write About Another Theme from *Summit English Language Arts 5 Activity Book*. They are to identify another theme in the book and explain the textual details and events that led them to this theme. They should include direct quotations from the text to support their answer.

LEARNING COACH CHECK-IN This activity page contains an open-ended question, so it's important that you review students' responses. Give students feedback, using the sample answer provided to guide you.

TRY IT
A Wrinkle in Time (H)

Write About Another Theme

Write your response in complete sentences.

Think about what you have read so far in *A Wrinkle in Time*. Think about the problems the characters have faced, how they have reacted, and what they have realized or recognized, based on the events of the story. Then name one theme that the novel has conveyed to this point. Explain how you determined that L'Engle conveys this theme, and include at least one direct quotation from the book that supports it.

Answers will vary.

An example of a theme: The novel conveys the idea that it's good to be different. From the very start, for instance, Charles Wallace is described as being unique. He is special, and the novel celebrates that. Students should include at least one direct quotation that supports the theme they identified. A quote from Chapter 1 that supports the example theme is when Meg is recalling a conversation she had with her father. They are talking about Charles Wallace and Meg, and Meg is worried that Charles Wallace will struggle because he is different, as is Meg. Mr. Murry says, "You and Charles Wallace will be able to do pretty much whatever you like when you grow up to yourselves." The quote supports the idea that being different is an advantage.

A WRINKLE IN TIME (H) **145**

TRY IT Practice Words from *A Wrinkle in Time*, Chapter 11

Students will answer questions to demonstrate their understanding of the vocabulary words from the reading.

WRAP-UP

Questions About *A Wrinkle in Time*, Chapter 11

Students will answer questions to show that they understand the reading.

A Wrinkle in Time (I)

Lesson Overview

ACTIVITY	ACTIVITY TITLE	TIME	ONLINE/OFFLINE
GET READY	Introduction to *A Wrinkle in Time* (I)	**1** minute	
	Spelling List 8 Review Game	**10** minutes	
	Recall *A Wrinkle in Time*, Chapter 11	**5** minutes	
	Before You Read *A Wrinkle in Time*, Chapter 12	**7** minutes	
READ	*A Wrinkle in Time*, Chapter 12	**20** minutes	
	Check-In: *A Wrinkle in Time*, Chapter 12	**5** minutes	
LEARN AND **TRY IT**	Crafting a Summary	**10** minutes	
	Summarize *A Wrinkle in Time*, Chapter 11	**10** minutes	
	Apply: Summarize Another Story	**15** minutes	
	Write About Chapter 12 **LEARNING COACH CHECK-IN**	**25** minutes	
	Practice Words from *A Wrinkle in Time*, Chapter 12	**7** minutes	
WRAP-UP	Questions About *A Wrinkle in Time*, Chapter 12	**5** minutes	

Content Background

Students will complete a spelling activity and finish reading *A Wrinkle in Time* by Madeleine L'Engle. They will then complete activities in which they learn more about writing effective summaries.

MATERIALS

Supplied
- *A Wrinkle in Time* by Madeleine L'Engle
- *Summit English Language Arts 5 Activity Book*
  - Write About Chapter 12

KEYWORDS

summarize – to tell in order the most important ideas or events of a text

A Wrinkle in Time, Chapter 12 Synopsis

The Mrs. Ws arrive on Ixchel, and it's decided that Meg must be the one to return to Camazotz to save Charles Wallace. He understands her, and she is closest to him. Meg finally stops blaming her father for leaving Charles Wallace behind, and she faces her test with courage. Before she leaves, the Mrs. Ws say things to help and encourage her. Mrs. Whatsit gives Meg her love, Mrs. Who tells her an inspirational quotation, and Mrs. Which tells her that she has something IT does not have. Meg wonders what this might be as she returns to Camazotz and goes to face IT. Once again, she is nearly overcome by IT's power. But at the last moment, she realizes what she has and IT does not: love. She loves Charles Wallace. So she tells Charles Wallace that she loves him, over and over, and she manages to free his mind from IT's grasp. He recognizes Meg, and they hug. In an instant, the brother and sister are then transported back home to Earth. They wind up in their backyard, where they are soon joined by Calvin and Mr. Murry. The twins come out of the Murry house to find them, and the family is reunited.

Note: This novel is the first in a series of several novels written by Madeleine L'Engle that follow the lives of these characters. Students who enjoyed *A Wrinkle in Time* should be encouraged to seek out and read the other novels in this series.

Lesson Goals

- Practice all spelling words online.
- Finish reading *A Wrinkle in Time*.
- Summarize *A Wrinkle in Time*.

GET READY

Introduction to *A Wrinkle in Time* (I)

Students will get a glimpse of what they will learn about in the lesson. They will also read the lesson goals and keywords. Have students select each keyword and preview its definition.

Spelling List 8 Review Game

Students will practice all spelling words from the workshop.

Recall *A Wrinkle in Time*, Chapter 11

Students will answer some questions to review the reading that they have already completed.

Before You Read *A Wrinkle in Time*, **Chapter 12**

Students will be introduced to some key vocabulary words that they will encounter in the upcoming reading.

READ

A Wrinkle in Time, **Chapter 12**

Students will read Chapter 12 of *A Wrinkle in Time* by Madeleine L'Engle.

Check-In: *A Wrinkle in Time*, **Chapter 12**

Students will answer several questions to demonstrate their comprehension of Chapter 12 of *A Wrinkle in Time*.

LEARN AND TRY IT

LEARN   Crafting a Summary

Students will learn about how to write an effective summary, focusing on describing events in the proper order, what types of details to include, and what types of details to leave out.

TRY IT   Summarize *A Wrinkle in Time*, **Chapter 11**

Students will answer several questions online to demonstrate their understanding of how to write an effective summary.

TRY IT   Apply: Summarize Another Story

Students will apply to a new work what they've learned about summarizing.

TRY IT   Write About Chapter 12

Students will complete Write About Chapter 12 from *Summit English Language Arts 5 Activity Book*. They should write an effective summary of the final chapter of *A Wrinkle in Time*, detailing major events in order and including all key details while omitting minor details.

LEARNING COACH CHECK-IN   This activity page contains an open-ended question, so it's important that you review students' responses. Give students feedback, using the sample answer provided to guide you.

A Wrinkle in Time (I)

Write About Chapter 12

Write your responses in complete sentences.

Think about the final chapter of *A Wrinkle in Time*. Consider the most important events and details in the chapter. Then write a 1–2 paragraph summary of the chapter. Remember that your summary should describe events in the same order as Madeleine L'Engle's novel, and be sure to leave out descriptions of minor or unimportant figures and moments.

Answers will vary.

Some key events and details, in order, that should be included:

- The Mrs. Ws arrive and try to help figure out how to save Charles Wallace.

- It's decided that it must be Meg who goes back because she is closest with Charles Wallace; Meg comes to understand and accept her duty.

- Back on Camazotz, Meg is afraid, but she goes to find IT and Charles Wallace.

- Once again, Meg is nearly overtaken by IT. She fights back, realizing that she has love, and IT does not. She can love Charles Wallace, and IT cannot. So she focuses on her brother and how much she loves him.

- At last, IT's control over Charles Wallace is broken. He is himself again. In a flash, he and Meg are quickly transported away from Camazotz and back to Earth, where Calvin and Mr. Murry soon join them.

Who should I include?
Which details?
What's it about?

TRY IT Practice Words from *A Wrinkle in Time*, Chapter 12

Students will answer questions to demonstrate their understanding of the vocabulary words from the reading.

WRAP-UP

Questions About *A Wrinkle in Time*, Chapter 12

Students will answer questions to show that they understand the reading.

A Wrinkle in Time Wrap-Up

Lesson Overview

ACTIVITY	ACTIVITY TITLE	TIME	ONLINE/OFFLINE
GET READY	Introduction to *A Wrinkle in Time* Wrap-Up	**1** minute	🛜
TRY IT	Write About *A Wrinkle in Time* **LEARNING COACH CHECK-IN**	**29** minutes	📄
	Read and Record	**10** minutes	🛜
	Review *A Wrinkle in Time*	**20** minutes	🛜
QUIZ	*A Wrinkle in Time*	**30** minutes	🛜
	Spelling List 8	**10** minutes	🛜
WRAP-UP	Keyboarding	**10** minutes	🛜
	More Language Arts Practice	**10** minutes	🛜

Advance Preparation

During the Keyboarding activity, students will practice their keyboarding skills using an external website or program. **You will need to work with students to select an appropriate keyboarding practice website or program; K12 does not specify which resource to use.** A few suggestions are provided in the online activity.

Depending on which program you choose, students may need to set up an account to save their progress. If needed, assist students in setting up and running their chosen keyboarding practice program.

MATERIALS

Supplied
- *Summit English Language Arts 5 Activity Book*
  - Write About *A Wrinkle in Time*

Lesson Goals

- Write about *A Wrinkle in Time*.
- Review *A Wrinkle in Time*.
- Take a quiz on *A Wrinkle in Time*.
- Take a spelling quiz.

GET READY

Introduction to *A Wrinkle in Time* Wrap-Up

Students will read the lesson goals.

TRY IT

Write About *A Wrinkle in Time*

Students will complete Write About *A Wrinkle in Time* in *Summit English Language Arts 5 Activity Book* to write a book review on Madeleine L'Engle's text.

LEARNING COACH CHECK-IN   This activity page contains an open-ended question, so it's important that you review students' responses. Give students feedback, using the sample answers provided to guide you.

TRY IT
A Wrinkle in Time Wrap-Up

Write About *A Wrinkle in Time*

Write a book review of *A Wrinkle in Time* by Madeleine L'Engle. Write your response in complete sentences.

Follow these guidelines in writing your review:

- Your review should be at least three paragraphs long.
- Describe several of the most important events, characters, and ideas in the novel.
- Include specific examples and direct quotations from the text.
- Explain why others should read the book.

NOTE: Remember that the goal of this review is to encourage others to read the novel, not to explain every moment or event. For example, you don't need to describe the ending of the novel in your review because readers can enjoy discovering that for themselves.

Answers will vary.

The review should relate the adventure that Meg, Charles Wallace, and Calvin go on to find Mr. Murry. It should give brief but accurate descriptions for each of the main characters. Meg is bright but difficult and sad over her father's absence. Charles Wallace is precocious and uniquely perceptive and intelligent. Calvin is thoughtful and kind and friendly. The review should detail how the Mrs. Ws help the children and teach them about the evil that threatens

A WRINKLE IN TIME WRAP-UP **149**

150 A WRINKLE IN TIME WRAP-UP

the universe. It should also cover what can or is being done to fight it. Students' response should include specific examples related to several places the children go. It should tell what they learn about fighting evil as the novel progresses. It should contain direct quotations that illustrate their points. The review does not have to touch on the ending of the novel since that might spoil the experience of reading it for those who haven't.

Read and Record

Good readers read quickly, smoothly, and with expression. This is called *fluency*. Students will record themselves reading aloud. They will listen to their recording and think about how quick, smooth, and expressive they sound.

TIP   Encourage students to rerecord as needed.

Review *A Wrinkle in Time*

Students will answer questions to review what they have learned about themes, characters, settings, making inferences, and using direct quotations and to demonstrate their comprehension of *A Wrinkle in Time*.

A Wrinkle in Time

Students will complete the *A Wrinkle in Time* quiz.

Spelling List 8

Students will complete the Spelling List 8 quiz.

Keyboarding

Students will practice their keyboarding skills using an external website or program.

More Language Arts Practice

Students will practice skills according to their individual needs.

Informational Writing Skills (A)

Lesson Overview

ACTIVITY	ACTIVITY TITLE	TIME	ONLINE/OFFLINE
GET READY	Introduction to Informational Writing Skills (A)	**1** minute	🖥️
	Spelling List 9 Pretest **LEARNING COACH CHECK-IN**	**10** minutes	🖥️ and 📄
	Look Back at Conjunctions	**8** minutes	🖥️
LEARN AND **TRY IT**	Coordinating and Subordinating Conjunctions	**15** minutes	🖥️
	Function of a Conjunction	**15** minutes	🖥️
	Explore the Writing in *Mesmerized*	**15** minutes	🖥️
	Explore the Writing in *Where Is Niagara Falls?*	**15** minutes	🖥️
	Write About a Celestial Body **LEARNING COACH CHECK-IN**	**15** minutes	📄
WRAP-UP	Questions About Conjunctions and Introductions	**6** minutes	🖥️
	Go Read!	**20** minutes	🖥️ or 📄

Content Background

Informational text is factual text written for sharing information. Students will analyze how authors write informational text. Then they will apply those skills to their own informational writing. In this lesson, students will learn how writers begin and organize informational text.

Writers introduce informational text with a *hook*, something that grabs readers' attention. Writers also clearly introduce the main idea of the text. Writers then organize ideas logically to support the main idea.

Grammar, Usage, and Mechanics Students will learn about coordinating and subordinating conjunctions.

There are seven **coordinating conjunctions**: *for, and, nor, but, or, yet, so.* A coordinating conjunction can connect the parts of a compound subject, predicate, or object.

> **Compound subject: Amir and Carrie** are watching the Animal Olympics.

Compound predicate: The woodchucks **ski and skate** well.

Compound object: Winners received **medals or trophies.**

A coordinating conjunction can also connect two independent clauses to create a compound sentence.

Compound sentence: The cheetah almost won the race, **but** she tripped before the finish line.

A **subordinating conjunction** is a word that introduces a dependent clause to create a complex sentence. Common subordinating conjunctions are *before*, *because*, *since*, and *until*.

Complex sentence: The kangaroo's win surprised everyone **since** the giraffe was ahead most of the game.

Advance Preparation

During the Go Read! activity, students will have the option of using the digital library. Allow extra time for students to make their reading selection, or have students make a selection before beginning the lesson.

Lesson Goals

- Take a spelling pretest.
- Explore coordinating and subordinating conjunctions.
- Explore how to introduce topics and organize ideas in informational writing.
- Begin to write an informational paragraph.
- Read for pleasure.

GET READY

Introduction to Informational Writing Skills (A)

Students will get a glimpse of what they will learn about in the lesson. They will also read the lesson goals and keywords. Have students select each keyword and preview its definition.

Spelling List 9 Pretest

Students will take a spelling pretest.

LEARNING COACH CHECK-IN   Have students turn to Spelling List 9 Pretest in *Summit English Language Arts 5 Activity Book* and open the online Spelling Pretest activity. Online, students will listen to the spelling word, type the word in the space indicated, and then check their answer. In the activity book, students will write the correct spelling of the word in the tables provided and indicate with a ✓ or an ✗ if they spelled the word correctly or incorrectly online. Students will repeat this process with the remaining words.

As needed, help students with the interaction between the online activity and the activity book page until they become comfortable with what they need to do. As students practice their spelling words throughout the workshop, they should pay special attention to words they spelled incorrectly on the pretest.

This is the complete list of words students will be tested on.

Homophones		Heart Words
aisle	rain	millionaire
I'll	reign	reservoir
isle	rein	turquoise
forth	vein	
fourth	vain	
mayor	assistance	
mare	assistants	

NOTE   Have students keep their completed activity page in a safe place so they can refer to it later.

Look Back at Conjunctions

Students will practice the prerequisite skill of recognizing and using conjunctions.

LEARN AND TRY IT

LEARN Coordinating and Subordinating Conjunctions

Students will explore the functions of coordinating and subordinating conjunctions.

TIP Students can use the mnemonic FANBOYS to recall the seven coordinating conjunctions:

F or
A nd
N or
B ut
O r
Y et
S o

TRY IT Function of a Conjunction

Students will answer questions about the functions of subordinating and coordinating conjunctions. They will receive feedback on their answers.

LEARN Explore the Writing in *Mesmerized*

Students will examine some of the elements of *Mesmerized: How Ben Franklin Solved a Mystery that Baffled All of France*, an informational text about Benjamin Franklin and the scientific method. They will focus on the author's use of a hook, introduction, and organizational structure.

TRY IT Explore the Writing in *Where Is Niagara Falls?*

Students will answer questions about how a writer grabs the attention of readers and organizes information. They will receive feedback on their answers.

TRY IT Write About a Celestial Body

Students will complete Write About a Celestial Body from *Summit English Language Arts 5 Activity Book*.

LEARNING COACH CHECK-IN This activity page contains open-ended questions, so it's important that you review students' responses. Give students feedback, using the sample answers provided to guide you.

NOTE Have students keep their completed activity page in a safe place so they can refer to it later.

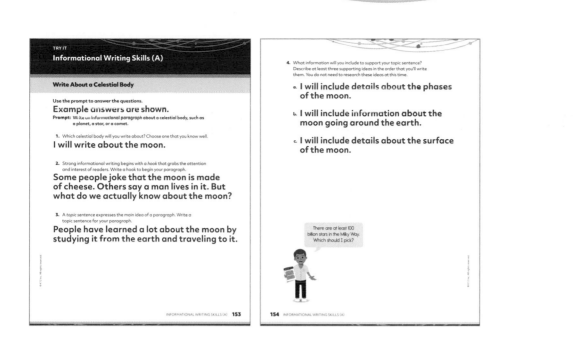

WRAP-UP

Questions About Conjunctions and Introductions

Students will answer questions to show that they understand how to create an effective introduction to a piece of informational writing and the functions of coordinating and subordinating conjunctions.

Go Read!

Students will read for pleasure. They should choose a book or a magazine that interests them, or they may choose a selection from the digital library, linked in the online lesson.

Students should read for the entire time. Have students select something to read ahead of time to help them stay focused.

Informational Writing Skills (B)

Lesson Overview

ACTIVITY	ACTIVITY TITLE	TIME	ONLINE/OFFLINE
GET READY	Introduction to Informational Writing Skills (B)	**2** minute	🖥
	Spelling List 9 Activity Bank	**10** minutes	📄
LEARN AND **TRY IT**	Correlative Conjunctions	**10** minutes	🖥
	Use Correlative Conjunctions	**10** minutes	📄
	Formatting and Media in *Mesmerized*	**15** minutes	🖥
	Formatting and Media in *Where Is Niagara Falls?*	**15** minutes	🖥
	Develop Your Topic **LEARNING COACH CHECK-IN**	**30** minutes	📄
WRAP-UP	Questions About Correlative Conjunctions and Relevant Facts	**8** minutes	🖥
	Go Read!	**20** minutes	🖥 or 📄

Content Background

Students will continue learning about informational writing by analyzing the work of expert writers and then applying those skills to their own writing. In this lesson, they will learn how writers use relevant information, headings, and images to support the ideas in informational texts.

Students will learn about the evidence that informational writers use, such as relevant facts, details, quotations, definitions, and examples. They will learn how writers effectively use headings to guide and focus readers. Finally, students will explore how writers use graphics, such as pictures and diagrams, to support their main idea. Graphics have a purpose beyond decoration, and students will learn that they should think critically about how they choose graphics to support their own informational writing.

Grammar, Usage, and Mechanics **Correlative conjunctions** work in pairs to connect parts of a sentence. *Both/and*, *either/or*, and *neither/nor* are common correlative conjunctions.

MATERIALS

Supplied
- *Summit English Language Arts 5 Activity Book*
  - Spelling List 9 Activity Bank
  - Develop Your Topic
- *Mesmerized: How Ben Franklin Solved a Mystery that Baffled All of France* by Mara Rockliff

Also Needed
- completed Spelling List 9 Pretest activity page from Informational Writing Skills (A)
- completed Write About a Celestial Body activity page from Informational Writing Skills (A)
- reading material for Go Read!

Students will learn how to use correlative conjunctions to effectively combine sentences.

Before: Mom loves pickles. Dad loves pickles.

After: Both Mom **and** Dad love pickles.

Advance Preparation

Gather students' completed Spelling List 9 Pretest activity page from Informational Writing Skills (A). Students will refer to this page during Get Ready: Spelling List 9 Activity Bank.

Gather *Mesmerized: How Ben Franklin Solved a Mystery that Baffled All of France*. During the Learn: Formatting and Media in *Mesmerized* activity, students will refer to page 9 in the book. Have students turn to the page before beginning the lesson.

Gather students' completed Write About a Celestial Body activity page from Informational Writing Skills (A). Students will refer to this page during Try It: Develop Your Topic.

During the Go Read! activity, students will have the option of using the digital library. Allow extra time for students to make their reading selection, or have students make a selection before beginning the lesson.

Lesson Goals

- Practice all spelling words offline.
- Use correlative conjunctions.
- Explore how to support ideas in informational writing.
- Continue to write an informational paragraph.
- Read for pleasure.

KEYWORDS

correlative conjunction – one part of a pair of conjunctions that connects words or groups of words; example pairs: either/or, neither/nor, both/and

heading – title within the body of a text that tells the reader something important about a section of the text

GET READY

Introduction to Informational Writing Skills (B)

Students will get a glimpse of what they will learn about in the lesson. They will also read the lesson goals and keywords. Have students select each keyword and preview its definition.

Spelling List 9 Activity Bank

Students will practice all spelling words by completing Spelling List 9 Activity Bank from *Summit English Language Arts 5 Activity Book*. Make sure students have their completed Spelling List 9 Pretest activity page from Informational Writing Skills (A) to refer to during this activity.

Remind students to pay special attention to words they spelled incorrectly on the Spelling Pretest.

LEARN AND TRY IT

LEARN   Correlative Conjunctions

Students will learn when and how to use correlative conjunctions.

TRY IT   Use Correlative Conjunctions

Students will answer questions about correctly using correlative conjunctions. They will receive feedback on their answers.

LEARN   Formatting and Media in *Mesmerized*

Students will continue to examine some of the elements of *Mesmerized: How Ben Franklin Solved a Mystery that Baffled All of France*, an informational text about Benjamin Franklin and the scientific method. They will focus on the piece's supporting details and images, and how those details and images help convey and reinforce main ideas.

Students will need to refer to page 9 in *Mesmerized: How Ben Franklin Solved a Mystery that Baffled All of France* during this activity. Have students turn to the page before beginning the activity.

TRY IT   Formatting and Media in *Where Is Niagara Falls?*

Students will answer questions about how a writer uses supporting details, headings, and images to convey and reinforce main ideas. They will receive feedback on their answers.

TRY IT   Develop Your Topic

Students will complete Develop Your Topic from *Summit English Language Arts 5 Activity Book*. Make sure students have their completed Write About a Celestial Body activity page from Informational Writing Skills (A) to refer to during this activity.

LEARNING COACH CHECK-IN   This activity page contains open-ended questions, so it's important that you review students' responses. Give students feedback, using the sample answers provided to guide you.

TIP   Students may need to do research in order to develop their supporting ideas. Work together with students to locate trustworthy websites, such as those run by city and state governments or government organizations, or trustworthy print sources, such as as encyclopedias.

NOTE   Have students keep their completed activity page in a safe place so they can refer to it later.

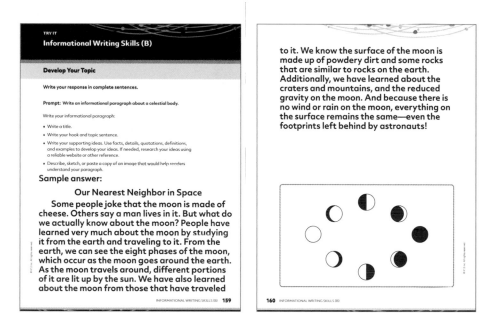

Questions About Correlative Conjunctions and Relevant Facts

Students will answer questions to show that they understand how to use correlative conjunctions and why writers of informational texts include relevant facts in their work.

Go Read!

Students will read for pleasure. They should choose a book or a magazine that interests them, or they may choose a selection from the digital library, linked in the online lesson.

Students should read for the entire time. Have students select something to read ahead of time to help them stay focused.

Informational Writing Skills (C)

Lesson Overview

ACTIVITY	ACTIVITY TITLE	TIME	ONLINE/OFFLINE
GET READY	Introduction to Informational Writing Skills (C)	**2** minutes	🖥️
	Spelling List 9 Review Game	**10** minutes	🖥️
	A Song in Space	**15** minutes	📶
LEARN AND **TRY IT**	Clarity and Conclusions in *Mesmerized*	**15** minutes	🖥️
	Clarity and Conclusions in *Where Is Niagara Falls?*	**15** minutes	🖥️
	Clear Up and Conclude Your Paragraph **LEARNING COACH CHECK-IN**	**30** minutes	📄
WRAP-UP	Question About Transitions in Informational Writing	**8** minutes	📶
	Go Read!	**25** minutes	🖥️ or 📄

Content Background

Students will continue learning about informational writing by analyzing how authors write informational texts and then applying those skills to their own writing. In this lesson, they will focus on using precise and domain-specific language, as well as transitions to connect ideas. They'll also learn how to write an effective conclusion to an informational text.

The term *precise language* refers to language that clearly and concisely describes complex content. *Domain-specific language* refers to the use of terms that are related to a particular field or subject. Using domain-specific language is something that helps establish the authority or expertise of a writer. *Transitions* link categories of information. For example, the transition *because* shows reason, and the transition *also* shows similarity. The transition *for example* tells the reader that the upcoming text is an example of the previous text.

A conclusion is the end of a text. It's not necessarily a single paragraph or a single sentence. The length of a conclusion can vary. A strong conclusion to an informational text wraps up the text, often covering the most recent events if the text is organized chronologically or stressing the meaning or importance of the subject.

MATERIALS

Supplied
- *Summit English Language Arts 5 Activity Book*
  - Clear Up and Conclude Your Paragraph

Also Needed
- completed Write About a Celestial Body activity page from Informational Writing Skills (A)
- completed Develop Your Topic activity page from Informational Writing Skills (B)
- reading material for Go Read!

KEYWORDS

transition – a word, phrase, or clause that connects ideas

Advance Preparation

Gather students' completed Write About a Celestial Body activity page from Informational Writing Skills (A) and completed Develop Your Topic activity page from Informational Writing Skills (B). Students will refer to these pages during Clear Up and Conclude Your Paragraph.

During the Go Read! activity, students will have the option of using the digital library. Allow extra time for students to make their reading selection, or have students make a selection before beginning the lesson.

Lesson Goals

- Practice all spelling words online.
- Practice grammar skills by editing a passage.
- Explore how to use domain-specific language, connect ideas, and write a conclusion to informational writing.
- Finish writing an informational paragraph.
- Read for pleasure.

GET READY

Introduction to Informational Writing Skills (C)

Students will get a glimpse of what they will learn about in the lesson. They will also read the lesson goals and keywords. Have students select each keyword and preview its definition.

Spelling List 9 Review Game

Students will practice all spelling words from the workshop.

A Song in Space

Students will edit a short passage to practice applying grammar skills. This passage contains errors and opportunities to improve the writing related to incomplete sentences. Students will also work with coordinating, subordinating, and correlative conjunctions within the paragraph.

LEARN Clarity and Conclusions in *Mesmerized*

Students will continue examining some of the elements of *Mesmerized: How Ben Franklin Solved a Mystery that Baffled All of France*, an informational text about Ben Franklin and the scientific method. They will focus on the writer's use of precise and domain-specific language, as well as transitions. They will also focus on how the writer concludes the text by stressing the subject's importance and meaning.

TRY IT Clarity and Conclusions in *Where Is Niagara Falls?*

Students will answer questions about how a writer uses precise and domain-specific language in an informational text, as well as transitions. They will also answer questions about how a writer concludes an informational text. Students will receive feedback on their answers.

TRY IT Clear Up and Conclude Your Paragraph

Students will complete Clear Up and Conclude Your Paragraph from *Summit English Language Arts 5 Activity Book*. Make sure students have their completed Write About a Celestial Body activity page from Informational Writing Skills (A) and Develop Your Topic activity page from Informational Writing Skills (B) to refer to during this activity.

LEARNING COACH CHECK-IN This activity page contains open-ended questions, so it's important that you review students' responses. Give students feedback, using the sample answers provided to guide you.

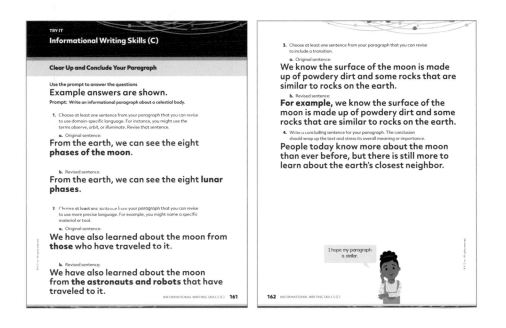

Question About Transitions in Informational Writing

Students will answer a question to show that they understand why writers of informational texts use transitions in their work.

Go Read!

Students will read for pleasure. They should choose a book or a magazine that interests them, or they may choose a selection from the digital library, linked in the online lesson.

Students should read for the entire time. Have students select something to read ahead of time to help them stay focused.

Informational Writing Skills Wrap-Up

Lesson Overview

ACTIVITY	ACTIVITY TITLE	TIME	ONLINE/OFFLINE
GET READY	Introduction to Informational Writing Skills Wrap-Up	**1** minute	
TRY IT	Use Informational Writing Skills **LEARNING COACH CHECK-IN**	**30** minutes	
	Review Conjunctions	**20** minutes	
QUIZ	Conjunctions and Informational Writing Skills	**30** minutes	
	Spelling List 9	**10** minutes	
WRAP-UP	Keyboarding	**10** minutes	
	More Language Arts Practice	**19** minutes	

Advance Preparation

During the Keyboarding activity, students will practice their keyboarding skills using an external website or program. **You will need to work with students to select an appropriate keyboarding practice website or program; K12 does not specify which resource to use.** A few suggestions are provided in the online activity.

Depending on which program you choose, students may need to set up an account to save their progress. If needed, assist students in setting up and running their chosen keyboarding practice program.

MATERIALS

Supplied
- *Summit English Language Arts 5 Activity Book*
  - Use Informational Writing Skills

Lesson Goals

- Review coordinating, subordinating, and correlative conjunctions, and informational writing skills.
- Take a quiz on conjunctions and informational writing skills.
- Take a spelling quiz.

Introduction to Informational Writing Skills Wrap-Up

Students will read the lesson goals.

Use Informational Writing Skills

Students will complete Use Informational Writing Skills in *Summit English Language Arts 5 Activity Book* to review the writing objectives that will be assessed on the quiz.

LEARNING COACH CHECK-IN   This activity page contains open-ended questions, so it's important that you review students' responses. Give students feedback, using the sample answers provided to guide you.

TRY IT

Informational Writing Skills Wrap-Up

Use Informational Writing Skills

Use the prompt and the facts to answer the questions.
Example answers are shown.
Prompt: Write an informational paragraph about the International Space Station.

Facts:

- Travels at 5 miles per second
- Orbits (circles) the earth once every 90 minutes, or 16 times each day
- 16 countries helped build it
- Travels about 250 miles above the earth
- Built in space
- Russia launched first piece in 1998
- Astronauts live onboard
- First astronauts moved in on November 2, 2000
- Astronauts continued to add pieces to the space station
- Finally completed in 2011
- Scientists onboard perform experiments inside and outside of the space station

INFORMATIONAL WRITING SKILLS WRAP-UP **163**

---

1. A hook grabs readers' attention. Write a hook to begin your informational paragraph about the International Space Station.

You have probably seen a construction site at some point. Maybe you have seen workers building a new home or a restaurant. But did you know people build things in space, too?

2. The topic sentence states the main idea of the paragraph. Write a topic sentence that states the main idea of your informational paragraph.

Many countries worked together to build the International Space Station to have a place to live and learn in space.

3. Using the facts provided, write at least three sentences to support your main idea. You do not need to include every fact.

Construction of the International Space Station (ISS) began in 1998. People from 16 countries worked for two years to build the ISS. Finally, on November 2, 2000, the space station was ready for the first astronauts to move in. As astronauts lived on the space station, they continued to add pieces to it. Construction was finally completed in 2011. But astronauts were not finished working at the space station. Even today, scientists live and work on the ISS.

164 INFORMATIONAL WRITING SKILLS WRAP-UP

---

4. Transitions connect and relate ideas in an informational text.

a. List at least one transition you included in your answer to Question 3.

"Finally," "But," and "Even today" are all transitions used to connect ideas in the sentences. Other transitions that might have been used include "For example," "As a result," or "Next."

b. Explain how the transition improves reader understanding.

"Finally" improves reader understanding by showing the order of events. "But" helps readers understand that a different or contrasting idea will follow. "Even today" emphasizes the previous idea.

5. An informational paragraph uses precise language.

a. Rewrite one sentence in your paragraph to make the language more precise.

Even today, scientists **aboard the ISS perform experiments inside and outside of the space station.**

b. Rewrite at least one sentence in your paragraph to language that is domain-specific.

Astronauts from 16 countries worked for two years to build the ISS.

INFORMATIONAL WRITING SKILLS WRAP-UP **165**

---

6. Write a short conclusion to your paragraph. Your conclusion should help readers understand why your main idea is important.

What scientists learn at the ISS does not help only those astronauts or only their countries. That important information helps scientists all over the world. So even those who cannot travel to the ISS are able to benefit from the incredible research that takes place there.

7. Informational writing often contains graphics. These graphics help readers understand the subject or give them a clear mental picture of people or events. Describe one helpful graphic that you could include in your informational paragraph about the International Space Station.

a photograph of the International Space Station; a photograph of astronauts aboard the International Space Station

This picture will help clarify my ideas.

166 INFORMATIONAL WRITING SKILLS WRAP-UP

---

200 ENGLISH LANGUAGE ARTS 5

Review Conjunctions

Students will answer questions to review what they have learned about coordinating, subordinating, and correlative conjunctions.

QUIZ

Conjunctions and Informational Writing Skills

Students will complete the Conjunctions and Informational Writing Skills quiz.

Spelling List 9

Students will complete the Spelling List 9 quiz.

WRAP-UP

Keyboarding

Students will practice their keyboarding skills using an external website or program.

More Language Arts Practice

Students will practice skills according to their individual needs.

Big Ideas: Mini-Project

Lesson Overview

Big Ideas lessons provide students the opportunity to further apply the knowledge acquired and skills learned throughout the unit workshops. Each Big Ideas lesson consists of these parts:

1. **Cumulative Review:** Students keep their skills fresh by reviewing prior content.

2. **Preview:** Students practice answering the types of questions they will commonly find on standardized tests.

3. **Synthesis:** Students complete an assignment that allows them to connect and apply what they have learned. Synthesis assignments vary throughout the course.

   In the Synthesis portion of this Big Ideas lesson, students will complete a small creative project that ties together concepts and skills they have encountered across workshops. These small projects are designed to deepen students' understanding of those concepts and skills.

   LEARNING COACH CHECK-IN   Make sure students complete, review, and submit the assignment to their teacher.

All materials needed for this lesson are linked online and not provided in the Activity Book.

Finding Their Way

Figurative Language

Lesson Overview

ACTIVITY	ACTIVITY TITLE	TIME	ONLINE/OFFLINE
GET READY	Finding Their Way Unit Overview	**1** minute	
	Introduction to Figurative Language	**1** minute	
	Look Back at Similes, Metaphors, and Onomatopoeia	**4** minutes	
LEARN AND **TRY IT**	Similes, Metaphors, and Onomatopoeia	**10** minutes	
	Practice Using Similes, Metaphors, and Onomatopoeia	**10** minutes	
	Apply: Comparisons and Sound Words **LEARNING COACH CHECK-IN**	**15** minutes	
	Go Write!	**15** minutes	
	Review Figurative Language	**15** minutes	
QUIZ	Figurative Language	**15** minutes	
WRAP-UP	Keyboarding	**10** minutes	
	More Language Arts Practice	**9** minutes	
	Go Read!	**15** minutes	

Content Background

Students will learn about recognizing, decoding, and using figurative language. The word list for this workshop contains examples of onomatopoeia, similes, and metaphors.

Advance Preparation

During the Keyboarding activity, students will practice their keyboarding skills using an external website or program. **You will need to work with students to select an appropriate keyboarding practice website or program; K12 does not specify which resource to use.** A few suggestions are provided in the online activity.

Depending on which program you choose, students may need to set up an account to save their progress. If needed, assist students in setting up and running their chosen keyboarding practice program.

MATERIALS

Supplied
- *Summit English Language Arts 5 Activity Book*
  - Apply: Comparisons and Sound Words

Also Needed
- reading material for Go Read!

During the Go Read! activity, students will have the option of using the digital library. Allow extra time for students to make their reading selection, or have students make a selection before beginning the lesson.

Lesson Goals

- Interpret figurative language, including similes, metaphors, and examples of onomatopoeia.
- Use context clues to help determine meaning of unknown words.
- Read for pleasure.

GET READY

Finding Their Way Unit Overview

Students will read a summary of what they will learn in the Finding Their Way unit.

Introduction to Figurative Language

Students will get a glimpse of what they will learn about in the lesson. They will also read the lesson goals and keywords. Have students select each keyword and preview its definition.

Look Back at Similes, Metaphors, and Onomatopoeia

Students will practice the prerequisite skill of identifying several types of figurative language.

LEARN AND TRY IT

LEARN   Similes, Metaphors, and Onomatopoeia

Students will learn what figurative language is and why writers use it. Then they will focus on how to identify and interpret examples of similes, metaphors, and onomatopoeia.

TRY IT   Practice Using Similes, Metaphors, and Onomatopoeia

Students will answer questions to develop their ability to understand and use similes, metaphors, and onomatopoeia.

TRY IT   Apply: Comparisons and Sound Words

Students will complete Apply: Comparisons and Sound Words from *Summit English Language Arts 5 Activity Book*.

This activity page contains open-ended questions, so it's important that you review students' responses. Give students feedback, using the sample answers provided to guide you.

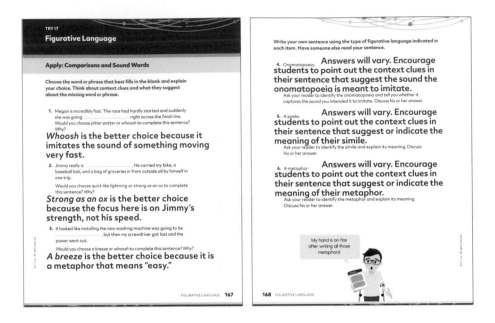

TRY IT Go Write!

Students will write independently for pleasure. As they write, they should consider opportunities to use figurative language, including similes, metaphors, and onomatopoeia.

TRY IT Review Figurative Language

Students will answer questions to review what they have learned about figurative language.

QUIZ

Figurative Language

Students will complete the Figurative Language quiz.

Keyboarding

Students will practice their keyboarding skills using an external website or program.

More Language Arts Practice

Students will practice skills according to their individual needs.

Go Read!

Students will read for pleasure. They should choose a book or a magazine that interests them, or they may choose a selection from the digital library, linked in the online lesson.

Students should read for the entire time. Have students select something to read ahead of time to help them stay focused.

You Should Meet Katherine Johnson (A)

Lesson Overview

ACTIVITY	ACTIVITY TITLE	TIME	ONLINE/OFFLINE
GET READY	Introduction to *You Should Meet Katherine Johnson* (A)	**1** minute	🖥️
	Spelling List 10 Pretest **LEARNING COACH CHECK-IN**	**10** minutes	🖥️ and 📄
	Computers in 60 Seconds	**1** minute	🖥️
	Look Back at Main Idea and Key Details	**4** minutes	🖥️
	Before You Read *You Should Meet Katherine Johnson*, Chapters 1–3	**14** minutes	🖥️
READ	*You Should Meet Katherine Johnson*, Chapters 1–3	**30** minutes	📄
	Check-In: *You Should Meet Katherine Johnson*, Chapters 1–3	**5** minutes	🖥️
LEARN AND **TRY IT**	Text Structure	**10** minutes	🖥️
	Examine Text Structure	**10** minutes	🖥️
	Apply: Explore the Structure of Another Work	**15** minutes	🖥️
	Create a Time Line, Chapters 1–3 **LEARNING COACH CHECK-IN**	**10** minutes	📄
	Practice Words from Chapters 1–3	**8** minutes	🖥️
WRAP-UP	Questions About Chapters 1–3	**2** minutes	🖥️

Content Background

Students will complete a spelling activity and begin to read *You Should Meet Katherine Johnson* by Thea Feldman. They will then complete activities in which they learn about the book's structure.

MATERIALS

Supplied
- *You Should Meet Katherine Johnson* by Thea Feldman
- *Summit English Language Arts 5 Activity Book*
  - Spelling List 10 Pretest
  - Create a Time Line, Chapters 1–3

Katherine Johnson, Chapters 1–3 Synopsis

Katherine Johnson is born in West Virginia in 1918. Her parents value education highly, and Katherine demonstrates advanced intelligence and an early interest in math. Because there is no high school for African American students in her hometown, the family relocates to a place where Katherine and her siblings can go to school. She graduates and attends West Virginia State College, where she majors in math and French. After college, though, a job as a research mathematician is hard to find. Katherine works as a French teacher and a piano instructor as she raises her own family. Finally, in 1953, she begins work for NACA (National Advisory Committee for Aeronautics) as a research mathematician. Though the agency is segregated, Katherine is able to work on several special projects, and she impresses the engineers with her skill. In the late 1950s, Katherine begins to work on the projects that aim to make space exploration possible.

Lesson Goals

- Take a spelling pretest.

- Begin to read *You Should Meet Katherine Johnson* by Thea Feldman.

- Examine the key details, main ideas, structure, and vocabulary in *You Should Meet Katherine Johnson*.

- Make inferences about and quote accurately from *You Should Meet Katherine Johnson*.

GET READY

Introduction to *You Should Meet Katherine Johnson* (A)

Students will get a glimpse of what they will learn about in the lesson. They will also read the lesson goals and keywords. Have students select each keyword and preview its definition.

Spelling List 10 Pretest

Students will take a spelling pretest.

LEARNING COACH CHECK-IN   Have students turn to Spelling List 10 Pretest in the activity book and open the online Spelling Pretest activity. Online, students will listen to the spelling word, type the word in the space indicated, and then check their answer. In the activity book, students will write the correct spelling of the word in the tables provided and indicate with a ✓ or an ✗ if they spelled the word correctly or incorrectly online. Students will repeat this process with the remaining words.

This is the complete list of words students will be tested on.

Adding *ion* to Base Words	Heart Words
congregate	all right
congregation	a lot
erode	a while
erosion	
inform	
information	
obsess	
obsession	
persuade	
persuasion	
prevent	
prevention	
propose	
proposition	

NOTE Have students keep their completed activity page in a safe place so they can refer to it later.

Computers in 60 Seconds

Students will watch a short video designed to spark their interest in upcoming topics.

Look Back at Main Idea and Key Details

Students will review what a main idea is and how key details support and help convey main ideas.

Before You Read *You Should Meet Katherine Johnson*, Chapters 1–3

Students will be introduced to some key vocabulary words that they will encounter in the upcoming reading, they will learn more about biographies, and they will answer a question to help them set a purpose for their reading.

READ

You Should Meet Katherine Johnson, Chapters 1–3

Students will read the introduction and the first three chapters of *You Should Meet Katherine Johnson* by Thea Feldman.

Check-In: *You Should Meet Katherine Johnson*, Chapters 1–3

Students will answer several questions to demonstrate their comprehension of the first three chapters of *You Should Meet Katherine Johnson*.

LEARN AND TRY IT

LEARN   Text Structure

Students will complete an online activity to learn about chronological order and how it affects reader understanding of a text.

TRY IT   Examine Text Structure

Students will complete an online activity in which they examine the structure of several passages from *You Should Meet Katherine Johnson* to explore the effect of that structure.

TRY IT   Apply: Explore the Structure of Another Work

Students will apply to a new work what they've learned about identifying the structure of a text and how that structure affects their understanding of people and events in the text.

TRY IT Create a Time Line, Chapters 1–3

Students will complete Create a Time Line, Chapters 1–3 from *Summit English Language Arts 5 Activity Book*.

LEARNING COACH CHECK-IN This activity page contains open-ended questions, so it's important that you review students' responses. Give students feedback, using the sample answers provided to guide you.

TRY IT

You Should Meet Katherine Johnson (A)

Create a Time Line, Chapters 1–3

Review what you have read in Chapters 1–3 of *You Should Meet Katherine Johnson*. Then choose three sentences from each chapter that contain key details. Write those sentences in chronological order, placing them within quotation marks, on the lines provided. Be sure to copy the sentences exactly. When you are finished, you should have a time line in quotations from the first three chapters of the book.

Chapter 1

Chapter 2   **See right.**

Chapter 3

YOU SHOULD MEET KATHERINE JOHNSON (A) **171**

Additional answers

- Answers will vary. Students' response should be three accurate quotations of lines that contain key details in the chapter, listed in chronological order. For instance, students might choose to quote one line about Katherine loving to count, a second line about her living in a place where there was no high school for African Americans, and a third line about her father moving the family so that Katherine and her siblings could attend high school.

- Answers will vary. Students' response should be three accurate quotations of lines that contain key details in the chapter, listed in chronological order. For instance, students might choose to quote one line about Katherine initially wanting to study French, a second line about her deciding to study mathematics, and then a third line about her difficulty in finding a good job after college.

- Answers will vary. Students' response should be three accurate quotations of lines that contain key details in the chapter, listed in chronological order. For instance, students might choose to quote one line about Katherine joining a group of twelve African American research mathematicians, a second line about her impressing the engineers on a special project, and then a third line about Katherine working for NACA when it turned its focus to space exploration.

TRY IT Practice Words from Chapters 1–3

Students will complete an online activity in which they answer questions to demonstrate their understanding of the vocabulary words from the reading.

WRAP UP

Questions About Chapters 1–3

Students will answer questions to show that they understand the structure of this text, as well as one of its main ideas and the details that support it.

You Should Meet Katherine Johnson (B)

Lesson Overview

ACTIVITY	ACTIVITY TITLE	TIME	ONLINE/OFFLINE
GET READY	Introduction to *You Should Meet Katherine Johnson* (B)	**1** minute	🖥️
	Spelling List 10 Activity Bank	**10** minutes	📄
	Recall *You Should Meet Katherine Johnson*, Chapters 1–3	**5** minute	🖥️
	Before You Read *You Should Meet Katherine Johnson*, Chapters 4–5	**10** minutes	🖥️
READ	*You Should Meet Katherine Johnson*, Chapters 4–5	**30** minutes	📄
	Check-In: *You Should Meet Katherine Johnson*, Chapters 4–5	**5** minutes	🖥️
LEARN AND **TRY IT**	Supporting Points with Reasons and Evidence	**10** minutes	🖥️
	Identify Points, Reasons, and Evidence	**10** minutes	🖥️
	Apply: Points, Reasons, and Evidence	**15** minutes	🖥️
	Create a Time Line, Chapters 4–5 **LEARNING COACH CHECK-IN**	**15** minutes	📄
	Practice Words from Chapters 4–5	**7** minutes	🖥️
WRAP-UP	Questions About Chapters 4–5	**2** minutes	🖥️

Content Background

Students will complete a spelling activity and continue to read *You Should Meet Katherine Johnson* by Thea Feldman. They will then complete activities in which they learn about identifying important points made by authors and recognizing the reasons and evidence authors use to support their points.

Advance Preparation

Gather students' completed Spelling List 10 Pretest activity page from *You Should Meet Katherine Johnson* (A). Students will refer to this page during Get Ready: Spelling List 10 Activity Bank.

MATERIALS

Supplied

- *You Should Meet Katherine Johnson* by Thea Feldman
- *Summit English Language Arts 5 Activity Book*
  - Spelling List 10 Activity Bank
  - Create a Time Line, Chapters 4–5

Also Needed

- completed Spelling List 10 Pretest activity page from *You Should Meet Katherine Johnson* (A)

Katherine Johnson, Chapters 4–5 Synopsis

As the space race heats up, Katherine works on several important missions at NASA, including the *Friendship 7* mission that puts John Glenn into orbit and the *Apollo 11* mission that lands astronauts on the moon. All the while, Katherine pushes to attend important meetings and be included in key discussions. She is greatly respected and works on every space mission until her retirement in 1986. After she stops working, Katherine receives several honors and takes time to speak to young people to encourage them to achieve their full potential.

KEYWORDS

summary – a short retelling that includes only the most important ideas or events of a text

supporting detail – a detail that gives more information about a main idea

Lesson Goals

- Practice all spelling words offline.

- Finish reading *You Should Meet Katherine Johnson* by Thea Feldman.

- Identify the most important points and quote accurately when summarizing *You Should Meet Katherine Johnson*.

- Understand the vocabulary in *You Should Meet Katherine Johnson*.

GET READY

Introduction to *You Should Meet Katherine Johnson* (B)

Students will get a glimpse of what they will learn about in the lesson. They will also read the lesson goals and keywords. Have students select each keyword and preview its definition.

Spelling List 10 Activity Bank

Students will practice all spelling words by completing Spelling List 10 Activity Bank from *Summit English Language Arts 5 Activity Book*. Make sure students have their completed Spelling List 10 Pretest activity page from *You Should Meet Katherine Johnson* (A) to refer to during this activity.

Remind students to pay special attention to words they spelled incorrectly on the Spelling Pretest.

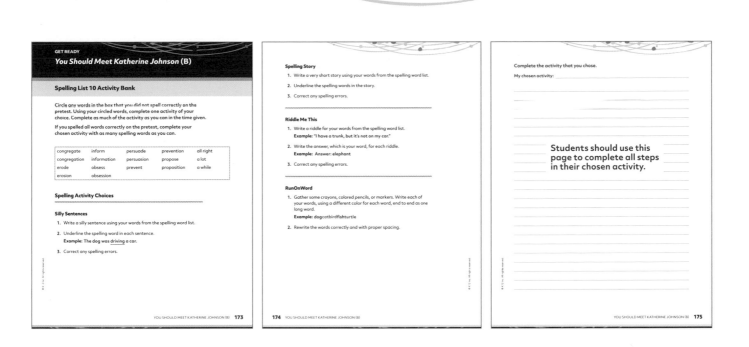

Recall *You Should Meet Katherine Johnson*, Chapters 1–3

Students will answer questions to review the reading that they have already completed.

Before You Read *You Should Meet Katherine Johnson,* Chapters 4–5

Students will be introduced to some key vocabulary words that they will encounter in the upcoming reading.

READ

You Should Meet Katherine Johnson, Chapters 4–5

Students will read Chapters 4–5 of *You Should Meet Katherine Johnson* by Thea Feldman.

Check-In: *You Should Meet Katherine Johnson,* Chapters 4–5

Students will answer several questions to demonstrate their comprehension of Chapters 4–5 of *You Should Meet Katherine Johnson*.

LEARN AND TRY IT

LEARN   Supporting Points with Reasons and Evidence

Students will complete an online activity to learn about identifying the points authors make and finding the reasons and evidence they provide to support their points.

TRY IT Identify Points, Reasons, and Evidence

Students will complete an online activity in which they practice identifying Thea Feldman's points and how she supports them in passages from *You Should Meet Katherine Johnson*.

TRY IT Apply: Points, Reasons, and Evidence

Students will apply to a new work what they've learned about identifying an author's points and the reasons and evidence he or she provides to support those points.

TRY IT Create a Time Line, Chapters 4–5

Students will complete Create a Time Line, Chapters 4–5 from *Summit English Language Arts 5 Activity Book*.

LEARNING COACH CHECK-IN This activity page contains open-ended questions, so it's important that you review students' responses. Give students feedback, using the sample answers provided to guide you.

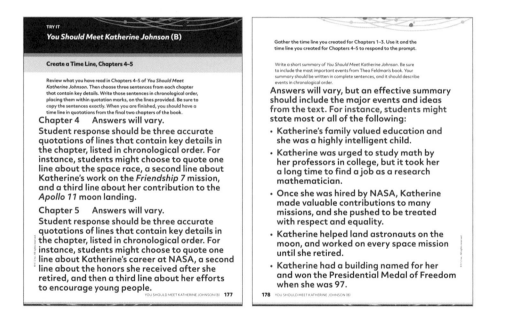

TRY IT

You Should Meet Katherine Johnson (B)

Create a Time Line, Chapters 4–5

Review what you have read in Chapters 4–5 of *You Should Meet Katherine Johnson*. Then choose three sentences from each chapter that contain key details. Write those sentences in chronological order, placing them within quotation marks, on the lines provided. Be sure to copy the sentences exactly. When you are finished, you should have a time line in quotations from the final two chapters of the book.

Chapter 4   Answers will vary.
Student response should be three accurate quotations of lines that contain key details in the chapter, listed in chronological order. For instance, students might choose to quote one line about the space race, a second line about Katherine's work on the *Friendship 7* mission, and a third line about her contribution to the *Apollo 11* moon landing.

Chapter 5   Answers will vary.
Student response should be three accurate quotations of lines that contain key details in the chapter, listed in chronological order. For instance, students might choose to quote one line about Katherine's career at NASA, a second line about the honors she received after she retired, and then a third line about her efforts to encourage young people.

YOU SHOULD MEET KATHERINE JOHNSON (B) **177**

Gather the time line you created for Chapters 1–3. Use it and the time line you created for Chapters 4–5 to respond to the prompt.

Write a short summary of *You Should Meet Katherine Johnson*. Be sure to include the most important events from Thea Feldman's book. Your summary should be written in complete sentences, and it should describe events in chronological order.

Answers will vary, but an effective summary should include the major events and ideas from the text. For instance, students might state most or all of the following:

- Katherine's family valued education and she was a highly intelligent child.
- Katherine was urged to study math by her professors in college, but it took her a long time to find a job as a research mathematician.
- Once she was hired by NASA, Katherine made valuable contributions to many missions, and she pushed to be treated with respect and equality.
- Katherine helped land astronauts on the moon, and worked on every space mission until she retired.
- Katherine had a building named for her and won the Presidential Medal of Freedom when she was 97.

178 YOU SHOULD MEET KATHERINE JOHNSON (B)

TRY IT Practice Words from Chapters 4–5

Students will complete an online activity in which they answer questions to demonstrate their understanding of the vocabulary words from the reading.

WRAP-UP

Questions About Chapters 4–5

Students will answer questions to show that they understand how to identify an author's points in a passage, how to spot the reasons and evidence provided to support those points, and how to briefly summarize a passage.

You Should Meet Katherine Johnson (C)

Lesson Overview

ACTIVITY	ACTIVITY TITLE	TIME	ONLINE/OFFLINE
GET READY	Introduction to *You Should Meet Katherine Johnson* (C)	**1** minute	🖥️
	Spelling List 10 Review Game	**10** minutes	📶
	Recall *You Should Meet Katherine Johnson*, Chapters 4–5	**5** minutes	📶
	Before You Read Katherine Johnson Articles	**10** minutes	🖥️
READ	Katherine Johnson Articles	**30** minutes	📄
	Check-In: Katherine Johnson Articles	**5** minutes	📶
LEARN AND **TRY IT**	Explore Multiple Texts on One Subject	**10** minutes	🖥️
	Compare and Contrast Texts About Katherine Johnson	**10** minutes	📶
	Apply: Examine Two New Texts on One Subject	**15** minutes	🖥️
	Write About Katherine Johnson **LEARNING COACH CHECK-IN**	**15** minutes	📄
	Practice Words from Articles About Katherine Johnson	**7** minutes	📶
WRAP-UP	Questions About Katherine Johnson Articles	**2** minutes	📶

Content Background

Students will complete a spelling activity and read two articles about Katherine Johnson in *Expeditions in Reading*. They will then complete activities in which they learn about comparing and contrasting multiple texts about a single subject and consulting multiple sources to answer questions.

MATERIALS

Supplied
- *You Should Meet Katherine Johnson* by Thea Feldman
- *Summit English Language Arts 5 Expeditions in Reading*
- *Summit English Language Arts 5 Activity Book*
  - Write About Katherine Johnson

Katherine Johnson Articles Synopsis

The articles in this lesson are both brief pieces about Katherine Johnson. "Katherine Johnson Biography" describes Johnson's early life and education, as well as her career at NACA/NASA and the major contributions she made while working on missions including *Friendship 7* and *Apollo 11*. "Mathematician Katherine Johnson at Work" is a shorter piece that focuses on Johnson's career at NACA/NASA and her legacy.

Lesson Goals

- Practice all spelling words online.

- Analyze articles about Katherine Johnson, identifying important points made by their authors.

- Compare and contrast multiple texts about Katherine Johnson.

GET READY

Introduction to *You Should Meet Katherine Johnson* (C)

Students will get a glimpse of what they will learn about in the lesson. They will also read the lesson goals.

Spelling List 10 Review Game

Students will practice all spelling words from the workshop.

Recall *You Should Meet Katherine Johnson,* Chapters 4–5

Students will answer questions to review the reading that they have already completed.

Before You Read Katherine Johnson Articles

Students will be introduced to some key vocabulary words that they will encounter in the upcoming reading. Then they will learn about how to recognize when online sources of information are credible and reliable and when they are not.

READ

Katherine Johnson Articles

Students will read two articles about Katherine Johnson in *Expeditions in Reading*: "Katherine Johnson Biography" and "Mathematician Katherine Johnson at Work."

Check-In: Katherine Johnson Articles

Students will answer several questions to demonstrate their comprehension of "Katherine Johnson Biography" and "Mathematician Katherine Johnson at Work."

LEARN AND TRY IT

LEARN   Explore Multiple Texts on One Subject

Students will complete an online activity to learn about comparing and contrasting multiple texts on the same subject and using multiple texts to answer questions.

TRY IT   Compare and Contrast Texts About Katherine Johnson

Students will complete an online activity in which they practice comparing and contrasting multiple texts on the same subject and using multiple texts to answer questions.

TRY IT   Apply: Examine Two New Texts on One Subject

Students will read other works on a single subject and practice comparing and contrasting them and using them to answer questions.

TRY IT   Write About Katherine Johnson

Students will complete Write About Katherine Johnson from *Summit English Language Arts 5 Activity Book*.

LEARNING COACH CHECK-IN   This activity page contains an open-ended question, so it's important that you review students' responses. Give students feedback, using the sample answers provided to guide you.

TRY IT
You Should Meet Katherine Johnson (C)

Write About Katherine Johnson

Write your response in complete sentences in the space provided.

Based on your reading in this workshop, what do you think Katherine Johnson's most important accomplishment was? Describe that accomplishment and explain its importance. In your description, include at least one direct quotation from one of the texts you read.

See right.

YOU SHOULD MEET KATHERINE JOHNSON (C)   **179**

Answers will vary.

- Students should start with the accomplishment they consider Katherine Johnson's most important. Perhaps that will be helping to integrate West Virginia University, or getting hired by NACA/NASA, or working on John Glenn's mission, or working on the *Apollo 11* mission, or inspiring and encouraging young people to pursue careers in science and technology.

- Students should then explain that accomplishment's importance. For instance, if students chose Katherine Johnson's work on the mission as her most important accomplishment, they might describe how her work helped protect the lives of the astronauts and establish the United States as the leader in the space race.

- Students should include at least one direct quotation from a text in the workshop. If students were writing about Katherine's work on the *Apollo 11* mission, they might quote Thea Feldman: "The little girl from White Sulphur Springs who loved to count had helped the U.S. make world history! The U.S. was now the clear leader in the Space Race."

TRY IT   Practice Words from Articles About Katherine Johnson

Students will complete an online activity in which they answer questions to demonstrate their understanding of the vocabulary words from the reading.

WRAP-UP

Questions About Katherine Johnson Articles

Students will answer questions to show that they understand how to compare and contrast multiple texts on one subject and how to use multiple texts to answer questions.

You Should Meet Katherine Johnson Wrap-Up

Lesson Overview

ACTIVITY	ACTIVITY TITLE	TIME	ONLINE/OFFLINE
GET READY	Introduction to *You Should Meet Katherine Johnson* Wrap-Up	**1** minute	🖥️
TRY IT	Write a Review **LEARNING COACH CHECK-IN**	**30** minutes	📄
	Read and Record	**10** minutes	🖥️
	Review Katherine Johnson	**20** minutes	🖥️
QUIZ	Katherine Johnson	**30** minutes	🖥️
	Spelling List 10	**10** minutes	🖥️
WRAP-UP	Keyboarding	**10** minutes	🖥️
	More Language Arts Practice	**9** minutes	🖥️

Advance Preparation

During the Keyboarding activity, students will practice their keyboarding skills using an external website or program. **You will need to work with students to select an appropriate keyboarding practice website or program; K12 does not specify which resource to use.** A few suggestions are provided in the online activity.

Depending on which program you choose, students may need to set up an account to save their progress. If needed, assist students in setting up and running their chosen keyboarding practice program.

MATERIALS

Supplied
- *You Should Meet Katherine Johnson* by Thea Feldman
- *Summit English Language Arts 5 Expeditions in Reading*
- *Summit English Language Arts 5 Activity Book*
  - Write a Review

Lesson Goals

- Review *You Should Meet Katherine Johnson*, "Katherine Johnson Biography," and "Mathematician Katherine Johnson at Work."

- Take a spelling quiz.

- Take a quiz on *You Should Meet Katherine Johnson*, "Katherine Johnson Biography," and "Mathematician Katherine Johnson at Work."

Introduction to *You Should Meet Katherine Johnson* Wrap-Up

Students will read the lesson goals.

Write a Review

Students will complete Write a Review from *Summit English Language Arts 5 Activity Book*.

LEARNING COACH CHECK-IN   This activity page contains an open-ended question, so it's important that you review students' responses. Give students feedback, using the sample answers provided to guide you.

TRY IT

You Should Meet Katherine Johnson Wrap-Up

Write a Review

Write your response in complete sentences in the space provided.

You have read three pieces about Katherine Johnson in this workshop. Choose one of those works and write a review of it now. In your review, be sure to do the following:

- State at least one main idea of the piece.
- Include at least two key details that support the main idea.
- Quote directly and accurately from the text to support one of your points.
- Explain how the piece you chose is different from the others you read in this workshop.

Answers will vary.

Students should review either *You Should Meet Katherine Johnson*, "Katherine Johnson Biography," or "Mathematician Katherine Johnson at Work."

- The response should identify at least one main idea of the piece. For example, if the student is reviewing *You Should Meet Katherine Johnson*, one main idea that students might mention is that Katherine was encouraged by her parents, who placed a high value on their children receiving an education.

YOU SHOULD MEET KATHERINE JOHNSON WRAP-UP **181**

- Students should then find and use at least two details that support the main idea they cited. For instance, if students cite the main idea that Katherine was encouraged by her parents, who placed a high value on their children receiving an education, their response might then describe how Katherine was taught to read even before she began school and how the family moved more than one hundred miles away so that Katherine and her siblings could attend high school.

- Students should include at least one direct quotation from a text in the workshop. For example, students might quote from the text, which states, "Institute had a high school for African Americans, and Katherine's mother and father made sure all their children graduated from it."

- Finally, students should explain what makes the piece they decided to review unique. Using the example above, students might state that *You Should Meet Katherine Johnson* is different from the two articles in that it goes into greater depth when discussing Katherine's childhood and her time at college, when she considered studying a subject other than math.

182   YOU SHOULD MEET KATHERINE JOHNSON WRAP-UP

Read and Record

Good readers read quickly, smoothly, and with expression. This is called *fluency*. Students will record themselves reading aloud. They will listen to their recording and think about how quick, smooth, and expressive they sound.

NOTE   Encourage students to rerecord as needed.

Review Katherine Johnson

Students will answer questions to review what they have learned about Katherine Johnson from the texts in this workshop.

QUIZ

Katherine Johnson

Students will complete the Katherine Johnson quiz.

Spelling List 10

Students will complete the Spelling List 10 quiz.

WRAP-UP

Keyboarding

Students will practice their keyboarding skills using an external website or program.

More Language Arts Practice

Students will practice skills according to their individual needs.

Informational Writing: Prewriting (A)

Lesson Overview

ACTIVITY	ACTIVITY TITLE	TIME	ONLINE/OFFLINE
GET READY	Introduction to Informational Writing: Prewriting (A)	**1** minute	🛜
	Spelling List 11 Pretest **LEARNING COACH CHECK-IN**	**10** minutes	🖥️ and 📄
	Look Back at Interjections	**10** minutes	🛜
LEARN AND **TRY IT**	Interjections	**15** minutes	🛜
	Interjections in the Wild	**15** minutes	🛜
	Explore a Student's Science Report	**15** minutes	🛜
	Brainstorming for a Science Report	**20** minutes	🛜
	Brainstorm for Your Science Report **LEARNING COACH CHECK-IN**	**30** minutes	📄
WRAP-UP	Questions About Brainstorming and Interjections	**4** minutes	🛜

Content Background

Students will begin working on an **informational essay**, specifically a science report about a subject of their choice. They will complete this assignment over the course of several lessons by following the writing process. Students will begin by prewriting.

Writing Process

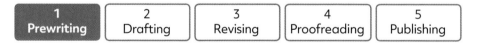

| 1 Prewriting | 2 Drafting | 3 Revising | 4 Proofreading | 5 Publishing |

During **prewriting**, writers choose a topic, conduct research, and create a plan for their writing assignment. In this lesson, students will complete the first part of prewriting: choosing a topic. To do that, they'll **brainstorm** by creating an idea web and evaluating several different topics.

Grammar, Usage, and Mechanics   Students will learn how to recognize and use interjections. An interjection is a word or phrase that expresses a strong feeling. It is set off with some form of punctuation.

> **Examples: Wow!** It is so sunny this afternoon!
>
> **Oh,** I guess I need sunscreen.

MATERIALS

Supplied
- *Summit English Language Arts 5 Activity Book*
  - Spelling List 11 Pretest
  - Brainstorm for Your Science Report
- Science Report Instructions (printout)

Also Needed
- folder for organizing informational writing assignment pages

Advance Preparation

Gather a folder that students can use to keep all notes and activity pages related to their science report.

Lesson Goals

- Take a spelling pretest.
- Learn how to use interjections.
- Explore a model informational essay.
- Analyze how an author brainstorms.
- Brainstorm topics for your science report.

GET READY

Introduction to Informational Writing: Prewriting (A)

Students will get a glimpse of what they will learn about in the lesson. They will also read the lesson goals and keywords. Have students select each keyword and preview its definition.

Spelling List 11 Pretest

Students will take a spelling pretest.

LEARNING COACH CHECK-IN   Have students turn to Spelling List 11 Pretest in *Summit English Language Arts 5 Activity Book* and open the online Spelling Pretest activity. Online, students will listen to the spelling word, type the word in the space indicated, and then check their answer. In the activity book, students will write the correct spelling of the word in the tables provided and indicate with a ✓ or an ✗ if they spelled the word correctly or incorrectly online. Students will repeat this process with the remaining words.

As needed, help students with the interaction between the online activity and the activity book page until they become comfortable with what they need to do. As students practice their spelling words throughout the workshop, they should pay special attention to words they spelled incorrectly on the pretest.

This is the complete list of words students will be tested on.

ch = /sh/	que = /k/	sc = /s/	Prefix out–
brochure	antique	adolescent	outgoing
chef	plaque	ascend	outreach
chivalry	technique	scenery	outspoken
chute	unique	scepter	
mustache	critique	scenic	
parachute			
chandelier			
crochet			

NOTE Have students keep their completed activity page in a safe place so they can refer to it later.

LEARN AND TRY IT

LEARN Interjections
Students will learn how to recognize and use interjections appropriately.

TRY IT Interjections in the Wild
Students will answer questions about recognizing and using interjections to express strong feelings. They will receive feedback on their answers.

LEARN Explore a Student's Science Report
To help them better understand their writing assignment, students will read a model science report and explore the elements that make it successful.

LEARN Brainstorming for a Science Report

Students will closely investigate brainstorming, which is the first part of the prewriting step of the writing process.

There are many ways to brainstorm. This activity introduces students to one effective brainstorming technique: creating an idea web.

TRY IT Brainstorm for Your Science Report

Students will complete Brainstorm for Your Science Report from *Summit English Language Arts 5 Activity Book*.

LEARNING COACH CHECK-IN   Review students' responses. Ensure that students have selected a topic for their science report that meets the criteria listed in Question 5 of the activity page. When students have completed the page, they should store it in a folder so that they can refer to it throughout the writing process.

NOTE   In addition to the brainstorming activity, this activity page contains the instructions for the science report. Students should read the instructions carefully, but in this lesson, they should complete the brainstorming activity only (not the entire assignment). If you or students wish, you can download and print another copy of the Science Report Instructions online.

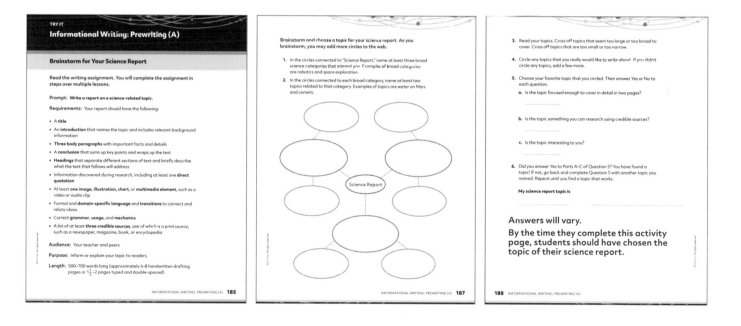

WRAP-UP

Questions About Brainstorming and Interjections

Students will answer questions to show that they understand how to brainstorm a topic for a science report and how to recognize and use interjections.

Informational Writing: Prewriting (B)

Lesson Overview

ACTIVITY	ACTIVITY TITLE	TIME	ONLINE/OFFLINE
GET READY	Introduction to Informational Writing: Prewriting (B)	**1** minute	📶
	Spelling List 11 Activity Bank	**10** minutes	📄
LEARN AND **TRY IT**	Prepositions	**10** minutes	📶
	Prepositions in the Wild	**10** minutes	📶
	Researching a Science Report	**10** minutes	📶
	Research Your Science Report **LEARNING COACH CHECK-IN**	**60** minutes	📄
WRAP-UP	Questions About Research and Prepositions	**4** minutes	📶
	Go Read!	**15** minutes	📶 or 📄

Content Background

Students will continue to work on their **science report**, an assignment that they will complete over the course of several lessons by following the writing process.

Writing Process

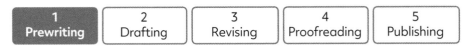

During **prewriting**, writers choose a topic, conduct research, and create a plan for their writing assignment. In this lesson, students will complete the second part of prewriting: conducting research.

First, students will create a **research question**, a question that will guide and focus their research and that their report will answer. Then they will find trustworthy print and digital sources with information about their topic. They will take notes on their topic, paraphrasing and summarizing information from at least three sources. They will also find at least one direct quotation to include in their report.

Grammar, Usage, and Mechanics   Students will learn how to recognize and use prepositions. A preposition begins a phrase that ends with a noun or pronoun. That noun or pronoun is called the object of the preposition. The preposition relates the object of the preposition to another word in a sentence.

In this example, the preposition *to* relates the object of the preposition, *kitchen*, to the word *walked*. It tells where the speaker walked.

> **Example:** I walked **to** the kitchen.

Advance Preparation

Gather students' completed Spelling List 11 Pretest activity page from Informational Writing: Prewriting (A). Students will refer to this page during Get Ready: Spelling List 11 Activity Bank.

Gather the folder that students are using to store the activity pages related to their science report. The folder should contain the following:

- Completed activity page Brainstorm for Your Science Report from Informational Writing: Prewriting (A)

Students will need to complete their own research during Research Your Science Report. Make sure students have access to trustworthy print and digital sources. You may choose to complete the activity at a library.

During the Go Read! activity, students will have the option of using the digital library. Allow extra time for students to make their reading selection, or have students make a selection before beginning the lesson.

Lesson Goals

- Practice spelling words offline.
- Learn how to use prepositions.
- Explore how to conduct research for an informational essay.
- Research the topic of your science report.
- Read for pleasure.

GET READY

Introduction to Informational Writing: Prewriting (B)

Students will get a glimpse of what they will learn about in the lesson. They will also read the lesson goals and keywords. Have students select each keyword and preview its definition.

Spelling List 11 Activity Bank

Students will practice all spelling words by completing Spelling List 11 Activity Bank from *Summit English Language Arts 5 Activity Book*. Make sure students have their completed Spelling List 11 Pretest activity page from Informational Writing: Prewriting (A) to refer to during this activity.

Remind students to pay special attention to words they spelled incorrectly on the Spelling Prestest.

GET READY

Informational Writing: Prewriting (B)

Spelling List 11 Activity Bank

Circle any words in the box that you did not spell correctly on the pretest. Using your circled words, complete one activity of your choice. Complete as much of the activity as you can in the time given.

If you spelled all words correctly on the pretest, complete your chosen activity with as many spelling words as you can.

brochure	parachute	unique	scenery	crochet
chef	antique	critique	scepter	outgoing
chivalry	plaque	adolescent	scenic	outreach
chute	technique	ascend	chandelier	outspoken
mustache				

Spelling Activity Choices

Hidden Words

1. Draw a picture and "hide" as many words from the Spelling Word List inside the picture as you can.

2. See if others can find the words within the picture.

Triangle Spelling

Write each word in a triangle.

Ghost Words

1. Use a white crayon to write each spelling word.

2. Go over the white crayon writing with a colored marker.

INFORMATIONAL WRITING: PREWRITING (B) **189**

Complete the activity that you chose.

My chosen activity:

Students should use this page to complete all steps in their chosen activity.

190 INFORMATIONAL WRITING: PREWRITING (B)

LEARN AND TRY IT

LEARN   Prepositions

Students will learn how to recognize and use prepositions appropriately.

TRY IT   Prepositions in the Wild

Students will answer questions about recognizing and using prepositions. They will receive feedback on their answers.

LEARN   Researching a Science Report

Students will learn about creating an effective research question and about conducting research, which is the second part of the prewriting step. They will focus on how to choose trustworthy sources and how to take notes by paraphrasing and summarizing information.

Tell students that major newspapers, such as the the *New York Times*, the *Washington Post*, and the *Chicago Tribune* are all trustworthy sources. Likewise, government websites, such as those run by the National Aeronautics and Space Administration (NASA), the Centers for Disease Control and Prevention (CDC), and other agencies contain reliable and useful information. Print reference books, such as *Encyclopedia Britannica* and the *World Book Encyclopedia*, are also credible sources of information.

TRY IT   Research Your Science Report

Students will complete Research Your Science Report from *Summit English Language Arts 5 Activity Book*.

LEARNING COACH CHECK-IN   Before students begin their research, ensure that they have written an effective research question that meets the criteria on the activity page. Assist students in identifying three appropriate and trustworthy sources, one of which should be a print source. When students have completed their research, they should store their Research Notes in the folder they are using to organize their writing assignment pages.

TIP   Supervise students as they complete online research.

NOTE   If you or students wish, you can download and print another copy of the Science Report Instructions online. Additional sheets for Research Notes are also available online.

TRY IT
Informational Writing: Prewriting (B)

Research Your Science Report

Follow these steps to write a research question.

1. A research question is the question that you will work to answer in your science report.

   Write three possible research questions for your science report.

   a. _____

   b. _____

   c. _____

2. Choose the research question that most interests you. Be sure that the question is one that you can answer in a 1–2 page report.

My research question: _____

Follow these steps to conduct research. Record information on the Research Notes pages that follow, using one page per source.

3. Gather or identify at least three sources. At least one source must be a print source, such as a book, an article originally published in a newspaper or magazine, or an encyclopedia article. The other sources may be digital sources found on the Internet. Record the title, author, publisher, and URL of each source.

4. As you read each source, take notes related to your topic and your research question. Paraphrase or summarize from the source. If you find a direct quotation that you think you might use in your report, record the quotation, word for word, in quotation marks. Also record the name of the person you are quoting. Remember, you must use at least one direct quotation in your report.

INFORMATIONAL WRITING: PREWRITING (B) **191**

Research Notes

Source

Title: _____

Author: _____

Published by: _____

URL (if necessary): _____

Notes

Paraphrase/Summary of Key Information:

_____

_____

_____

_____

_____

Direct quotation:

_____

_____

Person quoted: _____

192 INFORMATIONAL WRITING: PREWRITING (B)

Research Notes

Source

Title: _____

Author: _____

Published by: _____

URL (if necessary): _____

Notes

Paraphrase/Summary of Key Information:

_____
_____
_____
_____
_____
_____

Direct quotation:

_____
_____
_____

Person quoted: _____

Research Notes

Source

Title: _____

Author: _____

Published by: _____

URL (if necessary): _____

Notes

Paraphrase/Summary of Key Information:

_____
_____
_____
_____
_____
_____

Direct quotation:

_____
_____
_____

Person quoted: _____

WRAP-UP

Questions About Research and Prepositions

Students will answer questions to show that they understand how to create a research question and conduct research and how to recognize and use prepositions.

Go Read!

Students will read for pleasure. They should choose a book or a magazine that interests them, or they may choose a selection from the digital library, linked in the online lesson.

Students should read for the entire time. Have students select something to read ahead of time to help them stay focused.

Informational Writing: Prewriting (C)

Lesson Overview

ACTIVITY	ACTIVITY TITLE	TIME	ONLINE/OFFLINE
GET READY	Introduction to Informational Writing: Prewriting (C)	**1** minute	🖥️
	Spelling List 11 Practice	**10** minutes	🖥️
LEARN AND **TRY IT**	Titles of Works	**10** minutes	🖥️
	Format Titles of Works	**10** minutes	🖥️
	Outlining for a Science Report	**15** minutes	🖥️
	Outline for Your Science Report **LEARNING COACH CHECK-IN**	**50** minutes	📄
WRAP-UP	Questions About Outlining and Titles of Works	**4** minutes	🖥️
	Go Read!	**20** minutes	🖥️ or 📄

Content Background

Students will continue to work on their **science report**, an assignment that they will complete over the course of several lessons by following the writing process.

Writing Process

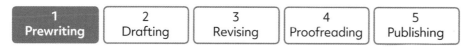

| 1 Prewriting | 2 Drafting | 3 Revising | 4 Proofreading | 5 Publishing |

During **prewriting**, writers choose a topic, conduct research, and create a plan for their writing assignment. In this lesson, students will complete the third part of prewriting: creating a plan in the form of an outline.

Students will use their research notes to help them create a plan for their science report by filling in the framework for an outline provided to them in their activity book. The outline will allow them to organize information in the same order that they will present it in their report. The outline will also help students group together related information.

Grammar, Usage, and Mechanics   Students will learn how to correctly format the titles of works. The titles of longer works, such as novels, books, newspapers, and magazines, should be italicized when typed and underlined when handwritten. The titles of shorter works, such as short stories, poems, and articles, should be placed within quotation marks.

Example (longer work, typed):
Sarah, Plain and Tall is a novel by Patricia McLachlan.

Example (longer work, handwritten):
Sarah, Plain and Tall is a novel by Patricia McLachlan.

Example (shorter work):
"Invitation" is a poem by Shel Silverstein.

Advance Preparation

Gather the folder that students are using to keep all notes and activity pages related to their science report. The folder should contain the following:

- Students' completed Brainstorm for Your Science Report activity page from Informational Writing: Prewriting (A)

- Students' completed research notes from Informational Writing: Prewriting (B)

During the Go Read! activity, students will have the option of using the digital library. Allow extra time for students to make their reading selection, or have students make a selection before beginning the lesson.

Lesson Goals

- Practice spelling words online.

- Learn how to format titles of works.

- Explore how to create an outline for an informational essay.

- Create an outline for your science report.

- Read for pleasure.

GET READY

Introduction to Informational Writing: Prewriting (C)
Students will get a glimpse of what they will learn about in the lesson. They will also read the lesson goals and keywords. Have students select each keyword and preview its definition.

Spelling List 11 Practice
Students will practice all spelling words from the workshop.

LEARN   Titles of Works

Students will learn how to correctly format the titles of both long and short works when typing them or writing them by hand.

TRY IT   Format Titles of Works

Students will answer questions about formatting titles of works correctly. They will receive feedback on their answers.

LEARN   Outlining for a Science Report

Students will learn about creating a useful outline, which is the third part of the prewriting step in the writing process. They will focus on how to use their notes to create the outline, how to order the outline to mirror the order of their draft, and how to group related information together.

TRY IT   Outline for Your Science Report

Students will complete Outline for Your Science Report from *Summit English Language Arts 5 Activity Book*.

LEARNING COACH CHECK-IN   Review students' responses. Ensure that students have incorporated their research into their outlines, followed the appropriate order for a five-paragraph essay, and grouped related information. When students have completed their outline, they should store it in the folder they are using to organize their writing assignment pages.

TIP   Remind students that it is not necessary to write in complete sentences when constructing an outline.

NOTE   If you or students wish, you can download and print another copy of the Science Report Instructions online.

TRY IT
Informational Writing: Prewriting (C)

Outline for Your Science Report

Use your research notes to complete an outline for your science report. You do not need to use complete sentences in your outline.

Note: Your report must include at least one direct quotation and one piece of media, such as a picture, chart, or video clip. You only need to fill in one blank labeled "Direct Quotation" and one blank labeled "Possible Use of Multimedia" in your outline.

Report Title:
Introduction:
Hook:
Background:
Thesis Statement:

Body Paragraph 1
Subtopic:
Related Information/Details:
Direct Quotation (if appropriate):
Image or Media (if appropriate)

Body Paragraph 2
Subtopic:
Related Information/Details:
Direct Quotation (if appropriate):
Image or Media (if appropriate)

Body Paragraph 3
Subtopic:
Related Information/Details:
Direct Quotation (if appropriate):
Image or Media (if appropriate)

Conclusion
Closing thoughts:
Short summary of key points:
Closing thoughts:

INFORMATIONAL WRITING: PREWRITING (C) **195**

196 INFORMATIONAL WRITING: PREWRITING (C)

INFORMATIONAL WRITING: PREWRITING (C) **197**

Questions About Outlining and Titles of Works

Students will answer questions to show that they understand how to create an outline and how to correctly format titles of works.

Go Read!

Students will read for pleasure. They should choose a book or a magazine that interests them, or they may choose a selection from the digital library, linked in the online lesson.

Students should read for the entire time. Have students select something to read ahead of time to help them stay focused.

Informational Writing: Drafting (A)

Lesson Overview

ACTIVITY	ACTIVITY TITLE	TIME	ONLINE/OFFLINE
GET READY	Introduction to Informational Writing: Drafting (A)	**1** minute	🖥️
	Spelling List 11 Review Game	**10** minutes	🖥️
	Staring Contest	**10** minutes	🖥️
LEARN AND **TRY IT**	Drafting a Science Report	**15** minutes	🖥️
	Draft Your Science Report **LEARNING COACH CHECK-IN**	**60** minutes	📄
WRAP-UP	Question About Drafting a Science Report	**4** minutes	🖥️
	Go Read!	**20** minutes	🖥️ or 📄

Content Background

Students will continue working on their **science report**. They will complete this assignment over the course of several lessons by following the writing process. In this lesson, students will begin drafting their report.

Writing Process

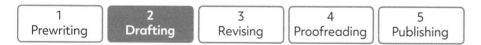

| 1 Prewriting | **2 Drafting** | 3 Revising | 4 Proofreading | 5 Publishing |

During **drafting**, students will use their notes and their completed outlines as guides as they write a rough draft of their science report. Students are expected to write about half of their rough draft in this lesson (although they may write more if they wish). They will have time to finish and turn in their draft in Informational Writing: Drafting (B).

Advance Preparation

Gather the folder that students are using to store the activity pages related to their science report. The folder should contain the following:

- Students' completed Brainstorm for Your Science Report activity page from Informational Writing: Prewriting (A)

- Students' completed research notes from Informational Writing: Prewriting (B)

> ### MATERIALS
>
> **Supplied**
> - *Summit English Language Arts 5 Activity Book*
>   - Draft Your Science Report
> - Science Report Instructions (printout)
> - Draft Paper (printout)
>
> **Also Needed**
> - folder in which students are storing science report writing assignment pages
> - reading material for Go Read!

- Students' completed Outline for Your Science Report activity page from Informational Writing: Prewriting (C)

During the Go Read! activity, students will have the option of using the digital library. Allow extra time for students to make their reading selection, or have students make a selection before beginning the lesson.

Lesson Goals

- Practice all spelling words online.
- Practice grammar skills by editing a passage.
- Analyze how an author writes a rough draft.
- Start the rough draft your science report.
- Read for pleasure.

GET READY

Introduction to Informational Writing: Drafting (A)
Students will get a glimpse of what they will learn about in the lesson. They will also read the lesson goals.

Spelling List 11 Review Game
Students will practice all spelling words from the workshop.

Staring Contest
Students will edit a short passage to practice applying grammar skills. This passage contains errors and opportunities to improve the writing related to interjections, prepositions, and the formats of titles.

LEARN AND TRY IT

LEARN   Drafting a Science Report
Students will investigate how a student uses an outline and research notes to draft a science report.

TRY IT   Draft Your Science Report
Students will complete half of their first draft using Draft Your Science Report in *Summit English Language Arts 5 Activity Book*. If students wish, they may complete more than half of their draft.

Make sure students have their completed Brainstorm for Your Science Report activity page from Informational Writing: Prewriting (A), their Research Your Science Report activity page (keeping in mind that students are only required to complete half of their draft at this time) from Informational Writing: Prewriting (B), and their Outline for Your Science Report activity page from Informational Writing: Prewriting (C) to refer to during this activity.

LEARNING COACH CHECK-IN Read students' draft to ensure it is in line with the assignment criteria outlined on the Brainstorm for Your Science Report activity page. If necessary, remind students not to focus on perfection at this stage of the writing process. Students should store their draft in the folder they are using to organize their writing assignment pages.

NOTE If you or students wish, you can download and print another copy of the Science Report Instructions online. Additional sheets of Drafting Paper are also available online.

TRY IT
Informational Writing: Drafting (A)

Draft Your Science Report

Using your notes and your outline to guide you, write the first draft of your science report. Write only on the white rows. You will use the purple rows for revisions later.

Title

start here ▶

Students should write their draft in the white rows only.

keep writing ▶

Draft Page 1

keep writing ▶

Draft Page 2

keep writing ▶

Draft Page 3

WRAP-UP

Question About Drafting a Science Report
Students will answer a question to show that they understand how to draft a science report.

Go Read!
Students will read for pleasure. They should choose a book or a magazine that interests them, or they may choose a selection from the digital library, linked in the online lesson.

Students should read for the entire time. Have students select something to read ahead of time to help them stay focused.

Informational Writing: Drafting (B)

Lesson Overview

ACTIVITY	ACTIVITY TITLE	TIME	ONLINE/OFFLINE
GET READY	Introduction to Informational Writing: Drafting (B)	**1** minute	🖥
TRY IT	Review Interjections, Prepositions, and Titles of Works	**10** minutes	🖥
QUIZ	Interjections, Prepositions, and Titles of Works	**20** minutes	🖥
	Spelling List 11	**10** minutes	🖥
TRY IT	Finish Drafting Your Science Report **LEARNING COACH CHECK-IN**	**58** minutes	📄
WRAP-UP	Turn In Your Science Report Draft	**1** minute	🖥
	Keyboarding	**10** minutes	🖥
	More Language Arts Practice	**10** minutes	🖥

Content Background

Students will continue working on their **science report** about a topic of their choice. In this lesson, students will finish and submit their rough draft. They will revise, proofread, and publish their report in a future workshop.

Writing Process

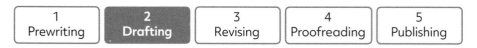

| 1
Prewriting | 2
Drafting | 3
Revising | 4
Proofreading | 5
Publishing |

Advance Preparation

Gather the folder that students are using to store the activity pages related to their science report. The folder should contain the following:

- Students' completed Brainstorm for Your Science Report activity page from Informational Writing: Prewriting (A)

- Students' completed research notes from Informational Writing: Prewriting (B)

- Students' completed Outline for Your Science Report activity page from Informational Writing: Prewriting (C)

- Students' in-progress Draft Your Science Report activity page from Informational Writing: Drafting (A)

MATERIALS

Supplied
- *Summit English Language Arts 5 Activity Book*
  - Drafting Your Science Report
- Science Report Instructions (printout)
- Draft Paper (printout)

Also Needed
- folder in which students are storing science report writing sassignment pages

During the Keyboarding activity, students will practice their keyboarding skills using an external website or program. **You will need to work with students to select an appropriate keyboarding practice website or program; K12 does not specify which resource to use.** A few suggestions are provided in the online activity.

Depending on which program you choose, students may need to set up an account to save their progress. If needed, assist students in setting up and running their chosen keyboarding practice program.

Lesson Goals

- Review how to use interjections and prepositions and how to correctly format titles of works.
- Take a grammer quiz.
- Take a spelling quiz.
- Finish and turn in the rough draft of your science report.

GET READY

Introduction to Informational Writing: Drafting (B)

Students will read the lesson goals.

TRY IT

Review Interjections, Prepositions, and Titles of Works

Students will answer questions to review what they have learned about interjections and prepositions and how to format the titles of works.

QUIZ

Interjections, Prepositions, and Titles of Works

Students will complete the Interjections, Prepositions, and Titles of Works quiz.

Spelling List 11

Students will complete the Spelling List 11 quiz.

Finish Drafting Your Science Report

Students will complete the rough draft of their science report. Students should gather the Draft Your Science Report activity page that they started in Informational Writing: Drafting (A) and complete it.

Make sure students also have their completed Brainstorm for Your Science Report activity page from Informational Writing: Prewriting (A), their Research Your Science Report activity page from Informational Writing: Prewriting (B), and their Outline for Your Science Report activity page from Informational Writing: Prewriting (C) to refer to during this activity.

LEARNING COACH CHECK-IN Read students' draft to ensure it is in line with the assignment criteria outlined on the Brainstorm for Your Science Report activity page. If necessary, remind students not to focus on perfection at this stage of the writing process. Students should store a copy of their draft in the folder they are using to organize their writing assignment pages.

NOTE If you or students wish, you can download and print another copy of the Science Report Instructions online. Additional sheets of Drafting Paper are also available online.

TRY IT
Informational Writing: Drafting (A)

Draft Your Science Report

Using your notes and your outline to guide you, write the first draft of your science report. Write only on the white rows. You will use the purple rows for revisions later.

Title

start here ▶

Students should write their draft in the white rows only.

keep writing ▶

Draft Page 1

INFORMATIONAL WRITING: DRAFTING (A) **199**

200 INFORMATIONAL WRITING: DRAFTING (A)

Draft Page 2

keep writing ▶

WRAP-UP

Turn In Your Science Report Draft

Students will submit their writing assignment to their teacher.

Keyboarding

Students will practice their keyboarding skills using an external website or program.

More Language Arts Practice

Students will practice skills according to their individual needs.

Hidden Figures (A)

Lesson Overview

ACTIVITY	ACTIVITY TITLE	TIME	ONLINE/OFFLINE
GET READY	Introduction to *Hidden Figures* (A)	**1** minute	🖥️
	Spelling List 12 Pretest **LEARNING COACH CHECK-IN**	**10** minutes	🖥️ and 📄
	Look Back at Using Evidence to Support an Analysis	**4** minutes	🖥️
	Before You Read *Hidden Figures*, Chapters 1, 2, and 6	**15** minutes	🖥️
READ	*Hidden Figures*, Prologue and Chapters 1, 2, and 6	**30** minutes	📄
	Check-In: *Hidden Figures*, Chapters 1, 2, and 6	**5** minutes	🖥️
LEARN AND **TRY IT**	Analyze *Hidden Figures*, Chapter 1	**10** minutes	🖥️
	Analyze *Hidden Figures*, Chapters 2 and 6	**10** minutes	🖥️
	Apply: Analyze Another Work	**15** minutes	🖥️
	Write About Miriam Mann **LEARNING COACH CHECK-IN**	**10** minutes	📄
	Practice Words from *Hidden Figures*, Chapters 1, 2, and 6	**8** minutes	🖥️
WRAP-UP	Questions About *Hidden Figures*, Chapters 1, 2, and 6	**2** minutes	🖥️

Content Background

Students will complete a spelling activity and begin to read *Hidden Figures* by Margot Lee Shetterly. They will then complete activities in which they learn about analyzing the text using details and evidence.

MATERIALS

Supplied
- *Hidden Figures* by Margot Lee Shetterly
- *Summit English Language Arts 5 Activity Book*
  - Spelling List 12 Pretest
  - Write About Miriam Mann

Hidden Figures, Chapters 1, 2, and 6 Synopsis

In the 1940s and 1950s, several African American women were hired to work as mathematicians for NACA (later NASA) to help the United States improve its understanding of flight and, eventually, space travel. These women made enormous contributions despite living and working in the South during a time when Jim Crow still existed and racial discrimination was commonplace. One reason many were hired was that when World War II broke out, jobs that had previously been held only by men became available. Agencies like NACA needed as many qualified people as they could find to help the war effort. So NACA hired a large number of female mathematicians—calling them "computers"—to do complex calculations in support of the agency's goals of improving America's planes. Some of these female mathematicians, including Dorothy Vaughan and Miriam Mann, were African American. They worked in the West Area Computing Unit, a segregated portion the NACA facility at Langley Laboratory. These women spent their days doing whatever complex calculations were assigned to them. Because they were black, they faced unique obstacles. But they fought against unfair treatment and supported one another, forging strong bonds and lifelong friendships.

Lesson Goals

- Take a spelling pretest.
- Begin to read *Hidden Figures* by Margot Lee Shetterly.
- Determine the key details and main ideas of the reading.
- Analyze *Hidden Figures* using evidence and direct quotations from it as support.
- Determine the meanings of unfamiliar words in *Hidden Figures*.

GET READY

Introduction to *Hidden Figures* (A)

Students will get a glimpse of what they will learn about in the lesson. They will also read the lesson goals.

Spelling List 12 Pretest

Students will take a spelling pretest.

LEARNING COACH CHECK-IN   Have students turn to Spelling List 12 Pretest in the activity book and open the online Spelling Pretest activity. Online, students will listen to the spelling word, type the word in the space indicated, and then check their answer. In the activity book, students will write the correct spelling of the word in the tables provided and indicate with indicate with a ✓ or an ✗ if they spelled the word correctly or incorrectly online. Students will repeat this process with the remaining words.

As needed, help students with the interaction between the online activity and the activity book page until they become comfortable with what they need to do. As students practice their spelling words throughout the workshop, they should pay special attention to words they spelled incorrectly on the pretest.

This is the complete list of words students will be tested on.

Root *brev*	Related Words
abbreviate	define
abbreviation	definite
brevity	definition
	oppose
	opposite
	personal
	personality
	practical
	practice
	related
	relative
	soft
	soften
	know
	knowledge
	overreach
	override
	overturn

NOTE   Have students keep their completed activity page in a safe place so they can refer to it later.

GET READY

Look Back at Using Evidence to Support an Analysis

Students will review how to use evidence from a text to support an analysis of that text.

Before You Read *Hidden Figures,* Chapters 1, 2, and 6

Students will be introduced to some key vocabulary words that they will encounter in the upcoming reading, they will learn some historical background, and they will answer a question to help them set a purpose for their reading.

READ

Hidden Figures, Prologue and Chapters 1, 2, and 6

Students will read the Prologue and Chapters 1, 2, and 6 of *Hidden Figures* by Margot Lee Shetterly.

Check-In: *Hidden Figures,* Prologue and Chapters 1, 2, and 6

Students will answer several questions to demonstrate their comprehension of the Prologue and Chapters 1, 2, and 6 of *Hidden Figures*.

LEARN AND TRY IT

LEARN   Analyze *Hidden Figures,* Chapter 1

Students will complete an online activity to learn about analyzing a text and using textual evidence as support.

TRY IT   Analyze *Hidden Figures*, Chapters 2 and 6

Students will answer several questions in which they use textual evidence to help them analyze Chapters 2 and 6 of *Hidden Figures*.

TRY IT   Apply: Analyze Another Work

Students will apply to a new work what they've learned about using textual evidence to develop and support an analysis.

TRY IT   Write About Miriam Mann

Students will complete Write About Miriam Mann from *Summit English Language Arts 5 Activity Book*.

LEARNING COACH CHECK-IN   This activity page contains an open-ended question, so it's important that you review students' responses. Give students feedback, using the sample answers provided to guide you.

TRY IT
Hidden Figures (A)

Write About Miriam Mann

Write your response in complete sentences.
Answers will vary. Students' answer should state that Chapter 6 describes how Miriam Mann repeatedly removed the "Colored Computers" sign that appeared in the cafeteria at Langley. Students should recognize that Shetterly depicts Mann's behavior positively. Her actions are shown to be admirable. Several details from the text affect reader understanding of Mann's behavior. For example, Shetterly describes Mann as a small person with a big personality. She makes it clear that standing up for herself and her fellow African American mathematicians was a risk for Mann, so readers realize that what she did took courage. Shetterly also describes how Mann removed the sign several times, which suggests her perseverance —another positive quality. Shetterly's language helps readers understand that the sign was hurtful, describing the sign as a "racial insult," "a subtle jab," and "particularly offensive." She also writes that the sign was a reminder that "some were more equal than others."

HIDDEN FIGURES (A)   **205**

TRY IT   Practice Words from *Hidden Figures*, Chapters 1, 2, and 6

Students will complete an online activity in which they answer questions to demonstrate their understanding of the vocabulary words from the reading.

WRAP UP

Questions About *Hidden Figures*, Chapters 1, 2, and 6

Students will answer questions to show that they understand how to use textual evidence to develop and support an analysis.

Hidden Figures (B)

Lesson Overview

ACTIVITY	ACTIVITY TITLE	TIME	ONLINE/OFFLINE
GET READY	Introduction to *Hidden Figures* (B)	**1** minute	online
	Spelling List 12 Activity Bank	**10** minutes	offline
	Recall *Hidden Figures*, Chapters 1, 2, and 6	**5** minutes	online
	Before You Read *Hidden Figures*, Chapters 10–12	**10** minutes	online
READ	*Hidden Figures*, Chapters 10–12	**30** minutes	offline
	Check-In: *Hidden Figures*, Chapters 10–12	**5** minutes	online
LEARN AND **TRY IT**	Analyze *Hidden Figures*, Chapter 10	**10** minutes	online
	Analyze *Hidden Figures*, Chapter 11	**10** minutes	online
	Apply: Keep Analyzing	**15** minutes	online
	Write About *Hidden Figures*, Chapters 10–12 **LEARNING COACH CHECK-IN**	**15** minutes	offline
	Practice Words from *Hidden Figures*, Chapters 10–12	**7** minutes	online
WRAP-UP	Questions About *Hidden Figures*, Chapters 10–12	**2** minutes	online

Content Background

Students will complete a spelling activity and continue to read *Hidden Figures* by Margot Lee Shetterly. They will then complete activities in which they learn more about analyzing the text using details and evidence before applying their analysis skills to today's reading.

Advance Preparation

Gather students' completed Spelling List 12 Pretest activity page from *Hidden Figures* (A). Students will refer to this page during Get Ready: Spelling List 12 Activity Bank.

MATERIALS

Supplied
- *Hidden Figures* by Margot Lee Shetterly
- *Summit English Language Arts 5 Activity Book*
  - Spelling List 12 Activity Bank
  - Write About *Hidden Figures,* Chapters 10–12

Also Needed
- completed Spelling List 12 Pretest activity page from *Hidden Figures* (A)

Hidden Figures, Chapters 10–12 Synopsis

Mary Jackson is a gifted mathematician who believes that all African Americans—and especially African American women and girls—must ignore or defy whatever limits are placed on them. She begins working at Langley Laboratory early in the 1950s, and she quickly demonstrates her skill, determination, and integrity. When she is treated poorly by some of her white coworkers, she gets upset and speaks openly to a white engineer about it. He responds with respect and consideration, and he offers her a job on his team, which tests airplanes flying faster than the speed of sound. Around the same time, Katherine Goble comes to work at Langley. Katherine is also a supremely talented mathematician who had been working as a public school teacher in a segregated school for several years. She believes deeply in trying to help African Americans advance, and she has a history of breaking racial barriers. She was one of just three African American graduate students who integrated West Virginia University. Katherine arrives at Langley and, by always being professional, wins the respect of her coworkers, both black and white.

Lesson Goals

- Practice all spelling words offline.
- Continue to read *Hidden Figures* by Margot Lee Shetterly.
- Determine the key details and main ideas of the reading.
- Analyze the text using evidence and direct quotations from it as support.
- Understand the vocabulary in *Hidden Figures*.

GET READY

Introduction to *Hidden Figures* (B)

Students will get a glimpse of what they will learn about in the lesson. They will also read the lesson goals.

Spelling List 12 Activity Bank

Students will practice all spelling words by completing Spelling List 12 Activity Bak *Summit English Language Arts 5 Activity Book* . Make sure students have their completed Spelling List 12 Pretest activity page from *Hidden Figures* (A) to refer to during this activity.

Remind students to pay special attention to words they spelled incorrectly on the Spelling Pretest.

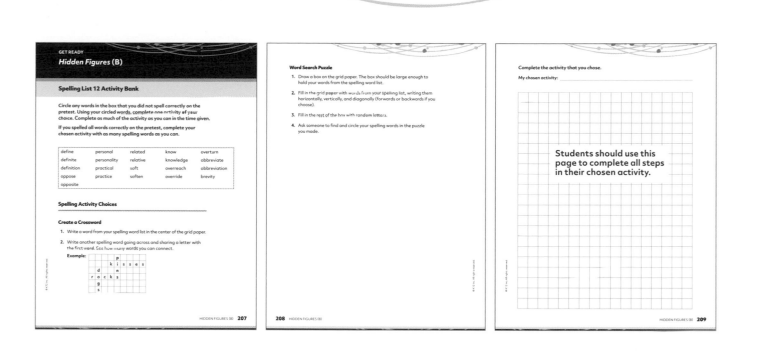

Recall *Hidden Figures,* Chapters 1, 2, and 6

Students will answer questions to review the reading that they have already completed.

Before You Read *Hidden Figures* Chapters 10–12

Students will be introduced to some key vocabulary words that they will encounter in the upcoming reading. They will also learn some important background information to prepare them for the upcoming chapters.

Hidden Figures, Chapters 10–12

Students will read Chapters 10–12 of *Hidden Figures* by Margot Lee Shetterly.

Check-In: *Hidden Figures,* Chapters 10–12

Students will answer several questions to demonstrate their comprehension of Chapters 10–12 of *Hidden Figures.*

LEARN   Analyze *Hidden Figures,* Chapter 10

Students will complete an online activity to continue to learn about analyzing a text and using textual evidence as support.

TRY IT   Analyze *Hidden Figures*, Chapter 11

Students will complete an online activity in which they practice using textual evidence to develop and support an analysis of what they've read.

TRY IT   Apply: Keep Analyzing

Students will apply to a new work what they've learned about using textual evidence to develop and support an analysis.

TRY IT   Write About *Hidden Figures*, Chapters 10–12

Students will complete Write About *Hidden Figures*, Chapters 10–12 from *Summit English Language Arts 5 Activity Book*.

LEARNING COACH CHECK-IN   This activity page contains an open-ended question, so it's important that you review students' responses. Give students feedback, using the sample answers provided to guide you.

TRY IT
Hidden Figures (B)

Write About *Hidden Figures*, Chapters 10–12

Write your response in complete sentences.
Answers will vary.

- Students' answer should state that Mary Jackson and Katherine Goble were alike in a number of ways. Both were highly intelligent and gifted mathematicians. Both believed in giving back to their community. Mary served as a Girl Scout troop leader, teaching the girls to make sure they "didn't put limits on themselves." Katherine taught in a segregated school because she "felt a sense of responsibility to 'advance the race' by giving her students the best possible education."
- Students should then describe which incidents show why both Mary Jackson and Katherine Goble were successful at NACA. They may cite the time Jackson stood by her work even when one of the division chiefs thought it was incorrect. She was vindicated, and her independence of mind and her confidence proved to be a great benefit to her. Students may cite Goble's experience on the Flight

HIDDEN FIGURES (B) **211**

Research Division team as one that illustrates why Goble was successful at NACA. Though a white male colleague initially seemed to be offended by her presence, she continued to do her job well, to be courteous, and to demonstrate her own decency. Her colleague soon changed his demeanor and became friends with Goble. By not stooping to the level of others or allowing them to change her, Goble earned others' respect.

- Finally, students should explain how reading about Jackson and Goble affected his or her understanding of the book. Answers will vary, but students should recognize that the chapters devoted to Jackson and Goble help convey the idea that these women were not merely smart and able mathematicians. They were also remarkable in other ways. They were people who wanted to help others, and they sought to bring about positive change, whether by leading young Girl Scouts or helping integrate a state university. They also were open-minded even when they were treated poorly by those who were not. And because they had confidence in themselves and were supportive of one another, they were able to accomplish amazing things.

212 HIDDEN FIGURES (B)

TRY IT   Practice Words from *Hidden Figures*, Chapters 10–12

Students will complete an online activity in which they answer questions to demonstrate their understanding of the vocabulary words from the reading.

WRAP UP

Questions About *Hidden Figures*, Chapters 10–12

Students will answer questions to show that they understand how to use textual evidence to develop and support an analysis.

Hidden Figures (C)

Lesson Overview

ACTIVITY	ACTIVITY TITLE	TIME	ONLINE/OFFLINE
GET READY	Introduction to *Hidden Figures* (C)	**1** minute	
	Spelling List 12 Review Game	**10** minutes	
	Recall *Hidden Figures*, Chapters 10–12	**5** minutes	
	Before You Read NASA Articles	**10** minutes	
READ	NASA Articles	**30** minutes	
	Check-In: NASA Articles	**5** minutes	
LEARN AND TRY IT	Integrate Information from Multiple Sources	**10** minutes	
	Integrate Information from Texts About Mary Jackson	**10** minutes	
	Apply: Practice Integrating Information	**15** minutes	
	Write About Women at NASA Then and Now **LEARNING COACH CHECK-IN**	**15** minutes	
	Practice Words from NASA Articles	**7** minutes	
WRAP-UP	Questions About Integrating Information	**2** minutes	

Content Background

Students will complete a spelling activity and read three articles published in *Expeditions in Reading* by NASA about women who worked or work for the agency. They will then complete activities in which they learn about integrating information from multiple texts about the same subject.

MATERIALS

Supplied

- *Hidden Figures* by Margot Lee Shetterly
- *Summit English Language Arts 5 Expeditions in Reading*
- *Summit English Language Arts 5 Activity Book*
  - Write About Women at NASA Then and Now

NASA Articles Synopsis

Two of the articles in this lesson are brief biographies of women students have already met in *Hidden Figures*: Dorothy Vaughan and Mary Jackson. Each tells about important accomplishments in its subject's life. The third article focuses on women who currently work for NASA, their feelings about the women of *Hidden Figures*, and the bond they feel, as women in a male-dominated field, with one another and those who came before them.

Lesson Goals

- Practice all spelling words online.
- Analyze multiple articles about Dorothy Vaughan, Mary Jackson, and others.
- Identify main points, draw information, and quote accurately from readings to explain important ideas and answer questions.

GET READY

Introduction to *Hidden Figures* (C)
Students will get a glimpse of what they will learn about in the lesson. They will also read the lesson goals.

Spelling List 12 Review Game
Students will practice all spelling words from the workshop.

Recall *Hidden Figures*, Chapters 10–12
Students will answer questions to review the reading that they have already completed.

Before You Read NASA Articles
Students will be introduced to some key vocabulary words that they will encounter in the upcoming reading.

NASA Articles

Students will read three articles in *Expeditions in Reading* published by NASA: "Dorothy Vaughan Biography," "Mary Jackson Biography," and "NASA Langley's Modern Figures Reflect on Changing Times and *Hidden Figures*."

Check-In: NASA Articles

Students will answer several questions to demonstrate their comprehension of "Dorothy Vaughan Biography," "Mary Jackson Biography," and "NASA Langley's Modern Figures Reflect on Changing Times and *Hidden Figures*."

LEARN AND TRY IT

LEARN   Integrate Information from Multiple Sources

Students will learn how to integrate—or combine—information from several texts on the same subject to develop and demonstrate their complete understanding of that subject.

TRY IT   Integrate Information from Texts About Mary Jackson

Students will practice integrating—or combining—information from several texts on Mary Jackson to develop their abilities in this area.

TRY IT   Apply: Practice Integrating Information

Students will apply to new works what they've learned about drawing and integrating information from them.

TRY IT   Write About Women at NASA Then and Now

Students will complete Write About Women at NASA Then and Now from *Summit English Language Arts 5 Activity Book*.

LEARNING COACH CHECK-IN   This activity page contains open-ended questions, so it's important that you review students' responses. Give students feedback, using the sample answers provided to guide you.

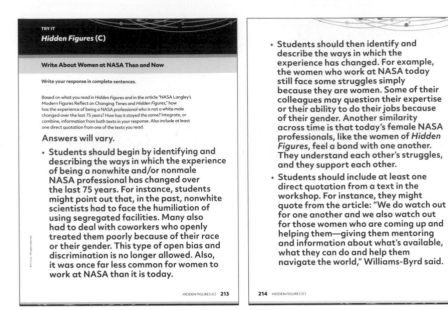

TRY IT   Practice Words from NASA Articles

Students will answer questions to demonstrate their understanding of the vocabulary words from the reading.

WRAP UP

Questions About Integrating Information

Students will answer questions to show that they understand why and how to integrate information from multiple texts.

Hidden Figures Wrap-Up

Lesson Overview

ACTIVITY	ACTIVITY TITLE	TIME	ONLINE/OFFLINE
GET READY	Introduction to *Hidden Figures* Wrap-Up	**1** minute	📶
TRY IT	Write About *Hidden Figures* **LEARNING COACH CHECK-IN**	**30** minutes	📄
	Read and Record	**10** minutes	📶
	Review *Hidden Figures* and NASA Articles	**20** minutes	📶
QUIZ	*Hidden Figures*	**30** minutes	📶
	Spelling List 12	**10** minutes	📶
WRAP-UP	Keyboarding	**10** minutes	📶
	More Language Arts Practice	**9** minutes	📶

Advance Preparation

During the Keyboarding activity, students will practice their keyboarding skills using an external website or program. **You will need to work with students to select an appropriate keyboarding practice website or program; K12 does not specify which resource to use.** A few suggestions are provided in the online activity.

Depending on which program you choose, students may need to set up an account to save their progress. If needed, assist students in setting up and running their chosen keyboarding practice program.

MATERIALS

Supplied
- *Hidden Figures* by Margot Lee Shetterly
- *Summit English Language Arts 5 Expeditions in Reading*
- *Summit English Language Arts 5 Activity Book*
- Write About *Hidden Figures*

Lesson Goals

- Review and take a quiz on *Hidden Figures*, "Dorothy Vaughan Biography," "Mary Jackson Biography," and "NASA Langley's Modern Figures Reflect on Changing Times and *Hidden Figures*."

- Take a spelling quiz.

Introduction to *Hidden Figures* Wrap-Up

Students will read the lesson goals.

Write About *Hidden Figures*

Students will complete Write About *Hidden Figures* from *Summit English Language Arts 5 Activity Book*.

LEARNING COACH CHECK-IN This activity page contains open-ended questions, so it's important that you review students' responses. Give students feedback, using the sample answers provided to guide you.

TRY IT
Hidden Figures Wrap-Up

Write About *Hidden Figures*

Write your responses in complete sentences in the space provided.

You have read several chapters from Margot Lee Shetterly's *Hidden Figures*, as well as additional articles about some of the women in the book.

- After reading and reflecting on these works, briefly explain why reading them is a valuable experience.
- What did you gain from reading about these women?
- Which parts of the readings did you find most meaningful or interesting? Why?
- How did reading more than one text on the same subject affect your understanding of it?
- Be sure to include at least one direct quotation from a text in this workshop in your response

Answers will vary.

- Students should begin by explaining why reading these works is a valuable experience. They might state that reading these works was valuable because it opened their eyes to people who made important contributions to American history and American achievements, but whose work and talents were not widely recognized in their own time.

HIDDEN FIGURES WRAP-UP **215**

- Students should then state what they gained from reading about these women. They may state that they gained an appreciation for the extraordinary intelligence of these women who did such complex math to advance the understanding of how planes and rockets fly. Or students may state that they developed greater respect for people who overcome obstacles—such as discrimination due to gender or race—to succeed in life.
- Next, students should describe which parts of the readings were most meaningful or interesting to them and why. They might state that the chapter in *Hidden Figures* that describes Mary Jackson's time as a Girl Scout leader and the influence she had on the young people in her troop was most interesting or meaningful because it shows how these women cared about and tried to help young people like themselves. Students might choose to include a direct quotation here.
- Finally, students should explain how reading multiple texts on a single subject affected their understanding of that subject. It is likely that students will state that it deepened their understanding of the subject.

216 HIDDEN FIGURES WRAP-UP

Read and Record

Good readers read quickly, smoothly, and with expression. This is called *fluency*. Students will record themselves reading aloud. They will listen to their recording and think about how quick, smooth, and expressive they sound.

TIP Encourage students to rerecord as necessary.

Review *Hidden Figures* and NASA Articles

Students will answer questions to review what they have learned about *Hidden Figures* and the NASA articles in this workshop.

QUIZ

Hidden Figures and NASA Articles

Students will complete the *Hidden Figures* and NASA Articles quiz.

Spelling List 12

Students will complete Spelling List 12 quiz.

WRAP-UP

Keyboarding

Students will practice their keyboarding skills using an external website or program.

More Language Arts Practice

Students will practice skills according to their individual needs.

Big Ideas: Critical Skills Assignment

Lesson Overview

Big Ideas lessons provide students the opportunity to further apply the knowledge acquired and skills learned throughout the unit workshops. Each Big Ideas lesson consists of these parts:

1. **Cumulative Review:** Students keep their skills fresh by reviewing prior content.

2. **Preview:** Students practice answering the types of questions they will commonly find on standardized tests.

3. **Synthesis:** Students complete an assignment that allows them to connect and apply what they have learned. Synthesis assignments vary throughout the course.

In the Synthesis portion of this Big Ideas lesson, students will read new selections. They will answer literal and inferential comprehension questions and complete writing questions that ask for short responses about the reading selections. Students should refer to the selections while answering the questions, because the questions emphasize using textual evidence. The questions call for students to demonstrate critical thinking, reading, and writing skills.

LEARNING COACH CHECK-IN   This is a graded assessment. Make sure students complete, review, and submit the assignment to their teacher.

All materials needed for this lesson are linked online and not provided in the Activity Book.

Moments
in History

"A Ride in the Night"

Lesson Overview

ACTIVITY	ACTIVITY TITLE	TIME	ONLINE/OFFLINE
GET READY	Moments in History Unit Overview	**1** minute	🖥
	Introduction to "A Ride in the Night"	**1** minute	🖥
	Spelling List 13 Pretest **LEARNING COACH CHECK-IN**	**10** minutes	🖥 and 📄
	Historical Fiction in 60 Seconds	**1** minute	🖥
	Look Back at Inferences	**4** minutes	🖥
	Before You Read "A Ride in the Night"	**14** minutes	🖥
READ	"A Ride in the Night"	**30** minutes	📄
	Check-In: "A Ride in the Night"	**5** minutes	🖥
LEARN AND **TRY IT**	Making Inferences Based on Details	**10** minutes	🖥
	Practice Making Inferences About "A Ride in the Night"	**9** minutes	🖥
	Apply: Inferences	**15** minutes	🖥
	Write About Will Clark **LEARNING COACH CHECK-IN**	**10** minutes	📄
	Practice Words from "A Ride in the Night"	**8** minutes	🖥
WRAP-UP	Questions About "A Ride in the Night"	**2** minutes	🖥

Content Background

Students will complete a spelling activity and read "A Ride in the Night" by Katharine E. Wilkie. They will then complete activities in which they learn about using textual details to make and support inferences.

MATERIALS

Supplied
- *Summit English Language Arts 5 Expeditions in Reading*
- *Summit English Language Arts 5 Activity Book*
  - Spelling List 13 Pretest
  - Write About Will Clark

"A Ride in the Night" Synopsis

Will Clark is a young boy of nine in 1779 when his father asks him to deliver horses to an inn. The horses are destined for George Washington's Continental Army, and Will must complete the mission with only another young person, an enslaved person named York, to help him. Together, Will and York ride through the night and reach the inn around dawn. Unfortunately, there are several British soldiers there, and they are looking for anyone who might try to deliver horses to the American side. Despite the suspicion of one particularly cruel soldier, Will convinces them that he is merely on his way to his aunt's home. When the soldiers leave the inn, Will and York successfully deliver the horses to the inn's owner, Mr. Coleman.

KEYWORDS

inference – a guess that readers make using the clues that authors give them in a piece of writing

Lesson Goals

- Take a spelling pretest.
- Read "A Ride in the Night" by Katharine E. Wilkie.
- Make inferences about figures and their behaviors.
- Write about young Will Clark.

GET READY

Moments in History Unit Overview
Students will read a summary of what they will learn in the Moments in History unit.

Introduction to "A Ride in the Night"
Students will get a glimpse of what they will learn about in the lesson. They will also read the lesson goals and keywords. Have students select each keyword and preview its definition.

Spelling List 13 Pretest
Students will take a spelling pretest.

LEARNING COACH CHECK-IN   Have students turn to Spelling List 13 Pretest in *Summit English Language Arts 5 Activity Book* and open the online Spelling Pretest activity. Online, students will listen to the spelling word, type the word in the space indicated, and then check their answer. In the activity book, students will write the correct spelling of the word in the tables provided and indicate with a ✓ or an ✗ ifs they spelled the word correctly or incorrectly online. Students will repeat this process with the remaining words.

As needed, help students with the interaction between the online activity and the activity book page until they become comfortable with what they need to do. As students practice their spelling words throughout the workshop, they should pay special attention to words they spelled incorrectly on the pretest.

This is the complete list of words students will be tested on.

Words That Are Often Confused			Root *bell*
adapt	conscience	picture	belligerent
adopt	conscious	pitcher	rebellion
advice	decent		rebellious
advise	descent		
allowed	effect		
aloud	affect		

NOTE   Have students keep their completed activity page in a safe place so they can refer to it later.

GET READY
"A Ride in the Night"

Spelling List 13 Pretest

1. Open the Spelling Pretest activity online. Listen to the first spelling word. Type the word. Check your answer.

2. Write the correct spelling of the word in the Word column of the Spelling Pretest table on the next page.

Word	✓	✗
1 blindfold		

3. Put a check mark in the ✓ column if you spelled the word correctly online.

Word	✓	✗
1 blindfold	✓	

Put an X in the ✗ column if you spelled the word incorrectly online.

Word	✓	✗
1 blindfold		X

4. Repeat Steps 1–3 for the remaining words in the Spelling Pretest.

"A RIDE IN THE NIGHT" **217**

"A Ride in the Night"

Spelling List 13 Pretest

Write each spelling word in the Word column, making sure to spell it correctly.

Word	✓	✗		Word	✓	✗
1 adapt				10 decent		
2 adopt				11 descent		
3 advice				12 effect		
4 advise				13 picture		
5 affect				14 pitcher		
6 allowed				15 belligerent		
7 aloud				16 rebellion		
8 conscience				17 rebellious		
9 conscious						

Students should use the ✓ and X columns to indicate whether they spelled each word correctly or incorrectly online.

218 "A RIDE IN THE NIGHT"

Historical Fiction in 60 Seconds
Students will watch a short video designed to spark their interest in upcoming topics.

Look Back at Inferences
Students will practice the prerequisite skill of making inferences.

Before You Read "A Ride in the Night"

Students will be introduced to some key vocabulary words that they will encounter in the upcoming reading, learn some important historical background related to the reading, and answer a question to help them set a purpose for their reading.

READ

"A Ride in the Night"

Students will read "A Ride in the Night" by Katharine E. Wilkie in *Expeditions in Reading*.

Check-In: "A Ride in the Night"

Students will answer several questions to demonstrate their comprehension of "A Ride in the Night."

LEARN AND TRY IT

LEARN   Making Inferences Based on Details

Students will learn how to make inferences about texts based on the details an author provides.

TRY IT   Practice Making Inferences About "A Ride in the Night"

Students will answer several questions online to develop their ability to make inferences and identify textual details and evidence that support those inferences.

TRY IT   Apply: Inferences

Students will apply to a new work what they've learned about using textual details and evidence to make and support inferences.

TRY IT   Write About Will Clark

Students will complete Write About Will Clark from *Summit English Language Arts 5 Activity Book*. Students will read a passage from the text, make an inference about Will Clark, and identify the textual details and evidence that support their inference.

LEARNING COACH CHECK-IN   This activity page contains open-ended questions, so it's important that you review students' responses. Give students feedback, using the sample answers provided to guide you.

Write About Will Clark

Read the excerpt from "A Ride in the Night" by Katharine E. Wilkie and answer the questions.

The soldier called Brown turned toward Will. His eyes were cold and dangerous. He twisted Will's shoulder crudely. "We're on the lookout for horses intended for the Continental Army. Do you know anything about them?"

"Ouch! You're hurting me!"

The man's roughness had brought real tears to Will's eyes. The boy was glad of it. The pain would excuse the look of fear on his face. But his great fear was for York, hidden back in the woods with the horses.

1. What can you infer about Will Clark based on this passage?

See right.

2. What evidence in the passage supports your inference?

See right.

Additional answers

Answers will vary.

1. Students may infer that Will is clever. Or students may infer that Will is unselfish. Both of these inferences are supported by the details of the passage.

2. If students inferred that Will is clever, the evidence from the text is that Will is glad that the soldier's roughness brought real tears to his eyes, since that helps explain why he looks afraid. If students inferred that Will is unselfish, the evidence from the text is that Will's greatest fear is for York, not for himself.

TRY IT   Practice Words from "A Ride in the Night"

Students will answer questions to demonstrate their understanding of the vocabulary words from today's reading.

WRAP-UP

Questions About "A Ride in the Night"

Students will answer questions to show that they understand how to make and support inferences using textual details.

"A Ride in the Night" Wrap-Up

Lesson Overview

ACTIVITY	ACTIVITY TITLE	TIME	ONLINE/OFFLINE
GET READY	Introduction to "A Ride in the Night" Wrap-Up	**1** minute	🛜
	Spelling List 13 Activity Bank **LEARNING COACH CHECK-IN**	**10** minutes	🛜 and 📄
TRY IT	Write About "A Ride in the Night" **LEARNING COACH CHECK-IN**	**30** minutes	📄
	Read and Record	**20** minutes	🛜
	Review Inferences	**10** minutes	🛜
QUIZ	"A Ride in the Night"	**20** minutes	🛜
WRAP-UP	Keyboarding	**10** minutes	📄
	More Language Arts Practice	**19** minutes	🛜

Advance Preparation

Gather students' completed Spelling List 13 Pretest activity page from "A Ride in the Night." Students will refer to this page during Spelling List 13 Activity Bank.

During the Keyboarding activity, students will practice their keyboarding skills using an external website or program. **You will need to work with students to select an appropriate keyboarding practice website or program; K12 does not specify which resource to use.** A few suggestions are provided in the online activity.

Depending on which program you choose, students may need to set up an account to save their progress. If needed, assist students in setting up and running their chosen keyboarding practice program.

MATERIALS

Supplied
- *Summit English Language Arts 5 Expeditions in Reading*
- *Summit English Language Arts 5 Activity Book*
  - Spelling List 13 Activity Bank
  - Write About "A Ride in the Night"

Also Needed
- completed Spelling List 13 Pretest activity page from "A Ride in the Night"

Lesson Goals

- Practice all spelling words offline.
- Summarize "A Ride in the Night."
- Review using textual details to make and support inferences.
- Take a quiz on "A Ride in the Night."

Introduction to "A Ride in the Night" Wrap-Up

Students will read the lesson goals.

Spelling List 13 Activity Bank

Students will practice all spelling words from the workshop by completing Spelling List 13 Activity Bank from *Summit English Language Arts 5 Activity Book*. Make sure students have their completed Spelling List 13 Pretest activity page from "A Ride in the Night" (A) to refer to during this activity.

Remind students to pay special attention to words they spelled incorrectly on the Spelling Pretest.

GET READY

"A Ride in the Night" Wrap-Up

Spelling List 13 Activity Bank

Circle any words in the box that you did not spell correctly on the pretest. Using your circled words, complete one activity of your choice. Complete as much of the activity as you can in the time given.

If you spelled all words correctly on the pretest, complete your chosen activity with as many spelling words as you can.

adapt	affect	conscious	effect	belligerent
adopt	allowed	decent	picture	rebellion
advice	aloud	descent	pitcher	rebellious
advise	conscience			

Spelling Activity Choices

Vowel-Free Words

1. In the left column, write only the consonants in each word and put a dot where each vowel should be.
2. Spell each word out loud, stating which vowels should be in the places you wrote dots.
3. In the right column, rewrite the entire spelling word.
4. Correct any spelling errors.

"A RIDE IN THE NIGHT" WRAP-UP **221**

Alphabetizing

1. In the left column, write your words from the spelling word list in alphabetical order.
2. Correct any spelling errors.

Parts of Speech

1. In the left column, write the words from your spelling list that are nouns.
2. In the right column, write all the other words from your spelling list and label each word's part of speech.
3. Correct any spelling errors.

Uppercase and Lowercase

1. In the left column, write each of your words in all capital letters, or all uppercase.
2. In the right column, write each of your words in all lowercase letters.
3. Correct any spelling errors.

222 "A RIDE IN THE NIGHT" WRAP-UP

Complete the activity that you chose.

My chosen activity: _____

1. _____
2. _____
3. _____
4. _____
5. _____
6. _____
7. _____
8. _____   Students should use this
9. _____   page to complete all steps
10. _____   in their chosen activity.
11. _____
12. _____
13. _____
14. _____
15. _____
16. _____
17. _____
18. _____
19. _____
20. _____
21. _____
22. _____
23. _____
24. _____

"A RIDE IN THE NIGHT" WRAP-UP **223**

TRY IT

TRY IT   Write About "A Ride in the Night"

Students will complete Write About "A Ride in the Night" in *Summit English Language Arts 5 Activity Book* to write a brief summary of the text.

This activity page contains an open-ended question, so it's important that you review students' responses. Give students feedback, using the sample answers provided to guide you.

TRY IT
"A Ride in the Night" Wrap-Up

Write About "A Ride in the Night"

A summary is a short retelling of the most important ideas or events in a text. Good summaries describe events in the same order as the text they summarize.

Summarize "A Ride in the Night" in two or three paragraphs.

See right.

"A RIDE IN THE NIGHT" WRAP-UP **225**

Additional answers

Answers will vary.

Effective summaries will include most of the following:

- Will's parents are reluctant to have him deliver the horses, but they are patriots and know that it is crucial the horses be delivered.
- Will and York must ride through the night, alone, in unfamiliar surroundings in order to reach the inn.
- When Will and York arrive at the inn, Will suspects that something is wrong and sends York to hide with the horses.
- Will enters the inn alone and finds several British soldiers inside, one of whom questions Will and is suspicious of him.
- Will lies to the soldiers and manages to convince them that he is not there to deliver horses.
- After the soldiers leave, Will returns to the inn and tells the owner that he has brought the horses.
- Will feels proud to have completed his mission and to have done something for his country.

Read and Record

Good readers read quickly, smoothly, and with expression. This is called *fluency*. Students will record themselves reading aloud. They will listen to their recording and think about how quick, smooth, and expressive they sound.

TIP Encourage students to rerecord as needed.

TRY IT   Review Inferences

Students will answer questions to review what they have learned about using textual details to make and support inferences.

QUIZ

"A Ride in the Night"

Students will complete the "A Ride in the Night" quiz.

WRAP-UP

Keyboarding

Students will practice their keyboarding skills using an external website or program.

More Language Arts Practice

Students will practice skills according to their individual needs.

"Run, Kate Shelley, Run"

Lesson Overview

ACTIVITY	ACTIVITY TITLE	TIME	ONLINE/OFFLINE
GET READY	Introduction to "Run, Kate Shelley, Run"	**1** minute	🖥️
	Spelling List 13 Review Game	**10** minutes	🖥️
	Look Back at Key Details	**4** minutes	🖥️
	Before You Read "Run, Kate Shelley, Run"	**15** minutes	🖥️
READ	"Run, Kate Shelley, Run"	**30** minutes	📄
	Check-In: "Run, Kate Shelley, Run"	**5** minutes	🖥️
LEARN AND **TRY IT**	Using Key Details to Infer Main Ideas	**10** minutes	🖥️
	Practice Inferring Main Ideas	**10** minutes	🖥️
	Apply: Main Idea and Key Details	**15** minutes	🖥️
	Write About Key Details and Main Ideas **LEARNING COACH CHECK-IN**	**10** minutes	📄
	Practice Words from "Run, Kate Shelley, Run"	**8** minutes	🖥️
WRAP-UP	Questions About "Run, Kate Shelley, Run"	**2** minutes	🖥️

Content Background

Students will complete a spelling activity and read "Run, Kate Shelley, Run" by Julia Pferdehirt. They will then complete activities in which they learn about using key details to make inferences about unstated main ideas.

MATERIALS

Supplied
- *Summit English Language Arts 5 Expeditions in Reading*
- *Summit English Language Arts 5 Activity Book*
  - Write About Key Details and Main Ideas

"Run, Kate Shelley, Run" Synopsis

Kate Shelley is fifteen years old in 1881 when a terrible storm strikes near her Iowa farmhouse. For days, the waters of nearby Honey Creek rise. Finally, one night, as an engine crosses a trestle bridge over Honey Creek, there is a terrible accident and the engine plunges into the water. Kate rushes to find two survivors, but before she can help them, she realizes that another train—this one carrying more than 200 people—will soon be traveling down the same tracks. Through the brutal storm, Kate sets off to warn the men working at the nearest train station so that they can stop the next train. To get there, she crosses a high trestle bridge on her hands and knees, in the dark and as the storm rages. She reaches the station in time and brings a rescue team back to Honey Creek to save the survivors of the engine crash. For her heroism, Kate receives many honors.

Lesson Goals

- Practice all spelling words online.

- Read "Run, Kate Shelley, Run" by Julia Pferdehirt.

- Make inferences and identify key details to determine and support main ideas.

- Write about key details and unstated main ideas in "Run, Kate Shelley, Run."

GET READY

Introduction to "Run, Kate Shelley, Run"

Students will get a glimpse of what they will learn about in the lesson. They will also read the lesson goals and keywords. Have students select each keyword and preview its definition.

Spelling List 13 Review Game

Students will practice all spelling words from the workshop.

Look Back at Key Details

Students will practice the prerequisite skill of identifying key details.

Before You Read "Run, Kate Shelley, Run"

Students will be introduced to some key vocabulary words that they will encounter in the upcoming reading, learn some important historical background related to the reading, and answer a question to help them set a purpose for their reading.

READ

"Run, Kate Shelley, Run"

Students will read "Run, Kate Shelley, Run" by Julia Pferdehirt in *Expeditions in Reading*.

Check-In: "Run, Kate Shelley, Run"

Students will answer several questions to demonstrate their comprehension of "Run, Kate Shelley, Run."

LEARN AND TRY IT

LEARN Using Key Details to Infer Main Ideas

Students will learn how to use key details provided in a text to make inferences about unstated main ideas.

TRY IT Practice Inferring Main Ideas

Students will answer several questions online to develop their ability to identify key details and then use them to infer unstated main ideas.

TRY IT Apply: Main Idea and Key Details

Students will apply to a new work what they've learned about using key details to make inferences about unstated main ideas.

TRY IT Write About Key Details and Main Ideas

Students will complete Write About Key Details and Main Ideas from *Summit English Language Arts 5 Activity Book*. Students will read a passage from the text, identify the key details in it, and use those key details to infer an unstated main idea in the passage.

LEARNING COACH CHECK-IN   This activity page contains open-ended questions, so it's important that you review students' responses. Give students feedback, using the sample answers provided to guide you.

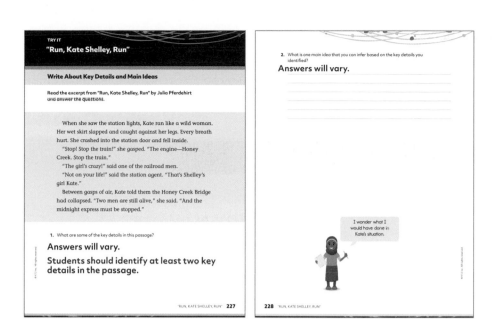

TRY IT Practice Words from "Run, Kate Shelley, Run"

Students will answer questions to demonstrate their understanding of the vocabulary words from today's reading.

WRAP-UP

Questions About "Run, Kate Shelley, Run"

Students will answer questions to show that they understand how to identify key details and determine main ideas.

"Run, Kate Shelley, Run" Wrap-Up

Lesson Overview

ACTIVITY	ACTIVITY TITLE	TIME	ONLINE/OFFLINE
GET READY	Introduction to "Run, Kate Shelley, Run" Wrap-Up	**1** minute	🖥
TRY IT	Write About "Run, Kate Shelley, Run" **LEARNING COACH CHECK-IN**	**30** minutes	📄
	Read and Record	**20** minutes	🖥
	Review Main Idea and Key Details	**10** minutes	🖥
QUIZ	"Run, Kate Shelley, Run"	**20** minutes	🖥
	Spelling List 13	**10** minutes	🖥
WRAP-UP	Keyboarding	**10** minutes	🖥
	More Language Arts Practice	**19** minutes	🖥

Advance Preparation

During the Keyboarding activity, students will practice their keyboarding skills using an external website or program. **You will need to work with students to select an appropriate keyboarding practice website or program; K12 does not specify which resource to use.** A few suggestions are provided in the online activity.

Depending on which program you choose, students may need to set up an account to save their progress. If needed, assist students in setting up and running their chosen keyboarding practice program.

MATERIALS

Supplied
- *Summit English Language Arts 5 Expeditions in Reading*
- *Summit English Language Arts 5 Activity Book*
  - Write About "Run, Kate Shelley, Run"

Lesson Goals

- Summarize "Run, Kate Shelley, Run."
- Review identifying textual details and using them to make inferences about unstated main ideas.
- Take a quiz on "Run, Kate Shelley, Run."
- Take a spelling quiz.

Introduction to "Run, Kate Shelley, Run"

Students will read the lesson goals.

TRY IT

TRY IT   Write About "Run, Kate Shelley, Run"

Students will complete Write About "Run, Kate Shelley, Run" in *Summit English Language Arts 5 Activity Book* to write a brief summary of the text.

LEARNING COACH CHECK-IN   This activity page contains an open-ended question, so it's important that you review students' responses. Give students feedback, using the sample answers provided to guide you.

TRY IT
"Run, Kate Shelley, Run" Wrap-Up

Write About "Run, Kate Shelley, Run"

Good summaries retell only the most important ideas or events in a text. They leave out minor or unimportant details, and they follow the same order as the text they summarize.

Summarize "Run, Kate Shelley, Run" in two or three paragraphs.

See right.

"RUN, KATE SHELLEY, RUN" WRAP-UP   229

Additional answers

Answers will vary. Students' response should be a 2 to 3 paragraph summary of "Run, Kate Shelley, Run." Effective summaries will contain include most of the following:

- It rained so much in July 1881 near Moingona, Iowa, that nearby rivers and creeks rose dangerously high.
- One night during a storm, the Honey Creek trestle bridge collapsed as an engine drove over it, plunging those on board into the river.
- Kate Shelley went to help the survivors, but soon realized that another train—a midnight express—would be traveling on the same tracks very soon.
- Kate made her way to the Moingona train station to warn the men working there so that they could halt the midnight express.
- To get there, Kate had to crawl over the Des Moines River bridge on her hands and knees in the dark while the storm was raging.
- Kate knew that the lives of those aboard the midnight express depended on her taking such risk. She reached the station, and the midnight express was stopped.
- For her heroism, Kate was honored by people across the country and by the railroad workers, who would even stop at her house whenever she needed to ride the train.

TRY IT   Read and Record

Good readers read quickly, smoothly, and with expression. This is called *fluency*. Students will record themselves reading aloud. They will listen to their recording and think about how quick, smooth, and expressive they sound.

TIP   Encourage students to rerecord as needed.

TRY IT   **Review Main Idea and Key Details**

Students will answer questions to review what they have learned about identifying key details and using them to make inferences about unstated main ideas.

QUIZ

"Run, Kate Shelley, Run"

Students will complete the "Run, Kate Shelley, Run" quiz.

Spelling List 13

Students will complete the Spelling List 13 quiz.

WRAP-UP

Keyboarding

Students will practice their keyboarding skills using an external website or program.

More Language Arts Practice

Students will practice skills according to their individual needs.

Informational Writing: Revising

Lesson Overview

ACTIVITY	ACTIVITY TITLE	TIME	ONLINE/OFFLINE
GET READY	Introduction to Informational Writing: Revising	**2** minutes	🖥️
	Look Back at Informational Writing Skills	**15** minutes	🖥️
LEARN AND **TRY IT**	Revising a Science Report	**20** minutes	🖥️
	Revise Your Science Report LEARNING COACH CHECK-IN	**60** minutes	📄
WRAP-UP	Question About Revising a Report	**3** minutes	🖥️
	Go Read!	**20** minutes	🖥️ or 📄

Content Background

Students will continue working on their **science report** about a science topic that fascinates them. In this lesson, students will **revise** their rough draft.

Writing Process

To revise their science report, students will use a checklist. The checklist focuses on organization (*Does my introduction clearly state the topic?*) and content (*Is my report factual and well researched, showing that I understand the topic?*). At the end of this lesson, students will be ready to proofread their science report for grammar, usage, and mechanics.

Students may not understand the difference between revising and proofreading. When revising, writers focus on large issues, such as the order of ideas, whether each idea is well supported with research, and whether the language is precise and domain-specific. When proofreading, writers fix errors in grammar, usage, and mechanics, such as spelling or punctuation mistakes. Encourage students to focus on revision during this lesson. In the next lesson, students will proofread their science report.

MATERIALS

Supplied
- *Summit English Language Arts 5 Activity Book*
  - Revise Your Science Report
- Science Report: Revision Feedback Sheet (printout)
- Science Report Instructions (printout)

Also Needed
- folder in which students are storing science report writing assignment pages
- reading material for Go Read!

Advance Preparation

Gather the folder that students are using to store the activity pages related to their science report. The folder should contain the following:

- Students' completed Brainstorm for Your Science report activity page from Informational Writing: Prewriting (A)

- Students' completed Conduct Research for Your Science Report activity page from Informational Writing: Prewriting (B)

- Students' completed Outline for Your Science Report activity page from Informational Writing: Prewriting (C)

- Students' completed rough draft from Informational Writing: Drafting (B)

Prior to the Revise Your Science Report activity in this lesson, read students' rough draft and complete Science Report: Revision Feedback Sheet.

During the Go Read! activity, students will have the option of using the digital library. Allow extra time for students to make their reading selection, or have students make a selection before beginning the lesson.

> ### KEYWORDS
>
> **informational text** – text written to explain and give information on a topic
>
> **revising** – the stage or step of the writing process in which the writer goes back, rereads the piece, and makes changes in content or organization

Lesson Goals

- Use a checklist to revise your science report.
- Read for pleasure.

GET READY

Introduction to Informational Writing: Revising

Students will get a glimpse of what they will learn about in the lesson. They will also read the lesson goals and keywords. Have students select each keyword and preview its definition.

Look Back at Informational Writing Skills

Students will review how to organize informational writing, including how to write a clear and effective introduction.

LEARN Revising a Science Report

Students will learn about revising, including how to use a revision checklist. Through a guided activity, they will explore how to revise a sample student science report.

TRY IT Revise Your Science Report

Students will complete Revise Your Science Report in *Summit English Language Arts 5 Activity Book*. They will need their completed rough draft from Informational Writing: Drafting (B). They should have their folder containing all of their work related to their report available in case they need to refer to the assignment instructions, their research notes, or their outline.

LEARNING COACH CHECK-IN Guide students through the revision process.

1. Use the Science Report: Revision Feedback Sheet that you filled out to guide a discussion with students.

   • Tell students the strengths of their science report. Provide positive comments about the ideas, language, detail, or other elements of the report that you enjoyed.

   • Share your constructive feedback with students.

   • As you discuss your feedback, encourage students to actively revise their draft in response. Reassure students that it's okay to remove or move around ideas and sentences. Students should revise their draft directly on the page, using the lines they left blank.

2. Have students review their draft once more, using the Revise Your Science Report activity page.

   • For students having difficulty recognizing areas they should revise, suggest a revision, and think aloud to model your revising. For example, *This detail doesn't sound right here. It really goes with the ideas in the second paragraph. Let's move it there, or else the reader might get confused. Can you find any other details that are out of place?*

3. Make sure students store their revised draft in the folder they are using to organize their writing assignment pages.

TIP Remind students to focus on the checklist questions. Emphasize that they should not worry about spelling, punctuation, grammar, and so on.

NOTE If you need a copy of the Science Report Instructions, you can download and print one online.

Informational Writing: Revising

Revise Your Science Report

Use the checklist as you revise your science report draft.

Students should check off each item as they make necessary changes in the draft of their science report.

Organization

☑ Does my report have an introduction, at least three body paragraphs, and a conclusion?

☑ Does my introduction clearly state the topic?

☑ Are supporting ideas grouped in the correct body paragraphs?

☑ Do appropriate headings separate the different sections of my report?

☑ Do I use clear and logical transitions?

Content

☑ Is my report factual and well researched, showing that I understand the topic?

☑ Do I use enough facts and supporting details, including at least one quotation, to explain ideas?

☑ Does my conclusion make sense and answer important questions?

☑ Are the words I use precise and domain-specific?

☑ Do I have a source list that includes at least three research sources, one of which is a print source?

INFORMATIONAL WRITING: REVISING **231**

WRAP-UP

Question About Revising a Report

Students will answer a question to show that they understand a key revision skill.

Go Read!

Students will read for pleasure. They should choose a book or a magazine that interests them, or they may choose a selection from the digital library, linked in the online lesson.

Students should read for the entire time. Have students select something to read ahead of time to help them stay focused.

Informational Writing: Proofreading

Lesson Overview

ACTIVITY	ACTIVITY TITLE	TIME	ONLINE/OFFLINE
GET READY	Introduction to Informational Writing: Proofreading	**2** minutes	🖥️
	Look Back at Titles of Works	**10** minutes	📶
LEARN AND **TRY IT**	Proofreading a Science Report	**20** minutes	📶
	Proofread Your Science Report ⬛ LEARNING COACH CHECK-IN	**60** minutes	📄
WRAP-UP	Question About Proofreading a Report	**3** minutes	🖥️
	Go Read!	**25** minutes	📶 or 📄

Content Background

Students will continue working on their **science report** about a science topic that fascinates them. In this lesson, students will **proofread** their revised rough draft.

Writing Process

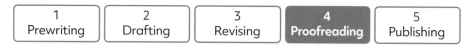

```
1            2            3            4              5
Prewriting   Drafting     Revising     Proofreading   Publishing
```

To proofread their science report, students will use a checklist. The checklist focuses on grammar, usage, and mechanics (*Are there any missing or extra words? Are titles of works formatted correctly?*). After completing this lesson, students will be ready to prepare a clean copy of their science report.

Proofreading is sometimes called *editing*.

Advance Preparation

Gather the folder that students are using to store the activity pages related to their science report. The folder should contain the following:

- Students' completed Brainstorm for Your Science report activity page from Informational Writing: Prewriting (A)

- Students' completed Conduct Research for Your Science Report activity page from Informational Writing: Prewriting (B)

MATERIALS

Supplied
- *Summit English Language Arts 5 Activity Book*
  - Proofread Your Science Report
- Science Report: Proofreading Feedback Sheet (printout)
- Science Report Instructions (printout)

Also Needed
- folder in which students are storing science report writing assignment pages
- reading material for Go Read!

- Students' completed Outline for Your Science Report activity page from Informational Writing: Prewriting (C)

- Students' revised rough draft from Informational Writing: Revising

Prior to the Proofread Your Science Report activity in this lesson, read students' revised rough draft and complete Science Report: Proofreading Feedback Sheet.

During the Go Read! activity, students will have the option of using the digital library. Allow extra time for students to make their reading selection, or have students make a selection before beginning the lesson.

Lesson Goals

- Use a checklist to proofread your science report.
- Read for pleasure.

GET READY

Introduction to Informational Writing: Proofreading

Students will get a glimpse of what they will learn about in the lesson. They will also read the lesson goals and keywords. Have students select each keyword and preview its definition.

Look Back at Titles of Works

Students will practice determining whether a title should be placed in quotation marks, italicized, or underlined. This is a skill that they will use when they proofread their science report.

LEARN AND TRY IT

LEARN Proofread a Science Report

Students will learn about proofreading, including how to use a proofreading checklist. Through a guided activity, they will explore how to proofread a sample student science report.

TRY IT Proofread Your Science Report

Students will complete Proofread Your Science Report in *Summit English Language Arts 5 Activity Book*. They will need their revised rough draft from Informational Writing: Revising. They should have their folder containing all of their work related to their report available in case they need to refer to any of that work (for instance, to check the spelling of a title or of the speaker of a direct quotation).

1. Have students read their draft aloud, listening for errors such as missing words, incomplete sentences, and verb tense errors. Have students fix any errors as they catch them.

   - For students having difficulty noticing errors as they read aloud, model the process. Slowly read a sentence aloud. Pause and model your thinking when you encounter an error. For example, *"Opened the door." This sentence sounds wrong. Who opened the door? The subject is missing. Since Joe opened the door, I'll write "Joe" at the beginning of the sentence and lowercase the word "Opened."*

2. Have students review their draft once more, using the Proofread Your Science Report activity page. Students should fix any additional errors that they find.

3. Review with students your comments on the Science Report: Proofreading Feedback Sheet. Praise students for the errors that they caught, and guide students to recognize any errors that they have not yet fixed.

4. Have students store their edited draft in the folder they are using to organize their writing assignment pages.

OPTIONAL Have students exchange revised reports with a peer and use the Proofread Your Science Report activity page to proofread each other's reports.

NOTE If you need a copy of the Science Report Instructions, you can download and print one online.

Question About Proofreading

Students will answer a question to show that they understand a key proofreading skill.

Go Read!

Students will read for pleasure. They should choose a book or a magazine that interests them, or they may choose a selection from the digital library, linked in the online lesson.

Students should read for the entire time. Have students select something to read ahead of time to help them stay focused.

Informational Writing: Publishing

Lesson Overview

ACTIVITY	ACTIVITY TITLE	TIME	ONLINE/OFFLINE
GET READY	Introduction to Informational Writing: Publishing	**2** minutes	📶
LEARN AND TRY IT	Publishing a Science Report	**15** minutes	📶
	Publish Your Science Report	**60** minutes	🖥️
WRAP-UP	Turn In Your Science Report	**1** minute	📶
	Keyboarding	**10** minutes	📶
	More Language Arts Practice	**17** minutes	🖥️
	Go Read!	**15** minutes	📶 or 📄

Content Background

Students will continue working on their report about a science topic they find fascinating. In this lesson, students will **publish** their report. Then they will submit their completed report to their teacher.

Writing Process

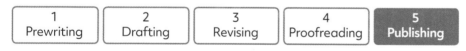

| 1 Prewriting | 2 Drafting | 3 Revising | 4 Proofreading | 5 Publishing |

They will complete an activity to review basic word-processing skills, such as using a keyboard and saving a document.

Advance Preparation

Gather the folder that students are using to store the activity pages related to their science report. The folder should contain the following:

- Students' completed Brainstorm for Your Science report activity page from Informational Writing: Prewriting (A)

- Students' completed Conduct Research for Your Science Report activity page from Informational Writing: Prewriting (B)

- Students' completed Outline for Your Science Report activity page from Informational Writing: Prewriting (C)

- Students' revised and edited rough draft from Informational Writing: Proofreading

During the Keyboarding activity, students will practice their keyboarding skills using an external website or program. **You will need to work with students to select an appropriate keyboarding practice website or program; K12 does not specify which resource to use.** A few suggestions are provided in the online activity.

Depending on which program you choose, students may need to set up an account to save their progress. If needed, assist students in setting up and running their chosen keyboarding practice program.

During the Go Read! activity, students will have the option of using the digital library. Allow extra time for students to make their reading selection, or have students make a selection before beginning the lesson.

Lesson Goals

- Type your science report.
- Submit your report to your teacher.

GET READY

Introduction to Informational Writing: Publishing

Students will get a glimpse of what they will learn about in the lesson. They will also read the lesson goals and keywords. Have students select each keyword and preview its definition.

LEARN AND TRY IT

LEARN   Publishing a Science Report

Students will learn about word-processing skills in preparation for typing their science report.

TRY IT   Publish Your Science Report

Students will type a final copy of their science report. Students should gather their revised and proofread draft, and they should type it using a word-processing program.

NOTE   If you need a copy of the Science Report Instructions, you can download and print one online.

Turn In Your Science Report

Students will submit their writing assignment to their teacher.

Keyboarding

Students will practice their keyboarding skills using an external website or program.

More Language Arts Practice

Students will practice skills according to their individual needs.

Go Read!

Students will read for pleasure. They should choose a book or a magazine that interests them, or they may choose a selection from the digital library, linked in the online lesson.

Students should read for the entire time. Have students select something to read ahead of time to help them stay focused.

Greek Roots and Affixes

Lesson Overview

ACTIVITY	ACTIVITY TITLE	TIME	ONLINE/OFFLINE
GET READY	Introduction to Greek Roots and Affixes	**1** minute	🖥️
	Look Back at Prefixes and Suffixes	**4** minutes	🖥️
LEARN AND **TRY IT**	Greek Roots and Affixes	**10** minutes	🖥️
	Greek Roots and Affixes	**10** minutes	🖥️
	Apply: Greek Roots and Affixes **LEARNING COACH CHECK-IN**	**15** minutes	📄
	Go Write!	**15** minutes	📄
	Review Greek Roots and Affixes	**15** minutes	🖥️
QUIZ	Greek Roots and Affixes	**15** minutes	🖥️
WRAP-UP	Keyboarding	**10** minutes	🖥️
	More Language Arts Practice	**10** minutes	🖥️
	Go Read!	**15** minutes	🖥️ or 📄

Content Background

Students will learn about recognizing and understanding the meanings of words with Greek roots. The word list for this workshop contains words whose Greek roots are *chron* (time), *sym* (together), and *graph* (written or drawn).

Advance Preparation

During the Keyboarding activity, students will practice their keyboarding skills using an external website or program. **You will need to work with students to select an appropriate keyboarding practice website or program; K12 does not specify which resource to use.** A few suggestions are provided in the online activity.

Depending on which program you choose, students may need to set up an account to save their progress. If needed, assist students in setting up and running their chosen keyboarding practice program.

MATERIALS

Supplied
- *Summit English Language Arts 5 Activity Book*
  - Apply: Greek Roots and Affixes

KEYWORDS

affix – a word part attached to a root or base word to create a new word

root – a word part that gives a word meaning and must have prefixes or suffixes added to it; *octo* is the root of octopus and octagon

During the Go Read! activity, students will have the option of using the digital library. Allow extra time for students to make their reading selection, or have students make a selection before beginning the lesson.

Lesson Goals

- Determine the meanings of words with Greek roots and affixes.
- Use context clues to help determine meaning of unknown words.
- Read for pleasure.

GET READY

Introduction to Greek Roots and Affixes

Students will get a glimpse of what they will learn about in the lesson. They will also read the lesson goals and keywords. Have students select each keyword and preview its definition.

LEARN AND TRY IT

LEARN   Look Back at Prefixes and Suffixes

Students will practice the prerequisite skill of identifying prefixes and suffixes.

LEARN   Greek Roots and Affixes

Students will learn what roots of words are and how knowing some common Greek roots and affixes can help them unlock the meanings of unfamiliar words.

TRY IT   Greek Roots and Affixes

Students will answer questions to develop their ability to use Greek roots and affixes to help them determine the meanings of words.

TRY IT   Apply: Greek Roots and Affixes

Students will complete Apply: Greek Roots and Affixes from *Summit English Language Arts 5 Activity Book*.

LEARNING COACH CHECK-IN   This activity page contains open-ended questions, so it's important that you review students' responses. Give students feedback, using the sample answers provided to guide you.

Page 235

Greek Roots and Affixes

Apply: Greek Roots and Affixes

Read the paragraph. Think about context clues and what they suggest about the missing word or phrase.

1. We've spent a long time trying to stop our dog's bad behavior, but he still won't obey. He spends most days chewing our shoes and most nights howling. He's acted this way since he was a puppy.

   a. Which word correctly fills in the blank? *chronic* or *chronological*

   b. Explanation:

   > See below.

2. My grandfather's pocket watch is dented on the outside and its face is cracked, but it is still ticking. I guess that's why I think of the watch as a _____ of my grandfather himself. Just like his watch, he isn't in perfect condition, but he's still going.

   a. Which word correctly fills in the blank? *symphony* or *symbol*

   b. Explanation:

   Symbol is the better choice because the sentence suggests that the watch represents or stands for the narrator's grandfather. A *symphony* is music written for several instruments playing together.

Page 236

3. When I turned on the TV, the first thing I saw was a _____ that showed the outline of a woman on a snowboard. Right away, I remembered that the Winter Olympics had started the day before.

   a. Which word correctly fills in the blank? *biography* or *graphic*

   b. Explanation:

   > See below.

Write a sentence using a word that comes from the given Greek root.
- Have someone else read your sentence.
- Explain to this person how the meaning of your word relates to the meaning of the given Greek root.
- Explain how any affixes that are part of your word affect the word's meaning.

4. *chron*

   Sentence:

   > See below.

5. *sym*

   Sentence:

   > See below.

6. *graph*

   Sentence:

   > See below.

Additional Answers

1b. *Chronic* is the better choice because it describes something that happens all the time. *Chronological* describes something related to or happening in time order.

3b. *Graphic* is the better choice because the sentence suggests that the narrator sees an image on the television. A *biography* is a written work that tells the story of a person's life.

4. Students should have used *chronic* or *chronological* in their sentence, but may have also used words such as *synchronize* or *chronicle*. Encourage students to explain how the word they chose is related to the root *chron*, which means "time," as well as how any affixes they used – such as *-ic* (it turns the word into an adjective) or *-logical* (speak or tell) – affect the word's meaning.

5. Students should have used *symbol* or *symphony* in their sentence, but may have also used words such as *symmetry* or *sympathy* or *symptoms*. Encourage students to explain how the word they chose is related to the root *sym*, which means "together," as well as how any affixes they used – such as *-phony* (sound) – affect the word's meaning.

6. Students should have used *graphic* or *biography* in their sentence, but may have also used words such as *photograph* or *autograph* or *geographic*. Encourage students to explain how the word they chose is related to the root *graph*, which means "written" or "drawn," as well as how any affixes they used – such as *bio-* (life) – affect the word's meaning.

TRY IT   Go Write!

Students will write independently for pleasure. As they write, they should consider opportunities to use words with Greek roots and affixes.

TRY IT   Review Greek Roots and Affixes

Students will answer questions to review what they have learned about Greek roots and affixes.

QUIZ

Greek Roots and Affixes

Students will complete the Greek Roots and Affixes quiz.

WRAP-UP

Keyboarding

Students will practice their keyboarding skills using an external website or program.

More Language Arts Practice

Students will practice skills according to their individual needs.

Go Read!

Students will read for pleasure. They should choose a book or a magazine that interests them, or they may choose a selection from the digital library, linked in the online lesson.

Students should read for the entire time. Have students select something to read ahead of time to help them stay focused.

"Young Frederick Douglass"

Lesson Overview

ACTIVITY	ACTIVITY TITLE	TIME	ONLINE/OFFLINE
GET READY	Introduction to "Young Frederick Douglass"	**1** minute	🖥️
	Spelling List 14 Pretest **LEARNING COACH CHECK-IN**	**10** minutes	📶 and 📄
	Before You Read "Young Frederick Douglass"	**18** minutes	📶
READ	"Young Frederick Douglass: The Slave Who Learned to Read"	**30** minutes	📄
	Check-In: "Young Frederick Douglass"	**5** minutes	📶
LEARN AND **TRY IT**	More Than One Main Idea	**10** minutes	📶
	Practice Finding Multiple Main Ideas	**10** minutes	📶
	Apply: More Than One Main Idea	**15** minutes	📶
	Write About Multiple Main Ideas **LEARNING COACH CHECK-IN**	**10** minutes	📄
	Practice Words from "Young Frederick Douglass"	**8** minutes	📶
WRAP-UP	Questions About "Young Frederick Douglass"	**3** minutes	📶

Content Background

Students will complete a spelling activity and read "Young Frederick Douglass: The Slave Who Learned to Read" by Linda Walvoord Girard. They will then complete activities in which they learn about using key details to identify multiple main ideas within a single passage.

MATERIALS

Supplied
- *Summit English Language Arts 5 Expeditions in Reading*
- *Summit English Language Arts 5 Activity Book*
  - Spelling List 14 Pretest
  - Write About Multiple Main Ideas

"Young Frederick Douglass" Synopsis

As a young boy, Frederick Douglass goes to Baltimore to serve as a slave in the home of Hugh Auld and his wife, Sophia. Soon after, Sophia begins to teach both her son and Frederick how to read, but she is reprimanded by her husband, who tells her that teaching an enslaved person to read is illegal and can lead to trouble. Frederick overhears this, and he becomes determined to learn how to read and write. With much ingenuity and hard work, he becomes literate. Then, after several more years of cruelty and bondage, he escapes to the North. Once free, Douglass becomes a prominent abolitionist and a great orator who gives speeches against slavery. He publishes his autobiography, and he even meets with President Lincoln during the Civil War.

> **KEYWORDS**
>
> **main idea** – the most important point the author makes; it may be stated or unstated
>
> **supporting detail** – a detail that gives more information about a main idea

Lesson Goals

- Take a spelling pretest.

- Read "Young Frederick Douglass: The Slave Who Learned to Read" by Linda Walvoord Girard.

- Use supporting details to determine multiple main ideas.

- Write about main ideas in the text.

GET READY

Introduction to "Young Frederick Douglass"

Students will get a glimpse of what they will learn about in the lesson. They will also read the lesson goals and keywords. Have students select each keyword and preview its definition.

Spelling List 14 Pretest

Students will take a spelling pretest.

LEARNING COACH CHECK-IN Have students turn to Spelling List 14 Pretest in *Summit English Language Arts 5 Activity Book* and open the online Spelling Pretest activity. Online, students will listen to the spelling word, type the word in the space indicated, and then check their answer. In the activity book, students will write the correct spelling of the word in the tables provided and indicate with a ✓ or an ✗ if they spelled the word correctly or incorrectly online. Students will repeat this process with the remaining words.

As needed, help students with the interaction between the online activity and the activity book page until they become comfortable with what they need to do. As students practice their spelling words throughout the workshop, they should pay special attention to words they spelled incorrectly on the pretest.

This is the complete list of words students will be tested on.

Plural Words		
echoes	radios	loaves
heroes	studios	scarves
potatoes	videos	shelves
tomatoes	zoos	wives
vetoes	calves	wolves
patios	knives	

NOTE Have students keep their completed activity page in a safe place so they can refer to it later.

GET READY
"Young Frederick Douglass"

Spelling List 14 Pretest

1. Open the Spelling Pretest activity online. Listen to the first spelling word. Type the word. Check your answer.

2. Write the correct spelling of the word in the Word column of the Spelling Pretest table on the next page.

Word		
1 blindfold		

3. Put a check mark in the ✓ column if you spelled the word correctly online.

Word		
1 blindfold	✓	

Put an X in the ✗ column if you spelled the word incorrectly online.

Word		
1 blindfold		X

4. Repeat Steps 1–3 for the remaining words in the Spelling Pretest.

"YOUNG FREDERICK DOUGLASS" **237**

"Young Frederick Douglass"

Spelling List 14 Pretest

Write each spelling word in the Word column, making sure to spell it correctly.

	Word	✓	✗		Word	✓	✗
1	echoes			10	zoos		
2	heroes			11	calves		
3	potatoes			12	knives		
4	tomatoes			13	loaves		
5	vetoes			14	scarves		
6	patios			15	shelves		
7	radios			16	wives		
8	studios			17	wolves		
9	videos						

Students should use the ✓ and X columns to indicate whether they spelled each word correctly or incorrectly online.

238 "YOUNG FREDERICK DOUGLASS"

Before You Read "Young Frederick Douglass"

Students will be introduced to some key vocabulary words that they will encounter in the upcoming reading, learn some important historical background related to the reading, and answer a question to help them set a purpose for their reading.

READ

"Young Frederick Douglass: The Slave Who Learned to Read"

Students will read "Young Frederick Douglass: The Slave Who Learned to Read" by Linda Walvoord Girard in *Expeditions in Reading*.

Check-In: "Young Frederick Douglass"

Students will answer several questions to demonstrate their comprehension of "Young Frederick Douglass: The Slave Who Learned to Read."

LEARN AND TRY IT

LEARN   More Than One Main Idea

Students will learn how to use several key details within a single passage to determine multiple main ideas in that passage.

TRY IT   Practice Finding Multiple Main Ideas

Students will complete an activity designed to develop their ability to determine multiple main ideas in a single passage based on the key details that passage contains.

TRY IT   Apply: More Than One Main Idea

Students will apply to a new work what they've learned about using key details to determine multiple main ideas within a passage or section of the text.

TRY IT   Write About Multiple Main Ideas

Students will complete Write About Multiple Main Ideas from *Summit English Language Arts 5 Activity Book*. Students will read a passage from the text and use several key details within the passage to determine two of its main ideas.

LEARNING COACH CHECK-IN   This activity page contains open-ended questions, so it's important that you review students' responses. Give students feedback, using the sample answers provided to guide you.

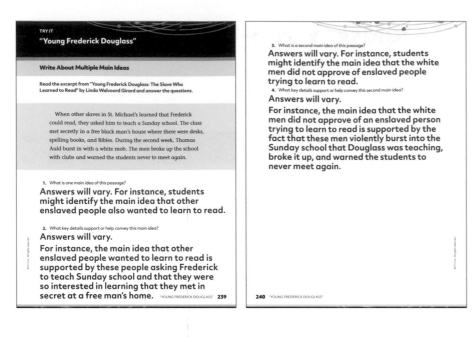

Write About Multiple Main Ideas

Read the excerpt from "Young Frederick Douglass: The Slave Who Learned to Read" by Linda Walvoord Girard and answer the questions.

> When other slaves in St. Michael's learned that Frederick could read, they asked him to teach a Sunday school. The class met secretly in a free black man's house where there were desks, spelling books, and Bibles. During the second week, Thomas Auld burst in with a white mob. The men broke up the school with clubs and warned the students never to meet again.

1. What is one main idea of this passage?

Answers will vary. For instance, students might identify the main idea that other enslaved people also wanted to learn to read.

2. What key details support or help convey this main idea?

Answers will vary.

For instance, the main idea that other enslaved people wanted to learn to read is supported by these people asking Frederick to teach Sunday school and that they were so interested in learning that they met in secret at a free man's home.   "YOUNG FREDERICK DOUGLASS" **239**

3. What is a second main idea of this passage?

Answers will vary. For instance, students might identify the main idea that the white men did not approve of enslaved people trying to learn to read.

4. What key details support or help convey this second main idea?

Answers will vary.

For instance, the main idea that the white men did not approve of an enslaved person trying to learn to read is supported by the fact that these men violently burst into the Sunday school that Douglass was teaching, broke it up, and warned the students to never meet again.

240 "YOUNG FREDERICK DOUGLASS"

TRY IT   Practice Words from "Young Frederick Douglass"

Students will answer questions to demonstrate their understanding of the vocabulary words from today's reading.

WRAP-UP

Questions About "Young Frederick Douglass"

Students will answer questions to show that they understand how to identify key details in a passage and determine multiple main ideas conveyed by the passage.

"Young Frederick Douglass" Wrap-Up

Lesson Overview

ACTIVITY	ACTIVITY TITLE	TIME	ONLINE/OFFLINE
GET READY	Introduction to "Young Frederick Douglass" Wrap-Up	**1** minute	🖥️
	Spelling List 14 Activity Bank **LEARNING COACH CHECK-IN**	**10** minutes	📄
TRY IT	Write About "Young Frederick Douglass" **LEARNING COACH CHECK-IN**	**30** minutes	📄
	Read and Record	**10** minutes	🖥️
	Review "Young Frederick Douglass"	**10** minutes	🖥️
QUIZ	"Young Frederick Douglass"	**30** minutes	🖥️
WRAP-UP	Keyboarding	**10** minutes	🖥️
	More Language Arts Practice	**19** minutes	🖥️

Advance Preparation

Gather students' completed Spelling List 14 Pretest activity page from "Young Frederick Douglass." Students will refer to this page during Spelling List 14 Activity Bank.

During the Keyboarding activity, students will practice their keyboarding skills using an external website or program. **You will need to work with students to select an appropriate keyboarding practice website or program; K12 does not specify which resource to use.** A few suggestions are provided in the online activity.

Depending on which program you choose, students may need to set up an account to save their progress. If needed, assist students in setting up and running their chosen keyboarding practice program.

MATERIALS

Supplied
- *Summit English Language Arts 5 Expeditions in Reading*
- *Summit English Language Arts 5 Activity Book*
  - Spelling List 14 Activity Bank
  - Write About "Young Frederick Douglass"

Also Needed
- completed Spelling List 14 Pretest activity page from "Young Frederick Douglass"

Lesson Goals

- Practice all spelling words offline.

- Summarize " Young Frederick Douglass: The Slave Who Learned to Read."

- Review using key details to determine multiple main ideas.

- Take a quiz on " Young Frederick Douglass: The Slave Who Learned to Read."

GET READY

Introduction to "Young Frederick Douglass"

Students will read the lesson goals.

Spelling List 13 Activity Bank

Students will practice all spelling words from the workshop by completing Spelling List 14 Activity Bank from *Summit English Language Arts 5 Activity Book*. Make sure students have their completed Spelling List 14 Pretest activity page from "Young Frederick Douglass" (A) to refer to during this activity.

Remind students to pay special attention to words they spelled incorrectly on the Spelling Pretest.

Write About "Young Frederick Douglass"

Students will complete Write About "Young Frederick Douglass" in *Summit English Language Arts 5 Activity Book* to write a brief summary of the text.

LEARNING COACH CHECK-IN This activity page contains an open-ended question, so it's important that you review students' responses. Give students feedback, using the sample answers provided to guide you.

Read and Record

Good readers read quickly, smoothly, and with expression. This is called *fluency*. Students will record themselves reading aloud. They will listen to their recording and think about how quick, smooth, and expressive they sound.

TIP Encourage students to rerecord as needed.

Review "Young Frederick Douglass"

Students will answer questions to review what they have learned about identifying key details and using them to determine multiple main ideas in a passage, as well as to demonstrate their understanding of Douglass as a person.

"Young Frederick Douglass"

Students will complete the "Young Frederick Douglass" quiz.

Keyboarding

Students will practice their keyboarding skills using an external website or program.

More Language Arts Practice

Students will practice skills according to their individual needs.

"The Most Famous Woman in America"

Lesson Overview

ACTIVITY	ACTIVITY TITLE	TIME	ONLINE/OFFLINE
GET READY	Introduction to "The Most Famous Woman in America"	**1** minute	online
	Spelling List 14 Review Game	**10** minutes	online
	Look Back at Fact vs. Opinion	**4** minutes	online
	Before You Read "The Most Famous Woman in America"	**15** minutes	online
READ	"The Most Famous Woman in America"	**30** minutes	offline
	Check-In: "The Most Famous Woman in America"	**5** minutes	online
LEARN AND **TRY IT**	Fact vs. Opinion	**10** minutes	online
	Fact or Opinion?	**10** minutes	online
	Apply: Fact vs. Opinion	**15** minutes	online
	Write About Facts and Opinions `LEARNING COACH CHECK-IN`	**10** minutes	offline
	Practice Words from "The Most Famous Woman in America"	**8** minutes	online
WRAP-UP	Questions About "The Most Famous Woman in America"	**2** minutes	online

Content Background

Students will complete a spelling activity and read "The Most Famous Woman in America" by Augusta Stevenson. They will then complete activities in which they learn about facts and opinions and how to distinguish between the two.

MATERIALS

Supplied
- *Summit English Language Arts 5 Expeditions in Reading*
- *Summit English Language Arts 5 Activity Book*
  - Write About Facts and Opinions

"The Most Famous Woman in America" Synopsis

In 1867, a large crowd gathers to hear Clara Barton deliver an address about the need to continue to care for veterans who were injured during the Civil War. The people in the audience take turns sharing what they know of Barton and their experiences with her. They speak of how she changed the way wounded soldiers were treated by moving medical supplies and professionals closer to the battlefields, and they speak about the courage Barton showed in coming to the front lines to rescue and care for soldiers who had been hurt. It is clear that Barton is deeply admired and beloved. Then the text jumps forward in time, to 1881, at another gathering at which Barton is going to speak. This time the occasion is the founding of the American Red Cross. The people in the crowd again describe the efforts that Barton made to establish the American Red Cross and the work that the organization will do, both for those injured in conflict and those affected by natural disasters such as floods, hurricanes, tornadoes, and earthquakes. As before, it is obvious that Barton's selfless efforts have won her the deep and lasting respect of everyone.

Lesson Goals

- Practice all spelling words online.

- Read "The Most Famous Woman in America" by Augusta Stevenson.

- Distinguish between facts and opinions in "The Most Famous Woman in America."

- Write about facts and opinions in "The Most Famous Woman in America."

GET READY

Introduction to "The Most Famous Woman in America"

Students will get a glimpse of what they will learn about in the lesson. They will also read the lesson goals and keywords. Have students select each keyword and preview its definition.

Spelling List 14 Review Game

Students will practice all spelling words from the workshop.

Look Back at Fact vs. Opinion

Students will practice the prerequisite skill of knowing the difference between facts and opinions.

Before You Read "The Most Famous Woman in America"

Students will be introduced to some key vocabulary words that they will encounter in the upcoming reading, learn some important biographical information about Clara Barton, and answer a question to help them set a purpose for their reading.

READ

"The Most Famous Woman in America"

Students will read "The Most Famous Woman in America" by Augusta Stevenson in *Expeditions in Reading*.

Check-In: "The Most Famous Woman in America"

Students will answer several questions to demonstrate their comprehension of "The Most Famous Woman in America."

LEARN AND TRY IT

LEARN   Fact vs. Opinion

Students will learn why writers of nonfiction texts include both facts and opinions in their work, as well as how to identify both and distinguish between the two.

TRY IT   Fact or Opinion?

Students will answer several questions online to develop their ability to distinguish between facts and opinions in "The Most Famous Woman in America."

TRY IT   Apply: Fact vs. Opinion

Students will apply to a new work what they've learned about distinguishing between facts and opinions.

TRY IT   Write About Facts and Opinions

Students will complete Write About Facts and Opinions from *Summit English Language Arts 5 Activity Book*. Students will read several lines from "The Most Famous Woman in America" and decide whether those lines state facts or express opinions. Then they will answer questions to explain their reasoning and to demonstrate their understanding of the text's main ideas.

LEARNING COACH CHECK-IN   This activity page contains open-ended questions, so it's important that you review students' responses. Give students feedback, using the sample answers provided to guide you.

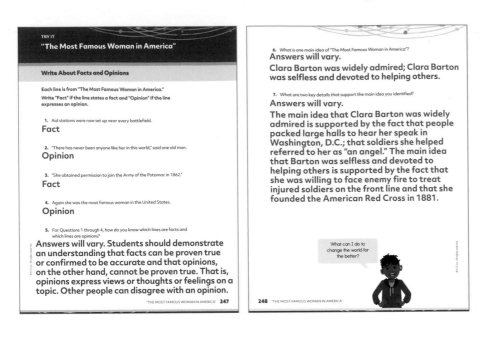

TRY IT

"The Most Famous Woman in America"

Write About Facts and Opinions

Each line is from "The Most Famous Woman in America."

Write "Fact" if the line states a fact and "Opinion" if the line expresses an opinion.

1. Aid stations were now set up near every battlefield.

Fact

2. "There has never been anyone like her in this world," said one old man.

Opinion

3. "She obtained permission to join the Army of the Potomac in 1862."

Fact

4. Again she was the most famous woman in the United States.

Opinion

5. For Questions 1 through 4, how do you know which lines are facts and which lines are opinions?

Answers will vary. Students should demonstrate an understanding that facts can be proven true or confirmed to be accurate and that opinions, on the other hand, cannot be proven true. That is, opinions express views or thoughts or feelings on a topic. Other people can disagree with an opinion.

"THE MOST FAMOUS WOMAN IN AMERICA" **247**

6. What is one main idea of "The Most Famous Woman in America"?

Answers will vary.

Clara Barton was widely admired; Clara Barton was selfless and devoted to helping others.

7. What are two key details that support the main idea you identified?

Answers will vary.

The main idea that Clara Barton was widely admired is supported by the fact that people packed large halls to hear her speak in Washington, D.C.; that soldiers she helped referred to her as "an angel." The main idea that Barton was selfless and devoted to helping others is supported by the fact that she was willing to face enemy fire to treat injured soldiers on the front line and that she founded the American Red Cross in 1881.

What can I do to change the world for the better?

248 "THE MOST FAMOUS WOMAN IN AMERICA"

TRY IT   Practice Words from "The Most Famous Woman in America"

Students will answer questions to demonstrate their understanding of the vocabulary words from the reading.

WRAP-UP

Questions About "The Most Famous Woman in America"

Students will answer questions to show that they understand how to distinguish between lines that state facts and lines that express opinions.

"The Most Famous Woman in America" Wrap-Up

Lesson Overview

ACTIVITY	ACTIVITY TITLE	TIME	ONLINE/OFFLINE
GET READY	Introduction to "The Most Famous Woman in America" Wrap-Up	**1** minute	🖥️
TRY IT	Write About "The Most Famous Woman in America" LEARNING COACH CHECK-IN	**30** minutes	📄
	Read and Record	**10** minutes	🖥️
	Review "The Most Famous Woman in America"	**20** minutes	🖥️
QUIZ	"The Most Famous Woman in America"	**30** minutes	🖥️
	Spelling List 14	**10** minutes	🖥️
WRAP-UP	Keyboarding	**10** minutes	🖥️
	More Language Arts Practice	**9** minutes	🖥️

Advance Preparation

During the Keyboarding activity, students will practice their keyboarding skills using an external website or program. **You will need to work with students to select an appropriate keyboarding practice website or program; K12 does not specify which resource to use.** A few suggestions are provided in the online activity.

Depending on which program you choose, students may need to set up an account to save their progress. If needed, assist students in setting up and running their chosen keyboarding practice program.

MATERIALS

Supplied
- *Summit English Language Arts Expeditions in Reading*
- *Summit English Language Arts 5 Activity Book*
  - Write About "The Most Famous Woman in America"

Lesson Goals

- Practice all spelling words offline.
- Write about "The Most Famous Woman in America."
- Review distinguishing between facts and opinions.
- Take a quiz on "The Most Famous Woman in America."
- Take a spelling quiz.

Introduction to "The Most Famous Woman in America" Wrap-Up
Students will read the lesson goals.

TRY IT

Write About "The Most Famous Woman in America"
Students will complete Write About "The Most Famous Woman in America" in *Summit English Language Arts 5 Activity Book* to write about Augusta Stevenson's text.

LEARNING COACH CHECK-IN   This activity page contains open-ended questions, so it's important that you review students' responses. Give students feedback, using the sample answers provided to guide you.

Read and Record
Good readers read quickly, smoothly, and with expression. This is called *fluency*. Students will record themselves reading aloud. They will listen to their recording and think about how quick, smooth, and expressive they sound.

TIP   Encourage students to rerecord as needed.

Review "The Most Famous Woman in America"
Students will answer questions to review what they have learned about distinguishing facts from opinions, identifying key details and main ideas, and demonstrating their comprehension of "The Most Famous Woman in America."

QUIZ

"The Most Famous Woman in America"

Students will complete the "The Most Famous Woman in America" quiz.

Spelling List 14

Students will complete the Spelling List 14 quiz.

WRAP-UP

Keyboarding

Students will practice their keyboarding skills using an external website or program.

More Language Arts Practice

Students will practice skills according to their individual needs.

Big Ideas: Respond to a Prompt

Lesson Overview

Big Ideas lessons provide students the opportunity to further apply the knowledge acquired and skills learned throughout the unit workshops. Each Big Ideas lesson consists of these parts:

1. **Cumulative Review:** Students keep their skills fresh by reviewing prior content.

2. **Preview:** Students practice answering the types of questions they will commonly find on standardized tests.

3. **Synthesis:** Students complete an assignment that allows them to connect and apply what they have learned. Synthesis assignments vary throughout the course.

   In the Synthesis portion of this Big Ideas lesson, students will respond to an essay prompt based on reading selections. To respond meaningfully, students will need to use their own ideas as well as examples from the readings. Students' writing will be assessed in four categories: purpose and content; structure and organization; language and word choice; and grammar, usage, and mechanics.

   LEARNING COACH CHECK-IN   This is a graded assessment. Make sure students complete, review, and submit the assignment to their teacher.

All materials needed for this lesson are linked online and not provided in the Activity Book.

MATERIALS

Supplied
- Respond to a Prompt (printout)

Persuasion
and
Opinion

Microscopes (A)

Lesson Overview

ACTIVITY	ACTIVITY TITLE	TIME	ONLINE/OFFLINE
GET READY	Persuasion and Opinion Unit Overview	**1** minute	🖥️
	Introduction to Microscopes (A)	**1** minute	🖥️
	Spelling List 15 Pretest **LEARNING COACH CHECK-IN**	**10** minutes	🖥️ and 📄
	Opinions in 60 Seconds	**1** minute	🖥️
	Look Back at Facts and Opinions	**4** minutes	🖥️
	Before You Read "Make Your Own Microscope"	**13** minutes	🖥️
READ	"Make Your Own Microscope"	**30** minutes	📄
	Check-In: "Make Your Own Microscope"	**5** minutes	🖥️
LEARN AND **TRY IT**	Point of View and Author's Beliefs	**10** minutes	🖥️
	Examine a Passage	**10** minutes	🖥️
	Apply: Point of View and Author's Beliefs in Another Work	**15** minutes	🖥️
	Write About the Author's Beliefs **LEARNING COACH CHECK-IN**	**10** minutes	📄
	Practice Words from "Make Your Own Microscope"	**8** minutes	🖥️
WRAP-UP	Questions About "Make Your Own Microscope"	**2** minutes	🖥️

Content Background

Students will complete a spelling activity and read an opinion piece called "Make Your Own Microscope" in *Expeditions in Reading*. They will then complete activities in which they learn about identifying the text's point of view and the writer's beliefs to understand how these elements influence or affect the text.

MATERIALS

Supplied
- *Summit English Language Arts 5 Expeditions in Reading*
- *Summit English Language Arts 5 Activity Book*
  - Spelling List 15 Pretest
  - Write About the Author's Beliefs

"Make Your Own Microscope" Synopsis

This opinion piece, written by an 11-year-old girl, describes her effort to turn her smartphone into a microscope after her little sister broke her microscope. The writer expresses and supports her opinion that creating a smartphone microscope is a worthwhile endeavor because it is inexpensive, educational, and results in a tool that is effective, easy to use, and portable.

KEYWORDS

fact – something that can be proven true

opinion – something that a person thinks or believes, but which cannot be proven to be true

Lesson Goals

- Take a spelling pretest.
- Read "Make Your Own Microscope."
- Explore the text's point of view, as well as the author's beliefs and how they are supported.

GET READY

Persuasion and Opinion Unit Overview

Students will read a summary of what they will learn in the Persuasion and Opinion unit.

Introduction to Microscopes (A)

Students will get a glimpse of what they will learn about in the lesson. They will also read the lesson goals and keywords. Have students select each keyword and preview its definition.

Spelling List 15 Pretest

Students will take a spelling pretest.

LEARNING COACH CHECK-IN   Have students turn to Spelling List 15 Pretest in *Summit English Language Arts 5 Activity Book* and open the online Spelling Pretest activity. Online, students will listen to the spelling word, type the word in the space indicated, and then check their answer. In the activity book, students will write the correct spelling of the word in the tables provided andindicate with a ✓ or an ✗ if they spelled the word correctly or incorrectly online. Students will repeat this process with the remaining words.

As needed, help students with the interaction between the online activity and the activity book page until they become comfortable with what they need to do. As students practice their spelling words throughout the workshop, they should pay special attention to words they spelled incorrectly on the pretest.

This is the complete list of words students will be tested on.

Adding –ed or –ing Suffix to Two-Syllable Words		
angered	suffering	rebelled
covering	concurred	referring
gathering	deferring	canceled
labeled	occurring	traveled
mattered	preferred	altering
sheltered	propelling	

NOTE   Have students keep their completed activity page in a safe place so they can refer to it later.

Opinions in 60 Seconds

Students will watch a short video designed to spark their interest in upcoming topics.

Look Back at Facts and Opinions

Students will practice the prerequisite skill of distinguishing between facts and opinions.

Before You Read "Make Your Own Microscope"

Students will be introduced to some key vocabulary words that they will encounter in the upcoming reading, learn about opinion pieces, and answer a question to help them set a purpose for their reading.

"Make Your Own Microscope"

Students will read an opinion piece called "Make Your Own Microscope" in *Expeditions in Reading*.

Check-In: "Make Your Own Microscope"

Students will answer several questions to demonstrate their comprehension of "Make Your Own Microscope."

LEARN AND TRY IT

LEARN   Point of View and Author's Beliefs

Students will learn how to examine a passage to determine the influence that point of view and the author's beliefs have on the text.

TRY IT   Examine a Passage

Students will complete an activity in which they explore a passage from "Make Your Own Microscope" to demonstrate their understanding of how point of view and the author's beliefs influence the text.

TRY IT   Apply: Point of View and Author's Beliefs in Another Work

Students will apply to a new work what they've learned about how point of view and the author's beliefs affect the text.

TRY IT   Write About the Author's Beliefs

Students will complete Write About the Author's Beliefs from *Summit English Language Arts 5 Activity Book*. They will read a passage from "Make Your Own Microscope," describe one of the beliefs the writer expresses, and explain how the details in the text help convey and support that belief.

> **LEARNING COACH CHECK-IN**   This activity page contains an open-ended question, so it's important that you review students' responses. Give students feedback, using the sample answer provided to guide you.

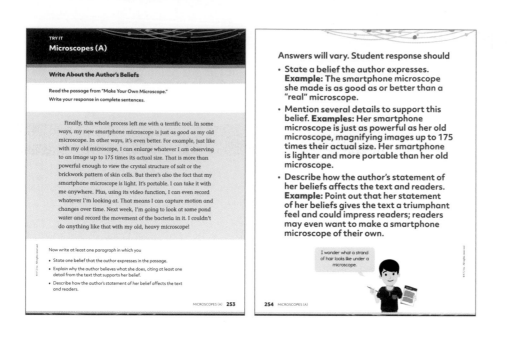

TRY IT   Practice Words from Make Your Own Microscope

Students will answer questions to demonstrate their understanding of the vocabulary words from the reading.

WRAP-UP

Questions About Make Your Own Microscope

Students will answer questions to show that they understand the reading.

Microscopes (B)

Lesson Overview

ACTIVITY	ACTIVITY TITLE	TIME	ONLINE/OFFLINE
GET READY	Introduction to Microscopes (B)	**1** minute	
	Spelling List 15 Activity Bank	**10** minutes	
	Recall "Make Your Own Microscope"	**4** minutes	
	Before You Read "Stick to Real Microscopes"	**15** minutes	
READ	"Stick to Real Microscopes"	**30** minutes	
	Check-In: "Stick to Real Microscopes"	**5** minutes	
LEARN AND **TRY IT**	How to Paraphrase	**10** minutes	
	Practice Paraphrasing	**10** minutes	
	Apply: Paraphrase Another Text	**15** minutes	
	Paraphrase a Passage **LEARNING COACH CHECK-IN**	**10** minutes	
	Practice Words from "Stick to Real Microscopes"	**8** minutes	
WRAP-UP	Questions About Paraphrasing	**2** minutes	

Content Background

Students will complete a spelling activity and read an opinion piece called "Stick to Real Microscopes" in *Expeditions in Reading*. They will then complete activities in which they learn about paraphrasing a text effectively.

Advance Preparation

Gather students' completed Spelling List 15 Pretest activity page from Microscopes (A). Students will refer to this page during Get Ready: Spelling List 15 Activity Bank.

MATERIALS

Supplied

- *Summit English Language Arts 5 Expeditions in Reading*
- *Summit English Language Arts 5 Activity Book*
  - Spelling List 15 Activity Bank
  - Paraphrase a Passage

Also Needed

- completed Spelling List 15 Pretest activity page from Microscopes (A)

"Stick to Real Microscopes" Synopsis

This opinion piece, a response to another piece that stated that turning a smartphone into a microscope was a good way to create an effective and useful tool, takes the opposing view. It argues that smartphone microscopes are neither cheap nor particularly effective as research tools. The writer provides facts and details to support his position throughout the text, continually insisting that "real" microscopes are better in virtually all ways.

Lesson Goals

- Practice all spelling words offline.
- Read "Stick to Real Microscopes."
- Learn how to paraphrase the text effectively.

GET READY

Introduction to Microscopes (B)

Students will get a glimpse of what they will learn about in the lesson. They will also read the lesson goals and keywords. Have students select each keyword and preview its definition.

Spelling List 15 Activity Bank

Students will practice all spelling words from the workshop by completing Spelling List 15 Activity Bank from *Summit English Language Arts 5 Activity Book*. Make sure students have their completed Spelling List 15 Pretest activity page from Microscopes (A) to refer to during this activity.

Remind students to pay special attention to words they spelled incorrectly on the Spelling Pretest.

Recall "Make Your Own Microscope"

Students will answer some questions to review the reading that they have already completed.

Before You Read "Stick to Real Microscopes"

Students will be introduced to some key vocabulary words that they will encounter in the upcoming reading, learn about ordering ideas in a text, and answer questions to help them set a purpose for their reading.

READ

"Stick to Real Microscopes"

Students will read an opinion piece in *Expeditions in Reading* called "Stick to Real Microscopes."

Check-In: "Stick to Real Microscopes"

Students will answer several questions to demonstrate their comprehension of "Stick to Real Microscopes."

LEARN AND TRY IT

LEARN   How to Paraphrase

Students will learn how to effectively paraphrase a text and how to touch on its most important points in the proper order while avoiding plagiarism.

TRY IT Practice Paraphrasing

Students will answer several questions online to develop their ability to paraphrase a passage.

TRY IT Apply: Paraphrase Another Text

Students will apply to a new work what they've learned about paraphrasing, expressing key ideas in their own words, and avoiding plagiarism.

TRY IT Paraphrase a Passage

Students will complete Paraphrase a Passage from *Summit English Language Arts 5 Activity Book*. Their paraphrase should cover—in order—the most important ideas in the passage provided, but should express those ideas in the students' own words.

LEARNING COACH CHECK-IN This activity page contains an open-ended question, so it's important that you review students' responses. Give students feedback, using the sample answer provided to guide you.

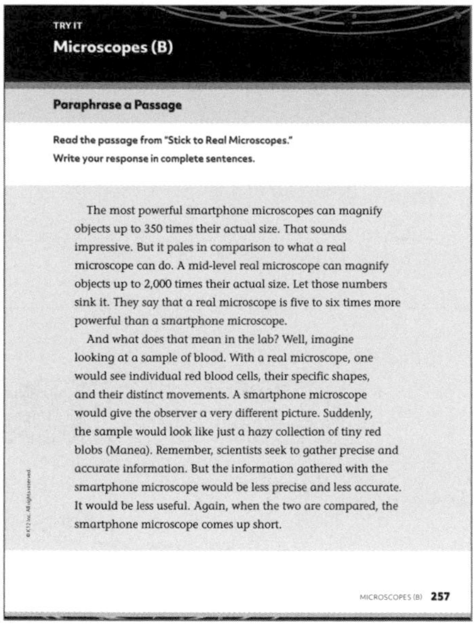

TRY IT

Microscopes (B)

Paraphrase a Passage

Read the passage from "Stick to Real Microscopes."
Write your response in complete sentences.

The most powerful smartphone microscopes can magnify objects up to 350 times their actual size. That sounds impressive. But it pales in comparison to what a real microscope can do. A mid-level real microscope can magnify objects up to 2,000 times their actual size. Let those numbers sink it. They say that a real microscope is five to six times more powerful than a smartphone microscope.

And what does that mean in the lab? Well, imagine looking at a sample of blood. With a real microscope, one would see individual red blood cells, their specific shapes, and their distinct movements. A smartphone microscope would give the observer a very different picture. Suddenly, the sample would look like just a hazy collection of tiny red blobs (Manea). Remember, scientists seek to gather precise and accurate information. But the information gathered with the smartphone microscope would be less precise and less accurate. It would be less useful. Again, when the two are compared, the smartphone microscope comes up short.

© K12 Inc. All rights reserved.

MICROSCOPES (B) 257

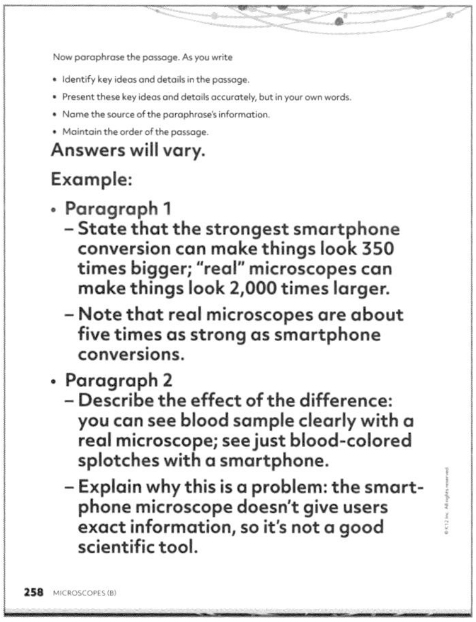

Now paraphrase the passage. As you write

- Identify key ideas and details in the passage.
- Present these key ideas and details accurately, but in your own words.
- Name the source of the paraphrase's information.
- Maintain the order of the passage.

Answers will vary.

Example:

- **Paragraph 1**
  - **State that the strongest smartphone conversion can make things look 350 times bigger; "real" microscopes can make things look 2,000 times larger.**
  - **Note that real microscopes are about five times as strong as smartphone conversions.**
- **Paragraph 2**
  - **Describe the effect of the difference: you can see blood sample clearly with a real microscope; see just blood-colored splotches with a smartphone.**
  - **Explain why this is a problem: the smart-phone microscope doesn't give users exact information, so it's not a good scientific tool.**

© K12 Inc. All rights reserved.

258 MICROSCOPES (B)

TRY IT Practice Words from "Stick to Real Microscopes"

Students will answer questions to demonstrate their understanding of the vocabulary words from the reading.

WRAP-UP

Questions About Paraphrasing

Students will answer questions to show that they understand the reading.

Microscopes (C)

Lesson Overview

ACTIVITY	ACTIVITY TITLE	TIME	ONLINE/OFFLINE
GET READY	Introduction to Microscopes (C)	**1** minute	🖥️
	Spelling List 15 Review Game	**10** minutes	🖥️
	Recall "Stick to Real Microscopes"	**5** minutes	🖥️
LEARN AND **TRY IT**	The Value of Differing Opinions	**10** minutes	🖥️
	Practice Treating Different Opinions Fairly	**10** minutes	🖥️
	Two Opinions About Microscopes	**15** minutes	🖥️
	Compare and Contrast Opinion Pieces	**15** minutes	🖥️
	Apply: Similarities and Differences	**30** minutes	🖥️
	Plan to Write About Microscopes **LEARNING COACH CHECK-IN**	**22** minutes	📄
WRAP-UP	Questions About Comparing and Contrasting	**2** minutes	🖥️

Content Background

Students will complete a spelling activity and learn about treating differing opinions fairly. They will then complete activities to compare and contrast the two opinion pieces about microscopes that they read in this workshop.

Lesson Goals

- Practice all spelling words online.

- Examine the importance of treating different viewpoints fairly.

- Compare and contrast opinion texts.

- Write about two texts, drawing information and ideas from each.

MATERIALS

Supplied
- *Summit English Language Arts 5 Expeditions in Reading*
- *Summit English Language Arts 5 Activity Book*
  - Plan to Write About Microscopes

KEYWORDS

paraphrase – to restate information in one's own words

summarize – to tell in order the most important ideas or events of a text

Introduction to Microscopes (C)

Students will get a glimpse of what they will learn about in the lesson. They will also read the lesson goals and keywords. Have students select each keyword and preview its definition.

Spelling List 15 Review Game

Students will practice all spelling words from the workshop.

Recall "Stick to Real Microscopes"

Students will answer some questions to review the reading that they have already completed.

LEARN   The Value of Differing Opinions

Students will learn about the importance of treating differing opinions fairly when attempting to fully understand a topic.

TRY IT   Practice Treating Different Opinions Fairly

Students will answer several questions to demonstrate their understanding of the importance of treating differing opinions fairly.

LEARN   Two Opinions About Microscopes

Students will learn about comparing and contrasting both the structure and content of texts by examining the similarities and differences between "Make Your Own Microscope" and "Stick to Real Microscopes."

TRY IT   Compare and Contrast Opinion Pieces

Students will explore several passages in "Make Your Own Microscope" and "Stick to Real Microscopes" to practice comparing and contrasting both the structure and content of the texts.

TRY IT   Apply: Similarities and Differences

Students will apply to a new work what they've learned about comparing and contrasting structures and content of texts.

TRY IT   Plan to Write About Microscopes

Students will complete Plan to Write About Microscopes from *Summit English Language Arts 5 Activity Book*. They should complete the graphic organizer by paraphrasing the important information from each text and noting the ways in which they are alike and different.

LEARNING COACH CHECK-IN This activity page contains an open-ended question, so it's important that you review students' responses. Give students feedback, using the sample answer provided to guide you. Note that students will use this page to complete their writing assignment in Microscopes Wrap-Up, so be sure that they keep their completed sheet in a safe place.

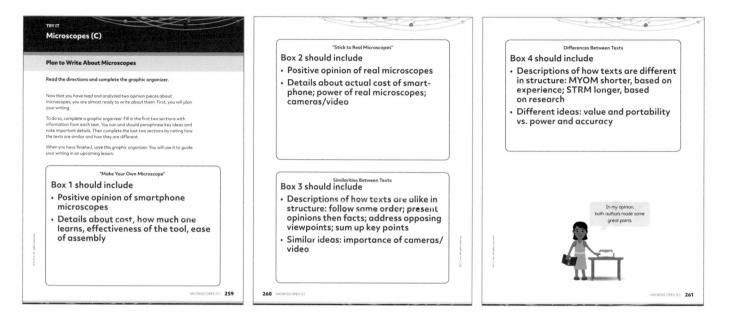

TRY IT
Microscopes (C)

Plan to Write About Microscopes

Read the directions and complete the graphic organizer.

Now that you have read and analyzed two opinion pieces about microscopes, you are almost ready to write about them. First, you will plan your writing.

To do so, complete a graphic organizer. Fill in the first two sections with information from each text. You can and should paraphrase key ideas and note important details. Then complete the last two sections by noting how the texts are similar and how they are different.

When you have finished, save this graphic organizer. You will use it to guide your writing in an upcoming lesson.

"Make Your Own Microscope"
Box 1 should include
- Positive opinion of smartphone microscopes
- Details about cost, how much one learns, effectiveness of the tool, ease of assembly

MICROSCOPES (C) **259**

"Stick to Real Microscopes"
Box 2 should include
- Positive opinion of real microscopes
- Details about actual cost of smartphone; power of real microscopes; cameras/video

Similarities Between Texts
Box 3 should include
- Descriptions of how texts are alike in structure: follow same order; present opinions then facts; address opposing viewpoints; sum up key points
- Similar ideas: importance of cameras/video

260 MICROSCOPES (C)

Differences Between Texts
Box 4 should include
- Descriptions of how texts are different in structure: MYOM shorter, based on experience; STRM longer, based on research
- Different ideas: value and portability vs. power and accuracy

In my opinion, both authors made some great points.

MICROSCOPES (C) **261**

WRAP-UP

Questions About Comparing and Contrasting

Students will answer questions to show that they understand the important concepts in this lesson.

Microscopes Wrap-Up

Lesson Overview

ACTIVITY	ACTIVITY TITLE	TIME	ONLINE/OFFLINE
GET READY	Introduction to Microscopes Wrap-Up	**1** minute	🖥️
TRY IT	Write About Microscopes **LEARNING COACH CHECK-IN**	**30** minutes	📄
	Read and Record	**10** minutes	🖥️
	Review Opinions About Microscopes	**20** minutes	🖥️
QUIZ	Microscopes	**30** minutes	🖥️
	Spelling List 15	**10** minutes	🖥️
WRAP-UP	Keyboarding	**10** minutes	🖥️
	More Language Arts Practice	**9** minutes	🖥️

Advance Preparation

Gather students' completed Plan to Write About Microscopes activity page from Microscopes (C). Students will refer to this page during Write About Microscopes.

During the Keyboarding activity, students will practice their keyboarding skills using an external website or program. **You will need to work with students to select an appropriate keyboarding practice website or program; K12 does not specify which resource to use.** A few suggestions are provided in the online activity.

Depending on which program you choose, students may need to set up an account to save their progress. If needed, assist students in setting up and running their chosen keyboarding practice program.

MATERIALS

Supplied
- *Summit English Language Arts 5 Activity Book*
  - Write About Microscopes

Also Needed
- completed Plan to Write About Microscopes activity page from Microscopes (C)

Lesson Goals

- Compare and contrast "Make Your Own Microscope" and "Stick to Real Microscopes."

- Review how point of view and author beliefs influence texts, as well as how to distinguish between facts and opinions.

- Explore main ideas and supporting details, as well as how to paraphrase and summarize texts.

- Take a quiz on this workshop's readings.

- Take a spelling quiz.

GET READY

Introduction to Microscopes Wrap-Up

Students will read the lesson goals.

TRY IT

TRY IT Write About Microscopes

Students will complete Write About Microscopes in *Summit English Language Arts 5 Activity Book* to compare and contrast "Make Your Own Microscope" and "Stick to Real Microscopes." Make sure students have their completed Plan to Write About Microscopes activity page from Microscopes (C) to refer to during this activity.

LEARNING COACH CHECK-IN This activity page contains an open-ended assignment, so it's important that you review students' responses. Give students feedback, using the sample response provided to guide you.

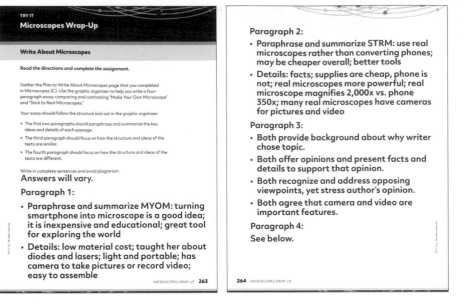

Additional answers

Paragraph 4:

- "Make Your Own Microscope" (MYOM) is shorter than "Stick to Real Microscopes" (STRM).

- MYOM has personal experience; STRM relies on research.

- MYOM focuses on low cost, portability, learning, camera; super-powerful magnification is not necessary.

- STRM focuses on true cost, need for more powerful magnification; portability not as important; both have cameras and video.

TRY IT   Read and Record

Good readers read quickly, smoothly, and with expression. This is called *fluency*. Students will record themselves reading aloud. They will listen to their recording and think about how quick, smooth, and expressive they sound.

TIP   Encourage students to rerecord as needed.

TRY IT   Review Opinions About Microscopes

Students will answer questions to review what they have learned about distinguishing between fact and opinion, recognizing the influence of point of view and an author's beliefs, identifying main ideas and supporting details, and paraphrasing texts. They will also show their understanding of the importance of treating different views fairly and demonstrate their overall comprehension of this workshop's readings.

QUIZ

Microscopes
Students will complete the Microscopes quiz.

Spelling List 15
Students will complete the Spelling List 15 quiz.

WRAP-UP

Keyboarding
Students will practice their keyboarding skills using an external website or program.

More Language Arts Practice
Students will practice skills according to their individual needs.

Latin Roots and Affixes

Lesson Overview

ACTIVITY	ACTIVITY TITLE	TIME	ONLINE/OFFLINE
GET READY	Introduction to Latin Roots and Affixes	**1** minute	🖥
	Look Back at Latin	**4** minutes	🖥
LEARN AND **TRY IT**	A Few Words Rooted in Latin	**10** minutes	🖥
	Figure Out Some Word Meanings	**10** minutes	🖥
	Apply: Practice Using Words with Latin Roots **LEARNING COACH CHECK-IN**	**15** minutes	📄
	Go Write!	**15** minutes	📄
	Review Latin Roots and Affixes	**15** minutes	🖥
QUIZ	Latin Roots and Affixes	**15** minutes	🖥
WRAP-UP	Keyboarding	**10** minutes	🖥
	More Language Arts Practice	**10** minutes	🖥
	Go Read!	**15** minutes	🖥 or 📄

Content Background

Students will learn about recognizing and understanding the meanings of words with Latin roots. The word list for this workshop contains words whose Latin roots are *struct* (build), *mal* (ill, bad), and *mut* (change).

Advance Preparation

During the Keyboarding activity, students will practice their keyboarding skills using an external website or program. **You will need to work with students to select an appropriate keyboarding practice website or program; K12 does not specify which resource to use.** A few suggestions are provided in the online activity.

Depending on which program you choose, students may need to set up an account to save their progress. If needed, assist students in setting up and running their chosen keyboarding practice program.

MATERIALS

Supplied

- *Summit English Language Arts 5 Activity Book*
  - Apply: Practice Using Words with Latin Roots

Also Needed

- reading material for Go Read!

During the Go Read! activity, students will have the option of using the digital library. Allow extra time for students to make their reading selection, or have students make a selection before beginning the lesson.

Lesson Goals

- Determine the meanings of words with Latin roots and affixes.

- Use context clues to help determine meaning of unknown words.

- Take a Latin Roots and Affixes quiz.

- Read for pleasure.

GET READY

Introduction to Latin Roots and Affixes

Students will get a glimpse of what they will learn about in the lesson. They will also read the lesson goals and keywords. Have students select each keyword and preview its definition.

Look Back at Latin

Students will review the importance of using context clues to help them determine the meanings of unfamiliar words and be reminded that many words in English have their roots in Latin.

LEARN AND TRY IT

LEARN   A Few Words Rooted in Latin

Students will learn some common Latin roots and explore how using their knowledge of these roots and context clues can help them unlock the meanings of unfamiliar words.

TRY IT   Figure Out Some Word Meanings

Students will practice recognizing common Latin roots and use their knowledge of those roots and context clues to help them determine the meanings of words.

TRY IT   Apply: Practice Using Words with Latin Roots

Students will complete Apply: Practice Using Words with Latin Roots from *Summit English Language Arts 5 Activity Book*.

LEARNING COACH CHECK-IN   This activity page contains open-ended questions, so it's important that you review students' responses. Give students feedback, using the sample answers provided to guide you.

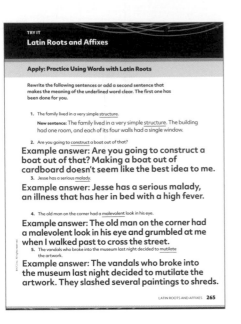

TRY IT Go Write!

Students will write independently for pleasure. As they write, they should think about using words with Latin roots in their writing.

TRY IT Review Latin Roots and Affixes

Students will answer questions to review what they have learned about words with Latin roots.

QUIZ

Latin Roots and Affixes

Students will complete the Latin Roots and Affixes quiz.

WRAP-UP

Keyboarding

Students will practice their keyboarding skills using an external website or program.

More Language Arts Practice

Students will practice skills according to their individual needs.

Go Read!

Students will read for pleasure. They should choose a book or a magazine that interests them, or they may choose a selection from the digital library, linked in the online lesson.

Students should read for the entire time. Have students select something to read ahead of time to help them stay focused.

Opinion Writing Skills (A)

Lesson Overview

ACTIVITY	ACTIVITY TITLE	TIME	ONLINE/OFFLINE
GET READY	Introduction to Opinion Writing Skills (A)	**2** minutes	🖥️
	Spelling List 16 Pretest **LEARNING COACH CHECK-IN**	**10** minutes	🖥️ and 📄
	Look Back at Lists	**5** minutes	🖥️
LEARN AND **TRY IT**	Items in a Series	**15** minutes	🖥️
	Punctuate Items in a Series	**15** minutes	📄
	Explore the Writing in "Make Your Own Microscope"	**15** minutes	🖥️
	Analyze the Writing in "Stick to Real Microscopes"	**15** minutes	🖥️
	Begin Your Opinion Piece **LEARNING COACH CHECK-IN**	**20** minutes	📄
WRAP-UP	Questions About Punctuating Lists and Introductions	**3** minutes	🖥️
	Go Read!	**20** minutes	🖥️ or 📄

Content Background

Your opinion is what your think or feel about something. One way we can share our opinions with others is by writing about them. This type of writing is called *opinion writing*. Students will analyze how authors write opinion pieces and then apply those skills to their own opinion writing. In this lesson, students will focus on the introduction and organization of an opinion piece.

Grammar, Usage, and Mechanics   Students will learn to use commas to separate items in a series of three or more items.

While some grammarians debate whether it's necessary, students will learn to always use a comma before the conjunction in a list. The comma before the conjunction in a series is known as the serial comma. In the example, the serial comma provides clarity. Without the comma, readers may wonder if both the flowers *and* the pinecones are purple.

> **Example:** We found pebbles, purple flowers**,** and pinecones on our walk.

MATERIALS

Supplied
- *Summit English Language Arts 5 Expeditions in Reading*
- *Summit English Language Arts 5 Activity Book*
  - Spelling List 16 Pretest
  - Begin Your Opinion Piece

Also Needed
- reading material for Go Read!

Advance Preparation

During the Go Read! activity, students will have the option of using the digital library. Allow extra time for students to make their reading selection, or have students make a selection before beginning the lesson.

Lesson Goals

- Take a spelling pretest.

- Use commas to separate items in a series.

- Explore how an author writes the introduction to and organizes an opinion piece.

- Begin writing your own opinion piece.

- Read for pleasure.

GET READY

Introduction to Opinion Writing Skills (A)

Students will get a glimpse of what they will learn about in the lesson. They will also read the lesson goals and keywords. Have students select each keyword and preview its definition.

Spelling List 16 Pretest

Students will take a spelling pretest.

LEARNING COACH CHECK-IN Have students turn to Spelling List 16 Pretest in *Summit English Language Arts 5 Activity Book* and open the online Spelling Pretest activity. Online, students will listen to the spelling word, type the word in the space indicated, and then check their answer. In the activity book, students will write the correct spelling of the word in the tables provided and indicate with a ✓ or an ✗ if they spelled the word correctly or incorrectly online. Students will repeat this process with the remaining words.

As needed, help students with the interaction between the online activity and the activity book page until they become comfortable with what they need to do. As students practice their spelling words throughout the workshop, they should pay special attention to words they spelled incorrectly on the pretest.

This is the complete list of words students will be tested on.

Words Ending with –*sion*	Root *cline*
supervision	decline
television	incline
pretension	recline
confession	
depression	
discussion	
inclusion	
impression	
revision	
transfusion	
possession	
profession	
progression	
division	

NOTE Have students keep their completed activity page in a safe place so they can refer to it later.

Look Back at Lists

Students will practice the prerequisite skill of correctly using a comma between items in a list.

LEARN   Items in a Series

Students will learn to correctly use a comma between items in a series.

TIP   The terms *series* and *list* have the same meaning. Students should be familiar with both terms.

TRY IT   Punctuate Items in a Series

Students will answer questions about using a comma between items in a series. They will receive feedback on their answers.

LEARN   Explore the Writing in "Make Your Own Microscope"

Students will learn what opinion writing is and that a successful opinion piece begins with a strong introduction. They will also briefly explore how opinion writing is organized.

TRY IT   Analyze the Writing in "Stick to Real Microscopes"

Students will answer questions about how a writer introduces and organizes an opinion piece. They will receive feedback on their answers.

TRY IT   Begin Your Opinion Piece

Students will complete Begin Your Opinion Piece in *Summit English Language Arts 5 Activity Book*.

TIP   Students are not expected to do research for this writing assignment. Encourage students to choose a topic about which they are knowledgeable.

LEARNING COACH CHECK-IN   This activity page contains open-ended questions, so it's important that you review students' responses. Give students feedback, using the sample answers provided to guide you.

NOTE   Have students keep their completed activity page in a safe place so they can refer to it later.

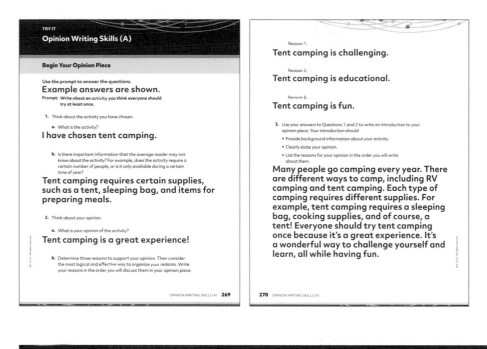

Questions About Punctuating Lists and Introductions

Students will answer questions to show that they understand how to use a comma between items in a list and the elements of an introduction to an opinion piece.

Go Read!

Students will read for pleasure. They should choose a book or a magazine that interests them, or they may choose a selection from the digital library, linked in the online lesson.

Students should read for the entire time. Have students select something to read ahead of time to help them stay focused.

Opinion Writing Skills (B)

Lesson Overview

ACTIVITY	ACTIVITY TITLE	TIME	ONLINE/OFFLINE
GET READY	Introduction to Opinion Writing Skills (B)	**2** minutes	🖥️
	Spelling List 16 Activity Bank	**10** minutes	📄
LEARN AND **TRY IT**	Introductory Elements	**10** minutes	🖥️
	Punctuate Introductory Elements	**10** minutes	🖥️
	Reasons and Evidence in "Make Your Own Microscope"	**15** minutes	🖥️
	Reasons and Evidence in "Stick to Real Microscopes"	**15** minutes	🖥️
	Order Reasons and Provide Evidence **LEARNING COACH CHECK-IN**	**30** minutes	📄
WRAP-UP	Questions About Commas and Evidence	**3** minutes	📄
	Go Read!	**25** minutes	🖥️ or 📄

Content Background

Students will continue analyzing how authors write opinion pieces and applying those skills to their own opinion writing. In this lesson, students will focus on supporting reasons for their opinions with facts and details.

Grammar, Usage, and Mechanics   An introductory element is a word, phrase, or clause that comes before the main clause of a sentence. Students will learn to use a comma after an introductory element.

> **Examples:** First**,** I wrote a poem.
>
> At the end of the poem**,** I drew a picture.
>
> When I finished my project**,** I was very satisfied with my work.

Advance Preparation

Gather students' completed Spelling List 16 Pretest activity page from Opinion Writing Skills (A). Students will refer to this page during Get Ready: Spelling List 16 Activity Bank.

MATERIALS

Supplied

- *Summit English Language Arts 5 Expeditions in Reading*
- *Summit English Language Arts 5 Activity Book*
  - Spelling List 16 Activity Bank
  - Order Reasons and Provide Evidence

Also Needed

- completed Spelling List 16 Pretest and Begin Your Opinion Piece activity pages from Opinion Writing Skills (A)
- reading material for Go Read!

Gather students' completed Begin Your Opinion Piece activity page from Opinion Writing Skills (A). Students will refer to this page during Order Reasons and Provide Evidence.

During the Go Read! activity, students will have the option of using the digital library. Allow extra time for students to make their reading selection, or have students make a selection before beginning the lesson.

Lesson Goals

- Practice all spelling words offline.
- Learn to use a comma after an introductory element.
- Explore how an author supports reasons for opinions with facts and details.
- Support reasons with facts and details in your opinion piece.
- Read for pleasure.

GET READY

Introduction to Opinion Writing Skills (B)

Students will get a glimpse of what they will learn about in the lesson. They will also read the lesson goals and keywords. Have students select each keyword and preview its definition.

Spelling List 16 Activity Bank

Students will practice all spelling words from the workshop by completing Spelling List 16 Activity Bank from *Summit English Language Arts 5 Activity Book*. Make sure students have their completed Spelling List 16 Pretest activity page from Opinion Writing Skills (A) to refer to during this activity.

Remind students to pay special attention to words they spelled incorrectly on the Spelling Pretest.

Opinion Writing Skills (B)

Spelling List 16 Activity Bank

Circle any words in the box that you did not spell correctly on the pretest. Using your circled words, complete one activity of your choice. Complete as much of the activity as you can in the time given.

If you spelled all words correctly on the pretest, complete your chosen activity with as many spelling words as you can.

supervision	depression	revision	profession	decline
television	discussion	transfusion	progression	incline
pretension	inclusion	possession	division	recline
confession	impression			

Spelling Activity Choices

Create a Crossword

1. Write a word from your spelling word list in the center of the grid paper.
2. Write another spelling word going across and sharing a letter with the first word. See how many words you can connect.

Example:

```
        p
      k i s s e s
    d   n
  r o c k s
    g
    s
```

Word Search Puzzle

1. Draw a box on the grid paper. The box should be large enough to hold your words from the spelling word list.
2. Fill in the grid paper with words from your spelling list, writing them horizontally, vertically, and diagonally (forward and backward if you choose).
3. Fill in the rest of the box with random letters.
4. Ask someone to find and circle your spelling words in the puzzle you made.

Complete the activity that you chose.

My chosen activity:

Students should use this page to complete all steps in their chosen activity.

LEARN AND TRY IT

LEARN Introductory Elements

Students will learn to use a comma to separate an introductory word, phrase, or clause from the rest of a sentence.

TRY IT Punctuate Introductory Elements

Students will answer questions about using a comma to separate an introductory word, phrase, or clause from the rest of a sentence. They will receive feedback on their answers.

LEARN Reasons and Evidence in "Make Your Own Microscope"

Students will learn how a writer supports opinions and reasons with facts and details in an opinion piece.

TIP   A fact is a true statement that can be proven. A detail may or may not be a fact. It may be an example, definition, or other piece of information that provides clarity.

Fact: Tomatoes grow best in sunny locations.

Detail: Our vegetables—especially our tomatoes—are growing really well because we planted our garden in the brightest part of our yard.

TRY IT Reasons and Evidence in "Stick to Real Microscopes"

Students will answer questions about how writers support reasons for their opinions with facts and details in an opinion piece. They will receive feedback on their answers.

TRY IT   Order Reasons and Provide Evidence

Students will complete Order Reasons and Provide Evidence from *Summit English Language Arts 5 Activity Book*. Make sure students have their completed Begin Your Opinion Piece activity page from Opinion Writing Skills (A) to refer to during this activity.

LEARNING COACH CHECK-IN   This activity page contains open-ended questions, so it's important that you review students' responses. Give students feedback, using the sample answers provided to guide you.

SUPPORT   If students have difficulty determining the best way to order their reasons, ask them questions to guide their thinking:

- Is there a time order to your reasons?
- Do any of your reasons give information that will help readers understand the other reasons?
- Is there a reason that will draw readers in?
- Is there a reason that you want to save until the end because you feel it will make your piece memorable?

Additional answers

Reason 2, supporting facts:

- Campers learn from the challenges. Each challenge conquered is a lesson that makes the next camping trip a little easier.
- Campers learn about nature. What they learn depends on the location and time of year, so each camping trip is a chance to learn something new.
- Campers learn about the wildlife around their campsite.

Reason 3, supporting facts:

- The challenges and learning are part of what makes camping fun.
- Camping activities, such as hiking, swimming, canoeing, and spending all day outdoors, are fun ways to spend time while camping.

Questions About Commas and Evidence

Students will answer questions to show that they understand how to use a comma to set off an introductory element and how to support reasons in opinion writing.

Go Read!

Students will read for pleasure. They should choose a book or a magazine that interests them, or they may choose a selection from the digital library, linked in the online lesson.

Students should read for the entire time. Have students select something to read ahead of time to help them stay focused.

Opinion Writing Skills (C)

Lesson Overview

ACTIVITY	ACTIVITY TITLE	TIME	ONLINE/OFFLINE
GET READY	Introduction to Opinion Writing Skills (C)	**2** minute	🛜
	Spelling List 16 Review Game	**10** minutes	🖥
	A Second Language	**15** minutes	🖥
LEARN AND **TRY IT**	The Language and Conclusion of "Make Your Own Microscope"	**15** minutes	🛜
	The Language and Conclusion of "Stick to Real Microscopes"	**15** minutes	🛜
	Link Ideas and Conclude Your Opinion Piece **LEARNING COACH CHECK-IN**	**30** minutes	📄
WRAP-UP	Questions About Linking Opinions and Reasons	**3** minutes	🖥
	Go Read!	**30** minutes	🛜 or 📄

Content Background

Students will continue analyzing how authors write opinion pieces and applying those skills to their own opinion writing. In this lesson, students will focus on using transitions and writing a conclusion.

Advance Preparation

Gather students' completed Begin Your Opinion Piece activity page from Opinion Writing Skills (A) and Order Reasons and Provide Evidence activity page from Opinion Writing Skills (B). Students will refer to these pages during Link Ideas and Conclude Your Opinion Piece.

During the Go Read! activity, students will have the option of using the digital library. Allow extra time for students to make their reading selection, or have students make a selection before beginning the lesson.

MATERIALS

Supplied

- *Summit English Language Arts 5 Expeditions in Reading*
- *Summit English Language Arts 5 Activity Book*
  - Link Ideas and Conclude Your Opinion Piece

Also Needed

- completed Begin Your Opinion Piece activity page from Opinion Writing Skills (A)
- completed Order Reasons and Provide Evidence activity page from Opinion Writing Skills (B)
- reading material for Go Read!

Lesson Goals

- Practice all spelling words online.
- Practice grammar skills by editing a passage.
- Explore how an author uses transitions and writes a conclusion in an opinion piece.
- Add transitions to your opinion piece, and write a conclusion.
- Read for pleasure.

GET READY

Introduction to Opinion Writing Skills (C)

Students will get a glimpse of what they will learn about in the lesson. They will also read the lesson goals and keywords. Have students select each keyword and preview its definition.

Spelling List 16 Review Game

Students will practice all spelling words from the workshop.

A Second Language

Students will edit a short passage to practice applying grammar skills. This passage contains errors and opportunities to improve the writing related to comma usage as well as to frequently confused words.

LEARN AND TRY IT

LEARN   The Language and Conclusion of "Make Your Own Microscope"

Students will learn how a writer uses transitions to connect ideas in an opinion piece. They will also learn how a writer concludes an opinion piece.

TIP   This table shows some purposes that transitions serve in opinion writing and examples of transitions for each purpose.

Purpose	Examples
Introduce opinion	*in my opinion*
Show order or importance of reasons	*first, next, additionally, finally*
Call out facts and details	*for example, in fact, consequently, specifically*
Conclude the piece	*in conclusion, to sum it up*

TRY IT The Language and Conclusion of "Stick to Real Microscopes"

Students will answer questions about how writers use transitions to connect ideas and write a conclusion in an opinion piece. They will receive feedback on their answers.

TRY IT Link Ideas and Conclude Your Opinion Piece

Students will complete Link Ideas and Conclude Your Opinion Piece from *Summit English Language Arts 5 Activity Book*. Make sure students have their completed Begin Your Opinion Piece activity page from Opinion Writing Skills (A) and Order Reasons and Provide Evidence activity page from Opinion Writing Skills (B) to refer to during this activity.

LEARNING COACH CHECK-IN   This activity page contains open-ended questions, so it's important that you review students' responses. Give students feedback, using the sample answers provided to guide you.

TRY IT
Opinion Writing Skills (C)
 	
Link Ideas and Conclude Your Opinion Piece
 	
Use the prompt to answer the questions.
Example answers are shown.
Prompt: **Write about an activity you think everyone should try at least once.**
 	
1. Write one body paragraph of your opinion piece.
 	
   a. Write a topic sentence that states your first reason. Begin the sentence with a transition that connects that reason to your opinion. Underline the transition.
 	
   <u>The first thing</u> that makes tent camping great is how challenging it is.
 	
   b. Write the remainder of that paragraph by supporting your reason with facts and details. Use at least one transition to connect your ideas. Underline the transitions.
 	
        See below.
 	
OPINION WRITING SKILLS (C) **277**
	2. Write the conclusion to your opinion piece.
	   • Start with a transition, such as "To sum it up," "In conclusion," "All in all," or "As you can see."
	   • State your opinion in words that are different from what you wrote in your introduction.
	   • Briefly restate the reasons for your opinion.
	   • Include any additional thoughts you have about the topic.
	
	All in all, tent camping is a wonderful activity that everyone should try at least once. It's a challenging, educational, and fun experience. And, no two camping trips are the same. There's always something new to learn or different ways to have fun. Anyone who misses out on tent camping is missing out on a great time!
	
	278 OPINION WRITING SKILLS (C)

Additional answer

1b. From the time you arrive until the time you leave your campsite, you will face challenges. <u>For example</u>, setting up a tent can be difficult, especially if it's your first time. Campfires are another challenge. You have to collect enough dry wood to burn for hours. <u>Then</u> you have to tend to the fire to make sure it doesn't burn out too quickly. All of that takes patience. And if those challenges have built up your appetite, don't expect a quick, easy meal. Cooking all your meals over a campfire or on a small camp stove is definitely more challenging than grabbing a quick bite at home. <u>Unlike cooking at home</u>, cooking while camping takes careful planning before arriving at the campsite and good organization during your stay.

Question About Linking Opinions and Reasons

Students will answer a question to show that they understand how to effectively use transitions in opinion writing.

Go Read!

Students will read for pleasure. They should choose a book or a magazine that interests them, or they may choose a selection from the digital library, linked in the online lesson.

Students should read for the entire time. Have students select something to read ahead of time to help them stay focused.

Opinion Writing Skills Wrap-Up

Lesson Overview

ACTIVITY	ACTIVITY TITLE	TIME	ONLINE/OFFLINE
GET READY	Introduction to Opinion Writing Skills Wrap-Up	**1** minute	🖥️
TRY IT	Use Opinion Writing Skills LEARNING COACH CHECK-IN	**30** minutes	📄
	Review Commas in Lists and After Introductory Elements	**20** minutes	🖥️
QUIZ	Commas and Opinion Writing Skills	**30** minutes	🖥️
	Spelling List 16	**10** minutes	🖥️
WRAP-UP	Keyboarding	**10** minutes	🖥️
	More Language Arts Practice	**19** minutes	🖥️

Advance Preparation

During the Keyboarding activity, students will practice their keyboarding skills using an external website or program. **You will need to work with students to select an appropriate keyboarding practice website or program; K12 does not specify which resource to use.** A few suggestions are provided in the online activity.

Depending on which program you choose, students may need to set up an account to save their progress. If needed, assist students in setting up and running their chosen keyboarding practice program.

MATERIALS

Supplied
- *Summit English Language Arts 5 Activity Book*
- Use Opinion Writing Skills

Lesson Goals

- Review opinion writing skills and how to use commas with lists and introductory elements.
- Take a quiz on commas and opinion writing skills.
- Take a spelling quiz.

Introduction to Opinion Writing Skills Wrap-Up

Students will read the lesson goals.

Use Opinion Writing Skills

Students will complete Use Opinion Writing Skills from *Summit English Language Arts 5 Activity Book* to review the writing objectives that will be assessed on the quiz.

LEARNING COACH CHECK-IN   This activity page contains open-ended questions, so it's important that you review students' responses. Give students feedback, using the sample answers provided to guide you.

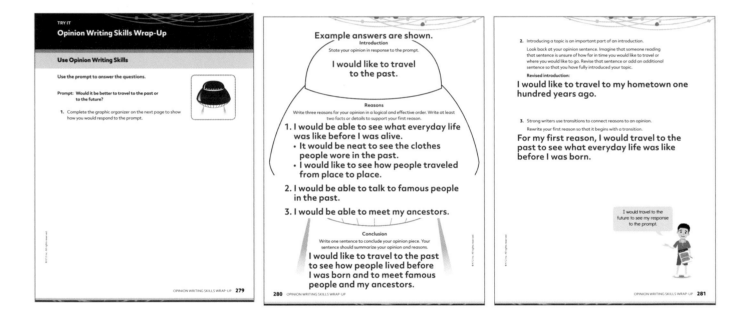

Review Commas in Lists and After Introductory Elements

Students will answer questions to show that they understand how to use commas in lists and after introductory elements.

QUIZ

Commas and Opinion Writing Skills

Students will complete the Commas and Opinion Writing Skills quiz.

Spelling List 16

Students will complete the Spelling List 16 quiz.

WRAP-UP

Keyboarding

Students will practice their keyboarding skills using an external website or program.

More Language Arts Practice

Students will practice skills according to their individual needs.

Solar Power (A)

Lesson Overview

ACTIVITY	ACTIVITY TITLE	TIME	ONLINE/OFFLINE
GET READY	Introduction to Solar Power (A)	**1** minute	🖥️
	Spelling List 17 Pretest **LEARNING COACH CHECK-IN**	**10** minutes	🖥️ and 📄
	Before You Read "Solar Power for Public Buildings	**14** minutes	🖥️
READ	"Solar Power for Public Buildings"	**30** minutes	📄
	Check-In: "Solar Power for Public Buildings"	**5** minutes	🖥️
LEARN AND **TRY IT**	How Writers Persuade Readers	**12** minutes	🖥️
	Analyze a Persuasive Piece	**12** minutes	🖥️
	Apply: Persuasion	**15** minutes	🖥️
	Write About a Persuasive Passage **LEARNING COACH CHECK-IN**	**10** minutes	📄
	Practice Words from "Solar Power for Public Buildings"	**8** minutes	🖥️
WRAP-UP	Questions About "Solar Power for Public Buildings"	**2** minutes	🖥️

Content Background

Students will complete a spelling activity and read a persuasive essay in *Expeditions in Reading* called "Solar Power for Public Buildings." They will then complete activities in which they learn about identifying the writer's position and the ways in which the writer presents ideas to convince readers to agree with that position.

> ### "Solar Power for Public Buildings" Synopsis
>
> This persuasive essay explains why the writer believes that California should lead the way in relying on solar energy. She states that California should take steps to ensure that all its public buildings will rely on solar power. The writer asserts that doing so will be good for the state's economy, its environment, and its people. The essay provides details and facts and reasons to support this position.

MATERIALS

Supplied
- *Summit English Language Arts 5 Expeditions in Reading*
- *Summit English Language Arts 5 Activity Book*
  - Spelling List 17 Pretest
  - Write About a Persuasive Passage

Lesson Goals

- Take a spelling pretest.
- Read "Solar Power for Public Buildings."
- Explore the text's main ideas and details, as well as the author's viewpoint and the relationship among her ideas.
- Distinguish between facts and opinions in the text.

GET READY

Introduction to Solar Power (A)

Students will get a glimpse of what they will learn about in the lesson. They will also read the lesson goals and keywords. Have students select each keyword and preview its definition.

Spelling List 17 Pretest

Students will take a spelling pretest.

LEARNING COACH CHECK-IN   Have students turn to Spelling List 17 Pretest in *Summit English Language Arts 5 Activity Book* and open the online Spelling Pretest activity. Online, students will listen to the spelling word, type the word in the space indicated, and then check their answer. In the activity book, students will write the correct spelling of the word in the tables provided and indicate with a ✓ or an ✗ if they spelled the word correctly or incorrectly online. Students will repeat this process with the remaining words.

As needed, help students with the interaction between the online activity and the activity book page until they become comfortable with what they need to do. As students practice their spelling words throughout the workshop, they should pay special attention to words they spelled incorrectly on the pretest.

This is the complete list of words students will be tested on.

Abbreviations	
hour; hr.	incorporated; inc.
month; mo.	number; no.
year; yr.	numbers; nos.
company; co.	
department; dept.	
government; govt.	

NOTE   Have students keep their completed activity page in a safe place so they can refer to it later.

Before You Read "Solar Power for Public Buildings"

Students will be introduced to some key vocabulary words that they will encounter in the upcoming reading, learn about why it's important to read persuasive essays, and answer a question to help them set a purpose for their reading.

READ

"Solar Power for Public Buildings"

Students will read a persuasive essay in *Expeditions in Reading* called "Solar Power for Public Buildings."

Check-In: "Solar Power for Public Buildings"

Students will answer several questions to demonstrate their comprehension of "Solar Power for Public Buildings."

LEARN AND TRY IT

LEARN   How Writers Persuade Readers

Students will learn how to examine a passage to determine a writer's position and explore some of the methods he or she uses to convince readers to agree with that position.

TRY IT   Analyze a Persuasive Piece

Students will complete an activity in which they explore a passage from "Solar Power for Public Buildings," recognizing the writer's position and examining the different methods she uses to convince readers to agree with that position.

TRY IT   Apply: Persuasion

Students will apply to a new work what they've learned about the ways in which the writer attempts to sway or convince readers to agree with a particular stance or position.

TRY IT   Write About a Persuasive Passage

Students will complete Write About a Persuasive Passage from *Summit English Language Arts 5 Activity Book*. They will read a short passage and identify the writer's position before explaining how he presents ideas to convince readers to agree with that position.

LEARNING COACH CHECK-IN   This activity page contains an open-ended question, so it's important that you review students' responses. Give students feedback, using the sample answer provided to guide you.

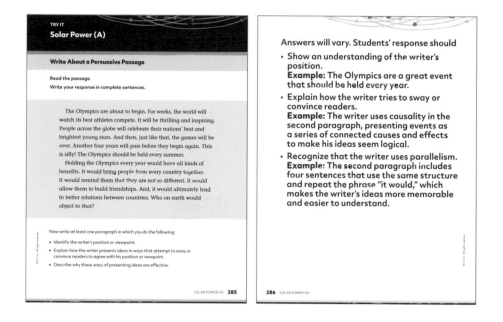

TRY IT   Practice Words from "Solar Power for Public Buildings"

Students will answer questions to demonstrate their understanding of the vocabulary words from today's reading.

WRAP-UP

Questions About "Solar Power for Public Buildings"

Students will answer questions to show that they understand today's reading.

Solar Power (B)

Lesson Overview

ACTIVITY	ACTIVITY TITLE	TIME	ONLINE/OFFLINE
GET READY	Introduction to Solar Power (B)	**1** minute	🖥️
	Spelling List 17 Activity Bank	**10** minutes	📄
	Recall "Solar Power for Public Buildings"	**4** minutes	🖥️
	Before You Read "Not So Fast, California!"	**14** minutes	🖥️
READ	"Not So Fast, California!"	**30** minutes	📄
	Check-In: "Not So Fast, California!"	**5** minutes	🖥️
LEARN AND **TRY IT**	Explore How Writers Support Positions	**10** minutes	🖥️
	Examine the Text Closely	**10** minutes	🖥️
	Apply: Logic, Reasoning, and Evidence	**15** minutes	🖥️
	Write About How a Writer Persuades Readers **LEARNING COACH CHECK-IN**	**10** minutes	📄
WRAP-UP	Practice Words from "Not So Fast, California!"	**8** minutes	🖥️
	Questions About "Not So Fast, California!"	**2** minutes	🖥️

Content Background

Students will complete a spelling activity and read a persuasive essay in *Expeditions in Reading* called "Not So Fast, California!" They will then complete activities in which they learn about determining how writers support their positions in ways that convince readers.

Advance Preparation

Gather students' completed Spelling List 17 Pretest activity page from Solar Power (A). Students will refer to this page during Get Ready: Spelling List 17 Activity Bank.

MATERIALS

Supplied
- *Summit English Language Arts 5 Expeditions in Reading*
- *Summit English Language Arts 5 Activity Book*
  - Spelling List 17 Activity Bank
  - Write About How a Writer Persuades Readers

Also Needed
- completed Spelling List 17 Pretest activity page from from Solar Power (A)

"Not So Fast, California!" Synopsis

This persuasive essay, a response to another piece that stated that California should take steps to power its public buildings with solar energy, argues the opposite position. It asserts that using solar electricity to power public buildings will cost the state a lot of money and that the state already creates too much electricity. The writer supports his position with evidence and logic.

KEYWORDS

evidence – a specific detail, such as a fact or expert opinion, that supports a reason

persuasive essay – an essay in which the writer tries to convince readers to agree with a stand on an issue

Lesson Goals

- Practice all spelling words offline.

- Read "Not So Fast, California!"

- Explore the logic, evidence, and reasoning that supports the writer's position in a persuasive essay.

GET READY

Introduction to Solar Power (B)

Students will get a glimpse of what they will learn about in the lesson. They will also read the lesson goals and keywords. Have students select each keyword and preview its definition.

Spelling List 17 Activity Bank

Students will practice all spelling words from the workshop by completing Spelling List 17 Activity Bank from *Summit English Language Arts 5 Activity Book*. Make sure students have their completed Spelling List 17 Pretest activity page from Solar Power (A) to refer to during this activity.

Remind students to pay special attention to words they spelled incorrectly on the Spelling Pretest.

Recall "Solar Power for Public Buildings"

Students will answer some questions to review the reading that they have already completed.

Before You Read "Not So Fast, California!"

Students will be introduced to some key vocabulary words that they will encounter in the upcoming reading and answer a question to help them understand the writer's purpose.

READ

"Not So Fast, California!"

Students will read the persuasive essay "Not So Fast, California!" in *Expeditions in Reading*.

Check-In: "Not So Fast, California!"

Students will answer several questions to demonstrate their comprehension of "Not So Fast, California!"

LEARN AND TRY IT

LEARN   Explore How Writers Support Positions

Students will learn how writers convince readers to agree with their positions in persuasive essays. They will focus on the use of evidence and logic.

TRY IT   Examine the Text Closely

Students will answer several questions online to develop their ability to understand how the writer of "Not So Fast, California!" convinces readers to agree with his position.

TRY IT   Apply: Logic, Reasoning, and Evidence

Students will apply to a new work what they've learned about identifying a writer's position and the methods he or she uses to convince readers to agree with that position.

TRY IT   Write About How a Writer Persuades Readers

Students will complete Write About How a Writer Persuades Readers from *Summit English Language Arts 5 Activity Book*. Their responses should demonstrate their ability to recognize what a writer's position is and their understanding of how the writer tries to convince readers to agree with that position.

LEARNING COACH CHECK-IN   This activity page contains open-ended questions, so it's important that you review students' responses. Give students feedback, using the sample answer provided to guide you.

TRY IT
Solar Power (B)

Write About How a Writer Persuades Readers

Read the passage. Then write your responses in complete sentences.

It's nearly summer, and that means that Fun Zone will soon open its doors. Hopefully, this is the last year that this statement is true. Why? Fun Zone is an overpriced, unsafe amusement park that no one should visit.

Let's start with the cost of visiting Fun Zone, which is outrageous. Adults must pay $120 to get in the front gate. Admission for children is $80. So, it would cost a family of four $400 just to visit Fun Zone. That number doesn't even take into account the fact that food and drinks in the park are wildly expensive. A hot dog costs $9. A bottle of water is $6. Oh, Fun Zone also charges visitors $35 for parking. If you add it all up, a single day at Fun Zone could easily cost that family of four over $500. That's far more than many families in our town can afford to spend.

The high prices aren't the only issue with Fun Zone. The park is also full of dangerous rides. Last year, 50 people were hurt when the Looptacular Roller Coaster hopped the tracks and skidded into the platform. Two women hurt their backs when they slipped on a wet bathroom floor. The Ferris wheel broke down and stranded dozens of visitors more than 100 feet in the air for six hours. And an ostrich escaped from the petting zoo and pecked a little boy's arms, causing bruises and nightmares.

SOLAR POWER (B)   **291**

1. What stance or position does the writer take in this passage?
Answers will vary. Students' response should demonstrate an understanding of the writer's position. The writer thinks: Fun Zone is overly expensive and dangerous.

2. How does the writer support his or her position? Cite specific examples from the text.

See right.

3. Why is the support the writer provides persuasive?
Answers will vary. Student's response should demonstrate an understanding that the support is persuasive because it shows how expensive and dangerous Fun Zone is. The support

- **Includes large numbers to make readers agree that the cost is beyond the reach of many families.**
- **Lists injuries and incidents that lead readers to agree with the writer's logic and view Fun Zone as dangerous.**

292   SOLAR POWER (B)

Additoinal answers

2. Answers will vary. Student responses should recognize that the writer supports the position with facts and information. The writer

- States "it would cost a family of four $400 just to visit Fun Zone."

- Uses logic by suggesting that spending more than $500 for a day at an amusement park is too costly for many families.

- Gives details about injuries and incidents at Fun Zone.

TRY IT   Practice Words from "Not So Fast, California!"

Students will answer questions to demonstrate their understanding of the vocabulary words from today's reading.

WRAP-UP

Questions About "Not So Fast, California!"

Students will answer questions to show that they understand today's reading.

Solar Power (C)

Lesson Overview

ACTIVITY	ACTIVITY TITLE	TIME	ONLINE/OFFLINE
GET READY	Introduction to Solar Power (C)	**1** minute	🖥️
	Spelling List 17 Review Game	**15** minutes	🖥️
	Recall "Not So Fast, California!"	**5** minutes	📶
LEARN AND **TRY IT**	Exaggerations and Other Misleading Statements	**15** minutes	🖥️
	Spot Exaggerations and Misleading Statements	**15** minutes	🖥️
	Claims, Evidence, and Purpose	**15** minutes	📶
	Link Claims to Evidence and Purpose	**15** minutes	📶
	Apply: Explore Claims, Evidence, and Purpose in a New Text	**20** minutes	📶
	Plan to Write About Solar Power **LEARNING COACH CHECK-IN**	**17** minutes	📄
WRAP-UP	Questions About Claims, Evidence, and Purpose	**2** minutes	🖥️

Content Background

Students will complete a spelling activity and learn about exaggerations and other misleading statements they may encounter in persuasive texts. They will then complete activities in which they learn about the relationship among claims, evidence, and the writer's purpose in crafting a persuasive essay.

MATERIALS

Supplied
- *Summit English Language Arts Grade 5 Expeditions in Reading*
- *Summit English Language Arts 5 Activity Book*
  - Plan to Write About Solar Power

Lesson Goals

- Practice all spelling words online.
- Identify exaggerations or misleading statements in persuasive texts.
- Determine how well an author achieves his or her purpose.
- Describe how evidence and reasons in a persuasive text support its claims.
- Write about two texts, drawing information and ideas from each.

Introduction to Solar Power (C)

Students will get a glimpse of what they will learn about in the lesson. They will also read the lesson goals and keywords. Have students select each keyword and preview its definition.

Spelling List 17 Review Game

Students will practice all spelling words from the workshop.

Recall "Not So Fast, California!"

Students will answer some questions to review the reading that they have already completed.

evidence – a specific detail, such as a fact or expert opinion, that supports a reason

claim – an idea or opinion presented, or a stand taken, in an argument

paraphrase – to restate information in one's own words

LEARN AND TRY IT

LEARN   Exaggerations and Other Misleading Statements

Students will learn about the importance of identifying exaggerations and misleading statements in texts, as well as the influence of both.

TRY IT   Spot Exaggerations and Misleading Statements

Students will answer several questions to demonstrate their ability to recognize exaggerations, misleading statements, and their effect.

LEARN   Claims, Evidence, and Purpose

Students will learn how to recognize claims in a persuasive text, as well as how certain evidence supports specific claims. Students will also explore how presenting claims and evidence effectively can help writers achieve their purpose in a persuasive text.

TRY IT   Link Claims to Evidence and Purpose

Students will answer several questions to demonstrate their ability to identify a claim and the evidence that supports it, as well as their understanding of how claims and evidence can help a writer achieve his or her purpose.

TRY IT   Apply: Explore Claims, Evidence, and Purpose in a New Text

Students will apply to a new work what they've learned about identifying claims and the evidence that supports them, as well as how these elements help the author to achieve his or her purpose.

TRY IT   Plan to Write About Solar Power

Students will complete Plan to Write About Solar Power from *Summit English Language Arts 5 Activity Book*. They should complete the graphic organizer by paraphrasing important information from each text, and noting the ways in which the texts are alike and different.

LEARNING COACH CHECK-IN   This activity page contains an open-ended question, so it's important that you review students' responses. Give students feedback, using the sample answer provided to guide you. Note that students will use this page to complete their writing assignment in Solar Power Wrap-Up, so be sure that they keep their completed sheet in a safe place.

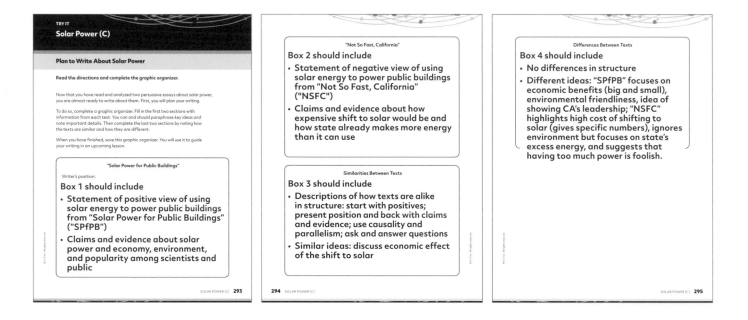

TRY IT
Solar Power (C)

Plan to Write About Solar Power

Read the directions and complete the graphic organizer.

Now that you have read and analyzed two persuasive essays about solar power, you are almost ready to write about them. First, you will plan your writing.

To do so, complete a graphic organizer. Fill in the first two sections with information from each text. You can and should paraphrase key ideas and note important details. Then complete the last two sections by noting how the texts are similar and how they are different.

When you have finished, save this graphic organizer. You will use it to guide your writing in an upcoming lesson.

"Solar Power for Public Buildings"

Writer's position:

Box 1 should include
- Statement of positive view of using solar energy to power public buildings from "Solar Power for Public Buildings" ("SPfPB")
- Claims and evidence about solar power and economy, environment, and popularity among scientists and public

SOLAR POWER (C)   **293**

"Not So Fast, California"

Box 2 should include
- Statement of negative view of using solar energy to power public buildings from "Not So Fast, California" ("NSFC")
- Claims and evidence about how expensive shift to solar would be and how state already makes more energy than it can use

Similarities Between Texts

Box 3 should include
- Descriptions of how texts are alike in structure: start with positives; present position and back with claims and evidence; use causality and parallelism; ask and answer questions
- Similar ideas: discuss economic effect of the shift to solar

294   SOLAR POWER (C)

Differences Between Texts

Box 4 should include
- No differences in structure
- Different ideas: "SPfPB" focuses on economic benefits (big and small), environmental friendliness, idea of showing CA's leadership; "NSFC" highlights high cost of shifting to solar (gives specific numbers), ignores environment but focuses on state's excess energy, and suggests that having too much power is foolish.

SOLAR POWER (C)   **295**

WRAP-UP

Questions About Claims, Evidence, and Purpose

Students will answer questions to show that they understand the important concepts in this lesson.

Solar Power Wrap-Up

Lesson Overview

ACTIVITY	ACTIVITY TITLE	TIME	ONLINE/OFFLINE
GET READY	Introduction to Solar Power Wrap-Up	**1** minute	📶
TRY IT	Write About Solar Power **LEARNING COACH CHECK-IN**	**30** minutes	📄
	Read and Record	**10** minutes	📶
	Review Solar Power	**20** minutes	📶
QUIZ	Solar Power	**30** minutes	🖥️
	Spelling List 17	**10** minutes	📶
WRAP-UP	Keyboarding	**10** minutes	📶
	More Language Arts Practice	**19** minutes	📶

Advance Preparation

Gather students' completed Plan to Write About Solar Power activity page from Solar Power (C). Students will refer to this page during Write About Solar Power.

During the Keyboarding activity, students will practice their keyboarding skills using an external website or program. **You will need to work with students to select an appropriate keyboarding practice website or program; K12 does not specify which resource to use.** A few suggestions are provided in the online activity.

Depending on which program you choose, students may need to set up an account to save their progress. If needed, assist students in setting up and running their chosen keyboarding practice program.

MATERIALS

Supplied
- *Summit English Language Arts 5 Expeditions in Reading*
- *Summit English Language Arts 5 Activity Book*
  - Write About Solar Power

Also Needed
- completed Plan to Write About Solar Power activity page from Solar Power (C)

Lesson Goals

- Compare and contrast "Solar Power for Public Buildings" and "Not So Fast, California!"

- Review how writers persuade readers and support their positions with logic, reasoning, and evidence.

- Demonstrate understanding of how exaggerations and misleading statements affect a text, as well as the relationship between claims, evidence, and purpose.

- Take a quiz on this workshop's readings.

- Take a spelling quiz.

GET READY

Introduction to Solar Power Wrap-Up

Students will read the lesson goals.

TRY IT

Write About Solar Power

Students will complete Write About Solar Power in *Summit English Language Arts 5 Activity Book* to compare and contrast "Solar Power for Public Buildings" and "Not So Fast, California!" Note that students should use the graphic organizer that they completed during the Solar Power (C) lesson to guide their writing. That graphic organizer is on the Plan to Write About Solar Power page, so make sure students have access to their graphic organizers.

LEARNING COACH CHECK-IN   This activity page contains an open-ended assignment, so it's important that you review students' responses. Give students feedback, using the sample response provided to guide you.

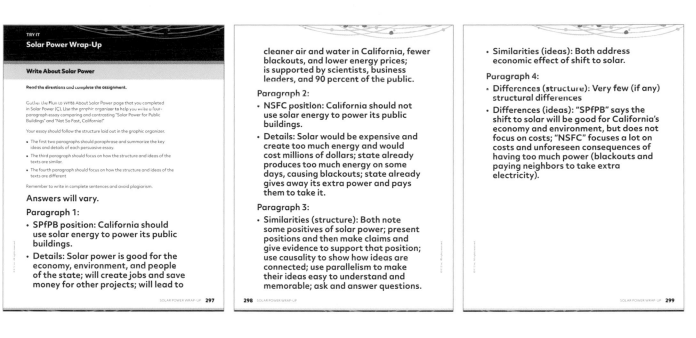

Read and Record

Good readers read quickly, smoothly, and with expression. This is called *fluency*. Students will record themselves reading aloud. They will listen to their recording and think about how quick, smooth, and expressive they sound.

TIP Encourage students to rerecord as needed.

Review Solar Power

Students will answer questions to review what they have learned about how writers persuade readers and support their positions with logic, reasoning, and evidence. They will also show their understanding of how exaggerations and misleading statements affect a text, as well as the relationship between claims, evidence, and purpose. Finally, they will demonstrate their overall comprehension of this workshop's readings.

QUIZ

Solar Power

Students will complete the Solar Power quiz.

Spelling List 17

Students will complete the Spelling List 17 quiz.

WRAP-UP

Keyboarding

Students will practice their keyboarding skills using an external website or program.

More Language Arts Practice

Students will practice skills according to their individual needs.

Big Ideas: Mini-Project

Lesson Overview

Big Ideas lessons provide students the opportunity to further apply the knowledge acquired and skills learned throughout the unit workshops. Each Big Ideas lesson consists of these parts:

1. **Cumulative Review:** Students keep their skills fresh by reviewing prior content.

2. **Preview:** Students practice answering the types of questions they will commonly find on standardized tests.

3. **Synthesis:** Students complete an assignment that allows them to connect and apply what they have learned. Synthesis assignments vary throughout the course.

   In the Synthesis portion of this Big Ideas lesson, students will complete a small creative project that ties together concepts and skills they have encountered across workshops. These small projects are designed to deepen students' understanding of those concepts and skills.

   LEARNING COACH CHECK-IN   Make sure students complete, review, and submit the assignment to their teacher.

All materials needed for this lesson are linked online and not provided in the Activity Book.

MATERIALS

Supplied
- Mini-Project Instructions (printout)

Get to Know
a Supreme Court
Justice

Who Is Sonia Sotomayor? (A)

Lesson Overview

ACTIVITY	ACTIVITY TITLE	TIME	ONLINE/OFFLINE
GET READY	Get to Know a Supreme Court Justice Unit Overview	**1** minute	🖥️
	Introduction to *Who Is Sonia Sotomayor?* (A)	**1** minute	🖥️
	Spelling List 18 Pretest **LEARNING COACH CHECK-IN**	**10** minutes	🖥️ and 📄
	The Supreme Court in 60 Seconds	**1** minute	🖥️
	Before You Read *Who Is Sonia Sotomayor?* Chapters 1–3	**13** minutes	🖥️
READ	*Who Is Sonia Sotomayor?* Chapters 1–3	**34** minutes	📄
	Check-In: *Who Is Sonia Sotomayor?* Chapters 1–3	**5** minutes	🖥️
LEARN AND **TRY IT**	Structure and Point of View in Biographies	**10** minutes	🖥️
	Examine Structure and Point of View	**10** minutes	🖥️
	Apply: Structure and Point of View	**15** minutes	🖥️
	Write About Events in Your Biography **LEARNING COACH CHECK-IN**	**10** minutes	📄
	Practice Words from *Who Is Sonia Sotomayor?* Chapters 1–3	**8** minutes	🖥️
WRAP-UP	Questions About Structure and Point of View	**2** minutes	🖥️

Content Background

Students will complete a spelling activity and read the introduction and first three chapters of a biography entitled *Who Is Sonia Sotomayor?* They will then complete activities in which they learn about how the structure and narrative point of view of a text can help them understand what they read.

MATERIALS

Supplied
- *Who Is Sonia Sotomayor?* by Megan Stine
- *Summit English Language Arts 5 Activity Book*
  - Spelling List 18 Pretest
  - Write About Events in Your Biography

Who Is Sonia Sotomayor? Chapters 1–3 Synopsis

This part of the biography begins with a brief description of the day that Sonia Sotomayor learned that she was being nominated to the Supreme Court. Then it returns to her early life, detailing her childhood in the Bronx, the struggles she faced due to poverty and the death of her father, and how she made her way to Princeton University, where she excelled.

KEYWORDS

biography – the story of someone's life written by another person

inference – a guess that readers make, using the clues that authors give them, in a piece of writing

third-person point of view – the telling of a story by someone outside of the action, using the third-person pronouns *he*, *she*, and *they*

Lesson Goals

- Take a spelling pretest.
- Read the introduction and Chapters 1–3 of *Who Is Sonia Sotomayor?*
- Explore the structure and point of view of *Who Is Sonia Sotomayor?*

GET READY

Get to Know a Supreme Court Justice Unit Overview

Students will read a summary of what they will learn in the Get to Know a Supreme Court Justice unit.

Introduction to *Who Is Sonia Sotomayor?* (A)

Students will get a glimpse of what they will learn about in the lesson. They will also read the lesson goals and keywords. Have students select each keyword and preview its definition.

Spelling List 18 Pretest

Students will take a spelling pretest.

LEARNING COACH CHECK-IN   Have students turn to Spelling List 18 Pretest in *Summit English Language Arts 5 Activity Book* and open the online Spelling Pretest activity. Online, students will listen to the spelling word, type the word in the space indicated, and then check their answer. In the activity book, students will write the correct spelling of the word in the tables provided and indicate with a ✓ or an ✘ if if they spelled the word correctly or incorrectly online. Students will repeat this process with the remaining words.

As needed, help students with the interaction between the online activity and the activity book page until they become comfortable with what they need to do. As students practice their spelling words throughout the workshop, they should pay special attention to words they spelled incorrectly on the pretest.

This is the complete list of words students will be tested on.

Adding Suffixes to Words Ending in *y* or silent *e*	Root *cert*	Suffix *–ical*
forgiving	certain	alphabetical
displaced	certificate	biographical
replacing	certify	comical
creating	ascertain	cubical
wisely		typical
bossiness		
homeless		
replacement		
cleanliness		
craziness		
emptiness		
happiness		
healthier		
muddier		
noisiest		
tinier		

NOTE Have students keep their completed activity page in a safe place so they can refer to it later.

The Supreme Court in 60 Seconds

Students will watch a short video designed to spark their interest in upcoming topics.

Before You Read *Who Is Sonia Sotomayor?* Chapters 1–3

Students will be introduced to some key vocabulary words that they will encounter in the upcoming reading, learn about opinion pieces, and answer a question to help them set a purpose for their reading.

READ

Who Is Sonia Sotomayor? Chapters 1–3

Students will read the introduction and Chapters 1–3 of *Who Is Sonia Sotomayor?* by Megan Stine.

Check-In: *Who Is Sonia Sotomayor?* Chapters 1–3

Students will answer several questions to demonstrate their comprehension of the introduction and Chapters 1–3 of *Who Is Sonia Sotomayor?*

LEARN AND TRY IT

LEARN   Structure and Point of View in Biographies

Students will learn how to examine a passage to determine the effect that its structure and narrative point of view have on their understanding of its content.

TRY IT   Examine Structure and Point of View

Students will complete an activity in which they explore a passage from *Who Is Sonia Sotomayor?* to demonstrate their ability to make inferences based on their understanding of the book's structure and narrative point of view.

TRY IT   Apply: Structure and Point of View

Students will apply to a new work what they've learned about making inferences about its content, based on its structure and narrative point of view.

TRY IT   Write About Events in Your Biography

Students will complete Write About Events in Your Biography from *Summit English Language Arts 5 Activity Book*. They will imagine what events from their own lives might be included in a biography and answer a question about writing such a biography.

LEARNING COACH CHECK-IN   This activity page contains open-ended questions, so it's important that you review students' responses. Give students feedback, using the sample answers provided to guide you.

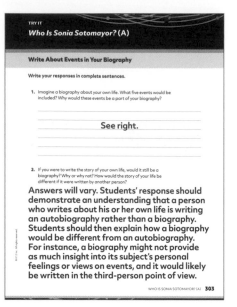

TRY IT
Who Is Sonia Sotomayor? (A)

Write About Events in Your Biography

Write your responses in complete sentences.

1. Imagine a biography about your own life. What five events would be included? Why would these events be a part of your biography?

See right.

2. If you were to write the story of your own life, would it still be a biography? Why or why not? How would the story of your life be different if it were written by another person?

Answers will vary. Students' response should demonstrate an understanding that a person who writes about his or her own life is writing an autobiography rather than a biography. Students should then explain how a biography would be different from an autobiography. For instance, a biography might not provide as much insight into its subject's personal feelings or views on events, and it would likely be written in the third-person point of view.

WHO IS SONIA SOTOMAYOR? (A) **303**

Additional answers

1. Answers will vary. Students should name five events from their own lives that might be included in a biography, such as their birth, early milestones, athletic or academic achievements, or other important occasions (family moves, births of siblings, and so on).

Student should then explain why these events would be part of their biography, demonstrating their understanding that biographies focus on significant events in their subjects' lives.

TRY IT   Practice Words from *Who Is Sonia Sotomayor?* Chapters 1–3

Students will answer questions to demonstrate their understanding of the vocabulary words from the reading.

WRAP-UP

Questions About Structure and Point of View

Students will answer questions to show that they understand the reading.

Who Is Sonia Sotomayor? (B)

Lesson Overview

ACTIVITY	ACTIVITY TITLE	TIME	ONLINE/OFFLINE
GET READY	Introduction to *Who Is Sonia Sotomayor?* (B)	**1** minute	
	Spelling List 18 Activity Bank **LEARNING COACH CHECK-IN**	**10** minutes	
	Recall *Who Is Sonia Sotomayor?* Chapters 1–3	**4** minutes	
	Before You Read *Who Is Sonia Sotomayor?* Chapters 4–7	**10** minutes	
READ	*Who Is Sonia Sotomayor?* Chapters 4–7	**30** minutes	
	Check-In: *Who Is Sonia Sotomayor?* Chapters 4–7	**5** minutes	
LEARN AND **TRY IT**	Verifying Facts and Supporting Opinions	**10** minutes	
	Examine Facts and Opinions	**10** minutes	
	Apply: Explore Facts and Opinions in Another Work	**15** minutes	
	Write About Facts and Opinions **LEARNING COACH CHECK-IN**	**15** minutes	
	Practice Words from *Who Is Sonia Sotomayor?* Chapters 4–7	**8** minutes	
WRAP-UP	Questions About Facts and Opinions	**2** minutes	

Content Background

Students will complete a spelling activity and read Chapters 4–7 of *Who Is Sonia Sotomayor?* by Megan Stine. They will then complete activities in which they learn about distinguishing between facts and opinions, as well as how to verify facts and how to find support for opinions.

Advance Preparation

Gather students' completed Spelling List 18 Pretest activity page from *Who Is Sonia Sotomayor?* (A). Students will refer to this page during Get Ready: Spelling List 18 Activity Bank.

MATERIALS

Supplied
- *Who Is Sonia Sotomayor?* by Megan Stine
- *Summit English Language Arts 5 Activity Book*
  - Spelling List 18 Activity Bank
  - Write About Facts and Opinions

Also Needed
- completed Spelling List 18 Pretest activity page from *Who Is Sonia Sotomayor?* (A)

Who Is Sonia Sotomayor? Chapters 4–7 Synopsis

These chapters of the book begin by focusing on Sonia's time at Yale Law School, where she excelled despite struggling her first year. After graduation, she began to work in the New York City district attorney's office as an assistant district attorney. Though she had to learn a lot on the job, Sonia was a successful and highly respected prosecutor, who was willing to work hard. The book then describes Sonia's work in the private sector, which she entered after leaving the DA's office in 1984. Working for a firm called Pavia & Harcourt, Sonia was able to travel around the world and work on many interesting cases. But she never forgot her roots, and she never gave up on her dream of being a judge. Finally, this section of the book describes how Sonia became a federal district court judge in 1992. It details the long and difficult process of being named to the federal bench, and it describes one of Sonia's most famous cases as a district court judge: one in which she helped end the Major League Baseball players' strike in 1995.

Lesson Goals

- Practice all spelling words offline.
- Continue to read *Who Is Sonia Sotomayor?*
- Identify facts and opinions in the text, as well as the details used to support them.

GET READY

Introduction to *Who Is Sonia Sotomayor?* (B)

Students will get a glimpse of what they will learn about in the lesson. They will also read the lesson goals and keywords. Have students select each keyword and preview its definition.

Spelling List 18 Activity Bank

Students will practice all spelling words from the workshop by completing Spelling List 18 Activity Bank from *Summit English Language Arts 5 Activity Book*. Make sure students have their completed Spelling List 18 Pretest activity page from *Who Is Sonia Sotomayor?* (A) to refer to during this activity.

Remind students to pay special attention to words they spelled incorrectly on the spelling pretest.

Spelling List 18 Activity Bank

Circle any words in the box that you did not spell correctly on the pretest. Using your circled words, complete one activity of your choice. Complete as much of the activity as you can in the time given.

If you spelled all words correctly on the pretest, complete your chosen activity with as many spelling words as you can.

forgiving	bossiness	emptiness	tinier	alphabetical
displaced	homeless	happiness	certain	biographical
replacing	replacement	healthier	certificate	comical
creating	cleanliness	muddier	certify	cubical
wisely	craziness	noisiest	ascertain	typical

Spelling Activity Choices

Silly Sentencess

1. Write a silly sentence using your words from the spelling word list.
2. Underline the spelling word in each sentence.
   Example: The dog was underlined driving a car.
3. Correct any spelling errors.

Spelling Story

1. Write a very short story using your words from the spelling word list.
2. Underline the spelling words in the story.
3. Correct any spelling errors.

Riddle Me This

1. Write a riddle for your words from the spelling word list.
   Example: "I have a trunk, but it's not on my car."
2. Write the answer, which is your word, for each riddle.
   Example: Answer: elephant
3. Correct any spelling errors.

RunOnWord

1. Gather some crayons, colored pencils, or markers. Write each of your words, using a different color for each word, end to end as one long word.
   Example: dogcatbirdfishturtle
2. Rewrite the words correctly and with proper spacing.

Complete the activity that you chose.

My chosen activity:

Students should use this page to complete all steps in their chosen activity.

Recall *Who Is Sonia Sotomayor?* Chapters 1–3

Students will answer some questions to review the reading that they have already completed.

Before You Read *Who Is Sonia Sotomayor?* Chapters 4–7

Students will be introduced to some key vocabulary words that they will encounter in the upcoming reading and learn some background about the American legal system.

READ

Who Is Sonia Sotomayor? Chapters 4–7

Students will read Chapters 4–7 of *Who Is Sonia Sotomayor?* by Megan Stine.

Check-In: *Who Is Sonia Sotomayor?* Chapters 4–7

Students will answer several questions to demonstrate their comprehension of Chapters 4–7 of *Who Is Sonia Sotomayor?*

LEARN AND TRY IT

LEARN   Verifying Facts and Supporting Opinions

Students will learn about separating facts from opinions in a text, as well as some ways to verify facts and how to find textual support for opinions that they encounter.

TRY IT   Examine Facts and Opinions

Students will look at a few passages from *Who Is Sonia Sotomayor?* to practice distinguishing facts and opinions and to demonstrate their understanding of how to verify facts and find support for opinions.

TRY IT   Apply: Explore Facts and Opinions in Another Work

Students will apply to a new work what they've learned about identifying facts and opinions in it. They will also demonstrate their ability to verify facts and to find textual support for opinions.

TRY IT   Write About Facts and Opinions

Students will complete Write About Facts and Opinions from *Summit English Language Arts 5 Activity Book*. Their responses to the questions on this page should demonstrate their understanding of how to identify facts and opinions, as well as how facts can be verified and opinions can be supported.

LEARNING COACH CHECK-IN   This activity page contains an open-ended question, so it's important that you review students' responses. Give students feedback, using the sample answer provided to guide you.

TRY IT
Who Is Sonia Sotomayor? (B)

Write About Facts and Opinions

Write your responses in the spaces provided.

1. Read each line from *Who Is Sonia Sotomayor?* Then write "F" under those that state facts, and write "O" under those that express opinions.
"Morganthau was famous in New York. He was a tough prosecutor."
O

"Finally, in 1992, Congress approved her. President George H.W. Bush named her as a federal judge."
F

"So in 1984, she took a job at a law firm called Pavia & Harcourt."
F

"Her office was tiny and unpleasant. It was usually too hot or too cold."
O

2. How could you verify the facts you identified in Question 1? What details might support the opinions you identified?
See right.

WHO IS SONIA SOTOMAYOR? (B)   **309**

Additional answers

2. Answers will vary. Students should indicate that they could verify facts by checking official records about when Sonia was hired to Pavia & Harcourt or when (and by whom) she was appointed to be a federal judge. Students could also verify facts by finding reliable sources that back them up. Students should then explain the kinds of details that might support the opinions they identified. For instance, they might find newspaper stories about Morganthau that show he was well known and describe his toughness as a prosecutor. Likewise, students might find pictures or further descriptions of Sonia's office that highlight its small size and lack of charm.

TRY IT   Practice Words from *Who Is Sonia Sotomayor?* Chapters 4–7

Students will answer questions to demonstrate their understanding of the vocabulary words from the reading.

WRAP-UP

Questions About Facts and Opinions

Students will answer questions to show that they understand the reading.

Who Is Sonia Sotomayor? (C)

Lesson Overview

ACTIVITY	ACTIVITY TITLE	TIME	ONLINE/OFFLINE
GET READY	Introduction to *Who Is Sonia Sotomayor?* (C)	**1** minute	🖥
	Spelling List 18 Practice	**10** minutes	🖥
	Recall *Who Is Sonia Sotomayor?* Chapters 4–7	**5** minutes	🖥
	Before You Read *Who Is Sonia Sotomayor?* Chapters 8–9	**10** minutes	🖥
READ	*Who Is Sonia Sotomayor?* Chapters 8–9	**30** minutes	📄
	Check-In: *Who Is Sonia Sotomayor?* Chapters 8–9	**5** minutes	🖥
LEARN AND **TRY IT**	Text Features in Informational Texts	**10** minutes	🖥
	Using Text Features	**10** minutes	🖥
	Apply: Text Features	**15** minutes	🖥
	Write About Sonia Sotomayor Using Text Features **LEARNING COACH CHECK-IN**	**15** minutes	📄
	Practice Words from *Who Is Sonia Sotomayor?* Chapters 8–9	**7** minutes	🖥
WRAP-UP	Questions About Text Features	**2** minutes	🖥

Content Background

Students will complete a spelling activity and read Chapters 8 and 9 of *Who Is Sonia Sotomayor?* by Megan Stine. They will then complete activities in which they learn about using text features to improve their understanding of Stine's book.

MATERIALS

Supplied
- *Who Is Sonia Sotomayor?* by Megan Stine
- *Summit English Language Arts 5 Activity Book*
  - Write About Sonia Sotomayor Using Text Features

Who Is Sonia Sotomayor? Chapters 8 and 9 Synopsis

These chapters of the book begin by focusing on Sonia Sotomayor's promotion from a federal district court judge to an appellate judge. It describes the process she had to endure before being appointed to the higher court and the fact that the promotion allowed Sonia Sotomayor to serve with her mentor, José Cabranes. Then Stine describes how Sonia Sotomayor was elevated to the Supreme Court by President Barack Obama in 2009.

Lesson Goals

- Practice all spelling words online.

- Finish reading *Who Is Sonia Sotomayor?*

- Use text features to find information that improves understanding of *Who Is Sonia Sotomayor?*

GET READY

Introduction to *Who Is Sonia Sotomayor?* (C)

Students will get a glimpse of what they will learn about in the lesson. They will also read the lesson goals and keywords. Have students select each keyword and preview its definition.

Spelling List 18 Practice

Students will practice all spelling words from the workshop online.

Recall *Who Is Sonia Sotomayor?* Chapters 4–7

Students will answer some questions to review the reading that they have already completed.

Before You Read *Who Is Sonia Sotomayor?* Chapters 8–9

Students will be introduced to some key vocabulary words that they will encounter in the upcoming reading and learn some background about text features and why writers use them.

Who Is Sonia Sotomayor? Chapters 8–9

Students will read Chapters 8 and 9 of *Who Is Sonia Sotomayor?* by Megan Stine.

Check-In: *Who Is Sonia Sotomayor?* Chapters 8–9

Students will answer several questions to demonstrate their comprehension of Chapters 8 and 9 of *Who Is Sonia Sotomayor?*

LEARN AND TRY IT

LEARN   Text Features in Informational Texts

Students will learn about several text features that Megan Stine uses in *Who Is Sonia Sotomayor?* and how these can affect reader understanding of the text.

TRY IT   Using Text Features

Students will answer several questions online to develop their understanding of how to use various text features found in *Who Is Sonia Sotomayor?*

TRY IT   Apply: Text Features

Students will apply to a new work what they've learned about recognizing and using text features to improve their understanding of the text.

TRY IT   Write About Sonia Sotomayor Using Text Features

Students will complete Write About Sonia Sotomayor Using Text Features from *Summit English Language Arts 5 Activity Book*. Their responses to the questions on this page should demonstrate their ability to effectively use the book's various text features.

LEARNING COACH CHECK-IN   This activity page contains open-ended questions, so it's important that you review students' responses. Give students feedback, using the sample answers provided to guide you.

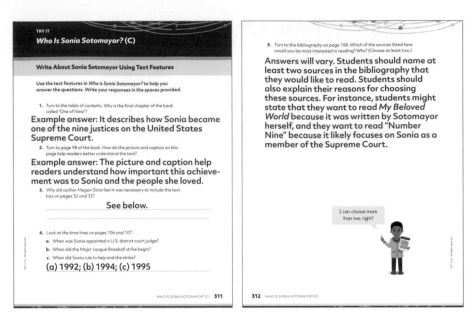

Additional answer

3. Example answer: The text box gives more information about affirmative action, a program that Sonia felt was very important to her having the opportunity to achieve her dreams.

TRY IT Practice Words from *Who Is Sonia Sotomayor?* Chapters 8–9

Students will answer questions to demonstrate their understanding of the vocabulary words from the reading.

WRAP-UP

Questions About Text Features

Students will answer questions to show that they understand the reading.

Who Is Sonia Sotomayor? Wrap-Up

Lesson Overview

ACTIVITY	ACTIVITY TITLE	TIME	ONLINE/OFFLINE
GET READY	Introduction to *Who Is Sonia Sotomayor?* Wrap-Up	**1** minute	📶
	Spelling List 18 More Practice	**10** minutes	📶
TRY IT	Write About *Who Is Sonia Sotomayor?* **LEARNING COACH CHECK-IN**	**30** minutes	📄
	Read and Record	**10** minutes	📶
	Review *Who Is Sonia Sotomayor?*	**20** minutes	📶
QUIZ	*Who Is Sonia Sotomayor?*	**30** minutes	📶
WRAP-UP	Keyboarding	**10** minutes	📶
	More Language Arts Practice	**9** minutes	📶

Advance Preparation

During the Keyboarding activity, students will practice their keyboarding skills using an external website or program. **You will need to work with students to select an appropriate keyboarding practice website or program; K12 does not specify which resource to use.** A few suggestions are provided in the online activity.

Depending on which program you choose, students may need to set up an account to save their progress. If needed, assist students in setting up and running their chosen keyboarding practice program.

MATERIALS

Supplied
- *Who Is Sonia Sotomayor?* by Megan Stine
- *Summit English Language Arts 5 Activity Book*
  - Write About *Who Is Sonia Sotomayor?*

Lesson Goals

- Practice all spelling words online.

- Summarize *Who Is Sonia Sotomayor?*

- Review how the text's language, devices, and structure influence readers' understanding of its content.

- Review how to separate facts from opinions and use text features to better understand the text.

- Take a quiz on *Who Is Sonia Sotomayor?*

GET READY

Introduction to *Who Is Sonia Sotomayor?* Wrap-Up

Students will get a glimpse of what they will learn about in the lesson. They will also read the lesson goals.

Spelling List 18 More Practice

Students will practice all spelling words from the workshop.

TRY IT

TRY IT Write About *Who Is Sonia Sotomayor?*

Students will complete Write About *Who Is Sonia Sotomayor?* in *Summit English Language Arts 5 Activity Book* to summarize *Who Is Sonia Sotomayor?* Their summaries should be about three paragraphs long and should be written in chronological order. They should describe the key figures and major events covered in Megan Stine's book.

LEARNING COACH CHECK-IN   This activity page contains an open-ended assignment, so it's important that you review students' responses. Give students feedback, using the sample response provided to guide you.

TRY IT   Read and Record

Good readers read quickly, smoothly, and with expression. This is called *fluency*. Students will record themselves reading aloud. They will listen to their recording and think about how quick, smooth, and expressive they sound.

TIP   Encourage students to rerecord as needed.

TRY IT   Review *Who Is Sonia Sotomayor?*

Students will answer questions to review what they have learned about how an informational text's structure, language, and devices affect readers' understanding of it. They will also show their ability to separate facts from opinions and their ability to use text features to answer questions about the work.

QUIZ

Who Is Sonia Sotomayor?

Students will complete the *Who Is Sonia Sotomayor?* quiz.

WRAP-UP

Keyboarding

Students will practice their keyboarding skills using an external website or program.

More Language Arts Practice

Students will practice skills according to their individual needs.

Sonia Sotomayor's Opening Statement

Lesson Overview

ACTIVITY	ACTIVITY TITLE	TIME	ONLINE/OFFLINE
GET READY	Introduction to Sonia Sotomayor's Opening Statement	**1** minute	🖥
	Spelling List 18 Review Game	**10** minutes	🖥
	Before You Read Opening Statement	**14** minutes	🖥
READ	Opening Statement to the Senate Judiciary Committee	**15** minutes	📄
	Check-In: Opening Statement	**5** minutes	🖥
LEARN AND **TRY IT**	Primary and Secondary Sources	**10** minutes	🖥
	Compare Sources	**10** minutes	🖥
	Focus on Structure and Language	**10** minutes	🖥
	Compare Structure and Language	**10** minutes	🖥
	Apply: Sources, Structure, and Language	**15** minutes	🖥
	Write About What You Learned **LEARNING COACH CHECK-IN**	**10** minutes	📄
	Practice Words from Opening Statement	**8** minutes	🖥
WRAP-UP	Questions About Sources and Structure	**2** minutes	🖥

Content Background

Students will complete a spelling review game and read a text written by Sonia Sotomayor. They will then complete activities in which they learn about different types of sources, as well how to compare and contrast the structure and language of different texts.

MATERIALS

Supplied
- *Summit English Language Arts 5 Expeditions in Reading*
- *Summit English Language Arts 5 Activity Book*
  - Write About What You Learned

Sonia Sotomayor's Opening Statement Synopsis

This text is a statement that Sonia Sotomayor delivered before Congress at the start of her Supreme Court confirmation hearings in 2009. In the statement, Sonia gives a brief overview of her life and experiences before describing her judicial philosophy and expressing her feelings about being nominated to serve on the Supreme Court.

Lesson Goals

- Practice all spelling words online.
- Read Opening Statement to the Senate Judiciary Committee.
- Determine the figurative meanings of words and phrases.
- Learn the difference between primary and secondary sources.
- Compare or contrast a primary source and a secondary source that address the same topic.

KEYWORDS

primary source – a record made by a person who saw or took part in an event or who lived at the time

secondary source – a record made by a person who did not see or take part in an event, or who made the record later

figurative language – words that describe something by comparing it to something completely different
For example: Rain fell in buckets and the streets looked like rivers.

GET READY

Introduction to Sonia Sotomayor's Opening Statement

Students will get a glimpse of what they will learn about in the lesson. They will also read the lesson goals and keywords. Have students select each keyword and preview its definition.

Spelling List 18 Review Game

Students will practice all spelling words from the workshop.

Before You Read Opening Statement to the Senate Judiciary Committee

Students will be introduced to some key vocabulary words that they will encounter in the upcoming reading and learn about figurative language.

READ

Opening Statement to the Senate Judiciary Committee

Students will read Opening Statement to the Senate Judiciary Committee by Sonia Sotomayor.

Check-In: Opening Statement to the Senate Judiciary Committee

Students will answer several questions to demonstrate their comprehension of Opening Statement to the Senate Judiciary Committee.

LEARN AND TRY IT

LEARN   Primary and Secondary Sources

Students will learn about the value of both primary and secondary sources and how to compare and contrast them.

TRY IT   Compare Sources

Students will complete an activity in which they examine a primary and a secondary source to demonstrate their understanding of each source's value and how to compare and contrast them.

LEARN   Focus on Structure and Language

Students will learn about how structure influences different texts on the same subject, as well as how to compare text structures. They will also learn about the effect of language in autobiographies and biographies.

TRY IT   Compare Structure and Language

Students will answer questions about how structure influences different texts on the same subject and about the effect of language in autobiographies and biographies.

TRY IT   Apply: Sources, Structure, and Language

Students will apply to new works what they've learned about comparing texts. They will decide what type of sources the texts are, what structure(s) they use, and the effect of their language on the text.

TRY IT   Write About What You Learned

Students will complete Write About What You Learned from *Summit English Language Arts 5 Activity Book*. Their responses to the questions on this page should demonstrate their understanding of how these texts differ and some of information that can be found in each work.

LEARNING COACH CHECK-IN   This activity page contains open-ended questions, so it's important that you review students' responses. Give students feedback, using the sample answer provided to guide you.

TRY IT

Sonia Sotomayor's Opening Statement

Write About What You Learned

Use both Opening Statement to the Senate Judiciary Committee by Sonia Sotomayor and Megan Stine's *Who Is Sonia Sotomayor?* to answer the questions. Write your responses in the spaces provided.

1. What does the statement reveal about Sonia's father?

See right.

2. What does Stine's book reveal about Sonia's father?

See right.

3. According to the statement, what does Sonia believe she owes her success to?

Example answer: Sonia thinks she owes her success to the values she learned as a child.

4. According to Stine's book, how did Sonia succeed in high school, college, law school, and her professional life?

Example answer: She asked for help when she needed it and worked hard.

5. According to the statement, which case was Sonia best known for deciding as a district court judge?

Example answer: the case involving the Major League Baseball strike in 1995

6. According to Stine's book, which case was one of the biggest of Sonia's career when she was an assistant district attorney?

Example answer: the "Tarzan murder case" in 1982

SONIA SOTOMAYOR'S OPENING STATEMENT **315**

Additional answers

1. Example answer: He left Puerto Rico during World War II, and he was a factory worker with a third-grade education.

2. Example answer: He struggled with alcohol addiction, but he took Sonia to Yankee games when she was a little girl.

TRY IT   Practice Words from Opening Statement

Students will answer questions to demonstrate their understanding of the vocabulary words from the reading.

WRAP-UP

Questions About Sources and Structure

Students will answer questions to show that they understand the important concepts in this lesson.

Sonia Sotomayor's Opening Statement Wrap-Up

Lesson Overview

ACTIVITY	ACTIVITY TITLE	TIME	ONLINE/OFFLINE
GET READY	Introduction to S. Sotomayor's Opening Statement Wrap-Up	**1** minute	🖥️
TRY IT	Write About Sonia Sotomayor, Supreme Court Justice **LEARNING COACH CHECK-IN**	**30** minutes	📄
	Read and Record	**10** minutes	🖥️
	Review Sonia Sotomayor's Opening Statement	**20** minutes	🖥️
QUIZ	Sonia Sotomayor's Opening Statement	**30** minutes	🖥️
	Spelling List 18	**10** minutes	🖥️
WRAP-UP	Keyboarding	**10** minutes	🖥️
	More Language Arts Practice	**9** minutes	🖥️

Advance Preparation

During the Keyboarding activity, students will practice their keyboarding skills using an external website or program. **You will need to work with students to select an appropriate keyboarding practice website or program; K12 does not specify which resource to use.** A few suggestions are provided in the online activity.

Depending on which program you choose, students may need to set up an account to save their progress. If needed, assist students in setting up and running their chosen keyboarding practice program.

MATERIALS

Supplied

- *Summit English Language Arts 5 Activity Book*
- Write About Sonia Sotomayor, Supreme Court Justice

Lesson Goals

- Write about Sonia Sotomayor.
- Review the important ideas and details of Opening Statement to the Senate Judiciary Committee.
- Differentiate between primary and secondary sources, comparing and contrasting information found in each type of source.
- Compare the structures of different texts.
- Take a quiz on this workshop's reading.
- Take a spelling quiz.

GET READY

Introduction to Sonia Sotomayor's Opening Statement Wrap-Up

Students will read the lesson goals.

TRY IT

Write About Sonia Sotomayor, Supreme Court Justice

Students will complete Write About Sonia Sotomayor, Supreme Court Justice in *Summit English Language Arts 5 Activity Book* to demonstrate their understanding of how Sonia's experiences led to her being named to the Supreme Court. Note that students should use details from Opening Statement to the Senate Judiciary Committee by Sonia Sotomayor and Megan Stine's *Who Is Sonia Sotomayor?* in their responses.

LEARNING COACH CHECK-IN   This activity page contains an open-ended assignment, so it's important that you review students' responses. Give students feedback, using the sample response provided to guide you.

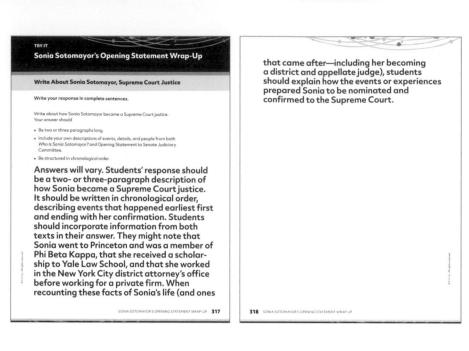

Read and Record

Good readers read quickly, smoothly, and with expression. This is called *fluency*. Students will record themselves reading aloud. They will listen to their recording and think about how quick, smooth, and expressive they sound.

TIP Encourage students to rerecord as needed.

Review Sonia Sotomayor's Opening Statement

Students will answer questions to review what they have learned about the main ideas and supporting details of this text. They will also show their understanding of how to distinguish primary sources from secondary sources. Finally, they will compare and contrast the statement with a biography of Sonia Sotomayor.

QUIZ

Sonia Sotomayor's Opening Statement

Students will complete the Sonia Sotomayor's Opening Statement quiz.

Spelling List 18

Students will complete the Spelling List 18 quiz.

WRAP-UP

Keyboarding

Students will practice their keyboarding skills using an external website or program.

More Language Arts Practice

Students will practice skills according to their individual needs.

Logical Relationships

Lesson Overview

ACTIVITY	ACTIVITY TITLE	TIME	ONLINE/OFFLINE
GET READY	Introduction to Logical Relationships	**1** minute	🖥️
	Look Back at Context Clues	**4** minutes	🖥️
LEARN AND **TRY IT**	Words That Signal Relationships	**10** minutes	🖥️
	Use Signal Words	**10** minutes	🖥️
	Apply: Write Sentences with Signal Words **LEARNING COACH CHECK-IN**	**15** minutes	📄
	Go Write!	**15** minutes	📄
	Review Logical Relationships	**15** minutes	🖥️
QUIZ	Logical Relationships	**15** minutes	🖥️
WRAP-UP	Keyboarding	**10** minutes	🖥️
	More Language Arts Practice	**10** minutes	🖥️
	Go Read!	**15** minutes	🖥️ or 📄

Content Background

Students will learn about recognizing and understanding the words that signal how ideas are related in a text. The word list for this workshop contains the following words: *however, moreover, although, additionally, nevertheless, similarly,* and *alternatively.*

Advance Preparation

During the Keyboarding activity, students will practice their keyboarding skills using an external website or program. **You will need to work with students to select an appropriate keyboarding practice website or program; K12 does not specify which resource to use.** A few suggestions are provided in the online activity.

Depending on which program you choose, students may need to set up an account to save their progress. If needed, assist students in setting up and running their chosen keyboarding practice program.

MATERIALS

Supplied
- *Summit English Language Arts 5 Activity Book*
  - Write Sentences with Signal Words

Also Needed
- reading material for Go Read!

KEYWORDS

context clue – a word or phrase in a text that helps you figure out the meaning of an unknown word

During the Go Read! activity, students will have the option of using the digital library. Allow extra time for students to make their reading selection, or have students make a selection before beginning the lesson.

Lesson Goals

- Use words that signal contrast, addition, or other logical relationships among ideas.
- Use context clues to help determine the meanings of unknown words.
- Take the Logical Relationships quiz.
- Read for pleasure.

GET READY

Introduction to Logical Relationships

Students will get a glimpse of what they will learn about in the lesson. They will also read the lesson goals and keywords. Have students select each keyword and preview its definition.

Look Back at Context Clues

Students will review the importance of using context clues to help them determine the meanings of unfamiliar words.

LEARN AND TRY IT

LEARN   Words That Signal Relationships

Students will learn some common words that writers use to signal relationships among ideas in texts. They will explore several examples of these types of words being used correctly and effectively.

TRY IT   Use Signal Words

Students will demonstrate their understanding of how signal words affect texts and practice correctly using words that signal relationships.

TRY IT   Apply: Write Sentences with Signal Words

Students will complete Write Sentences with Signal Words from *Summit English Language Arts 5 Activity Book*.

LEARNING COACH CHECK-IN   This activity page contains open-ended questions, so it's important that you review students' responses. Give students feedback, using the sample answers provided to guide you.

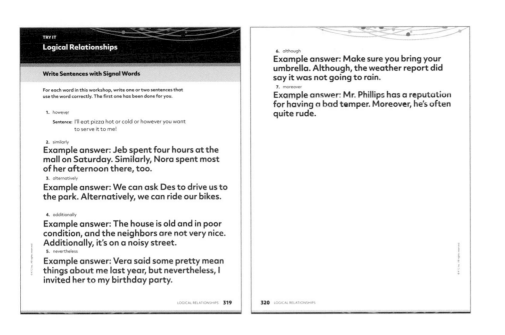

TRY IT   Go Write!

Students will write independently for pleasure. As they write, they should think about using words that signal the logical relationships between their ideas.

TRY IT   Review Logical Relationships

Students will answer questions to review what they have learned about words that signal logical relationships between ideas.

QUIZ

Logical Relationships

Students will complete the Logical Relationships quiz.

WRAP-UP

Keyboarding

Students will practice their keyboarding skills using an external website or program.

More Language Arts Practice

Students will practice skills according to their individual needs.

Go Read!

Students will read for pleasure. They should choose a book or a magazine that interests them, or they may choose a selection from the digital library, linked in the online lesson.

Students should read for the entire time. Have students select something to read ahead of time to help them stay focused.

Opinion Writing: Prewriting (A)

Lesson Overview

ACTIVITY	ACTIVITY TITLE	TIME	ONLINE/OFFLINE
GET READY	Introduction to Opinion Writing: Prewriting (A)	**2** minutes	🖥️
	Spelling List 19 Pretest **LEARNING COACH CHECK-IN**	**10** minutes	🖥️ and 📄
	Look Back at Commas	**10** minutes	🖥️
LEARN AND **TRY IT**	Direct Address	**15** minutes	🖥️
	Commas with Direct Address	**15** minutes	🖥️
	Explore a Student's Editorial	**20** minutes	🖥️
	Brainstorming for an Editorial	**15** minutes	🖥️
	Brainstorm for Your Editorial **LEARNING COACH CHECK-IN**	**30** minutes	📄
WRAP-UP	Questions About Commas and Editorials	**3** minutes	🖥️

Content Background

Students will begin working on an **editorial** about an issue that affects their community. An editorial is a type of opinion writing. The term derives from an editorial in a newspaper or a magazine, which is typically written by the editors of that publication and expresses the publication's stance on an issue. Students' editorial will express *their* opinion on an issue. Their editorial will also include a *call to action*, which is an appeal to readers to take a specific action related to the editorial.

Students will complete this writing assignment over the course of several lessons by following the writing process. Students will begin by prewriting.

Writing Process

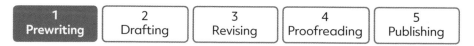

| 1 Prewriting | 2 Drafting | 3 Revising | 4 Proofreading | 5 Publishing |

During **prewriting**, writers choose a topic, conduct research, and create a plan for their writing assignment. In this lesson, students will complete the first part of prewriting, choosing a topic. To do that, they'll **brainstorm** by listing several possible topics and answering questions to evaluate them.

MATERIALS

Supplied
- *Summit English Language Arts 5 Activity Book*
  - Spelling List 19 Pretest
  - Brainstorm for Your Editorial
- Editorial Instructions (printout)

Also Needed
- folder for organizing editorial writing assignment pages

Grammar, Usage, and Mechanics   Students will learn how to punctuate a direct address, or text spoken directly to someone (or some*thing*). In a direct address, commas separate the name from the rest of the sentence.

> **Examples:** I am not hungry, **Dad**.
>
> Okay, **Chad,** I will finish your fries.
>
> **Fries,** you look delicious.

Advance Preparation

Gather a folder that students can use to keep all notes and activity pages related to their editorial.

> ## Lesson Goals
>
> - Take a spelling pretest.
> - Learn to punctuate a direct address.
> - Explore a model editorial.
> - Analyze how an author brainstorms.
> - Brainstorm topics for your editorial.

KEYWORDS

brainstorming – before writing, a way for the writer to come up with ideas

direct address – calling a person or animal by name or title
For example, Look, Mary, I found it! or Doctor, come here.

editorial – an article in a publication that gives an opinion held by its editor or editors; an opinion piece similar to such an article

opinion – something that a person thinks or believes, but which cannot be proven to be true

prewriting – the stage or step of writing in which a writer chooses a topic, gathers ideas, and plans what to write

GET READY

Introduction to Opinion Writing: Prewriting (A)

Students will get a glimpse of what they will learn about in the lesson. They will also read the lesson goals and keywords. Have students select each keyword and preview its definition.

Spelling List 19 Pretest

Students will take a spelling pretest.

LEARNING COACH CHECK-IN   Have students turn to Spelling List 19 Pretest in *Summit English Language Arts 5 Activity Book* and open the online Spelling Pretest activity. Online, students will listen to the spelling word, type the word in the space indicated, and then check their answer. In the activity book, students will write the correct spelling of the word in the tables provided and indicate with a ✓ or an ✗ if they spelled the word correctly or incorrectly online. Students will repeat this process with the remaining words.

As needed, help students with the interaction between the online activity and the activity book page until they become comfortable with what they need to do. As students practice their spelling words throughout the workshop, they should pay special attention to words they spelled incorrectly on the pretest.

This is the complete list of words students will be tested on.

Adding *able* and *ible*	Root *grat*	Suffix *–ism*
changeable	grateful	barbarism
knowledgeable	gratify	hypnotism
manageable	gratitude	patriotism
noticeable		tourism
replaceable		
admirable		
debatable		
inescapable		
mistakable		
admissible		
permissible		
invincible		
responsible		
reversible		

NOTE Have students keep their completed activity page in a safe place so they can refer to it later.

Look Back at Commas

Students will practice using commas to punctuate items in a series, introductory elements, and direct quotations.

LEARN AND TRY IT

LEARN   Direct Address

Students will learn that the name in a direct address should be separated from the rest of the sentence by commas.

TIP   Many funny grammar errors, including many Internet memes, relate to the use of commas with a direct address. Students might enjoy examples similar to the following:

> **Correct:** It's time to eat, Grandma! (The comma shows that the speaker is addressing Grandma.)

> **Incorrect:** It's time to eat Grandma! (Since there is no comma, it's not clear that the speaker is addressing Grandma. Yikes!)

TRY IT   Commas with Direct Address

Students will answer questions about using commas with a direct address. They will receive feedback on their answers.

LEARN   Explore a Student's Editorial

To help them better understand their writing assignment, students will read a model editorial and explore the elements that make it successful.

LEARN   Brainstorming for an Editorial

Students will closely investigate brainstorming, which is the first part of the prewriting step of the writing process.

TRY IT   Brainstorm for Your Editorial

Students will complete Brainstorm for Your Editorial from *Summit English Language Arts 5 Activity Book*.

LEARNING COACH CHECK-IN   Review students' responses. Ensure that students have selected a topic for their editorial that meets the criteria listed in Question 3 of the activity page. When students have completed the page, they should store it in a folder so that they can refer to it throughout the writing process.

NOTE   In addition to the brainstorming activity, this activity page contains the instructions for the editorial. Students should read the instructions carefully, but in this lesson, they should complete the brainstorming activity only (not the entire assignment). If you or students wish, you can download and print another copy of the Editorial Instructions online.

Opinion Writing: Prewriting (A)

Brainstorm for Your Editorial

Read the writing assignment. You will complete the assignment in steps over multiple lessons.

Prompt: Write an editorial about an issue in your community.

Requirements: Your editorial should include the following:

- A **title**
- An **introduction** that gives necessary background information, states your opinion, and provides an organizational structure
- **Three logically ordered body paragraphs**, each centered on a reason for your opinion
- **Facts and details** that support each reason and address possible audience questions
- Information discovered during **research** and relevant **personal experience**
- **Transitions** that link your opinion and reasons, and your reasons and evidence
- A **conclusion** that restates your opinion in different words and includes a call to action for the audience
- Correct **grammar**, **usage**, and **mechanics**
- A list of at least three trustworthy **research sources**

Audience: You will identify an appropriate audience for your editorial based on your topic, opinion, and call to action.

Purpose: Convince your audience to support your call to action.

Length: 500 to 600 words long (2 to 2½ typed, double-spaced pages)

Brainstorm and choose a topic for your editorial.

1. Think about your community. Think about the places, the rules, the traditions, the sports team, and more!

   a. List specific things you love about your community.

   b. List specific things you wish were different about your community.

---

2. Read your answers to Question 1.

   a. Circle the two topics that you listed that most interest you.

   b. For each topic you chose, try stating an opinion and a call to action. Two examples have been provided.

   > **Topic:** I love that my town has a food pantry.
   >
   > **Opinion:** Donating food to the town food pantry is important.
   >
   > **Call to Action:** At least once a month, donate food to the food pantry.

   > **Topic:** I dislike that there isn't a stop sign at the intersection near my house.
   >
   > **Opinion:** The intersection of Oak Leather Dr. and Burnside Landing Dr. needs a stop sign.
   >
   > **Call to Action:** Support me when I speak at the next town hall meeting.

   Topic 1:

   Opinion:

   Call to Action:

Topic 2:

Opinion:

Call to Action:

3. Decide which of the opinions you wrote in Question 2 interests you more. Then answer Yes or No to each question.

   a. Is your opinion focused enough to cover in detail in five paragraphs? _____

   b. Is your opinion something you can support with at least three reasons? _____

   c. Is there a realistic call to action related to your opinion? _____

4. Did you answer Yes to Parts A–C of Question 3? If so, you have found your editorial topic! If not, go back to the topics you listed in Question 1, choose a different topic, and follow the process described in Questions 2 and 3.

   The opinion that I am going to support in my editorial is

   Answers will vary. By the time they complete this activity page, students should have chosen the opinion that they will support in their editorial.

WRAP-UP

Questions About Commas and Editorials

Students will answer questions to show that they understand how to punctuate a direct address and how to brainstorm a topic for an editorial.

Opinion Writing: Prewriting (B)

Lesson Overview

ACTIVITY	ACTIVITY TITLE	TIME	ONLINE/OFFLINE
GET READY	Introduction to Opinion Writing: Prewriting (B)	**2** minutes	🖥️
	Spelling List 19 Activity Bank **LEARNING COACH CHECK-IN**	**10** minutes	📄
LEARN AND **TRY IT**	Tag Questions	**10** minutes	🖥️
	Commas with Tag Questions	**10** minutes	🖥️
	Researching an Editorial	**15** minutes	🖥️
	Research Your Editorial **LEARNING COACH CHECK-IN**	**50** minutes	📄
WRAP-UP	Questions About Commas and Research	**3** minutes	🖥️
	Go Read!	**20** minutes	🖥️ or 📄

Content Background

Students will continue to work on an **editorial**, an assignment they will complete over the course of several lessons by following the writing process.

Writing Process

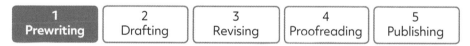

In this lesson, students will continue prewriting by conducting research. First, they will articulate reasons for their chosen opinion. For each reason, students will write a **research question** that they can answer to support that reason.

> **Example Reason:** Everyone deserves to have enough to eat.

> **Example Research Question:** What are the effects of not having enough to eat?

After writing their research questions, they will research using at least three trustworthy sources.

MATERIALS

Supplied
- *Summit English Language Arts 5 Activity Book*
  - Spelling List 19 Activity Bank
  - Research Your Editorial
- Research Notes (printout)
- Editorial Instructions (printout)

Also Needed
- completed Spelling List 19 Pretest activity page from Opinion Writing: Prewriting (A)
- folder for organizing editorial writing assignment pages
- reading material for Go Read!

Grammar, Usage, and Mechanics   Students will learn how to punctuate a tag question, which is a short question that's added to the end of a statement or a command. A comma separates the tag question from the rest of the sentence.

Examples: It's toasty in here**, isn't it?**
Open the window**, will you?**

Advance Preparation

Gather students' completed Spelling List 19 Pretest activity page from Opinion Writing: Prewriting (A). Students will refer to this page during Get Ready: Spelling List 19 Activity Bank.

Gather the folder that students are using to store the activity pages related to their editorial. The folder should contain the following:

- Students' completed Brainstorm for Your Editorial activity page from Opinion Writing: Prewriting (A)

Students will need to complete their own research during Research Your Editorial. Make sure students have access to trustworthy research sources. You may choose to complete the activity at a library.

During the Go Read! activity, students will have the option of using the digital library. Allow extra time for students to make their reading selection, or have students make a selection before beginning the lesson.

Lesson Goals

- Practice all spelling words offline.
- Learn how to punctuate a tag question.
- Learn how to conduct research for an editorial.
- Research your editorial.
- Read for pleasure.

GET READY

Introduction to Opinion Writing: Prewriting (B)
Students will get a glimpse of what they will learn about in the lesson. They will also read the lesson goals and keywords. Have students select each keyword and preview its definition.

Spelling List 19 Activity Bank

Students will practice all spelling words from the workshop by completing Spelling List 19 Activity Bank from *Summit English Language Arts 5 Activity Book*. Make sure students have their completed Spelling List 19 Pretest activity page from Opinion Writing: Prewriting (A) to refer to during this activity.

LEARNING COACH CHECK-IN Remind students to pay special attention to words they spelled incorrectly on the spelling pretest.

LEARN AND TRY IT

LEARN   Tag Questions

Students will learn that a tag question should be separated from the rest of a sentence by a comma.

TIP Writers can use tag questions to connect with the audience in an editorial.

TRY IT   Commas with Tag Questions

Students will answer questions about using commas with tag questions. They will receive feedback on their answers.

LEARN   Researching an Editorial

Students will learn how to come up with effective research questions for researching an opinion piece, such as an editorial. Additionally, they will learn about choosing search terms when conducting digital research.

Tell students that major newspapers, such as the *New York Times*, the *Washington Post*, and the *Chicago Tribune* are all trustworthy sources. Likewise, government websites, such as those run by the Library of Congress and other agencies contain reliable and useful information. Print reference books, such as *Encyclopedia Britannica* and the *World Book Encyclopedia*, are also credible sources of information.

NOTE A published editorial typically does not include a source list; however, a reputable publication keeps a detailed and organized list of research sources.

TRY IT   Research Your Editorial

Students will complete Research Your Editorial in *Summit English Language Arts 5 Activity Book*.

LEARNING COACH CHECK-IN Review students' responses. Ensure that students have created effective research questions before they begin their research. Then ensure that students have found and taken notes from appropriate and trustworthy sources. When students have completed the pages with their notes, they should store their notes in the folder they are using to organize their writing assignment pages.

NOTE If you or your students wish, you can download and print another copy of the Editorial Instructions online. Additional sheets for Research Notes are also available online.

TRY IT
Opinion Writing: Prewriting (B)

Research Your Editorial

Follow these steps to write research questions.
Answers will vary.

1. Write the opinion that you are going to support in your editorial.
   Sample Opinion: Donating food to the town food pantry is important.
   My Opinion:

2. List at least three reasons that you have for your opinion. Write questions that you can research to support each reason.

Reasons	Research Questions
Sample: Everyone deserves to have enough to eat.	**Sample:** What are the effects of not having enough to eat?

OPINION WRITING: PREWRITING (B)   **329**

Follow these steps to conduct research. Record information on the Research Notes pages that follow. Use one page per source.

3. Identify at least three sources (digital, print, or both) that you can use to answer your research questions. Record the title, author, publisher, and URL of each source.

4. As you read each source, take notes related to your research questions.
   • Write your notes in your own words.
   • If you find a direct quotation that you think you might use in your editorial, record the quotation, word for word, in quotation marks. Also record the name of the person you are quoting.

> Research can uncover surprises. You can adjust your research questions!

330   OPINION WRITING: PREWRITING (B)

Research Notes

Source

Title: _____

Author: _____

Published by: _____

URL (if necessary): _____

Notes

Key Information Written in Your Own Words:

_____
_____
_____
_____
_____
_____

Direct Quotation:

_____
_____

Person Quoted: _____

Research Notes

Source

Title: _____

Author: _____

Published by: _____

URL (if necessary): _____

Notes

Key Information Written in Your Own Words:

_____
_____
_____
_____
_____
_____

Direct Quotation:

_____
_____

Person Quoted: _____

WRAP-UP

Questions About Commas and Research

Students will answer questions to show that they understand how to punctuate a tag question and how to research an editorial.

Go Read!

Students will read for pleasure. They should choose a book or a magazine that interests them, or they may choose a selection from the digital library, linked in the online lesson.

Students should read for the entire time. Have students select something to read ahead of time to help them stay focused.

Opinion Writing: Prewriting (C)

Lesson Overview

ACTIVITY	ACTIVITY TITLE	TIME	ONLINE/OFFLINE
GET READY	Introduction to Opinion Writing: Prewriting (C)	**2** minutes	🖥️
	Spelling List 19 Practice	**10** minutes	🖥️
LEARN AND **TRY IT**	*Yes* and *No*	**10** minutes	🖥️
	Commas with *Yes* and *No*	**10** minutes	🖥️
	Planning an Editorial	**15** minutes	🖥️
	Plan Your Editorial **LEARNING COACH CHECK-IN**	**50** minutes	📄
WRAP-UP	Questions About Commas and Personal Experience	**3** minutes	🖥️
	Go Read!	**20** minutes	🖥️ or 📄

Content Background

Students will continue to work on their **editorial**, an assignment that they will complete over the course of several lessons by following the writing process.

Writing Process

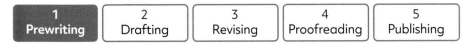

| 1 Prewriting | 2 Drafting | 3 Revising | 4 Proofreading | 5 Publishing |

So far, in **prewriting**, students have chosen a topic and conducted research. In this lesson, students will complete the final part of prewriting: creating a plan for their editorial.

Students will complete a graphic organizer provided to them in their activity book. The graphic organizer will help them to group related information from their research and logically organize that information in the same order that they will present it in their editorial.

Students will learn that personal experience—if relevant—is a powerful and valid form of research. Students will incorporate relevant personal information into their graphic organizer.

Remind students that it is not necessary to write in complete sentences when completing a graphic organizer.

MATERIALS

Supplied
- *Summit English Language Arts 5 Activity Book*
  - Plan Your Editorial
- Editorial Instructions (printout)

Also Needed
- folder for organizing editorial writing assignment pages
- reading material for Go Read!

Grammar, Usage, and Mechanics Students will learn that the words *yes* and *no* should be separated from the rest of a sentence with commas.

> **Examples: Yes,** you may ride your bike to Anna's house.
>
> **No,** I did not realize Anna lives 20 miles away.

Advance Preparation

Gather the folder that students are using to keep all notes and activity pages related to their editorial. The folder should contain the following:

- Students' completed Brainstorm for Your Editorial activity page from Opinion Writing: Prewriting (A)

- Students' completed research notes from Opinion Writing: Prewriting (B)

During the Go Read! activity, students will have the option of using the digital library. Allow extra time for students to make their reading selection, or have students make a selection before beginning the lesson.

Lesson Goals

- Practice spelling words online.

- Learn how to punctuate the words *yes* and *no* in a sentence.

- Learn how to logically organize an editorial.

- Explore how personal experience can strengthen an editorial.

- Complete a graphic organizer for your editorial.

- Read for pleasure.

KEYWORDS

detail – a fact or description that tells more about a topic

editorial – an article in a publication that gives an opinion held by its editor or editors; an opinion piece similar to such an article

fact – something that can be proven true

graphic organizer – a visual device, such as a diagram or chart, that helps a writer plan a piece of writing

opinion – something that a person thinks or believes, but which cannot be proven to be true

prewriting – the stage or step of writing in which a writer chooses a topic, gathers ideas, and plans what to write

GET READY

Introduction to Opinion Writing: Prewriting (C)

Students will get a glimpse of what they will learn about in the lesson. They will also read the lesson goals and keywords. Have students select each keyword and preview its definition.

Spelling List 19 Practice

Students will practice all spelling words from the workshop.

LEARN   Yes and No

Students will learn that the words *yes* and *no* should be separated from the rest of a sentence by a comma.

TIP   Challenge students to think of reasons a writer of an editorial might begin a sentence with the word *yes* or *no*.

TRY IT   Commas with *Yes* and *No*

Students will answer questions about using commas with the words *yes* and *no*. They will receive feedback on their answers.

LEARN   Planning an Editorial

Students will learn about completing a graphic organizer, which is the third part of the prewriting step in the writing process. They will focus on how to logically group and organize their research notes, as well as how to incorporate relevant personal experience into the plan for their editorial.

TRY IT   Plan Your Editorial

Students will complete Plan Your Editorial from *Summit English Language Arts 5 Activity Book*.

LEARNING COACH CHECK-IN   Review students' responses. Ensure that students have completed the graphic organizer in a way that meets the criteria on the activity page. When students have completed their graphic organizer, they should store it in the folder they are using to organize their writing assignment pages.

NOTE   If you or students wish, you can download and print another copy of the Editorial Instructions online.

TRY IT
Opinion Writing: Prewriting (C)

Plan Your Editorial

Review your research notes. Then complete the graphic organizer to plan your editorial. You do not need to use complete sentences.

- Top section: State your opinion.
- Middle sections: State your three supporting reasons. For each reason, list supporting facts and details you discovered during your research. Also, list any supporting personal experience.
- Bottom section: Restate your opinion, and state your call to action (what you want the audience to do).

Title: _____

Opinion:

Reason 1:

Evidence
Research: _____

Personal Experience: _____

Reason 2:

Evidence
Research: _____

Personal Experience: _____

Reason 3:

Evidence
Research: _____

Personal Experience: _____

Opinion, Reworded:

Call to Action:

OPINION WRITING: PREWRITING (C) **333**

334 OPINION WRITING: PREWRITING (C)

OPINION WRITING: PREWRITING (C) **335**

Questions About Commas and Personal Experience

Students will answer questions to show that they understand how to punctuate the words *yes* and *no* in a sentence and how to effectively use relevant personal experience in an editorial.

Go Read!

Students will read for pleasure. They should choose a book or a magazine that interests them, or they may choose a selection from the digital library, linked in the online lesson.

Students should read for the entire time. Have students select something to read ahead of time to help them stay focused.

Opinion Writing: Drafting (A)

Lesson Overview

ACTIVITY	ACTIVITY TITLE	TIME	ONLINE/OFFLINE
GET READY	Introduction to Opinion Writing: Drafting (A)	**2** minutes	📶
	Spelling List 19 Review Game	**10** minutes	📶
	Edit an Editorial	**10** minutes	📶
LEARN AND **TRY IT**	Drafting an Editorial	**15** minutes	📶
	Draft Your Editorial **LEARNING COACH CHECK-IN**	**60** minutes	📄
WRAP-UP	Question About Editorial Drafting	**3** minutes	📶
	Go Read!	**20** minutes	📶 or 📄

Content Background

Students will continue working on their **editorial**. They will complete this assignment over the course of several lessons by following the writing process. In this lesson, students will begin drafting their editorial.

Writing Process

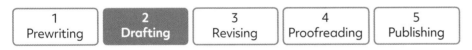

1 Prewriting	2 Drafting	3 Revising	4 Proofreading	5 Publishing

During **drafting**, students will use their notes and their completed graphic organizer as guides as they write a rough draft of their editorial. Students are expected to write about half of their rough draft in this lesson (although they may write more, if they wish). They will have time to finish and submit their draft in Opinion Writing: Drafting (B).

Advance Preparation

Gather the folder that students are using to store the activity pages related to their editorial. The folder should contain the following:

- Students' completed Brainstorm for Your Editorial activity page from Opinion Writing: Prewriting (A)

- Students' completed research notes from Opinion Writing: Prewriting (B)

MATERIALS

Supplied
- *Summit English Language Arts 5 Activity Book*
  - Draft Your Editorial
- Editorial Instructions (printout)
- Drafting Paper (printout)

Also Needed
- folder in which students are storing editorial writing assignment pages
- reading material for Go Read!

- Students' completed Plan Your Editorial activity page from Opinion Writing: Prewriting (C)

During the Go Read! activity, students will have the option of using the digital library. Allow extra time for students to make their reading selection, or have students make a selection before beginning the lesson.

Lesson Goals

- Practice all spelling words online.

- Practice grammar skills by editing a passage.

- Explore how to draft an editorial.

- Begin to draft your editorial.

- Read for pleasure.

GET READY

Introduction to Opinion Writing: Drafting (A)

Students will get a glimpse of what they will learn about in the lesson. They will also read the lesson goals and keywords. Have students select each keyword and preview its definition.

Spelling List 19 Review Game

Students will practice all spelling words from the workshop.

Edit an Editorial

Students will edit a short passage to practice applying grammar skills. This passage contains errors and opportunities to improve the writing related to pronoun-antecedent agreement, commas with direct address, tag questions, and the words *yes* and *no*.

LEARN AND TRY IT

LEARN   Drafting an Editorial

Students will explore how to draft an editorial using a completed graphic organizer and research notes. They will examine how they can target their writing to a particular audience.

TRY IT   Draft Your Editorial

Students will complete half of their first draft using Draft Your Editorial in *Summit English Language Arts 5 Activity Book*. If students wish, they may complete more than half of their draft.

Make sure students have their completed Brainstorm for Your Editorial activity page from Opinion Writing: Prewriting (A), their research notes from Opinion Writing: Prewriting (B), and their Plan Your Editorial activity page from Opinion Writing: Prewriting (C) to refer to during this activity.

LEARNING COACH CHECK-IN Review students' responses. Ensure that students' draft is in line with the assignment criteria outlined on the Brainstorm for Your Editorial activity page. If necessary, remind students not to focus on perfection at this stage of the writing process. Students should store their draft in the folder they are using to organize their writing assignment pages.

NOTE If you or students wish, you can download and print another copy of the Editorial Instructions online. Additional sheets of Drafting Paper are also available online.

TRY IT
Opinion Writing: Drafting (A)

Draft Your Editorial

Using your notes and your graphic organizer to guide you, write the first draft of your editorial. Write only on the white rows. You will use the purple rows for revisions later.

Note: List your sources at the end of your draft. For each source, include the title, author, publisher, and URL.

Title _____

start here ►

Students should write their draft in the white rows only.

keep writing ►

Draft Page 1

OPINION WRITING: DRAFTING (A) **337**

338 OPINION WRITING: DRAFTING (A)

keep writing ►

Draft Page 2

Draft Page 3

OPINION WRITING: DRAFTING (A) **339**

keep writing ►

Draft Page 4

340 OPINION WRITING: DRAFTING (A)

keep writing ►

Draft Page 5

OPINION WRITING: DRAFTING (A) **341**

Draft Page 6

342 OPINION WRITING: DRAFTING (A)

Question About Editorial Drafting

Students will answer a question to show that they understand how to draft an editorial.

Go Read!

Students will read for pleasure. They should choose a book or a magazine that interests them, or they may choose a selection from the digital library, linked in the online lesson.

Students should read for the entire time. Have students select something to read ahead of time to help them stay focused.

Opinion Writing: Drafting (B)

Lesson Overview

ACTIVITY	ACTIVITY TITLE	TIME	ONLINE/OFFLINE
GET READY	Introduction to Opinion Writing: Drafting (B)	**1** minute	🖥️
TRY IT	Review *Yes* and *No*, Tag Questions, and Direct Address	**10** minutes	🖥️
QUIZ	*Yes* and *No*, Tag Questions, and Direct Address	**20** minutes	🖥️
	Spelling List 19	**10** minutes	🖥️
TRY IT	Finish Drafting Your Editorial **LEARNING COACH CHECK-IN**	**50** minutes	📄
WRAP-UP	Turn In Your Editorial Draft	**1** minute	🖥️
	Keyboarding	**10** minutes	🖥️
	More Language Arts Practice	**18** minutes	🖥️

Content Background

Students will continue working on their **editorial**. In this lesson, students will finish and submit their rough draft. They will revise, proofread, and publish their editorial in a future workshop.

Writing Process

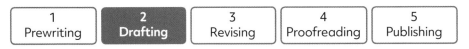

| 1 Prewriting | **2 Drafting** | 3 Revising | 4 Proofreading | 5 Publishing |

Advance Preparation

Gather the folder that students are using to store the activity pages related to their editorial. The folder should contain the following:

- Students' completed Brainstorm for Your Editorial activity page from Opinion Writing: Prewriting (A)

- Students' completed research notes from Opinion Writing: Prewriting (B)

- Students' completed Plan Your Editorial activity page from Opinion Writing: Prewriting (C)

- Students' in-progress Draft Your Editorial activity page from Opinion Writing: Drafting (A)

During the Keyboarding activity, students will practice their keyboarding skills using an external website or program. **You will need to work with students to select an appropriate keyboarding practice website or program; K12 does not specify which resource to use.** A few suggestions are provided in the online activity.

Depending on which program you choose, students may need to set up an account to save their progress. If needed, assist students in setting up and running their chosen keyboarding practice program.

Lesson Goals

- Review how to punctuate a direct address, tag question, and the words *yes* and *no* in a sentence.
- Take a quiz on punctuating a direct address, tag question, and the words *yes* and *no* in a sentence.
- Take a spelling quiz.
- Finish and submit the rough draft of your editorial.

GET READY

Introduction to Opinion Writing: Drafting (B)
Students will read the lesson goals.

TRY IT

Review *Yes* and *No*, Tag Questions, and Direct Address
Students will answer questions to review what they have learned about how to punctuate a direct address, tag question, and the words *yes* and *no* in a sentence.

QUIZ

Yes and *No*, Tag Questions, and Direct Address
Students will complete the *Yes* and *No*, Tag Questions, and Direct Address quiz.

Spelling List 19
Students will complete the Spelling List 19 quiz.

Finish Drafting Your Editorial

Students will complete the rough draft of their editorial. Students should gather the Draft Your Editorial activity page that they started in Opinion Writing: Drafting (A) and complete it.

Make sure students also have their completed Brainstorm for Your Editorial activity page from Opinion Writing: Prewriting (A), their research notes from Opinion Writing: Prewriting (B), and their Plan Your Editorial activity page from Opinion Writing: Prewriting (C) to refer to during this activity.

LEARNING COACH CHECK-IN Review students' draft. Ensure that students' draft is in line with the assignment criteria outlined on the Brainstorm for Your Editorial activity page. If necessary, remind students not to focus on perfection at this stage of the writing process. Students should store a copy of their draft in the folder they are using to organize their writing assignment pages.

NOTE If you or students wish, you can download and print another copy of the Editorial Instructions online. Additional sheets of Drafting Paper are also available online.

TRY IT

Opinion Writing: Drafting (A)

Draft Your Editorial

Using your notes and your graphic organizer to guide you, write the first draft of your editorial. Write only on the white rows. You will use the purple rows for revisions later.

Note: List your sources at the end of your draft. For each source, include the title, author, publisher, and URL.

Title _____

start here ▶

Students should write their draft in the white rows only.

keep writing ▶

Draft Page 1

OPINION WRITING: DRAFTING (A) **337**

---

338 OPINION WRITING: DRAFTING (A)

keep writing ▶

Draft Page 2

---

keep writing ▶

Draft Page 3

OPINION WRITING: DRAFTING (A) **339**

WRAP-UP

Turn In Your Editorial Draft

Students will submit their writing assignment to their teacher.

Keyboarding

Students will practice their keyboarding skills using an external website or program.

More Language Arts Practice

Students will practice skills according to their individual needs.

Big Ideas: Critical Skills Assignment

Lesson Overview

Big Ideas lessons provide students the opportunity to further apply the knowledge acquired and skills learned throughout the unit workshops. Each Big Ideas lesson consists of these parts:

1. **Cumulative Review:** Students keep their skills fresh by reviewing prior content.

2. **Preview:** Students practice answering the types of questions they will commonly find on standardized tests.

3. **Synthesis:** Students complete an assignment that allows them to connect and apply what they have learned. Synthesis assignments vary throughout the course.

   In the Synthesis portion of this Big Ideas lesson, students will read new selections. They will answer literal and inferential comprehension questions and complete writing questions that ask for short responses about the reading selections. Students should refer to the selections while answering the questions, because the questions emphasize using textual evidence. The questions call for students to demonstrate critical thinking, reading, and writing skills.

   LEARNING COACH CHECK-IN   This is a graded assessment. Make sure students complete, review, and submit the assignment to their teacher.

All materials needed for this lesson are linked online and not provided in the Activity Book.

Inside Out
and
Back Again

Homonyms and Homographs

Lesson Overview

ACTIVITY	ACTIVITY TITLE	TIME	ONLINE/OFFLINE
GET READY	*Inside Out and Back Again* Unit Overview	**1** minute	
	Introduction to Homonyms and Homographs	**1** minute	
	Look Back at Word Relationships	**4** minutes	
LEARN AND **TRY IT**	Discover Homonyms and Homographs	**10** minutes	
	Practice Using Homonyms and Homographs	**10** minutes	
	Apply: Homonyms and Homographs **LEARNING COACH CHECK-IN**	**15** minutes	
	Go Write!	**15** minutes	
	Review Homonyms and Homographs	**15** minutes	
QUIZ	Homonyms and Homographs	**15** minutes	
WRAP-UP	Keyboarding	**10** minutes	
	More Language Arts Practice	**14** minutes	
	Go Read!	**10** minutes	

Content Background

Students will use homonyms and homographs to determine the meaning of new words and to better understand words. Students will identify relationships between more complex homonyms and homographs. By understanding homonyms and homographs, students can improve their reading comprehension, spelling, and oral and written vocabulary.

Homonyms are words that have the same spelling and pronunciation but different meanings. *Homographs* have the same spelling but different pronunciations and meanings.

This is the word list for the workshop:

Homonyms	Homographs
duck	bow
pool	wind
point	lead

Advance Preparation

During the Keyboarding activity, students will practice their keyboarding skills using an external website or program. **You will need to work with students to select an appropriate keyboarding practice website or program; K12 does not specify which resource to use.** A few suggestions are provided in the online activity.

Depending on which program you choose, students may need to set up an account to save their progress. If needed, assist students in setting up and running their chosen keyboarding practice program.

During the Go Read! activity, students will have the option of using the digital library. Allow extra time for students to make their reading selection, or have students make a selection before beginning the lesson.

KEYWORDS

homographs – words spelled the same but pronounced differently and with different meanings

homonyms – words spelled the same and pronounced the same but with different meanings

Lesson Goals

- Use homonyms and homographs to determine the meaning of unknown words.
- Use homonyms and homographs correctly in writing.
- Identify relationships between homonyms and homographs.
- Read for pleasure.

GET READY

Inside Out and Back Again Unit Overview
Students will get a glimpse of what they will learn about in the unit.

Introduction to Homonyms and Homographs
Students will get a glimpse of what they will learn about in the lesson. They will also read the lesson goals and keywords. Have students select each keyword and preview its definition.

Look Back at Word Relationships
Students will practice the prerequisite skill of working with word relationships and multiple-meaning words.

LEARN Discover Homonyms and Homographs

Students will be introduced to the vocabulary words for the lesson. These words are either homonyms (spelled and pronounced the same but with different meanings) or homographs (spelled the same but pronounced differently and with different meanings).

TIP   The roots of the words *homonym* and *homograph* can help you remember their meanings.

- The root *nym* means "name." Homonyms have the same spelling and pronunciation. The word *duck* is a homonym—it can refer to the bird or the verb.

- The root *graph* means "writing." Homographs have the same spelling only. They are pronounced differently. The word *bow* is a homograph—it can refer to the pretty knot (pronounced with a long o sound) or the verb (pronounced with the /ow/ sound).

TRY IT Practice Using Homonyms and Homographs

Students will demonstrate their understanding of homonyms and homographs in context.

TRY IT Apply: Homonyms and Homographs

Students will complete Apply: Homonyms and Homographs from *Summit English Language Arts 5 Activity Book*.

LEARNING COACH CHECK-IN   This activity page contains open-ended questions, so it's important that you review students' responses. Give students feedback, using the sample answers provided to guide you.

TRY IT

Homonyms and Homographs

Apply: Homonyms and Homographs

Read the given word and sentence. Write a sentence using a homophone or homograph of the given word. The first one has been done for you.
Sample answers are shown.

1. Word: **bow**
   Sentence: The little girl has a pink **bow** in her hair.
   The audience clapped as the actor took a **bow**.

2. Word: **duck**
   Sentence: The mother **duck** walked her ducklings to the pond.
   I had to duck so that I wouldn't bump my head.

3. Word: **wind**
   Sentence: The **wind** was so strong it blew his hat off his head.
   We had to wind the toy car to make it move.

4. Word: **pool**
   Sentence: On a hot day, it is refreshing to jump into a **pool**.
   We need to pool our resources together to get the job done.

---

5. Word: **lead**
   Sentence: The owner will **lead** the horse to the water.
   Lead is a heavy type of metal.

6. Word: **point**
   Sentence: **Point** to the letter A on the page.
   Be careful with the point on the sharp pencil.

Did that bat just bat its eyes at me?

TRY IT   Go Write!

Students will write independently for pleasure. As they write, they should think about using homonyms and homographs.

TRY IT   Review Homonyms and Homographs

Students will answer questions to review what they have learned about homonyms and homographs.

QUIZ

Homonyms and Homographs

Students will complete the Homonyms and Homographs quiz.

WRAP-UP

Keyboarding

Students will practice their keyboarding skills using an external website or program.

More Language Arts Practice

Students will practice skills according to their individual needs.

Go Read!

Students will read for pleasure. They should choose a book or a magazine that interests them, or they may choose a selection from the digital library, linked in the online lesson.

Students should read for the entire time. Have students select something to read ahead of time to help them stay focused.

Inside Out and Back Again (A)

Lesson Overview

ACTIVITY	ACTIVITY TITLE	TIME	ONLINE/OFFLINE
GET READY	Introduction to *Inside Out and Back Again* (A)	**1** minute	🖥️
	Spelling List 20 Pretest **LEARNING COACH CHECK-IN**	**10** minutes	🖥️ and 📄
	Inside Out and Back Again in 60 Seconds	**1** minute	🖥️
	Look Back at Poetry	**4** minutes	🖥️
	Before You Read *Inside Out and Back Again*, Pages 1–31	**14** minutes	🖥️
READ	*Inside Out and Back Again*, Pages 1–31	**30** minutes	📄
	Check-In: *Inside Out and Back Again*, Pages 1–31	**5** minutes	🖥️
LEARN AND **TRY IT**	Form and Elements of Poetry	**10** minutes	🖥️
	Explore Poetry	**10** minutes	🖥️
	Apply: Poetry Knowledge	**15** minutes	🖥️
	Write About Visual Elements in Poetry **LEARNING COACH CHECK-IN**	**10** minutes	📄
	Practice Words from *Inside Out and Back Again*, Pages 1–31	**8** minutes	🖥️
WRAP-UP	Question About *Inside Out and Back Again*, Pages 1–31	**2** minutes	🖥️

Content Background

Students will begin reading *Inside Out and Back Again* by Thanhha Lai. This text is written as free verse poetry in a diary. Free verse poetry follows a natural speech pattern and does not follow typical poetic conventions, such as regular rhyme or meter. Students will complete activities to further examine poetry's form and visual elements to help them understand what they read.

MATERIALS

Supplied
- *Inside Out and Back Again* by Thanhha Lai
- *Summit English Language Arts 5 Activity Book*
  - Spelling List 20 Pretest
  - Write About Visual Elements in Poetry

Inside Out and Back Again Synopsis, Pages 1–31

Part 1 of this text takes place in Saigon. Through free verse poetry in a diary, we learn about what life is like for the main character, Hà. She lives with her mother and three brothers in Saigon. Her father left nine years before for a navy mission and did not return. Also, we learn about family friends who are fleeing their village because the Vietnam War is getting closer to Saigon.

Lesson Goals

- Take a spelling pretest.

- Begin to read *Inside Out and Back Again*.

- Differentiate between free verse and rhymed poetry.

- Explain how poetry's structure and visual elements support meaning.

GET READY

Introduction to *Inside Out and Back Again* (A)

Students will get a glimpse of what they will learn about in the lesson. They will also read the lesson goals and keywords. Have students select each keyword and preview its definition.

Spelling List 20 Pretest

Students will take a spelling pretest.

LEARNING COACH CHECK-IN   Have students turn to Spelling List 20 Pretest in *Summit English Language Arts 5 Activity Book* and open the online Spelling Pretest activity. Online, students will listen to the spelling word, type the word in the space indicated, and then check their answer. In the activity book, students will write the correct spelling of the word in the tables provided and indicate with a ✓ or an ✗ if they spelled the word correctly or incorrectly online. Students will repeat this process with the remaining words.

As needed, help students with the interaction between the online activity and the activity book page until they become comfortable with what they need to do. As students practice their spelling words throughout the workshop, they should pay special attention to words they spelled incorrectly on the pretest.

This is the complete list of words students will be tested on.

Words Ending with –tion	Words Beginning with init–
addiction	initial
attraction	initiate
conviction	initiative
correction	
projection	
deduction	
contraction	
reaction	
rejection	
celebration	
protection	
appreciation	
motivation	
regulation	

NOTE Have students keep their completed activity page in a safe place so they can refer to it later.

GET READY
Inside Out and Back Again (A)

Spelling List 20 Pretest

1. Open the Spelling Pretest activity online. Listen to the first spelling word. Type the word. Check your answer.

2. Write the correct spelling of the word in the Word column of the Spelling Pretest table on the next page.

Word	⊘	⊗
1 blindfold		

3. Put a check mark in the ⊘ column if you spelled the word correctly online.

Word	⊘	⊗
1 blindfold	✓	

Put an X in the ⊗ column if you spelled the word incorrectly online.

Word	⊘	⊗
1 blindfold		X

4. Repeat Steps 1–3 for the remaining words in the Spelling Pretest.

INSIDE OUT AND BACK AGAIN (A) **345**

Inside Out and Back Again (A)

Spelling List 20 Pretest

Write each spelling word in the Word column, making sure to spell it correctly.

Word	⊘	⊗
1 addiction		
2 attraction		
3 conviction		
4 correction		
5 projection		
6 deduction		
7 contraction		
8 reaction		
9 rejection		

Word	⊘	⊗
10 celebration		
11 protection		
12 appreciation		
13 motivation		
14 regulation		
15 initial		
16 initiate		
17 initiative		

Students should use the ✓ and X columns to indicate whether they spelled each word correctly or incorrectly online.

346 INSIDE OUT AND BACK AGAIN (A)

Inside Out and Back Again in 60 Seconds

Students will watch a short video designed to spark their interest in upcoming topics.

Look Back at Poetry

Students will review the some structural elements of poetry.

Before You Read *Inside Out and Back Again*, Pages 1–31

Students will be introduced to some key vocabulary words that they will encounter in the upcoming reading, learn some important historical background related to the reading, and answer questions to help them set a purpose for their reading.

TIP   Part 1 of this text starts with the celebration of Tết, the Vietnamese new year. There is also mention of the division of north and south Vietnam because of Communism.

READ

Inside Out and Back Again, Pages 1–31

Students will read pages 1–31 of *Inside Out and Back Again* by Thanhha Lai.

Check-In: *Inside Out and Back Again*, Pages 1–31

Students will answer several questions to demonstrate their comprehension of pages 1–31 of *Inside Out and Back Again*.

LEARN AND TRY IT

LEARN   Form and Elements of Poetry

Students will learn how form and elements of poetry affect their understanding of the poem. Students will identify and describe different forms of poems and differentiate between free verse and rhymed poetry.

TRY IT   Explore Poetry

Students will continue to examine the form and elements of poetry.

TRY IT   Apply: Poetry Knowledge

Students will apply to a new work their knowledge of form, structure, and visual elements of poetry.

TRY IT   Write About Visual Elements in Poetry

Students will complete Write About Visual Elements in Poetry from *Summit English Language Arts 5 Activity Book*.

LEARNING COACH CHECK-IN   This activity page contains open-ended questions, so it's important that you review students' responses. Give students feedback, using the sample answers provided to guide you.

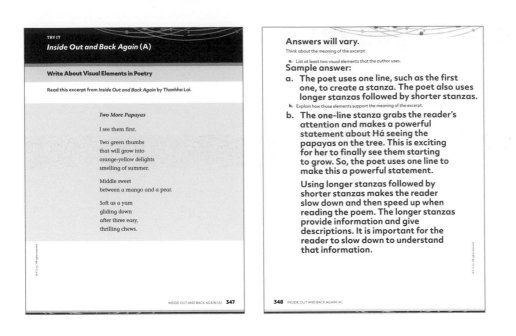

Write About Visual Elements in Poetry

Read this excerpt from *Inside Out and Back Again* by Thanhha Lai.

Two More Papayas

I see them first.

Two green thumbs
that will grow into
orange-yellow delights
smelling of summer.

Middle sweet
between a mango and a pear.

Soft as a yam
gliding down
after three easy,
thrilling chews.

Answers will vary.

Think about the meaning of the excerpt.

a. List at least two visual elements that the author uses.

Sample answer:

a. The poet uses one line, such as the first one, to create a stanza. The poet also uses longer stanzas followed by shorter stanzas.

b. Explain how those elements support the meaning of the excerpt.

b. The one-line stanza grabs the reader's attention and makes a powerful statement about Há seeing the papayas on the tree. This is exciting for her to finally see them starting to grow. So, the poet uses one line to make this a powerful statement.

Using longer stanzas followed by shorter stanzas makes the reader slow down and then speed up when reading the poem. The longer stanzas provide information and give descriptions. It is important for the reader to slow down to understand that information.

TRY IT   Practice Words from *Inside Out and Back Again*, Pages 1–31

Students will answer questions to demonstrate their understanding of the vocabulary from the reading.

WRAP-UP

Question About *Inside Out and Back Again*, Pages 1–31

Students will answer a question to demonstrate a skill they learned in the lesson.

Inside Out and Back Again (B)

Lesson Overview

ACTIVITY	ACTIVITY TITLE	TIME	ONLINE/OFFLINE
GET READY	Introduction to *Inside Out and Back Again* (B)	**1** minute	🛜
	Spelling List 20 Activity Bank	**10** minutes	📄
	Recall *Inside Out and Back Again*, Pages 1–31	**4** minutes	🖥
	Before You Read *Inside Out and Back Again*, Pages 32–69	**10** minutes	📄
READ	*Inside Out and Back Again*, Pages 32–69	**25** minutes	📄
	Check-In: *Inside Out and Back Again*, Pages 32–69	**5** minutes	🖥
LEARN AND **TRY IT**	Structure and Sound Elements in Poetry	**10** minutes	🖥
	Explore Structure and Sound Elements in Poetry	**5** minutes	🖥
	History, Politics, and Culture Affect Literature	**10** minutes	🖥
	Examine the Influence of History, Politics, and Culture	**10** minutes	🖥
	Apply: Influence of History, Politics, and Culture on Literature	**10** minutes	🖥
	Making a Prediction **LEARNING COACH CHECK-IN**	**10** minutes	📄
	Practice Words from *Inside Out and Back Again*, Pages 32–69	**8** minutes	🖥
WRAP-UP	Question About *Inside Out and Back Again*, Pages 32–69	**2** minutes	🖥

Content Background

Students will examine the effect of the poem's structure and sound elements on the meaning of the poem.

The structure of the poem is free verse. Free verse poetry does not follow regular rules of poetry, such as rhyming or syllable count. Sound elements include alliteration and onomatopoeia. *Alliteration* is the term for the first letter or sound being repeated, such as *Paula picks purple pansies*. *Onomatopoeia* is the term for words that show sounds, such as *smash* and *buzz*.

Students will also explore how history, politics, and culture affect *Inside Out and Back Again*.

Advance Preparation

Gather students' completed Spelling List 20 Pretest activity page from *Inside Out and Back Again* (A). Students will refer to this page during Get Ready: Spelling List 20 Activity Bank.

Gather *Summit English Language Arts 5 Activity Book* Making a Prediction page. Students will complete the first item before they read, and they will complete the second item after they read.

KEYWORDS

alliteration – the use of words with the same or close to the same beginning sounds

onomatopoeia – the use of words that show sounds
For example: *moo, woof, quack, squash*

Inside Out and Back Again Synopsis, Pages 32–69

Inside Out and Back Again is a fictional story set during real historical and political events. In this part of the text, Hà's family discusses leaving Saigon, but they decide not to leave. As the story continues, we learn about the president's resignation and the fall of Saigon to the North Vietnamese forces. This part ends with the family deciding to leave Saigon and destroying evidence of their existence.

Lesson Goals

- Practice spelling words.
- Continue to read *Inside Out and Back Again*.
- Make predictions using textual evidence.
- Confirm or modify predictions.
- Explore structure and sound elements in poetry.
- Explain how history, politics, and culture affect literature.

GET READY

Introduction to *Inside Out and Back Again* (B)

Students will get a glimpse of what they will learn about in the lesson. They will also read the lesson goals and keywords. Have students select each keyword and preview its definition.

Spelling List 20 Activity Bank

Students will practice spelling words by completing Spelling List 20 Activity Bank from *Summit English Language Arts 5 Activity Book*. Make sure students have their completed Spelling List 20 Pretest activity page from *Inside Out and Back Again* (A) to refer to during this activity.

Remind students to pay special attention to words they spelled incorrectly on the Spelling Pretest.

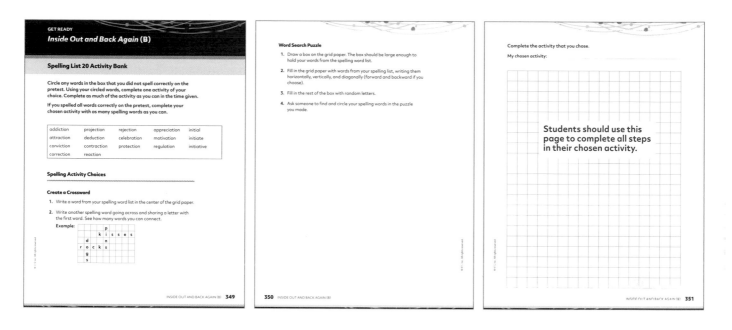

Recall *Inside Out and Back Again*, Pages 1–31

Students will answer some questions to review the reading that they have already completed.

Before You Read *Inside Out and Back Again*, Pages 32–69

Students will be introduced to some key vocabulary words that they will encounter in the upcoming reading and learn some important historical background related to the reading. Students will also complete the first item on Making a Prediction activity page from *Summit English Language Arts 5 Activity Book*.

READ

Inside Out and Back Again, Pages 32–69

Students will read pages 32–69 of *Inside Out and Back Again* by Thanhha Lai.

Check-In: *Inside Out and Back Again*, Pages 32–69

Students will answer several questions to demonstrate their comprehension of pages 32–69 of *Inside Out and Back Again*.

LEARN   Structure and Sound Elements in Poetry

Students will learn the differences between poetry and prose before examining the sound elements of *Inside Out and Back Again*.

TRY IT   Explore Structure and Sound Elements in Poetry

Students will complete an activity in which they explore the structure and sound elements of poetry.

TIP   Reading parts of the poem aloud helps to identify alliteration and onomatopoeia. Doing so may help the reader hear the repetitive beginning consonant sound (alliteration) and sound words (onomatopoeia).

LEARN   History, Politics, and Culture Affect Literature

Students will learn how to analyze passages to explain how history, politics, and culture affect the characters and the story development in *Inside Out and Back Again*.

TRY IT   Examine the Influence of History, Politics, and Culture

Students will complete an activity to explain the influence of the world's history, politics, and culture in *Inside Out and Back Again*.

TRY IT   Apply: Influence of History, Politics, and Culture on Literature

Students will apply to a new work their knowledge of how history, politics, and culture can affect a work of fiction.

TRY IT   Making a Prediction

Students will finish Making a Prediction from *Summit English Language Arts 5 Activity Book*. Students should have started this page during Get Ready: Before Your Read.

LEARNING COACH CHECK-IN   This activity page contains open-ended questions, so it's important that you review students' responses. Give students feedback, using the sample answers provided to guide you.

TRY IT   Practice Words from *Inside Out and Back Again*, Pages 32–69

Students will answer questions to demonstrate their understanding of the vocabulary words from the reading.

WRAP-UP

Question About *Inside Out and Back Again*, Pages 32–69

Students will answer a question to demonstrate a skill they learned in the lesson.

Inside Out and Back Again (C)

Lesson Overview

ACTIVITY	ACTIVITY TITLE	TIME	ONLINE/OFFLINE
GET READY	Introduction to *Inside Out and Back Again* (C)	**1** minute	📶
	Spelling List 20 Review Game	**10** minutes	📶
	Recall *Inside Out and Back Again*, Pages 32–69	**4** minutes	📶
	Before You Read *Inside Out and Back Again*, Pages 73–111	**10** minutes	📶
READ	*Inside Out and Back Again*, Pages 73–111	**25** minutes	📄
	Check-In: *Inside Out and Back Again*, Pages 73–111	**5** minutes	📶
LEARN AND **TRY IT**	Making Connections	**10** minutes	📶
	Examine Connections	**5** minutes	📶
	Use of Dialogue	**10** minutes	📶
	Examine Use of Dialogue	**10** minutes	📶
	Apply: Cause and Effect	**10** minutes	📶
	Special Delivery **LEARNING COACH CHECK-IN**	**10** minutes	📄
	Practice Words from *Inside Out and Back Again*, Pages 73–111	**8** minutes	📶
WRAP-UP	Question About *Inside Out and Back Again*, Pages 73–111	**2** minutes	📶

Content Background

Students will explore the cause-and-effect relationship between events in the story. Good readers process story events and determine the cause-and-effect relationships between them. One event (a cause) results in another event (effect). Thinking about cause and effect helps make sense of the story. In this lesson, students will also make connections with the text and real-world historical events to help them better understand the novel. Finally, students will explore the author's use of dialogue and how it helps to shape the meaning of the text.

MATERIALS

Supplied
- *Inside Out and Back Again* by Thanhha Lai
- *Summit English Language Arts 5 Activity Book*
- Special Delivery

Inside Out and Back Again Synopsis, Pages 73–111

In this part of *Inside Out and Back Again*, Hà's family continues their journey to safety. We learn of the hardships endured on the boat and the fall of South Vietnam. Eventually, the family arrives in Guam. While living in temporary housing (tents), they learn they need to figure out where they want to live. Some people choose France and others choose Canada. Hà's mom decides to go to America, with the hope that her sons will go to college. At the end of this part, Hà's family waits for a sponsor so they can go to America. Eventually, they are sponsored by a family in Alabama.

Lesson Goals

- Practice spelling words.

- Continue reading *Inside Out and Back Again*.

- Make connections between a text and the real world.

- Examine cause-and-effect relationships in a text.

- Identify how dialogue affects the meaning of a text.

GET READY

Introduction to *Inside Out and Back Again* (C)

Students will get a glimpse of what they will learn about in the lesson. They will also read the lesson goals.

Spelling List 20 Review Game

Students will practice spelling words from Spelling List 20.

Recall *Inside Out and Back Again*, Pages 32–69

Students will answer some questions to review the reading that they have already completed.

Before You Read *Inside Out and Back Again*, Pages 73–111

Students will be introduced to some key vocabulary words that they will encounter in the upcoming reading, learn some important historical background related to the reading, and answer questions to help them set a purpose for their reading.

Inside Out and Back Again, **Pages 73–111**

Students will read pages 73–111 of *Inside Out and Back Again* by Thanhha Lai.

Check-In: *Inside Out and Back Again,* **Pages 73–111**

Students will answer several questions to demonstrate their comprehension of pages 73–111 of *Inside Out and Back Again*.

LEARN AND **TRY IT**

LEARN   Making Connections

Students will learn how understanding *Inside Out and Back Again* can help readers understand the real world. Students will also explore the cause-and-effect relationships between events in the story.

TRY IT   Examine Connections

Students will continue to explore the cause-and-effect relationship between story events and text-to-world connections.

LEARN   Use of Dialogue

Students will learn how to examine the author's use of dialogue and its effect on the story.

> **TIP**   Remind students to focus on the word choice selected by the author when a character speaks. How the character speaks allows the reader to learn more about the character's personality, emotions, and actions.

TRY IT   Examine Use of Dialogue

Students will continue to explore the role of dialogue and its effect on the story.

TRY IT   Apply: Cause and Effect

Students will apply to a new work their knowledge of how real-world events can influence fiction and identify cause-and-effect events in a story.

TRY IT   Special Delivery

Students will complete Special Delivery from *Summit English Language Arts 5 Activity Book*.

> **LEARNING COACH CHECK-IN**   This activity page contain an open-ended question, so it's important that you review students' responses. Give students feedback, using the sample answer provided to guide you.

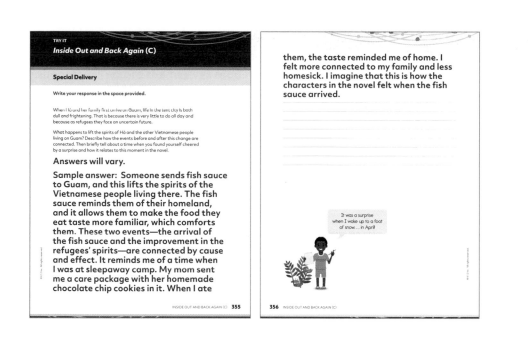

TRY IT Practice Words from *Inside Out and Back Again*, Pages 73–111

Students will answer questions to determine their understanding of the vocabulary from the reading.

Question About *Inside Out and Back Again*, Pages 73–111

Students will answer a question to demonstrate a skill they learned in the lesson.

Inside Out and Back Again (D)

Lesson Overview

ACTIVITY	ACTIVITY TITLE	TIME	ONLINE/OFFLINE
GET READY	Introduction to *Inside Out and Back Again* (D)	**1** minute	🖥️
QUIZ	Spelling List 20	**10** minutes	🖥️
GET READY	Recall *Inside Out and Back Again*, Pages 73–111	**4** minutes	🖥️
	Before You Read *Inside Out and Back Again*, Pages 115–141	**10** minutes	🖥️
READ	*Inside Out and Back Again*, Pages 115–141	**25** minutes	📄
	Check-In: *Inside Out and Back Again*, Pages 115–141	**5** minutes	🖥️
LEARN AND **TRY IT**	Identify Literary Devices	**10** minutes	🖥️
	Explain Literary Devices	**5** minutes	🖥️
	Themes of *Inside Out and Back Again*	**10** minutes	🖥️
	Examine Themes	**5** minutes	🖥️
	Apply: Figurative Language Adds Meaning	**15** minutes	🖥️
	Theme and Character Response **LEARNING COACH CHECK-IN**	**10** minutes	📄
	Practice Words from *Inside Out and Back Again*, Pages 115–141	**8** minutes	🖥️
WRAP-UP	Question About *Inside Out and Back Again*, Pages 115–141	**2** minutes	🖥️

Content Background

Students will explore literary devices and how they add meaning to text. Literary devices, such as sensory details and imagery, are words or phrases that authors use to fully describe the story using the five senses—see, hear, touch, taste, and feel. Literary devices allow readers to have a complete picture in their mind. Figurative language is another type of literary device. Figurative language includes similes, metaphors, personification, and onomatopoeia. For example, in *Inside Out and Back Again*, the author states a simile: "Mother's face crinkles like paper on fire."

> **MATERIALS**
>
> **Supplied**
> - *Inside Out and Back Again* by Thanhha Lai
> - *Summit English Language Arts 5 Activity Book*
>   - Theme and Character Response

Students will also begin to explore possible themes of the text and characters' involvement in developing themes. Themes are the big ideas that authors convey in a text that emerge and develop over the course of the story. To identify and interpret theme, good readers pay attention to what the characters in a story say and do. Themes are not single words; they are complete thoughts or statements. For example, the statement "Love is more important than money" is a theme.

Inside Out and Back Again Synopsis, Pages 115–141

This part of the text begins with Hà's family arriving in Alabama and acclimating to living in America. They are provided housing and begin to learn English. Hà's mother and brother begin working and the rest of the children start going to school, completing the last grade they left unfinished in Saigon. Hà is nervous to begin school, and this part ends with Hà's difficulty with her introduction to her teacher. They both struggle to say each other's names.

Lesson Goals

- Take a spelling quiz.

- Continue reading *Inside Out and Back Again*.

- Explain how an author uses literary devices to affect the meaning of a text.

- Examine themes and how characters help develop themes.

GET READY

Introduction to *Inside Out and Back Again* (D)
Students will get a glimpse of what they will learn about in the lesson. They will also read the lesson goals and keywords. Have students select each keyword and preview its definition.

QUIZ

Spelling List 20
Students will take the Spelling List 20 quiz.

Recall *Inside Out and Back Again*, **Pages 73–111**

Students will answer some questions to review the reading that they have already completed.

Before You Read *Inside Out and Back Again*, **Pages 115–141**

Students will be introduced to some key vocabulary words that they will encounter in the upcoming reading, learn some important historical background related to the reading, and answer questions to help them set a purpose for their reading.

READ

Inside Out and Back Again, **Pages 115–141**

Students will read pages 115–141 of *Inside Out and Back Again* by Thanhha Lai.

Check-In: *Inside Out and Back Again*, **Pages 115–141**

Students will answer several questions to demonstrate their comprehension of pages 115–141 of *Inside Out and Back Again*.

LEARN AND TRY IT

LEARN   Identify Literary Devices

Students will learn how to identify literary devices and examine how they add meaning to the text.

TRY IT   Explain Literary Devices

Students will examine passages to explain how literary devices add meaning to the text.

LEARN   Themes of *Inside Out and Back Again*

Students will determine possible themes for *Inside Out and Back Again* using details from the text.

TIP   Remind students that themes are not single words; they are complete thoughts or statements.

TRY IT   Examine Themes

Students will continue to examine possible themes for the text.

TRY IT   Apply: Figurative Language Adds Meaning

Students will apply to a new work what they've learned about identifying and explaining how figurative language adds meaning to a text.

TRY IT   Theme and Character Response

Students will complete Theme and Character Response from *Summit English Language Arts 5 Activity Book*.

LEARNING COACH CHECK-IN   This activity page contains open-ended questions, so it's important that you review students' responses. Give students feedback, using the sample answers provided to guide you.

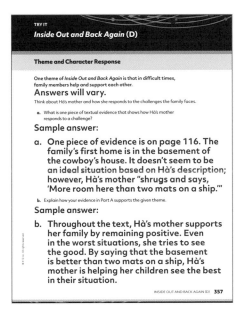

TRY IT   Practice Words from *Inside Out and Back Again*, Pages 115–141

Students will answer questions to determine their understanding of the vocabulary from the reading.

WRAP-UP

Question About *Inside Out and Back Again*, Pages 115–141

Students will answer a question to demonstrate a skill they learned in the lesson.

Inside Out and Back Again (E)

Lesson Overview

ACTIVITY	ACTIVITY TITLE	TIME	ONLINE/OFFLINE
GET READY	Introduction to *Inside Out and Back Again* (E)	**1** minute	🖥️
	Spelling List 21 Pretest `LEARNING COACH CHECK-IN`	**10** minutes	🖥️ and 📄
	Recall *Inside Out and Back Again*, Pages 115–141	**4** minutes	🖥️
	Before You Read *Inside Out and Back Again*, Pages 142–172	**10** minutes	🖥️
READ	*Inside Out and Back Again*, Pages 142–172	**25** minutes	📄
	Check-In: *Inside Out and Back Again*, Pages 142–172	**5** minutes	🖥️
LEARN AND **TRY IT**	Using Literary Devices	**10** minutes	🖥️
	Exploring Literary Devices	**5** minutes	🖥️
	Themes of *Inside Out and Back Again*	**10** minutes	🖥️
	Themes and Character Responses	**5** minutes	🖥️
	Apply: Author's Use of Figurative Language	**10** minutes	🖥️
	Identify Figurative Language `LEARNING COACH CHECK-IN`	**15** minutes	📄
	Practice Words from *Inside Out and Back Again*, Pages 142–172	**8** minutes	🖥️
WRAP-UP	Question About *Inside Out and Back Again*, Pages 142–172	**2** minutes	🖥️

Content Background

Students will continue to examine the author's use of literary devices and practice finding specific literary devices in the text that help support their understanding of how the characters feel. They will also identify figurative language used in a text. Figurative language is used by an author to describe something by comparing it to something completely different. It allows the author's words to be more effective in engaging the reader with the text. For example, rather than *It is cold outside*, an author might say *It's as cold as a freezer outside!* This gives the reader a more vivid mental picture and enables deeper engagement with the story. Students will also examine characters' responses to each other and to events in a text to learn about how authors develop themes.

MATERIALS

Supplied
- *Inside Out and Back Again* by Thanhha Lai
- *Summit English Language Arts 5 Activity Book*
  - Spelling List 21 Pretest
  - Identify Figurative Language

Inside Out and Back Again Synopsis, Pages 142–172

As the book continues, we learn about Hà's unpleasant experiences at school. She is teased and bullied by her peers for being different. Her teachers struggle to see her intellectual capabilities because of her limited ability with English, and Hà continues to be frustrated. Meanwhile, Hà's mother tries to continue to acclimate to their new American life by introducing herself and her family to their neighbors. One neighbor offers to tutor the family. Hà begins her lessons and slowly starts to learn English. However, as she learns more, Hà begins to understand how cruel the other kids are at school. This part ends with the family's neighbors convincing them to become members of the Del Ray Southern Baptist Church. They are baptized and become Christians.

Lesson Goals

- Complete a spelling pretest.
- Continue reading *Inside Out and Back Again*.
- Examine the author's use of literary devices.
- Find specific literary devices that support the meaning of the text.
- Explore themes, using evidence from the characters' responses.

GET READY

Introduction to *Inside Out and Back Again* (E)
Students will get a glimpse of what they will learn about in the lesson. They will also read the lesson goals.

Spelling List 21 Pretest
Students will take a spelling pretest.

LEARNING COACH CHECK-IN   Have students turn to Spelling List 21 Pretest in *Summit English Language Arts 5 Activity Book* and open the online Spelling Pretest activity. Online, students will listen to the spelling word, type the word in the space indicated, and then check their answer. In the activity book, students will write the correct spelling of the word in the tables provided and indicate with a ✓ or an ✗ if they spelled the word correctly or incorrectly online. Students will repeat this process with the remaining words.

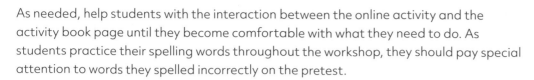

As needed, help students with the interaction between the online activity and the activity book page until they become comfortable with what they need to do. As students practice their spelling words throughout the workshop, they should pay special attention to words they spelled incorrectly on the pretest.

This is the complete list of words students will be tested on.

Homophones	More Homophones
coarse	boarder
course	border
flea	review
flee	revue
heal	right
heel	rite
loan	wright
lone	foul
pole	fowl
poll	
pore	
pour	

NOTE Have students keep their completed activity page in a safe place so they can refer to it later.

Recall *Inside Out and Back Again*, **Pages 115–141**

Students will answer some questions to review the reading that they have already completed.

Before You Read *Inside Out and Back Again*, **Pages 142–172**

Students will be introduced to some key vocabulary words that they will encounter in the upcoming reading and will be provided a purpose for reading the text.

READ

Read *Inside Out and Back Again*, **Pages 142–172**

Students will read pages 142–172 of *Inside Out and Back Again* by Thanhha Lai.

Check-In: *Inside Out and Back Again*, **Pages 142–172**

Students will answer several questions to demonstrate their comprehension of pages 142–172 of *Inside Out and Back Again*.

LEARN AND TRY IT

LEARN   Using Literary Devices

Students will determine which literary devices are used in a text and the purpose for using them.

TRY IT   Exploring Literary Devices

Students will continue exploring literary devices and how they add to understanding of the text.

LEARN   Themes of *Inside Out and Back Again*

Students will continue to focus on the development of themes, using evidence from what characters say and do throughout the text.

> **TIP**   Good readers focus on what the characters say or do throughout the text. Using this textual evidence, good readers can begin to form a possible theme of the text. Themes are not single words; they are complete thoughts or statements.

TRY IT   Themes and Character Responses

Students will explore characters' responses to themes in *Inside Out and Back Again*.

TRY IT   Apply: Identify Figurative Language

Students will apply to a new work what they've learned about identifying examples of figurative language in a story.

TRY IT   Identify Figurative Language

Students will complete Identify Figurative Language from *Summit English Language Arts 5 Activity Book*.

LEARNING COACH CHECK-IN   This activity page contains open-ended questions, so it's important that you review students' responses. Give students feedback, using the sample answers provided to guide you.

TRY IT
Inside Out and Back Again (E)

Identify Figurative Language

Read the phrase. Then read the excerpt from *Inside Out and Back Again* in which the phrase is used.

Identify which type of figurative language the phrase is an example of: *alliteration, metaphor, onomatopoeia,* or *simile*.

Example answers are shown.

1. Phrase: *like a caged puppy*

   Excerpt:

   But

   he looks

   more defeated than weak,

   more helpless than scared,

   like a caged puppy. (p. 226)

   Type of figurative language: **simile**

2. Phrase: *hush, hush*

   Excerpt:

   Hush, hush,

   hush, hush.

   She says it over and over,

   like a chant,

   slowly. (p. 210)

   Type of figurative language: **onomatopoeia**

---

3. Phrase: *misery keeps pouncing on me*

   Excerpt:

   It's time to tell Mother

   why misery

   keeps pouncing on me. (p. 213)

   Type of figurative language: **metaphor**

4. Phrase: *cool to a real whisper*

   Excerpt:

   Slowly

   the screams that never stopped

   inside my head

   cool to a real whisper. (p. 210)

   Type of figurative language: **metaphor**

5. Phrase: *drops from wet hair drip down*

   Excerpt:

   Drops from wet hair

   drip down my back. (p. 172)

   Type of figurative language: **alliteration**

6. Phrase: *clink clank*

   Excerpt:

   I hear the clink clank

   of Brother Khôi's bicycle (p. 154)

   Type of figurative language: **onomatopoeia**

TRY IT   Practice Words from *Inside Out and Back Again*, Pages 142–172

Students will answer questions to determine their understanding of the vocabulary from the reading.

WRAP-UP

Question About *Inside Out and Back Again*, Pages 142–172

Students will answer a question to demonstrate a skill they learned in the lesson.

Inside Out and Back Again (F)

Lesson Overview

ACTIVITY	ACTIVITY TITLE	TIME	ONLINE/OFFLINE
GET READY	Introduction to *Inside Out and Back Again* (F)	**1** minute	🖥️
	Spelling List 21 Activity Bank	**10** minutes	📄
	Recall *Inside Out and Back Again*, Pages 142–172	**4** minutes	🖥️
	Before You Read *Inside Out and Back Again*, Pages 173–202	**10** minutes	🖥️
READ	*Inside Out and Back Again*, Pages 173–202	**25** minutes	📄
	Check-In: *Inside Out and Back Again*, Pages 173–202	**5** minutes	🖥️
LEARN AND **TRY IT**	Author's Use of Dialogue and Imagery	**8** minutes	🖥️
	Explore Dialogue and Imagery	**8** minutes	🖥️
	Themes and Character Responses	**7** minutes	🖥️
	Examine Themes and Character Responses	**7** minutes	🖥️
	Apply: Dialogue and Imagery	**10** minutes	🖥️
	Plan a Narrative Poem **LEARNING COACH CHECK-IN**	**15** minutes	📄
	Practice Words from *Inside Out and Back Again*, Pages 173–202	**8** minutes	🖥️
WRAP-UP	Question About *Inside Out and Back Again*, Pages 173–202	**2** minutes	🖥️

Content Background

Students will explore how the author uses dialogue and imagery to enhance the meaning of a text. *Imagery* refers to words or phrases using the five senses that an author employs to create a picture in the reader's mind. For example, in *Inside Out and Back Again*, the author describes the main character riding on her brother's bike this way: *We glide and I feel as if I'm floating.* Students will also investigate characters' responses and how charaters develop the theme over the course of a text. Students will also begin planning their narrative poem. A narrative poem is a story written in the form of a poem.

> ### MATERIALS
>
> **Supplied**
> - *Inside Out and Back Again* by Thanhha Lai
> - *Summit English Language Arts 5 Activity Book*
>   - Spelling List 21 Activity Bank
>   - Plan a Narrative Poem
>
> **Also Needed**
> - completed Spelling List 21 Pretest activity page from *Inside Out and Back Again* (E)

Advance Preparation

Gather students' completed Spelling List 21 Pretest activity page from *Inside Out and Back Again* (E). Students will refer to this page during Get Ready: Spelling List 21 Activity Bank

Inside Out and Back Again Synopsis, Pages 173–202

This part of the book concerns Hà's mother yearning for the return of her husband. This is the first time the reader sees Hà's mother's lack of optimism. Hà continues to describe the complexity of learning English while sharing her miserable school experiences with her tutor, Miss Washington. Miss Washington encourages her and promises her it will get better. Hà remains doubtful. With a new lunch and new confidence, Hà begins to come out of her shell in school. However, Pink Boy continues to bully Hà. For the first time, Hà confides in her mother and bonds with her teacher.

Lesson Goals

- Practice spelling words.
- Continue reading *Inside Out and Back Again*.
- Identify how dialogue and imagery add meaning to a text.
- Explore themes and character responses to the challenges in a story.

GET READY

Introduction to *Inside Out and Back Again* (F)

Students will get a glimpse of what they will learn about in the lesson. They will also read the lesson goals and keywords. Have students select each keyword and preview its definition.

Spelling List 21 Activity Bank

Students will practice spelling words by completing Spelling List 21 Activity Bank from *Summit English Language Arts 5 Activity Book*. Make sure students have their completed Spelling List 21 Pretest activity page from *Inside Out and Back Again* (E) to refer to during this activity.

Remind students to pay special attention to words they spelled incorrectly on the Spelling Pretest.

Recall *Inside Out and Back Again*, Pages 142–172

Students will answer some questions to review the reading that they have already completed.

Before You Read *Inside Out and Back Again*, Pages 173–202

Students will be introduced to some key vocabulary words that they will encounter in the upcoming reading and will be provided a purpose for reading the text.

READ

Inside Out and Back Again, Pages 173–202

Students will read pages 173–202 of *Inside Out and Back Again* by Thanhha Lai.

Check-In: *Inside Out and Back Again*, Pages 173–202

Students will answer several questions to demonstrate their comprehension of pages 173–202 of *Inside Out and Back Again*.

LEARN AND TRY IT

LEARN   Author's Use of Dialogue and Imagery

Students will identify examples of dialogue and imagery used by the author to shape the meaning of a text.

TRY IT   Explore Dialogue and Imagery

Students will explore the author's use of dialogue and imagery, which add meaning to a text.

LEARN   Themes and Character Responses

Students will determine themes of *Inside Out and Back Again* and explain how characters' responses to challenges develop themes.

TRY IT   Examine Themes and Character Responses

Students will examine characters' responses and how characters' responses to challenges develop themes.

> **TIP**   Remind students that what characters say or do helps develop themes in a story.

TRY IT   Apply: Dialogue and Imagery

Students will apply to a new work what they've learned about an author's use of dialogue and imagery and how it adds to the overall meaning of a story.

TRY IT   Plan a Narrative Poem

Students will complete Plan a Narrative Poem from *Summit English Language Arts 5 Activity Book*.

> **LEARNING COACH CHECK-IN**   This activity page contains open-ended questions, so it's important that you review students' responses. Give students feedback as needed.

> **NOTE**   Have students keep their completed activity page in a safe place so they can refer to it later.

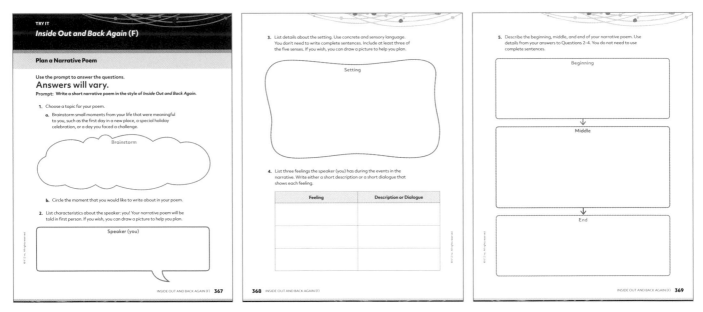

TRY IT   Practice Words from *Inside Out and Back Again*, Pages 173–202

Students will answer questions to determine their understanding of the vocabulary from the reading.

WRAP-UP

Question About *Inside Out and Back Again*, Pages 173–202

Students will answer a question to demonstrate a skill they learned in the lesson.

Inside Out and Back Again (G)

Lesson Overview

ACTIVITY	ACTIVITY TITLE	TIME	ONLINE/OFFLINE
GET READY	Introduction to *Inside Out and Back Again* (G)	**1** minute	🖥
	Spelling List 21 Practice	**10** minutes	🖥
	Recall *Inside Out and Back Again*, Pages 173–202	**4** minutes	📶
	Before You Read *Inside Out and Back Again*, Pages 203–234	**10** minutes	📶
READ	*Inside Out and Back Again*, Pages 203–234	**25** minutes	📄
	Check-In: *Inside Out and Back Again*, Pages 203–234	**5** minutes	📶
LEARN AND **TRY IT**	Sound Elements and Meaning	**8** minutes	🖥
	Investigate How Sound Elements Affect Meaning	**5** minutes	📶
	Apply: Sound Elements and Meaning	**12** minutes	📶
	Write a Narrative Poem **LEARNING COACH CHECK-IN**	**30** minutes	📄
	Practice Words from *Inside Out and Back Again*, Pages 203–234	**8** minutes	📶
WRAP-UP	Question About *Inside Out and Back Again*, Pages 203–234	**2** minutes	📶

Content Background

Students will continue to investigate how the author's use of sound elements in a poem enhances meaning. Sound elements include alliteration and onomatopoeia. Alliteration is the use of words having the same or similar beginning sound; for example, *drops drip down*. Onomatopoeia is the use of words that show sounds; for example, *smack, thud*.

Students will write a narrative poem about an important moment in their life. Students should write this poem in a sequential order with a speaker and should include precise, expressive language.

Advance Preparation

Gather students' completed Plan a Narrative Poem activity page from *Inside Out and Back Again* (F). Students will refer to this page during Write a Narrative Poem.

MATERIALS

Supplied
- *Inside Out and Back Again* by Thanhha Lai
- *Summit English Language Arts 5 Activity Book*
  - Write a Narrative Poem

Also Needed
- completed Plan a Narrative Poem activity page from *Inside Out and Back Again* (F)

Inside Out and Back Again Synopsis, Pages 203–234

This part of the book begins with the school intervening with Pink Boy's bullying of Hà. Despite this attempt, Hà continues to be harassed after school. Hà gets very angry, but Miss Washington is able to calm her down.

The family goes to the grocery store and encounters a butcher who refuses to serve them. Hà's mother is persistent and eventually he serves them. After school, Hà continues to be bullied. With the help of her brother, they devise a plan to end Pink Boy's bullying. The plan works and Hà is no longer tormented by him. By now, kids are more interested in being friends with her. This part ends with Hà's family receiving thoughtful Christmas gifts from the cowboy and Miss Washington.

KEYWORDS

narrative – a kind of writing that tells a story

narrative poem – a poem that tells a story

Lesson Goals

- Practice spelling words.

- Continue reading *Inside Out and Back Again*.

- Examine an author's use of sound elements and language to create meaning.

- Write a narrative poem.

GET READY

Introduction to *Inside Out and Back Again* (G)

Students will get a glimpse of what they will learn about in the lesson. They will also read the lesson goals and keywords. Have students select each keyword and preview its definition.

Spelling List 21 Practice

Students will practice spelling words from the workshop.

Recall *Inside Out and Back Again*, Pages 173–202

Students will answer some questions to review the reading that they have already completed.

Before You Read *Inside Out and Back Again*, Pages 203–234

Students will be introduced to some key vocabulary words that they will encounter in the upcoming reading and will be provided a purpose for reading the text.

Inside Out and Back Again, Pages 203–234

Students will read pages 203–234 of *Inside Out and Back Again* by Thanhha Lai.

Check-In: *Inside Out and Back Again*, Pages 203–234

Students will answer several questions to demonstrate their comprehension of pages 203–234 of *Inside Out and Back Again*.

LEARN AND TRY IT

LEARN   Sound Elements and Meaning

Students will explore the author's use of sound elements such as alliteration and onomatopoeia.

TIP   Have students try reading parts of the poem aloud to hear the alliteration (words having the same or similar beginning sound) and the onomatopoeia (words that show sounds).

TRY IT   Investigate How Sound Elements Affect Meaning

Students will continue to explore meaning of a text, using the sound elements selected by the author.

TRY IT   Apply: Sound Elements and Meaning

Students will apply to a new work what they've learned about how sound elements affect the meaning of a poem.

TRY IT   Write a Narrative Poem

Students will complete Write a Narrative Poem from *Summit English Language Arts 5 Activity Book*. Make sure students have their completed Plan a Narrative Poem activity page from *Inside Out and Back Again* (F) to refer to during this activity.

LEARNING COACH CHECK-IN   Review students' narrative poem. Ask students to point out the elements of narrative poetry that they used, including dialogue, imagery, figurative language, purposeful line breaks, and stanza breaks. Point out parts of the poem that you felt were particularly well done, and explain why.

NOTE   Have students keep their completed narrative poem in a safe place so they can refer to it later.

Write a Narrative Poem

Write the first draft of your narrative poem. Write only on the white rows. You will use the purple rows for revisions later.

Prompt: Write a short narrative poem in the style of *Inside Out and Back Again*.

As you write, use the following elements of narrative poetry: dialogue, imagery, figurative language, purposeful line breaks, and stanza breaks.

Title _____

start here ▶

Students should write their draft in the white rows only.

keep writing ▶

Draft Page 1

---

keep writing ▶

Draft Page 2

---

keep writing ▶

Draft Page 3

Draft Page 4

TRY IT   Practice Words from *Inside Out and Back Again*, Pages 203–234

Students will answer questions to determine their understanding of the vocabulary from the reading.

WRAP-UP

Question About *Inside Out and Back Again*, Pages 203–234

Students will answer a question to demonstrate a skill they learned in the lesson.

Inside Out and Back Again (H)

Lesson Overview

ACTIVITY	ACTIVITY TITLE	TIME	ONLINE/OFFLINE
GET READY	Introduction to *Inside Out and Back Again* (H)	**1** minute	🖥️
	Spelling List 21 Review Game	**10** minutes	🖥️
	Recall *Inside Out and Back Again*, Pages 203–234	**4** minutes	🖥️
	Before You Read *Inside Out and Back Again*, Pages 237–262	**10** minutes	🖥️
READ	*Inside Out and Back Again*, Pages 237–262	**25** minutes	📄
	Check-In: *Inside Out and Back Again*, Pages 237–262	**5** minutes	🖥️
LEARN AND **TRY IT**	Author's Word Choice	**8** minutes	🖥️
	Analyze Author's Word Choice	**7** minutes	🖥️
	Criteria for a Summary	**8** minutes	🖥️
	Understanding Summaries	**7** minutes	🖥️
	Apply: Summary Knowledge	**10** minutes	🖥️
	Revise and Publish a Narrative Poem **LEARNING COACH CHECK-IN**	**15** minutes	📄
	Practice Words from *Inside Out and Back Again*, Pages 237–262	**8** minutes	🖥️
WRAP-UP	Question About *Inside Out and Back Again*, Pages 237–262	**2** minutes	🖥️

Content Background

Students will analyze the author's word choice to establish the mood and highlight aspects of characters and setting. Students will also learn the criteria for a good summary and demonstrate their understanding of how to write an effective summary. A good or effective summary includes the major characters and events in the story. The summary is in sequential order and includes key details from the text. Often, the summary includes major themes of the text. Students will also revise and publish their narrative poem.

MATERIALS

Supplied
- *Inside Out and Back Again* by Thanhha Lai
- *Summit English Language Arts 5 Activity Book*
  - Revise and Publish a Narrative Poem

(continued on next page)

Advance Preparation

Gather students' completed Plan a Narrative Poem activity page from *Inside Out and Back Again* (F) and Write a Narrative Poem activity page from *Inside Out and Back Again* (G). Students will refer to these pages during Revise and Publish a Narrative Poem.

Inside Out and Back Again Synopsis, Pages 237–262

The beginning of this part of the book mentions that the Vietnam War has ended eight months before and the family has not heard from Hà's father. For Christmas, one of Hà's friends gives her a gift. She is happy but also embarrassed because she cannot give her friend a gift, too. The family continues to think about the whereabouts of their father, and Hà's mother continues hoping for a sign. One day, Hà's mother returns home from work without her treasured amethyst ring. She announces this is the sign that Father is gone.

The story continues with the start of a new year, the year of the dragon. The family prays for various things and is hopeful for this opportunity for a fresh start. The text concludes with an author's note, indicating that much of this story is based on the author's life.

Lesson Goals

- Practice spelling words.
- Continue reading *Inside Out and Back Again*.
- Analyze author's word choices.
- Demonstrate understanding of an effective summary.

Also Needed

- completed Plan a Narrative Poem activity page from *Inside Out and Back Again* (F)
- completed Write a Narrative Poem activity page from from *Inside Out and Back Again* (G)

KEYWORDS

narrative poem – a poem that tells a story

GET READY

Introduction to *Inside Out and Back Again* (H)

Students will get a glimpse of what they will learn about in the lesson. They will also read the lesson goals and keywords. Have students select each keyword and preview its definition.

Spelling List 21 Review Game

Students will practice spelling words from the workshop.

Recall *Inside Out and Back Again*, Pages 203–234

Students will answer some questions to review the reading that they have already completed.

Before You Read *Inside Out and Back Again*, Pages 237–262

Students will be introduced to some key vocabulary words that they will encounter in the upcoming reading and will be provided a purpose for reading the text.

READ

Inside Out and Back Again Pages, 237–262

Students will read pages 237–262 of *Inside Out and Back Again* by Thanhha Lai.

Check-In: *Inside Out and Back Again*, Pages 237–262

Students will answer several questions to demonstrate their comprehension of pages 237–262 of *Inside Out and Back Again*.

LEARN AND TRY IT

LEARN Author's Word Choice

Students will learn to examine the author's word choice, which establishes the mood and highlights aspects of characters and setting in the text.

TRY IT Analyze Author's Word Choice

Students will analyze the author's word choice, which establishes the mood and highlights aspects of the characters and setting in the text.

LEARN Criteria for a Summary

Students will learn about the criteria for a good summary.

> **TIP**   Remind students that an effective summary includes the major characters and events in the story. It is sequential and includes key details from the text. The summary also includes major themes of the text.

TRY IT Understanding Summaries

Students will answer questions to demonstrate their understanding of how to write an effective summary.

TRY IT Apply: Summary Knowledge

Students will read a summary and make necessary improvements based on their knowledge about effective summaries.

TRY IT   Revise and Publish a Narrative Poem

Students will complete Revise and Publish a Narrative Poem from *Summit English Language Arts 5 Activity Book*. Make sure students have their completed Plan a Narrative Poem activity page from *Inside Out and Back Again* (F) and Write a Narrative Poem activity page from *Inside Out and Back Again* (G).

LEARNING COACH CHECK-IN   Students will revise their narrative poem. Ask to read students' revised poem. Ask them to explain ways in which they revised their poem and why they made those revisions.

SUPPORT   For students having difficulty recognizing areas they should revise, suggest a revision, and think aloud to model your revising. For example: *This detail doesn't sound right here. It really goes with the ideas in the second stanza. Let's move it there, or else the reader might get confused. Can you find any other details that are out of place?*

TRY IT   Practice Words from *Inside Out and Back Again*, Pages 237–262

Students will answer questions to determine their understanding of the vocabulary from the reading.

WRAP-UP

Question About *Inside Out and Back Again*, Pages 237–262

Students will answer a question to demonstrate a skill they learned in the lesson.

Inside Out and Back Again Wrap-Up

Lesson Overview

ACTIVITY	ACTIVITY TITLE	TIME	ONLINE/OFFLINE
GET READY	Introduction to *Inside Out and Back Again* Wrap-Up	**1** minute	🖥
TRY IT	Summary of *Inside Out and Back Again* **LEARNING COACH CHECK-IN**	**30** minutes	📄
	Read and Record	**10** minutes	🖥
	Review *Inside Out and Back Again*	**20** minutes	🖥
QUIZ	*Inside Out and Back Again*	**30** minutes	🖥
	Spelling List 21	**10** minutes	🖥
WRAP-UP	Keyboarding	**10** minutes	🖥
	More Language Arts Practice	**9** minutes	🖥

Content Background

Students will create a summary of *Inside Out and Back Again*. An effective summary includes the major characters and events in the story. It is sequential and includes key details from the text. Often, the summary includes major themes of the text. Students will have an opportunity to review the text before demonstrating their knowledge on a quiz.

Advance Preparation

During the Keyboarding activity, students will practice their keyboarding skills using an external website or program. **You will need to work with students to select an appropriate keyboarding practice website or program; K12 does not specify which resource to use.** A few suggestions are provided in the online activity.

Depending on which program you choose, students may need to set up an account to save their progress. If needed, assist students in setting up and running their chosen keyboarding practice program.

MATERIALS

Supplied
- *Inside Out and Back Again* by Thanhha Lai
- *Summit English Language Arts 5 Activity Book*
  - Summary of *Inside Out and Back Again*

Lesson Goals

- Create an effective summary.
- Read and record text with fluency.
- Demonstrate knowledge on a quiz.
- Take a spelling quiz.

GET READY

Introduction to *Inside Out and Back Again* Wrap-Up

Students will read the lesson goals.

TRY IT

Summary of *Inside Out and Back Again*

Students will write a summary of *Inside Out and Back Again* and include the criteria of an effective summary.

LEARNING COACH CHECK-IN This activity page contains an open-ended question, so it's important that you review students' responses. Give students feedback, using the sample answers provided to guide you.

TRY IT
Inside Out and Back Again Wrap-Up

Summary of *Inside Out and Back Again*

Write your response in complete sentences.

Write a summary of *Inside Out and Back Again*. Write your ideas in sequential order, and include only the main characters, events, and key details.

Sample answer:

Answers may vary.

Inside Out and Back Again **is divided into four parts that are written as poems in a diary. In Part 1, we learn about the life of the main character, Hà. She lives with her mother and three brothers in Saigon. Her father left nine years before for a navy mission and did not return. They are in danger because of the Vietnam War, so they need to leave their home. In Part 2, Hà and her family take a difficult journey and end up in America. Part 3 begins with the family's new life in Alabama. Hà's mom starts working and the children go to school. However, we learn how difficult school is for Hà. She is bullied and teased.**

INSIDE OUT AND BACK AGAIN WRAP-UP **377**

378 INSIDE OUT AND BACK AGAIN WRAP-UP

The story continues with Hà's family adjusting to life in America. Hà continues to be bullied, but with the help of her family and their new friends, the problem is solved. In Part 4, we learn that the Vietnam War has ended and that most likely Hà's father has died. After mourning the loss of their father, the book ends with the family's hope for a fresh start with a new year.

Read and Record

Good readers read quickly, smoothly, and with expression. This is called *fluency*. Students will record themselves reading aloud. They will listen to their recording and think about how quick, smooth, and expressive they sound.

TIP Encourage students to rerecord as needed.

Review *Inside Out and Back Again*

Students will answer questions to review what they have learned about *Inside Out and Back Again*.

QUIZ

Inside Out and Back Again

Students will complete the *Inside Out and Back Again* quiz.

Spelling List 21

Students will take the Spelling List 21 quiz.

WRAP-UP

Keyboarding

Students will practice their keyboarding skills using an external website or program.

More Language Arts Practice

Students will practice skills according to their individual needs.

Opinion Writing: Revising

Lesson Overview

ACTIVITY	ACTIVITY TITLE	TIME	ONLINE/OFFLINE
GET READY	Introduction to Opinion Writing: Revising	**2** minute	🖥️
	Look Back at Opinion Writing Skills	**15** minutes	📶
LEARN AND TRY IT	Revising an Editorial	**20** minutes	📶
	Revise Your Editorial **LEARNING COACH CHECK-IN**	**60** minutes	📄
WRAP-UP	Question About Revising an Editorial	**3** minutes	🖥️
	Go Read!	**20** minutes	📶 or 📄

Content Background

Students will continue working on their **editorial** about a topic of their choice. In this lesson, students will **revise** their rough draft.

Writing Process

| 1 Prewriting | 2 Drafting | **3 Revising** | 4 Proofreading | 5 Publishing |

To revise their editorials, students will use a checklist. The checklist focuses on organization (*Are my body paragraphs in a logical order?*) and content (*Does each body paragraph focus on a reason that supports my opinion?*). At the end of this lesson, students will be ready to proofread their editorials for grammar, usage, and mechanics.

Students may not understand the difference between revising and proofreading. When revising, writers focus on large issues, such as the order of ideas or transitions. When proofreading, writers fix errors in grammar, usage, and mechanics, such as spelling or punctuation mistakes. Encourage students to focus on revision during this lesson. In the next lesson, students will proofread their editorials.

MATERIALS

Supplied
- *Summit English Language Arts 5 Activity Book*
  - Revise Your Editorial
- Editorial: Revision Feedback Sheet (printout)
- Editorial Instructions (printout)

Also Needed
- folder in which students are storing editorial writing assignment pages
- reading material for Go Read!

Advance Preparation

Gather the folder that students are using to store the activity pages related to their editorial. The folder should contain the following:

- Students' completed Brainstorm for Your Editorial activity page from Introduction to Opinion Writing: Prewriting (A)

- Students' completed research notes from Opinion Writing: Prewriting (B)

- Students' completed Plan Your Editorial activity page from Opinion Writing: Prewriting (C)

- Students' completed rough draft from Opinion Writing: Drafting (B)

Prior to the Revise Your Editorial activity in this lesson, read students' rough draft and complete Editorial: Revision Feedback Sheet.

During the Go Read! activity, students will have the option of using the digital library. Allow extra time for students to make their reading selection, or have students make a selection before beginning the lesson.

KEYWORDS

editorial – an article in a publication that gives an opinion held by its editor or editors; an opinion piece similar to such an article

opinion – something that a person thinks or believes, but which cannot be proven to be true

revising – the stage or step of the writing process in which the writer goes back, rereads the piece, and makes changes in content or organization

Lesson Goals

- Use a checklist to revise your editorial.

- Read for pleasure.

GET READY

Introduction to Opinion Writing: Revising

Students will get a glimpse of what they will learn about in the lesson. They will also read the lesson goals and keywords. Have students select each keyword and preview its definition.

Look Back at Opinion Writing Skills

Students will review how an expert writer uses evidence to support reasons in an opinion essay.

LEARN   Revising an Editorial

Students will learn about revising an editorial, including how to use a revision checklist. Through a guided activity, they will explore how to revise a sample student editorial.

TRY IT   Revise Your Editorial

Students will complete Revise Your Editorial from *Summit English Language Arts 5 Activity Book*. They will need their completed rough draft from Introduction to Opinion Writing: Drafting (B).

LEARNING COACH CHECK-IN   Guide students through the revision process.

1. Gather and use the Editorial: Revision Feedback Sheet that you filled out to guide a discussion with students.

   • Tell students the strengths of their editorial. Provide positive comments about the ideas, language, detail, or other elements of the editorial that you enjoyed.

   • Walk through your feedback with students.

   • As you discuss your feedback, encourage students to actively revise their draft in response. Reassure students that it's okay to remove or move around ideas and sentences. Students should revise their draft directly on the page, using the lines they left blank.

2. Have students review their draft once more, using the Revise Your Editorial activity page.

   • For students having difficulty recognizing areas they should revise, suggest a revision, and think aloud to model your revising. For example: *To understand Paragraph 3, readers really need to read Paragraph 4 first. Let's switch the order of those paragraphs. Can you find any other facts, details, sentences, or paragraphs that are out of place?*

3. Make sure students store their revised draft in the folder they are using to organize their writing assignment pages.

TIP   Remind students to focus on the checklist questions. Emphasize that they should not worry about spelling, punctuation, grammar, and so on.

NOTE   If you or students wish, you can download and print another copy of the Editorial Instructions online.

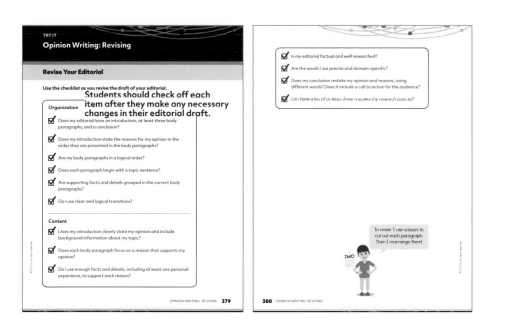

Question About Revising an Editorial

Students will answer a question to show that they understand a key editorial revision skill.

Go Read!

Students will read for pleasure. They should choose a book or a magazine that interests them, or they may choose a selection from the digital library, linked in the online lesson.

Students should read for the entire time. Have students select something to read ahead of time to help them stay focused.

Opinion Writing: Proofreading

Lesson Overview

ACTIVITY	ACTIVITY TITLE	TIME	ONLINE/OFFLINE
GET READY	Introduction to Opinion Writing: Proofreading	**2** minute	📶
LEARN AND **TRY IT**	Review Commas in Lists and After Introductory Elements	**15** minutes	📶
	Proofreading an Editorial	**20** minutes	📶
	Proofread Your Editorial **LEARNING COACH CHECK-IN**	**60** minutes	📄
WRAP-UP	Question About Proofreading an Editorial	**3** minutes	📶
	Go Read!	**20** minutes	📶 or 📄

Content Background

Students will continue working on their **editorial** about a topic of their choice. In this lesson, students will **proofread** their revised rough draft.

Writing Process

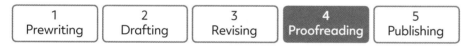

| 1 Prewriting | 2 Drafting | 3 Revising | 4 Proofreading | 5 Publishing |

To proofread their editorial, students will use a checklist. The checklist focuses on grammar, usage, and mechanics (*Are all sentences complete and correct? Are commas used correctly in series of items and to set off introductory elements?*). After completing this lesson, students will be ready to prepare a clean copy of their editorial.

Proofreading is sometimes called *editing*.

Advance Preparation

Gather the folder that students are using to store the activity pages related to their editorial. The folder should contain the following:

- Students' completed Brainstorm for Your Editorial activity page from Opinion Writing: Prewriting (A)

- Students' completed research notes from Opinion Writing: Prewriting (B)

- Students' completed Plan Your Editorial activity page from Opinion Writing: Prewriting (C)

- Students' revised draft from Opinion Writing: Revising

Prior to the Proofread Your Editorial activity in this lesson, read students' revised draft. As you read, complete Editorial: Proofreading Feedback Sheet.

During the Go Read! activity, students will have the option of using the digital library. Allow extra time for students to make their reading selection, or have students make a selection before beginning the lesson.

Lesson Goals

- Use a checklist to proofread your editorial.

- Read for pleasure.

GET READY

Introduction to Opinion Writing: Proofreading

Students will get a glimpse of what they will learn about in the lesson. They will also read the lesson goals and keywords. Have students select each keyword and preview its definition.

Review Commas in Lists and After Introductory Elements

Students will review how to correctly use commas in series and after introductory elements, two skills they will need as they proofread their editorial.

LEARN AND TRY IT

LEARN   Proofreading an Editorial

Students will learn about proofreading, including how to use a proofreading checklist. Through a guided activity, they will explore how to proofread a sample student editorial.

TRY IT   Proofread Your Editorial

Students will complete Proofread Your Editorial from *Summit English Language Arts 5 Activity Book*. They will need their revised rough draft from Opinion Writing: Revising.

LEARNING COACH CHECK-IN   Guide students through the proofreading process.

1. Have students read their draft aloud, listening for errors such as missing words or commas, incomplete sentences, and agreement errors. As students catch errors, have them fix the errors.

   - For students having difficultly noticing errors as they read aloud, model the process. Slowly read a sentence aloud. Pause and model your thinking when you encounter an error. For example, "*The people of this city need to change its attitude about recycling.*" This sentence sounds wrong. What needs to change? The noun *people* is plural, but the pronoun *its* is singular. I need to change *its* to *their* to fix the agreement error.

2. Have students review their revised draft once more, using the Proofread Your Editorial activity page.

3. Review with students your comments on the Editorial: Proofreading Feedback Sheet. Praise students for the errors that they caught, and guide students to recognize any errors that they have not yet fixed.

4. Have students store their edited draft in the folder they are using to organize their writing assignment pages.

OPTIONAL Have students exchange revised editorials with a peer and use the Proofread Your Editorial activity page to proofread each other's editorials.

NOTE If you or students wish, you can download and print another copy of the Editorial Instructions online.

TRY IT
Opinion Writing: Proofreading

Proofread Your Editorial

Use the checklist as you proofread your revised draft of your editorial.

Students should check off each item after they make any necessary changes in their editorial draft.

Grammar and Usage

☑ Are all sentences complete and correct?
☑ Are there any missing or extra words?
☑ Are all verbs in the appropriate tense?
☑ Are there other grammatical or usage errors?

Mechanics

☑ Is every word spelled correctly, including frequently confused words?
☑ Does every sentence begin with a capital letter and end with the appropriate punctuation?
☑ Are commas used correctly to set off tag questions, direct addresses, and the words yes and *no*?
☑ Are commas used correctly in series of items and to set off introductory elements?
☑ Is punctuation used thoughtfully and effectively?

OPINION WRITING: PROOFREADING **381**

☑ Are the titles of works in the source list capitalized and formatted correctly?
☑ Are direct quotations punctuated correctly?
☑ Are there other punctuation or capitalization errors?

382 OPINION WRITING: PROOFREADING

Question About Proofreading an Editorial

Students will answer a question to show that they understand a key editorial proofreading skill.

Go Read!

Students will read for pleasure. They should choose a book or a magazine that interests them, or they may choose a selection from the digital library, linked in the online lesson.

Students should read for the entire time. Have students select something to read ahead of time to help them stay focused.

Opinion Writing: Publishing

Lesson Overview

ACTIVITY	ACTIVITY TITLE	TIME	ONLINE/OFFLINE
GET READY	Introduction to Opinion Writing: Publishing	**1** minute	🖥️
LEARN AND **TRY IT**	Publishing an Editorial	**20** minutes	🖥️
	Publish Your Editorial	**60** minutes	🖥️
WRAP-UP	Turn In Your Editorial	**1** minute	🖥️
	Keyboarding	**10** minutes	🖥️
	More Language Arts Practice	**13** minutes	🖥️
	Go Read!	**15** minutes	🖥️ or 📄

Content Background

Students will continue working on their **editorial** about a topic of their choice. In this lesson, students will **publish** their editorial. Then they will submit their completed editorial to their teacher.

Writing Process

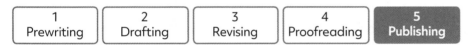

1 Prewriting	2 Drafting	3 Revising	4 Proofreading	**5 Publishing**

Students will need to type their editorial using a word-processing program. They will complete an activity to review basic word-processing skills, such as using a keyboard and saving a document.

Advance Preparation

Gather the folder that students are using to store the activity pages related to their editorial. The folder should contain the following:

- Students' completed Brainstorm for Your Editorial activity page from Opinion Writing: Prewriting (A)

- Students' completed research notes from Opinion Writing: Prewriting (B)

- Students' completed Plan Your Editorial activity page from Opinion Writing: Prewriting (C)

- Students' revised and edited draft from Opinion Writing: Proofreading

MATERIALS

Supplied
- Editorial Instructions (printout)

Also Needed
- folder in which students are storing editorial writing assignment pages
- reading material for Go Read!

KEYWORDS

editorial – an article in a publication that gives an opinion held by its editor or editors; an opinion piece similar to such an article

opinion – something that a person thinks or believes, but which cannot be proven to be true

publishing – the stage or step of the writing process in which the writer makes a clean copy of the piece and shares it

During the Keyboarding activity, students will practice their keyboarding skills using an external website or program. **You will need to work with students to select an appropriate keyboarding practice website or program; K12 does not specify which resource to use.** A few suggestions are provided in the online activity.

Depending on which program you choose, students may need to set up an account to save their progress. If needed, assist students in setting up and running their chosen keyboarding practice program.

During the Go Read! activity, students will have the option of using the digital library. Allow extra time for students to make their reading selection, or have students make a selection before beginning the lesson.

Lesson Goals

- Publish your editorial.

- Submit your editorial to your teacher.

GET READY

Introduction to Opinion Writing: Publishing

Students will read the lesson goals and keywords. Have students select each keyword and preview its definition.

LEARN AND TRY IT

LEARN   Publishing an Editorial

Students will learn about word-processing skills in preparation for typing their editorial.

TRY IT   Publishing Your Editorial

Students will type a final copy of their editorial. Students should gather their revised and proofread draft, and they should type it using a word-processing program.

NOTE   If you or students wish, you can download and print another copy of the Editorial Instructions online.

TIP   If appropriate, encourage students to try to publish their editorial. Suggest a local newspaper or a magazine geared toward children.

Turn In Your Editorial

Students will submit their writing assignment to their teacher.

Keyboarding

Students will practice their keyboarding skills using an external website or program.

More Language Arts Practice

Students will practice skills according to their individual needs.

Go Read!

Students will read for pleasure. They should choose a book or a magazine that interests them, or they may choose a selection from the digital library, linked in the online lesson.

Students should read for the entire time. Have students select something to read ahead of time to help them stay focused.

Big Ideas: Respond to a Prompt

Lesson Overview

Big Ideas lessons provide students the opportunity to further apply the knowledge acquired and skills learned throughout the unit workshops. Each Big Ideas lesson consists of these parts:

1. **Cumulative Review:** Students keep their skills fresh by reviewing prior content.

2. **Preview:** Students practice answering the types of questions they will commonly find on standardized tests.

3. **Synthesis:** Students complete an assignment that allows them to connect and apply what they have learned. Synthesis assignments vary throughout the course.

   In the Synthesis portion of this Big Ideas lesson, students will respond to an essay prompt based on reading selections. To respond meaningfully, students will need to use their own ideas as well as examples from the readings. Students' writing will be assessed in four categories: purpose and content; structure and organization; language and word choice; and grammar, usage, and mechanics.

   LEARNING COACH CHECK-IN This is a graded assessment. Make sure students complete, review, and submit the assignment to their teacher.

All materials needed for this lesson are linked online and not provided in the Activity Book.

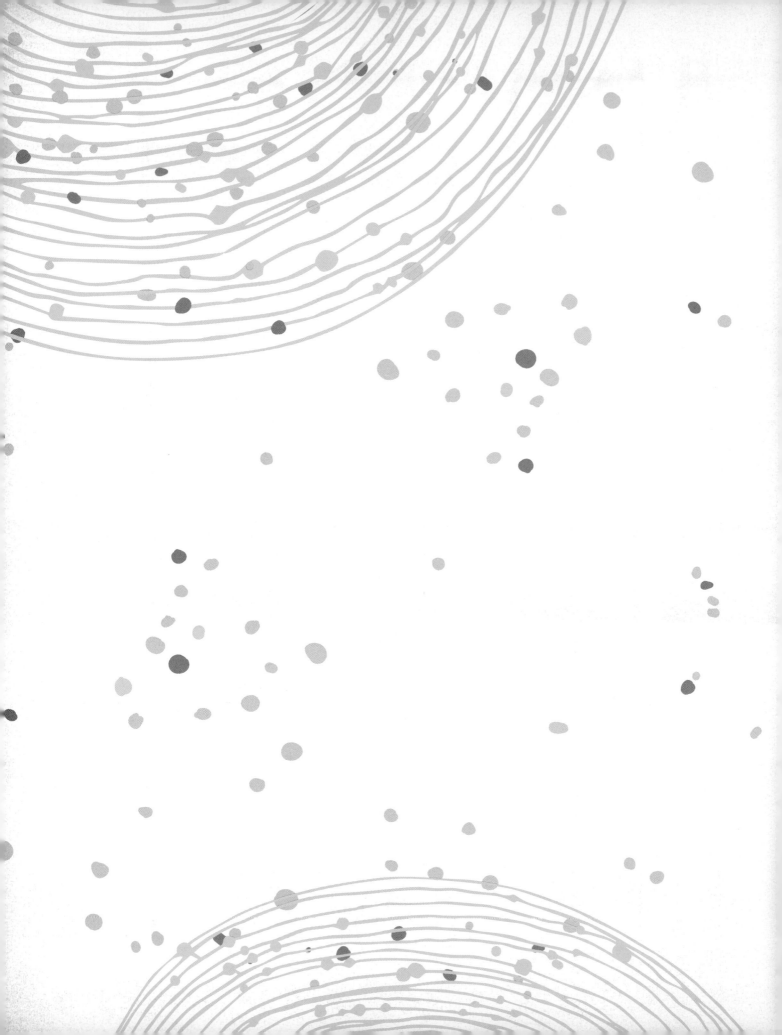

Choice
Reading Project

Choice Reading Project

Workshop Overview

This unique reading workshop is designed to build students' comprehension and critical-thinking skills as they read a work or works of their choice and complete a related project. Research indicates that opportunities for choice enhance student performance and motivate readers.

Students will select a project and corresponding book or books from a bank of options. All but one of the projects will require you to acquire a book on your own. The remaining project option will use a book or books available in the digital library linked in the online lesson. Discuss the choices with students to help ensure that they select an option that interests them. To help students make a choice, the online lessons include synopses of the books and descriptions of the related projects.

Other than the standard Spelling activities embedded throughout the workshop (and described on the following pages), students will encounter different lesson content depending on which project they choose. Therefore, this Lesson Guide does not contain detailed activity descriptions for each lesson of this workshop. Regardless of which project students choose, they will complete project work that includes reading, research, writing, and creation of a final product, which they will submit to their teacher.

All materials needed for the choice reading project are linked online and not provided in the Activity Book.

Advance Preparation

If students select a project that requires acquiring a book on your own, you will need to acquire the book before students begin the workshop.

MATERIALS
Supplied
• project packet (printout)
Also Needed
• students' chosen book or books

Choice Reading Project: Spelling

ACTIVITY	LESSON	ACTIVITY TITLE	TIME	ONLINE/OFFLINE
GET READY	1	Spelling List 22 Pretest **LEARNING COACH CHECK-IN**	**10** minutes	🖥 and 📄
	2	Spelling List 22 Activity Bank	**10** minutes	📄
	3	Spelling List 22 Review Game	**10** minutes	🖥
QUIZ	4	Spelling List 22	**10** minutes	🖥
GET READY	5	Spelling List 23 Pretest **LEARNING COACH CHECK-IN**	**10** minutes	🖥 and 📄
	6	Spelling List 23 Activity Bank	**10** minutes	📄
	7	Spelling List 23 Review Game	**10** minutes	🖥
QUIZ	8	Spelling List 23	**10** minutes	🖥

GET READY

Lesson 1   Spelling List 22 Pretest

Students will take a spelling pretest.

LEARNING COACH CHECK-IN   Have students turn to Spelling List 22 Pretest in *Summit English Language Arts 5 Activity Book* and open the online Spelling Pretest activity. Online, students will listen to the spelling word, type the word in the space indicated, and then check their answer. In the activity book, students will write the correct spelling of the word in the tables provided and indicate with a ✓ or an ✗ if they spelled the word correctly or incorrectly online. Students will repeat this process with the remaining words.

As needed, help students with the interaction between the online activity and the activity book page until they become comfortable with what they need to do. As students practice their spelling words throughout Lessons 2 and 3 of the workshop, they should pay special attention to words they spelled incorrectly on the pretest.

MATERIALS

Supplied

- *Summit English Language Arts 5 Activity Book*
  - Spelling List 22 Pretest
  - Spelling List 22 Activity Bank
  - Spelling List 23 Pretest
  - Spelling List 23 Activity Bank

This is the complete list of words students will be tested on in the Lesson 4 quiz.

Words That Are Related	
cycle	pleasure
cyclic	popular
cyclist	popularity
design	population
designation	public
muscle	publicity
muscular	sign
pleasant	signature
please	

NOTE Have students keep their completed activity page in a safe place so they can refer to it later.

GET READY
Choice Reading Project

Spelling List 22 Pretest

1. Open the Spelling Pretest activity online. Listen to the first spelling word. Type the word. Check your answer.

2. Write the correct spelling of the word in the Word column of the Spelling Pretest table on the next page.

Word	✓	✗
1 blindfold		

3. Put a check mark in the ✓ column if you spelled the word correctly online.

Word	✓	✗
1 blindfold	✓	

Put an X in the ✗ column if you spelled the word incorrectly online.

Word	✓	✗
1 blindfold		✗

4. Repeat Steps 1–3 for the remaining words in the Spelling Pretest.

CHOICE READING PROJECT **383**

Choice Reading Project

Spelling List 22 Pretest

Write each spelling word in the Word column, making sure to spell it correctly.

Word	✓	✗	Word	✓	✗
1 cycle			10 popularity		
2 cyclic			11 population		
3 cyclist			12 public		
4 muscle			13 publicity		
5 muscular			14 sign		
6 pleasant			15 signature		
7 please			16 design		
8 pleasure			17 designation		
9 popular					

Students should use the ✓ and X columns to indicate whether they spelled each word correctly or incorrectly online.

384 CHOICE READING PROJECT

Lesson 2   Spelling List 22 Activity Bank

Students will practice all spelling words from Spelling List 22 by completing Spelling List 22 Activity Bank from *Summit English Language Arts 5 Activity Book*. Make sure students have their completed Spelling List 22 Pretest activity page to refer to during this activity.

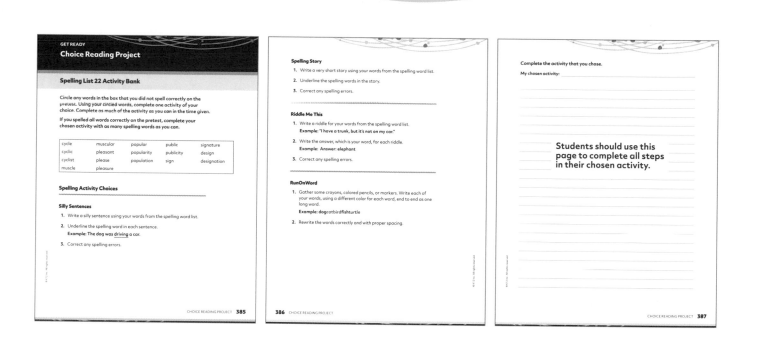

Lesson 3   Spelling List 22 Review Game

Students will practice all spelling words from Spelling List 22.

Lesson 4   Spelling List 22

Students will complete the Spelling List 22 quiz.

Lesson 5   Spelling List 23 Pretest

Students will take a spelling pretest.

LEARNING COACH CHECK-IN   Have students turn to Spelling List 23 Pretest in *Summit English Language Arts 5 Activity Book* and open the online Spelling Pretest activity. Online, students will listen to the spelling word, type the word in the space indicated, and then check their answer. In the activity book, students will write the correct spelling of the word in the tables provided and indicate with a ✓ or an ✗ if they spelled the word correctly or incorrectly online. Students will repeat this process with the remaining words.

As needed, help students with the interaction between the online activity and the activity book page until they become comfortable with what they need to do. As students practice their spelling words throughout Lessons 6 and 7 of the workshop, they should pay special attention to words they spelled incorrectly on the pretest.

This is the complete list of words students will be tested on in the Lesson 8 quiz.

Root *min*	Compound Words	
miniature	billfold	motorcycle
minimum	clothesline	newscast
minus	copyright	outstanding
	gentleman	peppermint
	grandparent	scarecrow
	household	whoever
	sideways	worthwhile

NOTE Have students keep their completed activity page in a safe place so they can refer to it later.

GET READY
Choice Reading Project

Spelling List 23 Pretest

1. Open the Spelling Pretest activity online. Listen to the first spelling word. Type the word. Check your answer.

2. Write the correct spelling of the word in the Word column of the Spelling Pretest table on the next page.

Word	✓	✗
1 blindfold		

3. Put a check mark in the ✓ column if you spelled the word correctly online.

Word	✓	✗
1 blindfold	✓	

Put an X in the ✗ column if you spelled the word incorrectly online.

Word	✓	✗
1 blindfold		X

4. Repeat Steps 1–3 for the remaining words in the Spelling Pretest.

CHOICE READING PROJECT **389**

Choice Reading Project

Spelling List 23 Pretest

Write each spelling word in the Word column, making sure to spell it correctly.

Word	✓	✗		Word	✓	✗
1 billfold			10	outstanding		
2 clothesline			11	peppermint		
3 copyright			12	scarecrow		
4 gentleman			13	whoever		
5 grandparent			14	worthwhile		
6 sideways			15	minimum		
7 household			16	miniature		
8 motorcycle			17	minus		
9 newscast						

Students should use the ✓ and X columns to indicate whether they spelled each word correctly or incorrectly online.

390 CHOICE READING PROJECT

Lesson 6   Spelling List 23 Activity Bank

Students will practice all spelling words from Spelling List 23 by completing Spelling List 23 Activity Bank from *Summit English Language Arts 5 Activity Book*. Make sure students have their completed Spelling List 23 Pretest activity page to refer to during this activity.

Remind students to pay special attention to words they spelled incorrectly on the Spelling Pretest.

Lesson 7　Spelling List 23 Review Game

Students will practice all spelling words from Spelling List 23.

QUIZ

Lesson 8　Spelling List 23

Students will complete the Spelling List 23 quiz.

Presentation Skills (A)

Lesson Overview

ACTIVITY	ACTIVITY TITLE	TIME	ONLINE/OFFLINE
GET READY	Introduction to Presentation Skills (A)	**2** minutes	🖥
	Look Back at Effective Language	**5** minutes	🖥
LEARN AND **TRY IT**	Combine Sentences	**10** minutes	🖥
	Practice Combining Sentences	**10** minutes	🖥
	Six Syllable Patterns	**15** minutes	🖥
	Speaking About an Opinion	**15** minutes	🖥
	Analyze an Opinion Speech	**10** minutes	🖥
	Present Your Opinion **LEARNING COACH CHECK-IN**	**30** minutes	🖥 and 📄
WRAP-UP	Questions About Combining Sentences and Opinion Speeches	**3** minutes	🖥
	Go Read!	**20** minutes	🖥 or 📄

Content Background

Students will explore presentation, or speaking, skills. They will explore skills related to the mechanics of speaking, such as speaking clearly and at an understandable pace. They will also explore skills related to the organization and content of a speech.

To organize a speech, students will learn the following: (1) Say what you're going to say; (2) Say it; (3) Say what you said. This simple and effective structure mirrors the beginning-middle-end structure students have used to organize writing assignments.

In the middle, or "Say it," section of a speech, students will learn to group related information and include relevant facts and details. They will learn that description, or details that evoke the five senses, are especially effective in a speech.

Students will have a chance to use the skills they learn to give their own short opinion speech. This speech will not require research.

MATERIALS

Supplied
- *Summit English Language Arts 5 Activity Book*
  - Present Your Opinion

Also Needed
- reading material for Go Read!

Grammar, Usage, and Mechanics Students are familiar with how to combine sentences using conjunctions. In this lesson, they will explore *why* good writers combine sentences. Writers combine sentences to help with meaning, engage readers, and express their style, depending on their purpose for writing.

By combining sentences, writers can make it clear how two sentences relate. By combining the sentences in the following example, the writer clarifies the order of the events.

> **Not Combined:** Lucy walked to the car. The rain stopped.

> **Combined for Meaning:** Lucy walked to the car before the rain stopped.

Writers also combine sentences for reader interest. Simply put, too many simple sentences in a row can be boring, causing readers to lose interest.

> **Not Combined:** A few minutes passed. The rain started again. Lucy watched the rain drops. She sighed.

> **Combined for Interest:** After a few minutes, the rain started again. Lucy watched the rain drops and sighed.

Writers combine sentences for style. A writer's style, or choice of words and sentence structure, depends on the purpose of a particular piece of writing. In a narrative, for example, a writer might combine sentences to sound conversational.

> **Not Combined:** Lucy stopped her car. She opened her driver's-side window. She placed her hand outside. She let the rain wash over her hand.

> **Combined for Style:** Lucy stopped her car and opened her driver's-side window. She placed her hand outside and let the rain wash over it.

Advance Preparation

During the Go Read! activity, students will have the option of using the digital library. Allow extra time for students to make their reading selection, or have students make a selection before beginning the lesson.

Lesson Goals

- Combine sentences for meaning, reading interest, and style.
- Learn the six syllable patterns.
- Analyze the ideas and organization of a speech.
- Give your own opinion speech.
- Read for pleasure.

description – writing that uses words that show how something looks, sounds, feels, tastes, or smells

opinion – something that a person thinks or believes, but which cannot be proven to be true

pace – the speed, and the change of speeds, of a speaker's delivery

style – the words a writer chooses and the way the writer arranges the words into sentences

syllable – a unit of spoken language; a syllable contains only one vowel sound

Introduction to Presentation Skills (A)

Students will get a glimpse of what they will learn about in the lesson. They will also read the lesson goals and keywords. Have students select each keyword and preview its definition.

Look Back at Effective Language

Students will practice the prerequisite skill of choosing words and phrases for effect.

LEARN AND TRY IT

LEARN   Combine Sentences

Students will learn how to purposely combine sentences for meaning, reader interest, and style.

TRY IT   Practice Combining Sentences

Students will practice combining sentences for meaning, reader interest, and style. They will receive feedback on their answers.

LEARN   Six Syllable Patterns

Students will learn the six syllable patterns. They will explore how understanding those patterns can help them read words correctly and fluently.

> **TIP**   Understanding syllable patterns can improve spelling skills.

LEARN   Speaking About an Opinion

Students will learn the elements of an effective opinion speech. They will focus on logical organization and using relevant facts and descriptive details that influence listeners. They will also explore what it means to speak clearly and at an understandable pace.

TRY IT   Analyze an Opinion Speech

Students will answer questions about an effective opinion speech. They will receive feedback on their answers.

TRY IT   Present Your Opinion

Students will complete Present Your Opinion from *Summit English Language Arts 5 Activity Book*.

> **NOTE**   This activity involves planning a short speech, recording that speech using the online recording tool, and then listening to the speech and answering reflection questions. Ensure that students have access to a computer while completing the activity.

Encourage students to present their speech to you. Or, if students prefer, you can listen to their recorded speech. Give students feedback, using Question 3 on the activity page as a guide.

TRY IT
Presentation Skills (A)

Present Your Opinion

Use the prompt to answer the questions.
Answers will vary.
Prompt: Give an opinion speech that is approximately one minute long.
Choose a topic that you do not need to research.

1. Write notes about what you will say in your speech.

> **Beginning: Say what you're going to say.**
> My opinion:
> My three reasons:
> ....
> **Middle: Say it!**
> Reason 1:
> Facts and descriptive details:
> **Reason 2:**
> Facts and descriptive details:
> **Reason 3:**
> Facts and descriptive details:
> ....
> **End: Say what you said.**
> My opinion and reasons restated:
> Final thoughts:

PRESENTATION SKILLS (A) **393**

2. Record your speech.
   • Refer to your graphic organizer from Question 1 as you speak.
   • Speak clearly, distinctly, and at an understandable pace.

3. Listen to your speech. Then answer these questions.
   a. Were your ideas well organized? Why or why not?

   _____

   b. Which details were most descriptive? Which details could be more descriptive?

   _____

   c. Were any details not relevant to your opinion? If so, which ones?

   _____

   d. Did you speak too quickly or too slowly during any parts of your speech? Identify one way you could improve your pace.

   _____

   e. Did you speak all words clearly and distinctly? Identify one way you could improve your speaking.

   _____

394 PRESENTATION SKILLS (A)

WRAP-UP

Questions About Combining Sentences and Opinion Speeches

Students will answer questions to show that they understand how to combine sentences for meaning, reader interest, or style and how to organize ideas in an opinion speech.

Go Read!

Students will read for pleasure. They should choose a book or a magazine that interests them, or they may choose a selection from the digital library, linked in the online lesson.

Students should read for the entire time. Have students select something to read ahead of time to help them stay focused.

Presentation Skills (B)

Lesson Overview

ACTIVITY	ACTIVITY TITLE	TIME	ONLINE/OFFLINE
GET READY	Introduction to Presentation Skills (B)	**2** minutes	🖥️
	Don't Fear Spiders	**15** minutes	🖥️
LEARN AND **TRY IT**	Pictures with Purpose	**20** minutes	🖥️
	Analyze Using Pictures with Purpose	**15** minutes	🖥️
	Add Pictures to Your Opinion Speech **LEARNING COACH CHECK-IN**	**40** minutes	📄
WRAP-UP	Question About Purposeful Visuals in a Speech	**3** minutes	🖥️
	Go Read!	**25** minutes	🖥️ or 📄

Content Background

Students will learn how to effectively use media, such as pictures, graphs, video clips, and music, in a speech or presentation. They will learn that media enhances a speech only if it directly supports a main idea or theme of the speech. Otherwise, the media can distract the audience.

Students will use the skills they learn to add a media element (or describe a media element that they would add) to their own opinion speech. Then they will present their opinion speech, including their media element, to you (the Learning Coach).

Advance Preparation

Gather students' completed Present Your Opinion activity page from Presentation Skills (A). Students will refer to this page during Add Pictures to Your Opinion Speech. In addition, Add Pictures to Your Opinion speech specifies that students deliver a speech to their Learning Coach.

During the Go Read! activity, students will have the option of using the digital library. Allow extra time for students to make their reading selection, or have students make a selection before beginning the lesson.

MATERIALS

Supplied
- *Summit English Language Arts 5 Activity Book*
  - Add Pictures to Your Opinion Speech

Also Needed
- completed Present Your Opinion activity page from Presentation Skills (A)
- reading material for Go Read!

KEYWORDS

description – writing that uses words that show how something looks, sounds, feels, tastes, or smells

opinion – something that a person thinks or believes, but which cannot be proven to be true

pace – the speed, and the change of speeds, of a speaker's delivery

Lesson Goals

- Practice grammar skills by editing a passage.
- Learn how to effectively use a visual in a speech.
- Add a purposeful visual to your opinion speech.
- Read for pleasure.

GET READY

Introduction to Presentation Skills (B)

Students will get a glimpse of what they will learn about in the lesson. They will also read the lesson goals and keywords. Have students select each keyword and preview its definition.

Don't Fear Spiders

Students will edit a short passage to practice applying grammar skills. This passage contains opportunities to improve the writing related to using precise language and combining sentences for meaning, reader interest, and style.

LEARN AND TRY IT

LEARN   Pictures with Purpose

Students will learn how media can effectively support the main idea or theme of a speech.

TRY IT   Analyze Using Pictures with Purpose

Students will answer questions about effective media use in a speech. They will receive feedback on their answers.

TRY IT   Add Pictures to Your Opinion Speech

Students will complete Add Pictures to Your Opinion Speech from *Summit English Language Arts 5 Activity Book*. Make sure students have their completed Present Your Opinion activity page from Presentation Skills (A) to refer to during this activity.

LEARNING COACH CHECK-IN   As part of this activity, students will deliver an opinion speech to you. Encourage students by pointing out things that they did well during their speech. Focus both on speaking skills, such as pace and clarity, and the content and organization of their speech. Point out strong, precise details that they used.

TIP Students can speak to an audience—even a virtual one! If possible, encourage students to present their speech to a friend or a relative near or far.

Presentation Skills (B)

Add Pictures to Your Opinion Speech

Use the prompt to answer the questions.
Answers will vary.
Prompt: Give an opinion speech that is approximately one minute long. Choose a topic that you do not need to research.

1. Think about a visual—such as a picture, diagram, map, or video clip— that would enhance your opinion speech.

   a. Describe, draw, or paste a copy of the visual.

b. At what part of your speech would it make sense to show your visual? For example, would you show it at the beginning? During Reason 1?

c. How does the visual support your opinion? Explain.

2. Read your answers to Question 3 of the Present Your Opinion activity page. List at least three ways you can improve your speech.

3. Deliver your speech to your Learning Coach.
   • Include the improvements you described in Question 2.
   • Display the visual you described in Question 1 (if possible) at the most logical point for it in your speech.

PRESENTATION SKILLS (B) **395**

396 PRESENTATION SKILLS (B)

WRAP-UP

Question About Purposeful Visuals in a Speech

Students will answer a question to show that they understand how to purposefully use a visual in a speech.

Go Read!

Students will read for pleasure. They should choose a book or a magazine that interests them, or they may choose a selection from the digital library, linked in the online lesson.

Students should read for the entire time. Have students select something to read ahead of time to help them stay focused.

Presentation Skills Wrap-Up

Lesson Overview

ACTIVITY	ACTIVITY TITLE	TIME	ONLINE/OFFLINE
GET READY	Introduction to Presentation Skills Wrap-Up	**1** minute	🛜
TRY IT	Use Presentation Skills **LEARNING COACH CHECK-IN**	**40** minutes	🖥️ and 📄
	Review Combining Sentences	**20** minutes	🖥️
QUIZ	Combining Sentences and Presentation Skills	**30** minutes	🖥️
WRAP-UP	Keyboarding	**10** minutes	🖥️
	More Language Arts Practice	**19** minutes	🖥️

Advance Preparation

During the Keyboarding activity, students will practice their keyboarding skills using an external website or program. **You will need to work with students to select an appropriate keyboarding practice website or program; K12 does not specify which resource to use.** A few suggestions are provided in the online activity.

Depending on which program you choose, students may need to set up an account to save their progress. If needed, assist students in setting up and running their chosen keyboarding practice program.

> ### MATERIALS
>
> **Supplied**
> - *Summit English Language Arts 5 Activity Book*
>   - Use Presentation Skills

Lesson Goals

- Review presentation skills by responding to a speaking prompt.
- Review how to combine sentences for meaning, reading interest, and style.
- Take a quiz on combining sentences and presentation skills.

GET READY

Introduction to Presentation Skills Wrap-Up

Students will read the lesson goals.

Use Presentation Skills

Students will complete Use Presentation Skills from *Summit English Language Arts 5 Activity Book*.

NOTE This activity involves planning a short speech, recording that speech using the online recording tool, and then listening to the speech and answering reflection questions. Ensure that students have access to a computer while completing the activity.

LEARNING COACH CHECK-IN Encourage students to present their speech to you. Or, if students prefer, you can listen to their recorded speech. Give them specific feedback about their speaking pace and clarity. Additionally, give them feedback about the content of their speech, including how well they organized their ideas, used descriptive details, and incorporated a purposeful visual aid.

Review Combining Sentences

Students will answer questions to review what they have learned about combining sentences for meaning, reader interest, and style.

Combining Sentences and Presentation Skills

Students will complete the Combining Sentences and Presentation Skills quiz.

Keyboarding

Students will practice their keyboarding skills using an external website or program.

More Language Arts Practice

Students will practice skills according to their individual needs.

Idioms

Lesson Overview

ACTIVITY	ACTIVITY TITLE	TIME	ONLINE/OFFLINE
GET READY	Introduction to Idioms	**1** minute	🖥️
	Look Back at Figurative Language	**4** minutes	🖥️
LEARN AND **TRY IT**	Idioms	**10** minutes	🖥️
	More on Idioms	**10** minutes	🖥️
	Apply: Idioms **LEARNING COACH CHECK-IN**	**15** minutes	📄
	Go Write!	**15** minutes	🖥️ or 📄
	Review Idioms	**15** minutes	🖥️
QUIZ	Idioms	**15** minutes	🖥️
WRAP-UP	Keyboarding	**10** minutes	🖥️
	More Language Arts Practice	**10** minutes	🖥️
	Go Read!	**15** minutes	🖥️ or 📄

Content Background

Idioms are used in writing and conversation to go beyond the literal level. They can create deeper meaning or humor, allowing writers to further engage readers.

Advance Preparation

During the Keyboarding activity, students will practice their keyboarding skills using an external website or program. **You will need to work with students to select an appropriate keyboarding practice website or program; K12 does not specify which resource to use.** A few suggestions are provided in the online activity.

Depending on which program you choose, students may need to set up an account to save their progress. If needed, assist students in setting up and running their chosen keyboarding practice program.

MATERIALS

Supplied
- *Summit English Language Arts 5 Activity Book*
  - Apply: Idioms

Also Needed
- reading material for Go Read!

During the Go Read! activity, students will have the option of using the digital library. Allow extra time for students to make their reading selection, or have students make a selection before beginning the lesson.

Lesson Goals

- Identify and explain common idioms.

- Read and write for pleasure.

GET READY

Introduction to Idioms

Students will get a glimpse of what they will learn about in the lesson. They will also read the lesson goals.

Look Back at Figurative Language

Students will practice the prerequisite skill of using context to determine the meaning of figurative language.

LEARN AND TRY IT

LEARN   Idioms

Students will practice identifying and explaining common idioms.

TRY IT   More on Idioms

Students will continue identifying and explaining other idioms.

TIP   Remind students to use context to help them understand the meaning of idioms.

TRY IT   Apply: Idioms

Students will complete Idioms from *Summit English Language Arts 5 Activity Book*.

LEARNING COACH CHECK-IN   This activity page contains open-ended questions, so it's important that you review students' responses.

TRY IT   Go Write!

Students will write independently for pleasure. As they write, they should think about using idioms.

TRY IT   Review Idioms

Students will review idioms.

QUIZ

Idioms

Students will complete the Idioms quiz.

WRAP-UP

Keyboarding

Students will practice their keyboarding skills using an external website or program.

More Language Arts Practice

Students will practice skills according to their individual needs.

Go Read!

Students will read for pleasure. They should choose a book or a magazine that interests them, or they may choose a selection from the digital library, linked in the online lesson.

Students should read for the entire time. Have students select something to read ahead of time to help them stay focused.

Big Ideas: Mini-Project

Lesson Overview

Big Ideas lessons provide students the opportunity to further apply the knowledge acquired and skills learned throughout the unit workshops. Each Big Ideas lesson consists of these parts:

1. **Cumulative Review:** Students keep their skills fresh by reviewing prior content.

2. **Preview:** Students practice answering the types of questions they will commonly find on standardized tests.

3. **Synthesis:** Students complete an assignment that allows them to connect and apply what they have learned. Synthesis assignments vary throughout the course.

   In the Synthesis portion of this Big Ideas lesson, students will complete a small creative project that ties together concepts and skills they have encountered across workshops. These small projects are designed to deepen students' understanding of those concepts and skills.

   LEARNING COACH CHECK-IN Make sure students complete, review, and submit the assignment to their teacher.

All materials needed for this lesson are linked online and not provided in the Activity Book.

> **MATERIALS**
>
> **Supplied**
> - Mini-Project Instructions (printout)

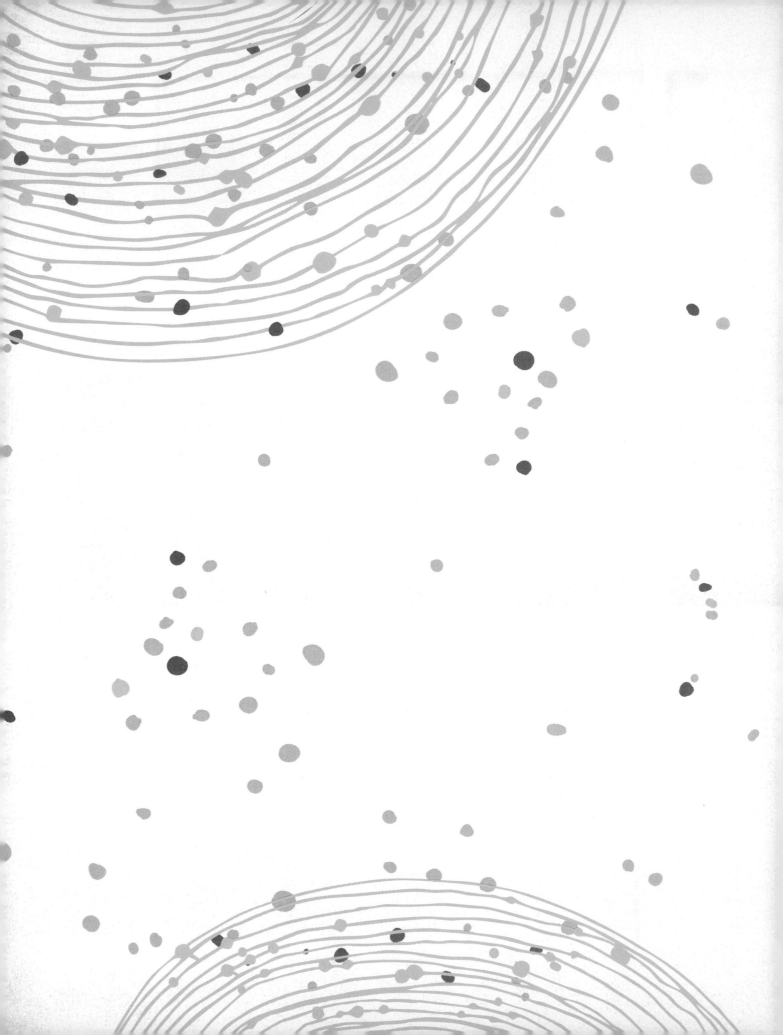

Money

"From Barter to Bitcoin"

Lesson Overview

ACTIVITY	ACTIVITY TITLE	TIME	ONLINE/OFFLINE
GET READY	Money Unit Overview	**1** minute	🖥️
	Introduction to "From Barter to Bitcoin"	**1** minute	📶
	Spelling List 24 Pretest **LEARNING COACH CHECK-IN**	**10** minutes	📶 and 📄
	Money in 60 Seconds	**1** minute	📶
	Before You Read "From Barter to Bitcoin"	**10** minutes	🖥️
READ	"From Barter to Bitcoin"	**30** minutes	📄
	Check-In: "From Barter to Bitcoin"	**5** minutes	📶
LEARN AND **TRY IT**	Text Structure	**10** minutes	🖥️
	Examine Structure and Organization	**10** minutes	🖥️
	Subtopics and Key Details	**5** minutes	🖥️
	Examine Subtopics and Key Details	**5** minutes	📶
	Apply: Subtopics and Key Details	**15** minutes	📶
	Write About Two Ways of Buying Goods **LEARNING COACH CHECK-IN**	**10** minutes	📄
	Practice Words from "From Barter to Bitcoin"	**5** minutes	🖥️
WRAP-UP	Questions About Structure and Subtopics	**2** minutes	📶

Content Background

Students will read an article called "From Barter to Bitcoin." They will examine how the text is structured chronologically—or in time order. They will then explore how the text is broken down into subtopics and how key details related to each subtopic are grouped together.

The article includes a few important terms related to the history of money. To *barter* is to trade goods or services. *Interest* refers to the fee that lenders charge for borrowing money.

"From Barter to Bitcoin" Synopsis

This magazine article provides students with a brief overview of the history of money and how it has been used over time. It begins with the use of bartering in ancient times and describes the concept of currency and some objects that have served as currency through the ages. The text then focuses on coins, paper money, modern ways to use money (such as credit and debit cards), and virtual money (cryptocurrencies).

KEYWORDS

structure – the way a piece of writing is organized

Lesson Goals

- Take a spelling pretest.
- Read "From Barter to Bitcoin."
- Examine the organization and structure of an informational article.
- Determine subtopics in an informational article and how key details support them.

GET READY

Money Unit Overview

Students will read a summary of what they will learn in the Money unit.

Introduction to "From Barter to Bitcoin"

Students will get a glimpse of what they will learn about in the lesson. They will also read the lesson goals and keywords. Have students select each keyword and preview its definition.

Spelling List 24 Pretest

Students will take a spelling pretest.

LEARNING COACH CHECK-IN   Have students turn to Spelling List 24 Pretest in *Summit English Language Arts 5 Activity Book* and open the online Spelling Pretest activity. Online, students will listen to the spelling word, type the word in the space indicated, and then check their answer. In the activity book, students will write the correct spelling of the word in the tables provided and indicate with a ✓ or an ✗ if they spelled the word correctly or incorrectly online. Students will repeat this process with the remaining words.

As needed, help students with the interaction between the online activity and the activity book page until they become comfortable with what they need to do. As students practice their spelling words throughout the workshop, they should pay special attention to words they spelled incorrectly on the pretest.

This is the complete list of words students will be tested on.

Homophones	Root *flam*
capital	flame
capitol	flammable
dual	inflammation
duel	
patience	
patients	
principal	
principle	
profit	
prophet	
stationary	
stationery	
weather	
whether	

NOTE Have students keep their completed activity page in a safe place so they can refer to it later.

GET READY
"From Barter to Bitcoin"

Spelling List 24 Pretest

1. Open the Spelling Pretest activity online. Listen to the first spelling word. Type the word. Check your answer.

2. Write the correct spelling of the word in the Word column of the Spelling Pretest table on the next page.

Word	✓	✗
1 blindfold		

3. Put a check mark in the ✓ column if you spelled the word correctly online.

Word	✓	✗
1 blindfold	✓	

Put an X in the ✗ column if you spelled the word incorrectly online.

Word	✓	✗
1 blindfold		X

4. Repeat Steps 1–3 for the remaining words in the Spelling Pretest.

"From Barter to Bitcoin"

Spelling List 24 Pretest

Write each spelling word in the Word column, making sure to spell it correctly.

Word	✓	✗		Word	✓	✗
1 capital				10 prophet		
2 capitol				11 stationary		
3 dual				12 stationery		
4 duel				13 weather		
5 patience				14 whether		
6 patients				15 flammable		
7 principal				16 flame		
8 principle				17 inflammation		
9 profit						

Students should use the ✓ and X columns to indicate whether they spelled each word correctly or incorrectly online.

Money in 60 Seconds

Students will watch a short video designed to spark their interest in upcoming topics.

Before You Read "From Barter to Bitcoin"

Students will be introduced to some key vocabulary words that they will encounter in the upcoming reading, learn some important prereading strategies, and answer a question to help them predict what the upcoming reading will cover.

READ

"From Barter to Bitcoin"

Students will read "From Barter to Bitcoin" in *K12 World: Money, Money, Money*.

Check-In: "From Barter to Bitcoin"

Students will answer several questions to demonstrate their comprehension of "From Barter to Bitcoin."

LEARN AND TRY IT

LEARN   Text Structure

Students will determine the structure and organization of a passage from the text. They will learn about how recognizing and understanding text structure can improve their understanding of the text.

TRY IT   Examine Structure and Organization

Students will answer questions in which they demonstrate their understanding of the structure and organization of an article and the effect of structure and organization on the ideas presented in the article.

LEARN   Subtopics and Key Details

Students will learn how to identify subtopics in a text and explore how those subtopics and key details are presented in an article.

TRY IT   Examine Subtopics and Key Details

Students will answer questions in which they demonstrate their ability to identify subtopics within a text and their understanding of how key details support those subtopics.

TRY IT   Apply: Subtopics and Key Details

Students will apply to a new work what they've learned about identifying subtopics within a text and exploring how key details support those subtopics.

TRY IT   Write About Two Ways of Buying Goods

Students will complete Write About Two Ways of Buying Goods from *Summit English Language Arts 5 Activity Book*. They will demonstrate their understanding of how the text conveys information, as well as the similarities and differences between these two methods of completing transactions.

LEARNING COACH CHECK-IN   This activity page contains an open-ended question, so it's important that you review students' responses. Give students feedback, using the sample answers provided to guide you.

TRY IT
"From Barter to Bitcoin"

Write About Two Ways of Buying Goods

Respond in complete sentences.

Based on "From Barter to Bitcoin," explain how bartering and bitcoin are related. How did people go from one to the other over time? How are they similar? How are they different?

Answers will vary. Student should note that

- Bartering and bitcoin are both ways to obtain things from others.
- Bartering was replaced by hard currency, such as coins and paper money.
- Bitcoin can now be used instead of coins or paper money.
- The two are similar in some ways: for instance, both involve giving something of value to get what one wants or needs.
- The two are different in some ways: for instance, bartering involves trading goods in person; using bitcoin means doing transactions on computers.

"FROM BARTER TO BITCOIN" **405**

TRY IT   Practice Words from "From Barter to Bitcoin"

Students will answer questions to demonstrate their understanding of the vocabulary words from the reading.

WRAP-UP

Questions About Structure and Subtopics

Students will answer questions to show that they understand the structure of the text and how to identify it, as well as the way key details support subtopics in the reading.

"From Barter to Bitcoin" Wrap-Up

Lesson Overview

ACTIVITY	ACTIVITY TITLE	TIME	ONLINE/OFFLINE
GET READY	Introduction to "From Barter to Bitcoin" Wrap-Up	**1** minute	🛜
	Spelling List 24 Activity Bank	**10** minutes	📄
TRY IT	Write About "From Barter to Bitcoin" **LEARNING COACH CHECK-IN**	**30** minutes	📄
	Read and Record	**10** minutes	🖥️
	Review "From Barter to Bitcoin"	**20** minutes	🖥️
QUIZ	"From Barter to Bitcoin"	**30** minutes	🖥️
WRAP-UP	Keyboarding	**10** minutes	🖥️
	More Language Arts Practice	**9** minutes	🖥️

Content Background

Students will complete a spelling activity and then write about the article they read. Students will then have an opportunity to review the texts from this workshop before demonstrating their knowledge of them on a quiz.

Advance Preparation

Gather students' completed Spelling list 24 Pretest activity page from "From Barter to Bitcoin." Students will refer to this page during Get Ready: Spelling List 24 Activity Bank.

During the Keyboarding activity, students will practice their keyboarding skills using an external website or program. **You will need to work with students to select an appropriate keyboarding practice website or program; K12 does not specify which resource to use.** A few suggestions are provided in the online activity.

Depending on which program you choose, students may need to set up an account to save their progress. If needed, assist students in setting up and running their chosen keyboarding practice program.

> ### MATERIALS
>
> **Supplied**
> - *K12 World: Money, Money, Money*
> - *Summit English Language Arts 5 Activity Book*
>   - Spelling List 24 Activity Bank
>   - Write About "From Barter to Bitcoin"
>
> **Also Needed**
> - completed Spelling List 24 Pretest activity page from "From Barter to Bitcoin"

Lesson Goals

- Practice all spelling words offline.
- Write about the organization of ideas in "From Barter to Bitcoin."
- Read and record text with fluency.
- Take a quiz on "From Barter to Bitcoin."
- Practice keyboarding and language arts skills.

GET READY

Introduction to "From Barter to Bitcoin" Wrap-Up

Students will read the lesson goals.

Spelling List 24 Activity Bank

Students will practice all spelling words from the workshop by completing Spelling List 24 Activity Bank from *Summit English Language Arts 5 Activity Book*. Make sure students have their completed Spelling List 24 Pretest activity page from "From Barter Bitcoin" to refer to during this activity.

Remind students to pay special attention to words they spelled incorrectly on the Spelling Pretest.

TRY IT

Write About "From Barter to Bitcoin"

Students will complete Write About "From Barter to Bitcoin" from *Summit English Language Arts 5 Activity Book*.

This activity page contains an open-ended question, so it's important that you review students' responses. Give students feedback, using the sample answers provided to guide you.

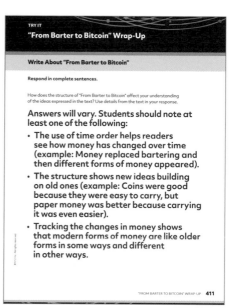

Read and Record

Good readers read quickly, smoothly, and with expression. This is called *fluency*. Students will record themselves reading aloud. They will listen to their recording and think about how quick, smooth, and expressive they sound.

TIP Encourage students to rerecord as needed.

Review "From Barter to Bitcoin"

Students will answer questions to review what they have learned in the "From Barter to Bitcoin" workshop.

QUIZ

"From Barter to Bitcoin"

Students will complete the "From Barter to Bitcoin" quiz.

WRAP-UP

Keyboarding

Students will practice their keyboarding skills using an external website or program.

More Language Arts Practice

Students will practice skills according to their individual needs.

"Making Money"

Lesson Overview

ACTIVITY	ACTIVITY TITLE	TIME	ONLINE/OFFLINE
GET READY	Introduction to "Making Money"	**1** minute	🖥
	Spelling List 24 Review Game	**10** minutes	🖥
	Before You Read "Making Money"	**9** minutes	🖥
READ	"Making Money"	**30** minutes	📄
	Check-In: "Making Money"	**5** minutes	🖥
LEARN AND TRY IT	Connections and Structure	**5** minutes	🖥
	Examine the Article	**5** minutes	🖥
	Interpreting Information	**10** minutes	🖥
	Interpret Facts and Details	**10** minutes	🖥
	Apply: Understanding a Scientific Text	**15** minutes	🖥
	Write About a Process **LEARNING COACH CHECK-IN**	**10** minutes	📄
	Practice Words from "Making Money"	**8** minutes	🖥
WRAP-UP	Questions About Connecting and Interpreting Information	**2** minutes	🖥

Content Background

Students will read an article called "Making Money." They will explore the structure of the text and the way the writer connects ideas within it. They will also learn strategies for interpreting facts and details within the text.

The article is a procedural text. It describes the steps of two processes in order, from start to finish.

MATERIALS

Supplied
- *K12 World: Money, Money, Money*
- *Summit English Language Arts 5 Activity Book*
  - Write About a Process

"Making Money" Synopsis

This magazine article provides students with explanations about the printing of paper money and the creation of coins. The text first explains why money must sometimes be taken out of circulation and then details the steps that occur when new paper money is made. The second half of the article focuses on coins, explaining how old coins are melted down and new ones are made from different metals.

Lesson Goals

- Practice all spelling words online.
- Read "Making Money."
- Analyze the way the text is organized, and interpret information based on the details and content of the article.

GET READY

Introduction to "Making Money"

Students will get a glimpse of what they will learn about in the lesson. They will also read the lesson goals.

Spelling List 24 Review Game

Students will practice all spelling words from the workshop.

Before You Read "Making Money"

Students will be introduced to some key vocabulary words that they will encounter in the upcoming reading and learn about the difference between a stated purpose and an implied purpose.

READ

"Making Money"

Students will read "Making Money" in *K12 World: Money, Money, Money*.

Check-In: "Making Money"

Students will answer several questions to demonstrate their comprehension of "Making Money."

LEARN   Connections and Structure

Students will explore the structure and organization of a text. They will then learn about making connections between related details and information to better understand that text.

TRY IT   Examine the Article

Students will answer questions in which they demonstrate their understanding of how a text is organized and how the ideas in that text are related.

LEARN   Interpreting Information

Students will learn how to interpret information in a text to answer questions, solve problems, and demonstrate their understanding of a subject.

TRY IT   Interpret Facts and Details

Students will answer questions in which they demonstrate their ability to interpret information in a text.

TRY IT   Apply: Understanding a Scientific Text

Students will apply to a new work what they've learned about explaining the way ideas in a text interact or are related.

TRY IT   Write About a Process

Students will complete Write About a Process from *Summit English Language Arts 5 Activity Book*. They will demonstrate their understanding of how coins are created and the relationship between the steps of the process.

LEARNING COACH CHECK-IN   This activity page contains an open-ended question, so it's important that you review students' responses. Give students feedback, using the sample answers provided to guide you.

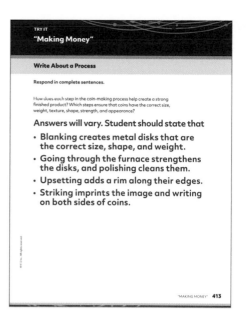

TRY IT   Practice Words from "Making Money"

Students will answer questions to demonstrate their understanding of the vocabulary words from the reading.

WRAP-UP

Questions About Connecting and Interpreting Information

Students will answer questions to show that they understand how to connect details in a text and interpret information that text includes.

"Making Money" Wrap-Up

Lesson Overview

ACTIVITY	ACTIVITY TITLE	TIME	ONLINE/OFFLINE
GET READY	Introduction to "Making Money" Wrap-Up	**1** minute	🖥️
TRY IT	Write About "Making Money" **LEARNING COACH CHECK-IN**	**30** minutes	📄
	Read and Record	**10** minutes	🖥️
	Review "Making Money"	**20** minutes	🖥️
QUIZ	"Making Money"	**30** minutes	🖥️
	Spelling List 24	**10** minutes	🖥️
WRAP-UP	Keyboarding	**10** minutes	🖥️
	More Language Arts Practice	**9** minutes	🖥️

Content Background

Students will write about "Making Money." They will then have an opportunity to review the other articles they've read before demonstrating their knowledge on a quiz. They will also take a spelling quiz.

Advance Preparation

During the Keyboarding activity, students will practice their keyboarding skills using an external website or program. **You will need to work with students to select an appropriate keyboarding practice website or program; K12 does not specify which resource to use.** A few suggestions are provided in the online activity.

Depending on which program you choose, students may need to set up an account to save their progress. If needed, assist students in setting up and running their chosen keyboarding practice program.

MATERIALS

Supplied
- *K12 World: Money, Money, Money*
- *Summit English Language Arts 5 Activity Book*
  - Write About "Making Money"

Lesson Goals

- Write about the organizational pattern used in "Making Money."
- Read and record text with fluency.
- Take a quiz on "Making Money."
- Take a spelling quiz.
- Practice keyboarding and language arts skills.

GET READY

Introduction to "Making Money" Wrap-Up

Students will read the lesson goals.

TRY IT

Write About "Making Money"

Students will complete Write About Making Money from *Summit English Language Arts 5 Activity Book*.

LEARNING COACH CHECK-IN   This activity page contains an open-ended question, so it's important that you review students' responses. Give students feedback, using the sample answers provided to guide you.

TRY IT
"Making Money" Wrap-Up

Write About "Making Money"

Respond in complete sentences.

How does the structure of "Making Money" affect your understanding of the text? How might this article be different with a different structure? Use examples from the text in your answer.

Answers will vary. Students should show their understanding that

- **The article is a procedural text that uses problem and solution. It explains two processes and describes the steps in each process. It tells how paper money is made, and it tells how coins are made.**

- **The structure helps readers understand each process clearly. Each step builds on the steps that came before. It lets readers see how the problem of having old, unfit money is solved.**

- **The piece would be very different if it had a different structure. Mostly, it would be harder to understand. The timing of each step would not be clear. How the parts of the process are related would not be clear. How the steps work together to create a finished coin or bill would not be clear.**

"MAKING MONEY" WRAP-UP **415**

Read and Record

Good readers read quickly, smoothly, and with expression. This is called *fluency*. Students will record themselves reading aloud. They will listen to their recording and think about how quick, smooth, and expressive they sound.

 TIP   Encourage students to rerecord as needed.

Review "Making Money"

Students will answer questions to review what they have learned in the article "Making Money."

QUIZ

"Making Money"

Students will complete the "Making Money" quiz.

Spelling List 24

Students will complete the Spelling List 24 quiz.

WRAP-UP

Keyboarding

Students will practice their keyboarding skills using an external website or program.

More Language Arts Practice

Students will practice skills according to their individual needs.

Economy Words

Lesson Overview

ACTIVITY	ACTIVITY TITLE	TIME	ONLINE/OFFLINE
GET READY	Introduction to Economy Words	**1** minute	🖥️
LEARN AND **TRY IT**	Words About Economy	**10** minutes	🖥️
	Explore Words About Economy	**10** minutes	🖥️
	Appy: Using Context Clues **LEARNING COACH CHECK-IN**	**15** minutes	📄
	Go Write!	**15** minutes	📄
	Review Economy Words	**15** minutes	🖥️
QUIZ	Economy Words	**15** minutes	🖥️
WRAP-UP	Keyboarding	**10** minutes	🖥️
	More Language Arts Practice	**9** minutes	🖥️
	Go Read!	**20** minutes	🖥️ or 📄

Content Background

Students will learn several words related to the economy. They will practice using context clues and word relationships to define and understand unknown words.

Advance Preparation

During the Keyboarding activity, students will practice their keyboarding skills using an external website or program. **You will need to work with students to select an appropriate keyboarding practice website or program; K12 does not specify which resource to use.** A few suggestions are provided in the online activity.

Depending on which program you choose, students may need to set up an account to save their progress. If needed, assist students in setting up and running their chosen keyboarding practice program.

During the Go Read! activity, students will have the option of using the digital library. Allow extra time for students to make their reading selection, or have students make a selection before beginning the lesson.

Lesson Goals

- Use context clues to understand new words.

- Apply knowledge of economy words to infer meaning of a text.

- Read and write for pleasure.

GET READY

Introduction to Economy Words

Students will get a glimpse of what they will learn about in the lesson. They will also read the lesson goals.

LEARN AND TRY IT

LEARN   Words About Economy

Students will practice using context clues to learn words about the economy.

TRY IT   Explore Words About Economy

Students will continue to work with economic words.

TRY IT   Apply: Using Context Clues

Students will complete Apply: Using Context Clues from *Summit English Language Arts 5 Activity Book*.

TIP   Remind students to read carefully around the word and to use the clues provided by the author to determine the meaning. Sometimes the word is clearly defined in the next sentence.

LEARNING COACH CHECK-IN   This activity page contains open-ended questions, so it's important that you review students' responses. Give students feedback, using the sample answers provided to guide you.

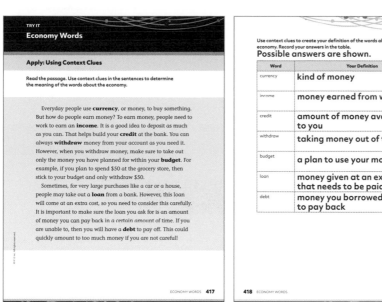

TRY IT   Go Write!

Students will write independently for pleasure. As they write, they should think about using words related to the economy.

TRY IT   Review Economy Words

Students will review economy words.

QUIZ

Economy Words

Students will complete the Economy Words quiz.

WRAP-UP

Keyboarding

Students will practice their keyboarding skills using an external website or program.

More Language Arts Practice

Students will practice skills according to their individual needs.

Go Read!

Students will read for pleasure. They should choose a book or a magazine that interests them, or they may choose a selection from the digital library, linked in the online lesson.

Students should read for the entire time. Have students select something to read ahead of time to help them stay focused.

Presentation: Digital Tools

Lesson Overview

ACTIVITY	ACTIVITY TITLE	TIME	ONLINE/OFFLINE
GET READY	Introduction to Presentation: Digital Tools	**2** minutes	🖥
	Spelling List 25 Pretest **LEARNING COACH CHECK-IN**	**10** minutes	🖥 and 📄
	Look Back at Choosing Effective Language	**5** minutes	🖥
LEARN AND **TRY IT**	Expand Sentences	**15** minutes	🖥
	Practice Expanding Sentences	**10** minutes	🖥
	Presentation Software	**15** minutes	🖥
	Use Presentation Software **LEARNING COACH CHECK-IN**	**40** minutes	🖥 and 📄
WRAP-UP	Questions About Expanding Sentences and Digital Tools	**3** minutes	🖥
	Go Read!	**20** minutes	🖥 or 📄

Content Background

Students will learn how to use presentation software. Through a demonstration, they will learn fundamentals, such as opening the software and saving a new file. They will also learn some basic skills: creating new slides, reordering slides, adding text, adding pictures, adding audio files, and viewing a presentation.

The focus of this lesson is familiarity with the software itself (as opposed to writing or giving a presentation).

Grammar, Usage, and Mechanics Students are familiar with different ways to expand sentences by adding clauses, phrases, and words. In this lesson, they will explore why good writers expand sentences (and why sometimes, they don't). Three reasons writers expand sentences are for meaning, reader interest, and style.

> ### MATERIALS
>
> **Supplied**
> - *Summit English Language Arts 5 Activity Book*
>   - Spelling List 25 Pretest
>   - Use Presentation Software
> - Use Presentation Software Answer Key (PowerPoint file)
>
> **Also Needed**
> - reading material for Go Read!

By expanding a sentence, writers can provide additional information and clarify the meaning of the sentence.

> **Not Expanded:** Kelsey only tried one of the desserts.

> **Expanded for Meaning:** Kelsey only tried one of the desserts because she is allergic to chocolate.

Writers also expand sentences for reader interest. For example, writers might use a series of adjectives or a prepositional phrase to paint a picture in the reader's mind. They might use an interjection to elicit a strong emotion.

> **Not Expanded:** She took a bite of a cupcake.

> **Expanded for Interest:** She cautiously took a bite of a tiny cupcake with pink icing.

Finally, writers expand sentences for style. A writer's style, including how much detail and what type of details to include, depends on the purpose of a particular piece of writing. In an informational text, for instance, a writer might expand a sentence to add relevant details that support the main idea. A writer might use a shorter, more succinct sentence to emphasize an important idea.

> **Not Expanded:** The number of children with food allergies has risen in recent years.

> **Expanded for Style:** The number of children with food allergies has risen by 50 percent over the last two decades.

Expanding a sentence does not always improve it. Wordiness can distract readers from important information and make a sentence difficult to read. Writers should strive to be concise and precise.

Advance Preparation

During the Go Read! activity, students will have the option of using the digital library. Allow extra time for students to make their reading selection, or have students make a selection before beginning the lesson.

Lesson Goals

- Take a spelling pretest.
- Expand sentences for meaning, reader interest, and style.
- Learn how to use presentation software.
- Practice using presentation software.
- Read for pleasure.

Introduction to Presentation: Digital Tools

Students will get a glimpse of what they will learn about in the lesson. They will also read the lesson goals.

Spelling List 25 Pretest

Students will take a spelling pretest.

LEARNING COACH CHECK-IN   Have students turn to Spelling List 25 Pretest in *Summit English Language Arts 5 Activity Book* and open the online Spelling Pretest activity. Online, students will listen to the spelling word, type the word in the space indicated, and then check their answer. In the activity book, students will write the correct spelling of the word in the tables provided and indicate with a ✓ or an ✗ if they spelled the word correctly or incorrectly online. Students will repeat this process with the remaining words.

As needed, help students with the interaction between the online activity and the activity book page until they become comfortable with what they need to do. As students practice their spelling words throughout the workshop, they should pay special attention to words they spelled incorrectly on the pretest.

This is the complete list of words students will be tested on.

Words ending with *tion* or *sion*	Root *nov*	Prefix *ir–*
addition	novel	irrational
clarification	novelty	irregular
collision	renovate	irreplaceable
combination		irresponsible
competition		
composition		
conclusion		
exclamation		
extension		
intrusion		
multiplication		
qualification		
relaxation		
transportation		

NOTE Have students keep their completed activity page in a safe place so they can refer to it later.

Look Back at Choosing Effective Language

Students will practice the prerequisite skill of choosing words and phrases for effect.

LEARN AND TRY IT

LEARN   Expand Sentences

Students will learn how to purposely expand sentences for meaning, reader interest, and style.

TRY IT   Practice Expanding Sentences

Students will practice expanding sentences for meaning, reader interest, and style. They will receive feedback on their answers.

LEARN   Presentation Software

Students will learn how to use presentation software. They will learn how to open a new presentation; give the presentation a file name and save it; create new slides; reorder slides; add titles, text, pictures, and audio; and view the presentation as a slide show.

TIP   The presentation software used in this activity is PowerPoint. The skills shown can be applied to other types of presentation software with some modification.

TRY IT   Use Presentation Software

Students will complete Use Presentation Software from *Summit English Language Arts 5 Activity Book*. Use Presentation Software Answer Key, which is an example completed presentation, is available online.

NOTE   Students will follow the directions on the activity page to practice using presentation software. Ensure that students have access to a computer while completing the activity.

LEARNING COACH CHECK-IN   Assist students as needed as they complete this activity, especially if this is their first time using presentation software. Give students feedback, using the sample completed presentation provided online to guide you.

WRAP-UP

Questions About Expanding Sentences and Digital Tools

Students will answer questions to show that they understand how to expand sentences for meaning, reader interest, or style and how to use presentation software.

Go Read!

Students will read for pleasure. They should choose a book or a magazine that interests them, or they may choose a selection from the digital library, linked in the online lesson.

Students should read for the entire time. Have students select something to read ahead of time to help them stay focused.

Presentation: Planning

Lesson Overview

ACTIVITY	ACTIVITY TITLE	TIME	ONLINE/OFFLINE
GET READY	Introduction to Presentation: Planning	**2** minutes	🖥️
	Spelling List 25 Activity Bank	**10** minutes	📄
LEARN AND **TRY IT**	Reduce Sentences	**10** minutes	🖥️
	Practice Reducing Sentences	**10** minutes	🖥️
	Explore a Student's Presentation	**15** minutes	🖥️
	Planning a Presentation	**15** minutes	🖥️
	Plan Your Presentation **LEARNING COACH CHECK-IN**	**35** minutes	📄
WRAP-UP	Questions About Reducing Sentences and Presentations	**3** minutes	🖥️
	Go Read!	**20** minutes	🖥️ or 📄

Content Background

Students will begin working on an **informational presentation about a historical figure** that they will create using presentation software. They will complete this assignment over the course of several lessons by following the writing process. Students will begin by prewriting, or planning.

Writing Process

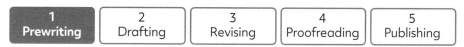

| 1 Prewriting | 2 Drafting | 3 Revising | 4 Proofreading | 5 Publishing |

During this step of the writing process, students will brainstorm and choose the topic of their informational presentation.

Grammar, Usage, and Mechanics Students will explore examples of how good writers shorten, or reduce, sentences for meaning, reader interest, and style.

By reducing a sentence, good writers convey their intended meaning without distracting readers. Good writers reread sentences and ask themselves if any of the information is irrelevant or repetitive. In the following example, "a hot cup of hot cocoa" is repetitive. The same is true for "white snow" and snow falling "from the sky."

MATERIALS

Supplied
- *Summit English Language Arts 5 Activity Book*
  - Spelling List 25 Activity Bank
  - Plan Your Presentation
- Presentation Instructions (printout)

Also Needed
- completed Spelling List 25 Pretest activity page from Presentation: Digital Tools
- folder in which students are storing presentation assignment pages
- reading material for Go Read!

The phrase "in his favorite mug" may be distracting depending on the context.

Not Reduced: Elijah drank a hot cup of hot cocoa in his favorite mug and watched the white snow fall from the sky.

Reduced for Meaning: Elijah drank a cup of hot cocoa and watched the snow fall.

Writers also reduce sentences for reader interest. Many long, rambling sentences can bore, or even frustrate, readers. In this example, the wording "The reason that _____ is" creates a wordy sentence. Reducing those words focuses the reader on the interesting part of the sentence.

Not Reduced: The reason that I am drinking cocoa is because I am very cold.

Reduced for Interest: I am drinking cocoa because I am very cold.

Another method for reducing writing for interest is substituting a wordy phrase for a single, precise word. Adverbs like *very* often begin phrases that can be reduced.

Not Reduced: I am drinking cocoa because I am very cold.

Reduced for Interest: I am drinking cocoa because I am freezing.

Finally, writers reduce sentences for style. A writer's style, include sentence length, depends on the purpose of a particular piece of writing. For example, formal writing tends to contain longer sentences, and informal writing tends to contain shorter sentences.

Not Reduced: Similarly, I often enjoy a bowl of soup on a night when the temperature, accounting for wind chill, dips below freezing.

Reduced for Style: I also like a bowl of soup on a cold night.

Advance Preparation

Gather students' completed Spelling List 25 Pretest activity page from Presentation: Digital Tools. Students will refer to this page during Get Ready: Spelling List 25 Activity Bank.

Gather a folder that students can use to keep all notes and activity pages related to their presentation.

During the Go Read! activity, students will have the option of using the digital library. Allow extra time for students to make their reading selection, or have students make a selection before beginning the lesson.

Lesson Goals

- Practice spelling words offline.
- Reduce sentences for meaning, reader interest, and style.
- Explore a model presentation.
- Begin planning your presentation.
- Read for pleasure.

Introduction to Presentation: Planning

Students will get a glimpse of what they will learn about in the lesson. They will also read the lesson goals and keywords. Have students select each keyword and preview its definition.

Spelling List 25 Activity Bank

Students will practice all spelling words from the workshop by completing Spelling List 25 Activity Bank from *Summit English Language Arts 5 Activity Book*. Make sure students have their completed Spelling List 25 Pretest activity page from Presentation: Digital Tools to refer to during this activity.

Remind students to pay special attention to words they spelled incorrectly on the Spelling Pretest.

GET READY
Presentation: Planning

Spelling List 25 Activity Bank

Circle any words in the box that you did not spell correctly on the pretest. Using your circled words, complete one activity of your choice. Complete as much of the activity as you can in the time given.

If you spelled all words correctly on the pretest, complete your chosen activity with as many spelling words as you can.

addition	composition	intrusion	transportation	irrational
clarification	conclusion	multiplication	novel	irregular
collision	exclamation	qualification	novelty	irresponsible
combination	extension	relaxation	renovate	irreplaceable
competition				

Spelling Activity Choices

Silly Sentences
1. Write a silly sentence using your words from the spelling word list.
2. Underline the spelling word in each sentence.
   Example: The dog was driving a car.
3. Correct any spelling errors.

PRESENTATION: PLANNING **423**

Spelling Story
1. Write a very short story using your words from the spelling word list.
2. Underline the spelling words in the story.
3. Correct any spelling errors.

Riddle Me This
1. Write a riddle for your words from the spelling word list.
   Example: "I have a trunk, but it's not on my car."
2. Write the answer, which is your word, for each riddle.
   Example: Answer: elephant
3. Correct any spelling errors.

RunOnWord
1. Gather some crayons, colored pencils, or markers. Write each of your words, using a different color for each word, end to end as one long word.
   Example: dogcatbirdfishturtle
2. Rewrite the words correctly and with proper spacing.

424 PRESENTATION: PLANNING

Complete the activity that you chose.

My chosen activity: _____

Students should use this page to complete all steps in their chosen activity.

PRESENTATION: PLANNING **425**

LEARN   Reduce Sentences

Students will learn how to purposely reduce sentences for meaning, reader interest, and style.

TRY IT   Practice Reducing Sentences

Students will practice reducing sentences for meaning, reader interest, and style. They will receive feedback on their answers.

LEARN   Explore a Student's Presentation

Students will be introduced to their assignment, which is to create an informational presentation about a historical figure using presentation software. To help them better understand the assignment, students will explore a model presentation and think about the elements that make it successful.

TRY IT   Planning a Presentation

Students will investigate how a student chooses a topic and begins planning a presentation.

TIP   Discuss historical figures that students have learned about in their courses. Encourage students to think about political figures, explorers, inventors, scientists, mathematicians, authors, poets, and artists.

TRY IT   Plan Your Presentation

Students will complete Plan Your Presentation from *Summit English Language Arts 5 Activity Book*.

LEARNING COACH CHECK-IN   Review students' responses. Ensure that students have selected a topic for their presentation that meets the criteria listed in Question 3 of the activity page. When students have completed the page, they should store it in a folder so that they can refer to it throughout the writing process.

NOTE   In addition to the planning activity, this activity page contains the instructions for the presentation. Students should read the instructions carefully, but in this lesson, they should complete the planning activity only (not the entire presentation assignment). If you or students wish, you can download and print another copy of the Presentation Instructions online.

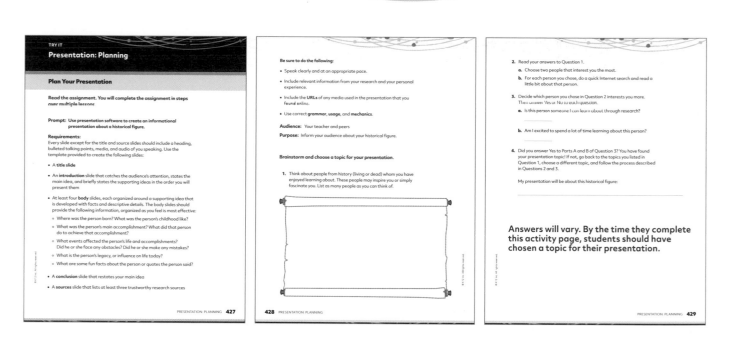

WRAP-UP

Questions About Reducing Sentences and Presentations

Students will answer questions to show that they understand how to reduce sentences for meaning, reader interest, or style and how to plan a presentation.

Go Read!

Students will read for pleasure. They should choose a book or a magazine that interests them, or they may choose a selection from the digital library, linked in the online lesson.

Students should read for the entire time. Have students select something to read ahead of time to help them stay focused.

Presentation: Research

Lesson Overview

ACTIVITY	ACTIVITY TITLE	TIME	ONLINE/OFFLINE
GET READY	Introduction to Presentation: Research	**2** minutes	🖥️
	Spelling List 25 Practice	**10** minutes	🖥️
	Baseball's Early Days	**10** minutes	🖥️
LEARN AND **TRY IT**	Researching a Presentation	**15** minutes	🖥️
	Research Your Presentation **LEARNING COACH CHECK-IN**	**60** minutes	🖥️ or 📄
WRAP-UP	Question About Researching a Presentation	**3** minutes	🖥️
	Go Read!	**20** minutes	🖥️ or 📄

Content Background

Students will continue working on an **informational presentation about a historical figure** that they will create using presentation software. They will complete this assignment over the course of several lessons by following the writing process.

Writing Process

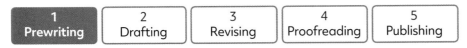

In this lesson, students will continue prewriting by conducting research. Students will continue to learn how to think critically about their research sources. In particular, they will analyze how mass media, such as movies and magazines, may promote messages that conflict with students' research goals.

Students will also continue to learn how to hone research questions. They will explore a few characteristics, such as how to determine whether a question is too narrow or too broad. A research question that is too narrow can be answered with a simple fact. One that is too broad cannot be answered in a typical assignment. Students will learn how to strive for a question that has the appropriate breadth.

Similarly, students will learn how to evaluate the breadth and depth of their research findings.

MATERIALS

Supplied
- *Summit English Language Arts 5 Activity Book*
  - Research Your Presentation
- Presentation Instructions (printout)
- Research Notes (printout)

Also Needed
- folder in which students are storing presentation assignment pages
- reading material for Go Read!

Advance Preparation

Gather the folder that students are using to store the activity pages related to their presentation. The folder should contain the following:

- Students' completed Plan for Your Presentation activity page from Presentation: Planning

Students will need to complete their own research during Try It: Research Your Presentation. Make sure students have access to trustworthy research sources. You may choose to complete the activity at a library.

During the Go Read! activity, students will have the option of using the digital library. Allow extra time for students to make their reading selection, or have students make a selection before beginning the lesson.

Lesson Goals

- Practice spelling words online.
- Practice grammar skills by editing a passage.
- Learn how to conduct research for a presentation.
- Research for your presentation.
- Read for pleasure.

GET READY

Introduction to Presentation: Research

Students will get a glimpse of what they will learn about in the lesson. They will also read the lesson goals and keywords. Have students select each keyword and preview its definition.

Spelling List 25 Practice

Students will practice all spelling words from the workshop.

Baseball's Early Days

Students will edit a short passage to practice applying grammar skills. This passage contains opportunities to improve the writing related to combining, expanding, and reducing sentences as well as using punctuation for effect.

LEARN   Researching a Presentation

Students will learn skills that will help them research their presentation. They will learn how to evaluate a media source for underlying messages and then to determine whether that source is appropriate for their research. They will also explore research questions, including how to write a question that isn't too narrow or too broad. Additionally, students will review important research skills, such as how to paraphrase information.

TIP   Tell students that major newspapers, such as the *New York Times*, the *Washington Post*, and the *Chicago Tribune* are all trustworthy sources. Likewise, government websites, such as those run by the Library of Congress and other agencies, contain reliable and useful information. Print reference books, such as *Encyclopedia Britannica* and the *World Book Encyclopedia*, are also credible sources of information.

TRY IT   Research Your Presentation

Students will complete Research Your Presentation from *Summit English Language Arts 5 Activity Book*. Make sure students have their completed Plan Your Presentation activity page from Presentation: Planning to refer to during this activity.

LEARNING COACH CHECK-IN   Assist students as needed in finding relevant, appropriate, and trustworthy research sources. When students have completed their research notes, they should store them in the folder they are using to organize their presentation assignment pages.

TIP   If you or your students wish, you can download and print another copy of the Presentation Instructions online. Additional sheets for Research Notes are also available online.

TRY IT
Presentation: Research

Research Your Presentation

Follow these steps to conduct research. Record information on the Research Notes pages that follow. Use one page per source.

Answers will vary.

1. Read the research questions that you need to answer in your presentation about a historical figure:
   a. Where was the person born? What was the person's childhood like?
   b. What was the person's main accomplishment? What did that person do to achieve that accomplishment?
   c. What events affected the person's life and accomplishments? Did he or she face any obstacles? Did he or she make any mistakes?
   d. What is the person's legacy, or influence on life today?
   e. What are some fun facts about the person or quotes the person said?

2. Identify at least three sources (digital, print, or both) that you can use to answer the research questions. Record the title, author, publisher, and URL of each source on the Research Notes pages that follow. Use one page per source.

3. As you read each source, take notes on the Research Notes pages related to the research questions.
   • Label each fact with the letter of the question that it answers.
   • Write your notes in your own words.
   • If you find a direct quotation that you think you might use in your presentation, record the quotation, word for word, in quotation marks. Also record the name of the person you are quoting.

PRESENTATION: RESEARCH **431**

---

432 PRESENTATION: RESEARCH

Research Notes

Source
Title: _____
Author: _____
Published by: _____
URL (if necessary): _____

Notes
Key Information Written in Your Own Words:
_____
_____
_____
_____
_____

Direct Quotations:
_____
_____

Person Quoted: _____

Research Notes

Source
Title: _____
Author: _____
Published by: _____
URL (if necessary): _____

Notes
Key Information Written in Your Own Words:
_____
_____
_____
_____
_____

Direct Quotations:
_____
_____

Person Quoted: _____

PRESENTATION: RESEARCH **433**

Research Notes

Source

Title: _____

Author: _____

Published by: _____

URL (if necessary): _____

Notes

Key Information Written in Your Own Words:

_____
_____
_____
_____
_____
_____

Direct Quotations:

_____
_____
_____

Person Quoted: _____

Reflect on your research.

4. What general conclusions can you draw from your research? Summarize your research in one to two sentences.

_____
_____
_____

5. Look back at the research questions.

   a. How well does your research answer each question?

   _____
   _____
   _____

   b. Did you answer any questions in addition to the research questions? If so, what?

   _____
   _____
   _____

   c. Based on your research, list what you believe will be the topic of each body slide in your presentation.

   _____
   _____
   _____

WRAP-UP

Question About Researching a Presentation

Students will answer a question to show that they understand how to research a presentation.

Go Read!

Students will read for pleasure. They should choose a book or a magazine that interests them, or they may choose a selection from the digital library, linked in the online lesson.

Students should read for the entire time. Have students select something to read ahead of time to help them stay focused.

Presentation: Drafting (A)

Lesson Overview

ACTIVITY	ACTIVITY TITLE	TIME	ONLINE/OFFLINE
GET READY	Introduction to Presentation: Drafting (A)	**2** minutes	🖥️
	Spelling List 25 Review Game	**10** minutes	🖥️
	Yurts	**10** minutes	🖥️
LEARN AND **TRY IT**	Drafting and Choosing Images for a Presentation	**20** minutes	🖥️
	Draft Your Presentation **LEARNING COACH CHECK-IN**	**55** minutes	🖥️
WRAP-UP	Question About Language in a Presentation	**3** minutes	🖥️
	Go Read!	**20** minutes	🖥️ or 📄

Content Background

Students will continue working on an **informational presentation about a historical figure**, an assignment that they will complete over the course of several lessons by following the writing process. In this lesson, students will begin drafting their presentation in PowerPoint.

Writing Process

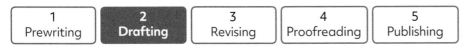

During **drafting**, students will use their research notes and other planning work to create a rough draft of their presentation. Students will draft directly in the presentation software—not on drafting paper. They will use a provided template that includes directions for what students need to do on each slide of the presentation.

Students will need to determine how to best group and order the information in their body slides. Sequential order is logical for a presentation about someone's life, but that isn't the only effective way students can organize the presentation. For instance, students might begin by presenting a problem and then show how their historical figure solved that problem. Or, students might compare and contrast their historical figure's setbacks and accomplishments. Students should think critically about structure and should feel empowered to experiment with different ways to structure their presentation.

MATERIALS

Supplied
- Model Presentation (PowerPoint file)
- Presentation Template (PowerPoint file)
- Presentation Instructions (printout)

Also Needed
- folder in which students are storing presentation assignment pages
- reading material for Go Read!

KEYWORDS

copyright – the right held by one person or company to publish, sell, distribute, and reproduce a work of art, literature, or music

draft – an early effort at a piece of writing, not the finished work

Students will learn guidelines for how to find images online that they can use in their presentations. Since copyright law is complicated and image rights sometimes change, **ensure that students do not publish their completed presentations online.** That includes sharing the presentation on a personal or family website or on social media. Students should share their presentation with their teacher and classmates only.

Students are expected to write about half of their rough draft in this lesson (although they may write more, if they wish). They will have time to finish and submit their draft in Presentation: Drafting (B).

Advance Preparation

Gather the folder that students are using to store the activity pages related to their presentation. The folder should contain the following:

- Students' completed Plan for Your Presentation activity page from Presentation: Planning

- Students' completed research notes from Presentation: Research

During the Go Read! activity, students will have the option of using the digital library. Allow extra time for students to make their reading selection, or have students make a selection before beginning the lesson.

Lesson Goals

- Practice spelling words online.
- Practice grammar skills by editing a passage.
- Learn how to create your presentation using a template.
- Learn how to choose images to include in a presentation.
- Begin to draft your presentation.
- Read for pleasure.

GET READY

Introduction to Presentation: Drafting (A)

Students will get a glimpse of what they will learn about in the lesson. They will also read the lesson goals and keywords. Have students select each keyword and preview its definition.

Spelling List 24 Review Game

Students will practice all spelling words from the workshop.

Yurts

Students will edit a short passage to practice applying grammar skills. This passage contains errors and opportunities to improve the writing related to combining, expanding, and reducing sentences; shifts in verb tense; and correctly punctuating items in a series.

LEARN AND TRY IT

LEARN   Drafting and Choosing Images for a Presentation

Students will learn how to use a template to create their informational presentation about a historical figure using presentation software. As they learn about the template, they will explore ways to structure their presentation, as well as determine whether formal or informal language is appropriate for the assignment. Students will also learn guidelines for finding images online that they can use in their presentation.

TIP   Students don't necessarily need to find images for their presentation online. They can use photos they take themselves (or photos for which they have a friend's or family member's permission to use). They can also create images, such as drawings, charts, and graphs, on the computer. Finally, students can draw on paper and photograph or scan those drawings.

TRY IT   Draft Your Presentation

Students will use the Presentation Template to begin drafting their presentation. Students should complete about half of their draft during this activity. If students wish, they may complete more than half of their draft.

Make sure students have their completed Plan Your Presentation activity page from Presentation: Planning and their research notes from Presentation: Research to refer to during this activity.

LEARNING COACH CHECK-IN   Ensure that students understand how to use the template (you may wish to supervise them as they complete one slide). If necessary, remind students not to focus on perfection at this stage of the writing process.

TIP   Help students create a folder on the computer in which to save their in-progress presentation.

NOTE   If you or students wish, you can download and print another copy of the Presentation Instructions online. The Model Presentation is also available online as a reference.

Question About Drafting a Presentation

Students will answer a question to show that they understand how to draft a presentation.

Go Read!

Students will read for pleasure. They should choose a book or a magazine that interests them, or they may choose a selection from the digital library, linked in the online lesson.

Students should read for the entire time. Have students select something to read ahead of time to help them stay focused.

Presentation: Drafting (B)

Lesson Overview

ACTIVITY	ACTIVITY TITLE	TIME	ONLINE/OFFLINE
GET READY	Introduction to Presentation: Drafting (B)	**1** minute	🖥️
TRY IT	Review Expanding and Reducing Sentences	**10** minutes	🖥️
QUIZ	Expanding and Reducing Sentences	**20** minutes	🖥️
	Spelling List 25	**10** minutes	🖥️
TRY IT	Finish Drafting Your Presentation **LEARNING COACH CHECK-IN**	**50** minutes	🖥️
WRAP-UP	Turn In Your Presentation Draft	**1** minute	🖥️
	Keyboarding	**10** minutes	🖥️
	More Language Arts Practice	**18** minutes	🖥️

Content Background

Students will continue working on an **informational presentation about a historical figure**, an assignment that they will complete over the course of several lessons by following the writing process. In this lesson, students will finish drafting their presentation in PowerPoint. They will complete the remaining steps of the writing process in a future workshop.

Writing Process

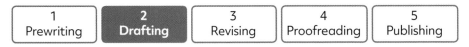

| 1 Prewriting | **2 Drafting** | 3 Revising | 4 Proofreading | 5 Publishing |

Advance Preparation

Help students locate their in-progress presentation that they saved to the computer in Presentation: Drafting (A).

Gather the folder that students are using to store the activity pages related to their presentation. The folder should contain the following:

- Students' completed Plan for Your Presentation activity page from Presentation: Planning

- Students' completed research notes from Presentation: Research

MATERIALS

Supplied
- Model Presentation (PowerPoint file)
- Presentation Template (PowerPoint file)
- Presentation Instructions (printout)

Also Needed
- students' in-progress presentation from Presentation: Drafting (A)
- folder in which students are storing presentation assignment pages

During the Keyboarding activity, students will practice their keyboarding skills using an external website or program. **You will need to work with students to select an appropriate keyboarding practice website or program; K12 does not specify which resource to use.** A few suggestions are provided in the online activity.

Depending on which program you choose, students may need to set up an account to save their progress. If needed, assist students in setting up and running their chosen keyboarding practice program.

Lesson Goals

- Review how to expand and reduce sentences for meaning, reader interest, and style.
- Take a quiz on expanding and reducing sentences for meaning, reader interest, and style.
- Take a spelling quiz.
- Finish and submit the rough draft of your presentation.

GET READY

Introduction to Presentation: Drafting (B)
Students will read the lesson goals.

TRY IT

Review Expanding and Reducing Sentences
Students will answer questions to review what they have learned about expanding and reducing sentences for meaning, reader interest, and style.

QUIZ

Expand and Reduce Sentences
Students will complete the Expand and Reduce Sentences quiz.

Spelling List 25
Students will complete the Spelling List 25 quiz.

Finish Drafting Your Presentation

Students will complete the rough draft of their presentation. Students should open the PowerPoint file they saved in Presentation: Drafting (A) and complete their draft.

Make sure students have their completed Plan Your Presentation activity page from Presentation: Planning and their research notes from Presentation: Research to refer to during this activity.

LEARNING COACH CHECK-IN   Review students' presentation draft. Ensure that students' draft is in line with the assignment criteria outlined on the Plan Your Presentation activity page. Students should save a copy of their presentation on their computer.

NOTE   If you or students wish, you can download and print another copy of the Presentation Instructions online. The Presentation Template and Model Presentation are also available online.

Turn In Your Presentation Draft

Students will submit their presentation draft to their teacher.

Keyboarding

Students will practice their keyboarding skills using an external website or program.

More Language Arts Practice

Students will practice skills according to their individual needs.

"The Value of Money"

Lesson Overview

ACTIVITY	ACTIVITY TITLE	TIME	ONLINE/OFFLINE
GET READY	Introduction to "The Value of Money"	**1** minute	🖥️
	Spelling List 26 Pretest **LEARNING COACH CHECK-IN**	**10** minutes	🖥️ and 📄
	Before You Read "The Value of Money"	**9** minutes	🖥️
READ	"The Value of Money"	**30** minutes	📄
	Check-In: "The Value of Money"	**5** minutes	🖥️
LEARN AND **TRY IT**	Cause and Effect	**5** minutes	🖥️
	Focus on Causes and Effects	**5** minutes	🖥️
	Using Graphs, Charts, and Other Features	**10** minutes	🖥️
	Focus on Features and Interpreting Information	**10** minutes	🖥️
	Apply: Cause-and-Effect Relationship	**15** minutes	🖥️
	Write About Two Texts **LEARNING COACH CHECK-IN**	**10** minutes	📄
	Practice Words From "The Value of Money"	**8** minutes	🖥️
WRAP-UP	Questions About Text Features and Cause and Effect	**2** minutes	🖥️

Content Background

Students will read an article entitled "The Value of Money." They will learn about causes and effects, as well as how text features and graphics (such as diagrams, charts, and other visual aids) help make the important ideas in a text easier to understand.

> **Cause:** Carol forgets to put a carton of ice cream in the freezer.
>
> **Effect:** The ice cream melts.

The article also covers a few important economic terms. *Inflation* refers to an increase in the price of goods and services. *Hyperinflation* describes an extremely rapid increase in those prices. *Deflation* refers to a decrease in the price of goods and services. *Supply shock* describes a situation in which a good or service suddenly becomes very scarce—and consequently more expensive.

MATERIALS

Supplied
- *K12 World: Money, Money, Money*
- *Summit English Language Arts 5 Activity Book*
  - Spelling List 26 Pretest
  - Write About Two Texts

"The Value of Money" Synopsis

This magazine article provides students with an explanation of how money's value can change over time. It describes inflation, its causes and effects, and hyperinflation. It also describes deflation and why it is also problematic.

KEYWORDS

cause and effect – a situation in which one condition or fact, the cause, results in another, the effect

Lesson Goals

- Take a spelling pretest.

- Read "The Value of Money."

- Examine how ideas and details in the text are related by cause and effect.

- Interpret information included in text features, and explore connections within and across works.

GET READY

Introduction to "The Value of Money"

Students will get a glimpse of what they will learn about in the lesson. They will also read the lesson goals and keywords. Have students select each keyword and preview its definition.

Spelling List 26 Pretest

Students will take a spelling pretest.

LEARNING COACH CHECK-IN   Have students turn to Spelling List 26 Pretest in *Summit English Language Arts 5 Activity Book* and open the online Spelling Pretest activity. Online, students will listen to the spelling word, type the word in the space indicated, and then check their answer. In the activity book, students will write the correct spelling of the word in the tables provided and indicate with a ✓ or an ✗ if they spelled the word correctly or incorrectly online. Students will repeat this process with the remaining words.

As needed, help students with the interaction between the online activity and the activity book page until they become comfortable with what they need to do. As students practice their spelling words throughout the workshop, they should pay special attention to words they spelled incorrectly on the pretest.

This is the complete list of words students will be tested on.

Words Often Confused	Root *mob*
desert	automobile
dessert	mobility
envelop	mobilize
envelope	
formally	
formerly	
flaunt	
flout	
morality	
mortality	
precede	
proceed	
hoard	
horde	

NOTE Have students keep their completed activity page in a safe place so they can refer to it later.

Before You Read "The Value of Money"

Students will be introduced to some key vocabulary words that they will encounter in the upcoming reading and learn some important strategies to use when reading a difficult or complex text.

"The Value of Money"

Students will read "The Value of Money" in *K12 World: Money, Money, Money*.

Check-In: "The Value of Money"

Students will answer several questions to demonstrate their comprehension of "The Value of Money."

LEARN AND TRY IT

LEARN   Cause and Effect

Students will determine the structure of a passage from the text. They will learn how to recognize causes and effects and explore the relationship between them.

TRY IT   Focus on Causes and Effects

Students will answer questions in which they demonstrate their understanding of cause-and-effect structure and how to recognize causes and effects.

LEARN   Using Graphs, Charts, and Other Features

Students will learn how to use text features, such as graphs and charts, to identify or gather key information. They will also explore how to make interpretations based on information in the text.

TRY IT   Focus on Features and Interpreting Information

Students will answer questions in which they demonstrate their ability to gather information from graphs and charts and to make interpretations based on information in the text.

TRY IT   Apply: Cause-and-Effect Relationship

Students will apply to a new work what they've learned about identifying cause-and-effect relationships in a text.

TRY IT   Write About Two Texts

Students will complete Write About Two Texts from *Summit English Language Arts 5 Activity Book*. They will demonstrate their understanding of the similarities and differences in structure of two texts in this unit.

LEARNING COACH CHECK-IN   This activity page contains an open-ended question, so it's important that you review students' responses. Give students feedback, using the sample answers provided to guide you.

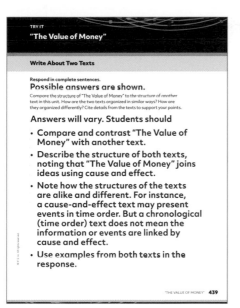

TRY IT   Practice Words From "The Value of Money"

Students will answer questions to demonstrate their understanding of the vocabulary words from the reading.

WRAP-UP

Questions About Text Features and Cause and Effect

Students will answer questions to show that they understand how to draw information from graphs and charts and that they can recognize cause-and-effect relationships.

"The Value of Money" Wrap-Up

Lesson Overview

ACTIVITY	ACTIVITY TITLE	TIME	ONLINE/OFFLINE
GET READY	Introduction to "The Value of Money" Wrap-Up	**1** minute	🖥️
	Spelling List 26 Activity Bank	**10** minutes	📄
TRY IT	Write About "The Value of Money" **LEARNING COACH CHECK-IN**	**30** minutes	📄
	Read and Record	**10** minutes	🖥️
	Review "The Value of Money"	**20** minutes	🖥️
QUIZ	"The Value of Money"	**30** minutes	🖥️
WRAP-UP	Keyboarding	**10** minutes	🖥️
	More Language Arts Practice	**9** minutes	🖥️

Content Background

Students will complete a spelling activity and then write about the articles they have read. Students will then have an opportunity to review the texts they've read before demonstrating their knowledge of them on a quiz.

Advance Preparation

Gather students' completed Spelling List 26 Pretest activity page from "The Value of Money." Students will refer to this page during Get Ready: Spelling List 26 Activity Bank.

During the Keyboarding activity, students will practice their keyboarding skills using an external website or program. **You will need to work with students to select an appropriate keyboarding practice website or program; K12 does not specify which resource to use.** A few suggestions are provided in the online activity.

Depending on which program you choose, students may need to set up an account to save their progress. If needed, assist students in setting up and running their chosen keyboarding practice program.

MATERIALS

Supplied

- *K12 World: Money, Money, Money*
- *Summit English Language Arts 5 Activity Book*
  - Spelling List 26 Activity Bank
  - Write About "The Value of Money"

Also Needed

- completed Spelling List 26 Pretest activity page from "The Value of Money"

Lesson Goals

- Practice all spelling words offline.
- Write about the ideas in "The Value of Money" and another text.
- Read and record text with fluency.
- Take a quiz on "The Value of Money."
- Practice keyboarding and language arts skills.

Introduction to "The Value of Money" Wrap-Up

Students will read the lesson goals.

Spelling List 26 Activity Bank

Students will practice all spelling words from the workshop by completing Spelling List 26 Activity Bank from *Summit English Language Arts 5 Activity Book*. Make sure students have their completed Spelling List 26 Pretest activity page from "The Value of Money" to refer to during this activity.

Remind students to pay special attention to words they spelled incorrectly on the Spelling Pretest.

Write About "The Value of Money"

Students will complete Write About "The Value of Money" from *Summit English Language Arts 5 Activity Book*.

LEARNING COACH CHECK-IN   This activity page contains an open-ended question, so it's important that you review students' responses. Give students feedback, using the sample answers provided to guide you.

> TRY IT
> ## "The Value of Money" Wrap-Up
>
> **Write About "The Value of Money"**
>
> Respond in complete sentences.
> ### Example answers are shown.
> Think about what you read in "The Value of Money" and at least one other text in this unit. Briefly describe what these texts taught you. Finally, write about the most important thing you learned about money. Use details from the texts in your response.
> ### Answers will vary. Students should
>
> - Describe at least two texts from this unit. As needed, they should note that "From Barter to Bitcoin" tells the history of money. "Making Money" explains how paper money and coins are created. "The Value of Money" provides information about how money's worth can change. "The Future of Money" is about digital money.
> - Name the most important thing they've learned about money. For example, students may write about how money is created to prevent counterfeiting. Or they may write about how credit cards have made physical money less common today than in the past.
> - Include details from the readings.
>
> "THE VALUE OF MONEY" WRAP-UP **445**

Read and Record

Good readers read quickly, smoothly, and with expression. This is called *fluency*. Students will record themselves reading aloud. They will listen to their recording and think about how quick, smooth, and expressive they sound.

TIP   Encourage students to rerecord as needed.

Review "The Value of Money"

Students will answer questions to review what they have learned from the "The Value of Money" article.

QUIZ

"The Value of Money"

Students will complete the "The Value of Money" quiz.

WRAP-UP

Keyboarding

Students will practice their keyboarding skills using an external website or program.

More Language Arts Practice

Students will practice skills according to their individual needs.

"The Future of Money"

Lesson Overview

ACTIVITY	ACTIVITY TITLE	TIME	ONLINE/OFFLINE
GET READY	Introduction to "The Future of Money"	**1** minute	🖥️
	Spelling List 26 Review Game	**10** minutes	🖥️
	Before You Read "The Future of Money"	**9** minutes	🖥️
READ	"The Future of Money"	**30** minutes	📄
	Check-In: "The Future of Money"	**5** minutes	🖥️
LEARN AND **TRY IT**	Comparisons and Contrasts	**5** minutes	🖥️
	Examine Comparisons and Contrasts	**5** minutes	🖥️
	Information Within and Across Texts	**10** minutes	🖥️
	Explore Multiple Works	**10** minutes	🖥️
	Apply: Compare-and-Contrast Relationship	**15** minutes	🖥️
	Write About Different Structures **LEARNING COACH CHECK-IN**	**10** minutes	📄
	Practice Words from "The Future of Money"	**8** minutes	🖥️
WRAP-UP	Questions About "The Future of Money"	**2** minutes	🖥️

Content Background

Students will read an article called "The Future of Money." They will explore how the author compares and contrasts ideas in the text. They will also learn strategies for finding information within a single text or across multiple texts.

The article includes a few important terms related to the latest developments in currency. *Cryptocurrency* is digital money that can be used to pay for goods and services via computers and smartphones. Complex coding and a network of computers that store records of online transactions —known as *blockchains*—work to ensure user security and prevent fraud and counterfeiting. *Bitcoin*, the most successful and widely used cryptocurrency, can be bought, sold, and used to complete transactions on the Internet.

> ### MATERIALS
>
> **Supplied**
> - *K12 World: Money, Money, Money*
> - *Summit English Language Arts 5 Activity Book*
>   - Write About Different Structures

"The Future of Money" Synopsis

This magazine article teaches students what cryptocurrency is, how it is used, and why it is important. It does so by comparing and contrasting cryptocurrency with traditional currency. The piece focuses mostly on the most well-known cryptocurrency: bitcoin.

Lesson Goals

- Practice all spelling words online.
- Read "The Future of Money."
- Analyze the way an article is organized.
- Connect and interpret ideas and information within and across texts.

GET READY

Introduction to "The Future of Money"
Students will get a glimpse of what they will learn about in the lesson. They will also read the lesson goals.

Spelling List 26 Review Game
Students will practice all spelling words from the workshop.

Before You Read "The Future of Money"
Students will be introduced to some key vocabulary words that they will encounter in the upcoming reading and learn about skimming a text before reading it.

READ

"The Future of Money"
Students will read "The Future of Money" in *K12 World: Money, Money, Money.*

Check-In: "The Future of Money"
Students will answer several questions to demonstrate their comprehension of "The Future of Money."

LEARN Comparisons and Contrasts

Students will explore how "The Future of Money" is structured. This article structure highlights the similarities and differences between cryptocurrency and traditional currency.

TRY IT Examine Comparisons and Contrasts

Students will answer questions in which they demonstrate their understanding of how a text is organized and how its ideas are related.

LEARN Information Within and Across Texts

Students will focus first on how to interpret information within a text and then on how to look across texts to develop a more complete understanding of an idea or subject.

TRY IT Explore Multiple Works

Students will answer questions in which they demonstrate their ability to interpret information within a single text and develop a greater understanding of an idea or subject by looking across texts.

TRY IT Apply: Compare and Contrast Relationship

Students will apply to a new work what they've learned about understanding ideas that are being compared and contrasted.

TRY IT Write About Different Structures

Students will complete Write About Different Structures from *Summit English Language Arts 5 Activity Book*. They will demonstrate their understanding of how each text in this unit is structured and why the writers chose to structure the texts that way.

LEARNING COACH CHECK-IN   This activity page contains open-ended questions, so it's important that you review students' responses. Give students feedback, using the sample answers provided to guide you.

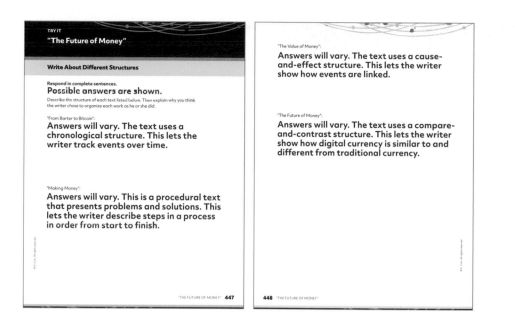

TRY IT   Practice Words from "The Future of Money"

Students will answer questions to demonstrate their understanding of the vocabulary words from the reading.

WRAP-UP

Questions About "The Future of Money"

Students will answer questions to show that they can recognize when a text uses compare-and-contrast structure and know how to develop a deeper understanding of a topic by using multiple texts.

"The Future of Money" Wrap-Up

Lesson Overview

ACTIVITY	ACTIVITY TITLE	TIME	ONLINE/OFFLINE
GET READY	Introduction to "The Future of Money" Wrap-Up	**1** minute	🖥️
TRY IT	Write About What You've Read **LEARNING COACH CHECK-IN**	**30** minutes	📄
	Read and Record	**10** minutes	🖥️
	Review "The Future of Money"	**20** minutes	🖥️
QUIZ	"The Future of Money"	**30** minutes	🖥️
	Spelling List 26	**10** minutes	🖥️
WRAP-UP	Keyboarding	**10** minutes	🖥️
	More Language Arts Practice	**9** minutes	🖥️

Content Background

Students will write about the article they read. Students will then have an opportunity to review the texts they've read before demonstrating their knowledge of them on a quiz. They will also take a spelling quiz.

Advance Preparation

During the Keyboarding activity, students will practice their keyboarding skills using an external website or program. **You will need to work with students to select an appropriate keyboarding practice website or program; K12 does not specify which resource to use.** A few suggestions are provided in the online activity.

Depending on which program you choose, students may need to set up an account to save their progress. If needed, assist students in setting up and running their chosen keyboarding practice program.

> ### MATERIALS
>
> **Supplied**
> - *K12 World: Money, Money, Money*
> - *Summit English Language Arts 5 Activity Book*
>   - Write About What You've Read

Lesson Goals

- Write about using text structures and features within and across texts.
- Read and record text with fluency.
- Take a quiz on "The Future of Money."
- Take a spelling quiz.
- Practice keyboarding and language arts skills.

GET READY

Introduction to "The Future of Money" Wrap-Up

Students will read the lesson goals.

TRY IT

Write About What You've Read

Students will complete Write About What You've Read from *Summit English Language Arts 5 Activity Book*.

LEARNING COACH CHECK-IN   This activity page contains open-ended questions, so it's important that you review students' responses. Give students feedback, using the sample answers provided to guide you. As necessary, remind students of some of the information texts they have read in this course, such as *The Mary Celeste: An Unsolved Mystery from History*, *Mesmerized*, *You Should Meet Katherine Johnson*, and *Who Is Sonia Sotomayor?*

Left activity page:

TRY IT
"The Future of Money" Wrap-Up

Write About What You've Read

Respond in complete sentences.

1. Think about the different text structures you've learned about in this unit. You've read articles in *Money, Money, Money* that organize ideas using chronological order, problem and solution, cause and effect, and compare and contrast. Each article also included several text features, such as headings, graphs, charts, diagrams, and illustrations.
   - Which article was your favorite? Why?
   - Which text feature was your favorite? Why?
   - Cite specific examples from the text in your response.

Answers will vary. Students should

- State which article and text feature they liked best; for example: "From Barter to Bitcoin" and its illustrations.
- Explain the reasons for selecting this article; for instance, the use of chronological order in this article makes it easy to understand the history of money. The pictures help readers visualize its subtopics.

"THE FUTURE OF MONEY" WRAP-UP   **449**

Right activity page:

2. Compare and contrast the structure and text features of an article in *Money, Money, Money* to the structure and text features in another informational text you've read in this course.
   - How are the pieces similar? How are they different?
   - Considering its structure and text features, which text do you think is more effective?

Answer will vary. Students should

- Compare an article from this unit to an informational text in the course. Possible texts to compare an article with are *Who Is Sonia Sotomayor?*, *The Mary Celeste: An Unsolved Mystery from History*, *Mesmerized*, *You Should Meet Katherine Johnson*, and others.
- Correctly identify the structure of the article and the other text (most use chronological order).
- Evaluate the effectiveness of both works, pointing out similarities and differences.
- Describe the features found in each text, noting how they affect reader understanding.

450   "THE FUTURE OF MONEY" WRAP-UP

Read and Record

Good readers read quickly, smoothly, and with expression. This is called *fluency*. Students will record themselves reading aloud. They will listen to their recording and think about how quick, smooth, and expressive they sound.

TIP Encourage students to rerecord as needed.

Review "The Future of Money"

Students will answer questions to review what they have learned from "The Future of Money" article.

QUIZ

"The Future of Money"

Students will complete the "The Future of Money" quiz.

Spelling List 26

Students will complete the Spelling List 26 quiz.

WRAP-UP

Keyboarding

Students will practice their keyboarding skills using an external website or program.

More Language Arts Practice

Students will practice skills according to their individual needs.

Big Ideas: Critical Skills Assignment

Lesson Overview

Big Ideas lessons provide students the opportunity to further apply the knowledge acquired and skills learned throughout the unit workshops. Each Big Ideas lesson consists of these parts:

1. **Cumulative Review:** Students keep their skills fresh by reviewing prior content.

2. **Preview:** Students practice answering the types of questions they will commonly find on standardized tests.

3. **Synthesis:** Students complete an assignment that allows them to connect and apply what they have learned. Synthesis assignments vary throughout the course.

    In the Synthesis portion of this Big Ideas lesson, students will read new selections. They will answer literal and inferential comprehension questions and complete writing questions that ask for short responses about the reading selections. Students should refer to the selections while answering the questions, because the questions emphasize using textual evidence. The questions call for students to demonstrate critical thinking, reading, and writing skills.

    LEARNING COACH CHECK-IN   This is a graded assessment. Make sure students complete, review, and submit the assignment to their teacher.

All materials needed for this lesson are linked online and not provided in the Activity Book.

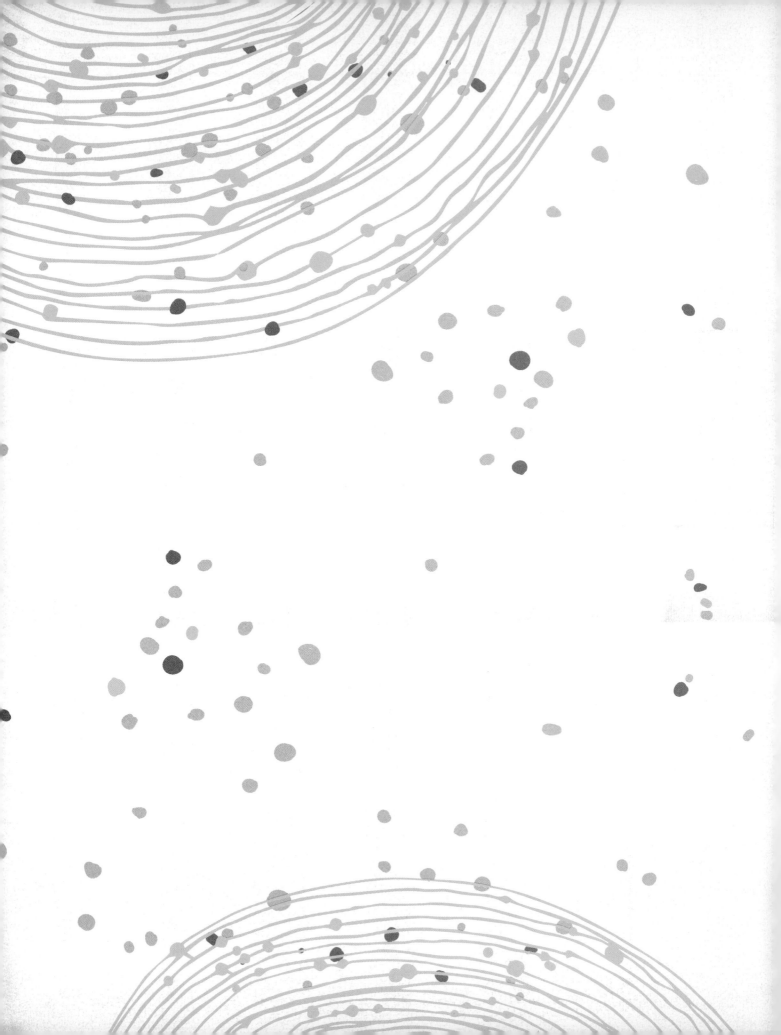

The Adventures of Sherlock Holmes

Sayings

Lesson Overview

ACTIVITY	ACTIVITY TITLE	TIME	ONLINE/OFFLINE
GET READY	The Adventures of Sherlock Holmes Unit Overview	**1** minute	🖥
	Introduction to Sayings	**1** minute	🖥
LEARN AND **TRY IT**	Common Sayings	**9** minutes	🖥
	Show Your Command of Common Sayings	**10** minutes	🖥
	Apply: Use Common Sayings **LEARNING COACH CHECK-IN**	**15** minutes	📄
	Go Write!	**15** minutes	📄
	Review Sayings	**15** minutes	🖥
QUIZ	Sayings	**15** minutes	🖥
WRAP-UP	Keyboarding	**10** minutes	🖥
	More Language Arts Practice	**15** minutes	🖥
	Go Read!	**14** minutes	🖥 or 📄

Content Background

Students will use logic and context clues to learn and explore the meanings of several common sayings. They will also practice using sayings in their own writing. By understanding sayings, students can improve their reading comprehension and vocabulary.

Let sleeping dogs lie.

Live and let live.

Nothing ventured, nothing gained.

Old habits die hard.

Once bitten, twice shy.

The leopard cannot change his spots.

The grass is always greener on the other side.

Strike while the iron is hot.

Advance Preparation

During the Keyboarding activity, students will practice their keyboarding skills using an external website or program. **You will need to work with students to select an appropriate keyboarding practice website or**

program; K12 does not specify which resource to use. A few suggestions are provided in the online activity.

Depending on which program you choose, students may need to set up an account to save their progress. If needed, assist students in setting up and running their chosen keyboarding practice program.

During the Go Read! activity, students will have the option of using the digital library. Allow extra time for students to make their reading selection, or have students make a selection before beginning the lesson.

Lesson Goals

- Identify and explain the meanings of common sayings.
- Read for pleasure.

GET READY

The Adventures of Sherlock Holmes Unit Overview

Students will read a summary of what they will learn about in the Adventures of Sherlock Holmes unit.

Introduction to Sayings

Students will get a glimpse of what they will learn about in the lesson. They will also read the lesson goals.

LEARN AND TRY IT

LEARN   Common Sayings

Students will be introduced to the vocabulary for the lesson. Each item is a common saying that offers some advice or piece of wisdom.

TRY IT   Show Your Command of Common Sayings

Students will demonstrate their understanding of the sayings they've learned by identifying them and their meanings in context.

TRY IT   Apply: Use Common Sayings

Students will complete Use Common Sayings from *Summit English Language Arts 5 Activity Book*.

LEARNING COACH CHECK-IN   This activity page contains open-ended questions, so it's important that you review students' responses. Give students feedback, using the sample answers provided to guide you.

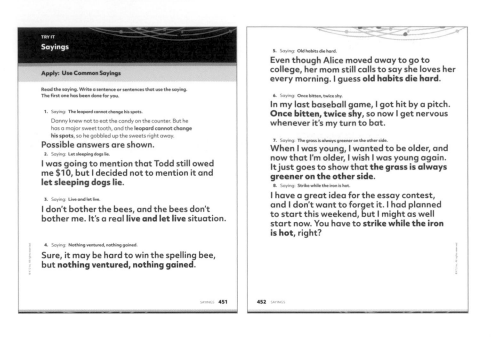

TRY IT   Go Write!

Students will write independently for pleasure. As they write, they should think about using common sayings.

TRY IT   Review Sayings

Students will answer questions to review what they have learned about the meanings of sayings.

Sayings

Students will complete the Sayings quiz.

Keyboarding

Students will practice their keyboarding skills using an external website or program.

More Language Arts Practice

Students will practice skills according to their individual needs.

Go Read!

Students will read for pleasure. They should choose a book or a magazine that interests them, or they may choose a selection from the digital library, linked in the online lesson.

Students should read for the entire time. Have students select something to read ahead of time to help them stay focused.

Meet Sherlock Holmes (A)

Lesson Overview

ACTIVITY	ACTIVITY TITLE	TIME	ONLINE/OFFLINE
GET READY	Introduction to Meet Sherlock Holmes (A)	**1** minute	🖥
	Spelling List 27 Pretest **LEARNING COACH CHECK-IN**	**10** minutes	🖥
	Sherlock Holmes in 60 Seconds	**1** minute	🖥
	Before You Read "The Red-Headed League," Part 1	**14** minutes	🖥
READ	"The Red-Headed League," Part 1	**30** minutes	🖥 or 📄
	Check-In: "The Red-Headed League," Part 1	**5** minutes	🖥
LEARN AND **TRY IT**	Drawing Conclusions	**10** minutes	🖥
	Practice Drawing Conclusions	**10** minutes	🖥
	Apply: Draw More Conclusions	**15** minutes	🖥
	Draw a Conclusion **LEARNING COACH CHECK-IN**	**15** minutes	📄
	Practice Words from "The Red-Headed League," Part 1	**8** minutes	🖥
WRAP-UP	Question About "The Red-Headed League," Part 1	**2** minutes	🖥

Content Background

Students will learn about detective fiction before starting to read a story about Sherlock Holmes called "The Red-Headed League." After reading the first section of the story, students will learn how to use textual evidence to draw conclusions and the importance of backing up their conclusions with accurate quotations from the text.

MATERIALS

Supplied
- *Summit English Language Arts 5 Expeditions in Reading*
- *Summit English Language Arts 5 Activity Book*
  - Spelling List 27 Pretest
  - Write About a Conclusion

"The Red-Headed League," Part 1 Synopsis

Dr. Watson arrives at the home of Sherlock Holmes to find Holmes with a tradesman named Mr. Jabez Wilson. Wilson, who has bright red hair, tells Holmes and Watson how he was recently hired to do a rather strange job—copy out entries from the encyclopedia—for four hours a day by a man named Duncan Ross, who runs an organization called the Red-Headed League. Wilson tells Holmes and Watson how his assistant, Vincent Spaulding, told him about the league and that he worked for the league for eight weeks. When Wilson went to work recently, he found a note stating that the league had been dissolved. He asks Holmes to help him make sense of the case. Holmes thinks he can do so and focuses his questions on Wilson's assistant, Vincent Spaulding.

Lesson Goals

- Take a spelling pretest.
- Learn about the detective fiction genre.
- Begin to read "The Red-Headed League."
- Draw conclusions based on textual evidence and direct quotations.
- Determine the meanings of unfamiliar words.

GET READY

Introduction to Meet Sherlock Holmes (A)

Students will get a glimpse of what they will learn about in the lesson. They will also read the lesson goals and keywords. Have students select each keyword and preview its definition.

Spelling List 27 Pretest

Students will take a spelling pretest.

LEARNING COACH CHECK-IN   Have students turn to Spelling List 27 Pretest in *Summit English Language Arts 5 Activity Book* and open the online Spelling Pretest activity. Online, students will listen to the spelling word, type the word in the space indicated, and then check their answer. In the activity book, students will write the correct spelling of the word in the tables provided and indicate with a ✓ or an ✗ if they spelled the word correctly or incorrectly online. Students will repeat this process with the remaining words.

As needed, help students with the interaction between the online activity and the activity book page until they become comfortable with what they need to do. As students practice their spelling words throughout the workshop, they should pay special attention to words they spelled incorrectly on the pretest.

This is the complete list of words students will be tested on.

Homographs			
tear	dove	record	produce
content	invalid	refuse	sewer
contract	minute	separate	
convict	moderate	wound	
moped	lead	present	

NOTE Have students keep their completed activity page in a safe place so they can refer to it later.

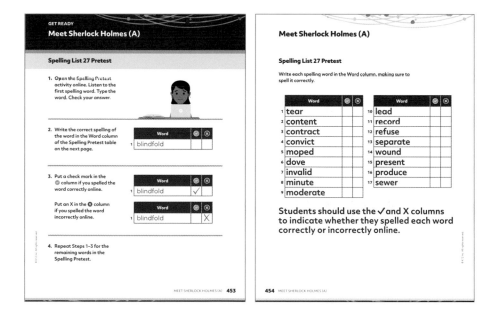

Sherlock Holmes in 60 Seconds

Students will watch a short video designed to spark their interest in upcoming topics.

Before You Read "The Red-Headed League," Part 1

Students will be introduced to some key vocabulary words that they will encounter in the upcoming reading and learn some important historical background related to the reading.

"The Red-Headed League," Part 1

Students will read Part 1 of "The Red-Headed League" in *Expeditions in Reading*.

Check-In: "The Red-Headed League," Part 1

Students will answer several questions to demonstrate their comprehension of Part 1 of "The Red-Headed League."

LEARN AND TRY IT

LEARN Drawing Conclusions

Students will examine a passage from the story and learn how to use evidence and textual details to draw conclusions based on it. They will also learn about using accurate quotations from the text to support any conclusion that they draw.

TRY IT Practice Drawing Conclusions

Students will answer questions in which they draw conclusions about an excerpt from "The Red-Headed League" and quote accurately from the text in support of those conclusions.

TRY IT Apply: Draw More Conclusions

Students will apply to a new work what they've learned about drawing and supporting conclusions.

TRY IT Draw a Conclusion

Students will complete Draw a Conclusion from *Summit English Language Arts 5 Activity Book*. In this activity, students will write about a conclusion they've drawn based on the reading and use details and evidence from the text (including accurate quotations) to support that conclusion.

LEARNING COACH CHECK-IN   This activity page contains open-ended questions, so it's important that you review students' responses. Give students feedback, using the sample answers provided to guide you.

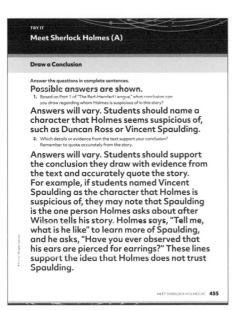

TRY IT   Practice Words from "The Red-Headed League," Part 1

Students will answer questions to demonstrate their understanding of the vocabulary words from today's reading.

WRAP-UP

Question About "The Red-Headed League," Part 1

Students will answer a question to show that they understand how to draw conclusions based on textual details and evidence, as well as how to support conclusions with accurate quotations.

Meet Sherlock Holmes (B)

Lesson Overview

ACTIVITY	ACTIVITY TITLE	TIME	ONLINE/OFFLINE
GET READY	Introduction to Meet Sherlock Holmes (B)	**1** minute	🖥️
	Spelling List 27 Activity Bank	**10** minutes	📄
	Recall "The Red-Headed League," Part 1	**5** minutes	🖥️
	Before You Read "The Red-Headed League," Parts 2 and 3	**10** minutes	🖥️
READ	"The Red-Headed League," Parts 2 and 3	**30** minutes	📄
	Check-In: "The Red-Headed League," Parts 2 and 3	**5** minutes	🖥️
LEARN AND **TRY IT**	Who Is Telling the Story?	**10** minutes	🖥️
	Examine the Importance of the Narrator	**10** minutes	📄
	Apply: Focus on the Narrator	**14** minutes	🖥️
	Write About a Different Narrator **LEARNING COACH CHECK-IN**	**15** minutes	📄
	Practice Words from "The Red-Headed League," Parts 2 and 3	**8** minutes	🖥️
WRAP-UP	Question About "The Red-Headed League," Parts 2 and 3	**2** minutes	🖥️

Content Background

Students will finish reading Sir Arthur Conan Doyle's "The Red-Headed League." They will learn about the importance and the influence of the story's narrator. They will also examine some of the story's vocabulary words.

MATERIALS

Supplied

- *Summit English Language Arts 5 Expeditions in Reading*
- *Summit English Language Arts 5 Activity Book*
  - Spelling List 27 Activity Bank
  - Write About a Different Narrator

Also Needed

- completed Spelling List 27 Pretest activity from Meet Sherlock Holmes (A)

"The Red-Headed League," Parts 2 and 3 Synopsis

Holmes and Watson go to Saxe-Coburg Square to see the home of Mr. Jabez Wilson. Holmes speaks briefly to Wilson's assistant, Vincent Spaulding, to get a look at the legs of the man's trousers. Then they examine the street behind Wilson's home and find that it is lined with businesses, including a bank. That night, Watson and Holmes meet up again and go to the bank, accompanied by the director of the bank and a police agent from Scotland Yard. They wait in the bank's vault and, in time, two would-be thieves tunnel into the vault from below. Holmes, Watson, and the police agent apprehend them, and Holmes explains what happened. Spaulding, alias John Clay, and Duncan Ross invented the Red-Headed League and hired Wilson to work for it so that he would be out of the house, and they could work on digging a tunnel from his home to the bank.

KEYWORDS

narrator – the teller of a story

Lesson Goals

- Practice all spelling words offline.
- Finish reading "The Red-Headed League."
- Explore the narrator of the story and how the narrative perspective affects the text.
- Use context clues to determine the meanings of unfamiliar words.

GET READY

Introduction to Meet Sherlock Holmes (B)

Students will get a glimpse of what they will learn about in the lesson. They will also read the lesson goals and keywords. Have students select each keyword and preview its definition.

Spelling List 27 Activity Bank

Students will practice all spelling words from the workshop by completing Spelling List 27 Activity Bank from *Summit English Language Arts 5 Activity Book*. Make sure students have their completed Spelling List 27 Pretest activity page from Meet Sherlock Holmes (A) to refer to during this activity.

Remind students to pay special attention to words they spelled incorrectly on the Spelling Pretest.

Recall "The Red-Headed League," Part 1

Students will answer some questions to review the reading that they have already completed.

Before You Read "The Red-Headed League," Parts 2 and 3

Students will be introduced to some key vocabulary words that they will encounter in the upcoming reading.

READ

"The Red-Headed League," Parts 2 and 3

Students will read Parts 2 and 3 of "The Red-Headed League" in *Expeditions in Reading*.

Check-In: "The Red-Headed League," Parts 2 and 3

Students will answer several questions to demonstrate their comprehension of Parts 2 and 3 of "The Red-Headed League."

LEARN AND TRY IT

LEARN   Who Is Telling the Story?

Students will examine the effect of having Dr. Watson as the narrator of stories about Sherlock Holmes.

TRY IT   Examine the Importance of the Narrator

Students will answer questions in which they demonstrate their understanding of how having Watson as the story's narrator affects their understanding of the text.

TRY IT   Apply: Focus on the Narrator

Students will apply to a new work what they've learned about how a narrator affects their understanding of events and characters in the text.

TRY IT   Write About a Different Narrator

Students will complete Write About a Different Narrator from *Summit English Language Arts 5 Activity Book*. They will consider how "The Red-Headed League" would be different if Holmes, rather than Watson, narrated the story.

LEARNING COACH CHECK-IN   This activity page contains an open-ended question, so it's important that you review students' responses. Give students feedback, using the sample answers provided to guide you.

> **TRY IT**
> **Meet Sherlock Holmes (B)**
>
> **Write About a Different Narrator**
>
> Answer the question in complete sentences.
>
> Dr. Watson is the narrator of "The Red-Headed League." But imagine that Holmes told the story. How would this tale be different if Holmes were the narrator?
>
> **Student responses should recognize that**
>
> - They would not know Watson's thoughts about Holmes or the other characters (unless expressed in dialogue).
> - There would be less mystery in the story, since Holmes's thoughts could be shared with readers much earlier. Readers would know that he suspected Spaulding was John Clay; they would know that he thought the criminals were attempting to tunnel into the bank; and so forth.
>
> MEET SHERLOCK HOLMES (B)   **459**

TRY IT   Practice Words from "The Red-Headed League," Parts 2 and 3

Students will answer questions to demonstrate their understanding of the vocabulary words from the reading.

WRAP-UP

Question About "The Red-Headed League," Parts 2 and 3

Students will answer a question to show that they understand how having Dr. Watson as a narrator affects their understanding of stories about Sherlock Holmes.

Meet Sherlock Holmes (C)

Lesson Overview

ACTIVITY	ACTIVITY TITLE	TIME	ONLINE/OFFLINE
GET READY	Introduction to Meet Sherlock Holmes (C)	**1** minute	🖥️
	Spelling List 27 Review Game	**10** minutes	📄
	Recall "The Red-Headed League"	**5** minutes	🖥️
	Before You Read "The Adventure of the Blue Carbuncle," Part 1	**10** minutes	🖥️
READ	"The Adventure of the Blue Carbuncle," Part 1	**30** minutes	📄
	Check-In: "The Adventure of the Blue Carbuncle," Part 1	**5** minutes	🖥️
LEARN AND TRY IT	Making Connections Between Stories	**10** minutes	🖥️
	Practice Making Connections	**10** minutes	🖥️
	Apply: Make More Connections	**14** minutes	🖥️
	Write About the Texts and Make a Prediction **LEARNING COACH CHECK-IN**	**15** minutes	📄
	Practice Words from "Blue Carbuncle," Part 1	**8** minutes	🖥️
WRAP-UP	Question About "The Adventure of the Blue Carbuncle," Part 1	**2** minutes	🖥️

Content Background

Students will begin reading Sir Arthur Conan Doyle's "The Adventure of the Blue Carbuncle." They will learn about comparing and contrasting characters, events, and ideas in different texts. They will also examine some of the story's vocabulary words.

MATERIALS

Supplied
- *Summit English Language Arts 5 Expeditions in Reading*
- *Summit English Language Arts 5 Activity Book*
  - Write About the Texts and Make a Prediction

"The Adventure of the Blue Carbuncle," Part 1 Synopsis

Watson goes to visit Sherlock Holmes two days after Christmas and finds Holmes examining a hat that a police commissioner named Peterson has brought to him. Just by observing the hat closely, Holmes can tell much about Henry Baker, the man who lost it. He explains that Baker lost the hat when he was set upon by a gang on the street and that Baker also lost his Christmas goose. Holmes wants to return the hat to Baker. Just then, Peterson arrives. He explains that there was a precious blue gemstone inside the goose that Baker dropped. Holmes knows that the stone was recently stolen, and he sets a plan in motion to try to apprehend the thief.

Lesson Goals

- Practice all spelling words online.

- Begin reading "The Adventure of the Blue Carbuncle."

- Make connections between "The Adventure of the Blue Carbuncle" and "The Red-Headed League," comparing and contrasting the two stories.

- Use context clues to determine the meanings of unfamiliar words.

GET READY

Introduction to Meet Sherlock Holmes (C)

Students will get a glimpse of what they will learn about in the lesson. They will also read the lesson goals.

Spelling List 27 Review Game

Students will practice all spelling words from the workshop.

Recall "The Red-Headed League"

Students will answer some questions to review the reading that they have already completed.

Before You Read "The Adventure of the Blue Carbuncle," Part 1

Students will be introduced to some key vocabulary words that they will encounter in the upcoming reading.

"The Adventure of the Blue Carbuncle," Part 1

Students will read Part 1 of "The Adventure of the Blue Carbuncle" in *Expeditions in Reading*.

Check-In: "The Adventure of the Blue Carbuncle," Part 1

Students will answer several questions to demonstrate their comprehension of Part 1 of "The Adventure of the Blue Carbuncle."

LEARN AND TRY IT

LEARN Making Connections Between Stories

Students will explore how to draw connections between "The Red-Headed League" and "The Adventure of the Blue Carbuncle" by comparing and contrasting characters, events, and ideas in the texts.

TRY IT Practice Making Connections

Students will answer questions in which they demonstrate their understanding of how to make connections between "The Red-Headed League" and "The Adventure of the Blue Carbuncle."

TRY IT Apply: Make More Connections

Students will apply to a new work what they've learned about making connections between its characters, events, and ideas and those in other works they have read.

TRY IT Write About the Texts and Make a Prediction

Students will complete Write About the Texts and Make a Prediction from *Summit English Language Arts 5 Activity Book*. They will consider how "The Red-Headed League" and "The Adventure of the Blue Carbuncle" are similar. Then they will make a prediction about what will happen in the remainder of "The Adventure of the Blue Carbuncle."

LEARNING COACH CHECK-IN This activity page contains open-ended questions, so it's important that you review students' responses. Give students feedback, using the sample answers provided to guide you.

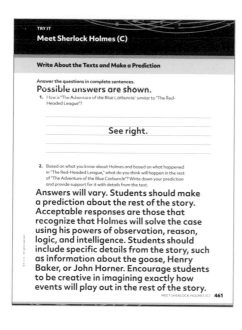

Additonal answers

1. Answers will vary.

   Similarities:

   • Both feature Sherlock Holmes and Dr. Watson.

   • Both are narrated by Watson.

   • Both relate a puzzling event/crime.

   • Both highlight Holmes's intelligence and ability to use logic.

TRY IT   Practice Words from "Blue Carbuncle," Part 1

Students will answer questions to demonstrate their understanding of the vocabulary words from the reading.

Question About "The Adventure of the Blue Carbuncle," Part 1

Students will answer a question to show that they understand how to make connections between "The Red-Headed League" and "The Adventure of the Blue Carbuncle."

Meet Sherlock Holmes (D)

Lesson Overview

ACTIVITY	ACTIVITY TITLE	TIME	ONLINE/OFFLINE
GET READY	Introduction to Meet Sherlock Holmes (D)	**1** minute	🖥️
QUIZ	Spelling List 27	**10** minutes	🖥️
GET READY	Recall "The Adventure of the Blue Carbuncle," Part 1	**5** minutes	🖥️
	Before You Read "Blue Carbuncle," Parts 2, 3, and 4	**10** minutes	🖥️
READ	"The Adventure of the Blue Carbuncle," Parts 2, 3, and 4	**30** minutes	📄
	Check-In: "Blue Carbuncle," Parts 2, 3, and 4	**5** minutes	🖥️
LEARN AND TRY IT	Implications, Consequences, and Summaries	**10** minutes	🖥️
	Explore Implications, Consequences, and Summaries	**10** minutes	🖥️
	Apply: Implications, Consequences, and Summaries	**14** minutes	🖥️
	Write a Summary of the Story **LEARNING COACH CHECK-IN**	**15** minutes	📄
	Practice Words from "Blue Carbuncle," Parts 2, 3, and 4	**8** minutes	🖥️
WRAP-UP	Question About "Blue Carbuncle," Parts 2, 3, and 4	**2** minutes	🖥️

Content Background

Students will finish reading Sir Arthur Conan Doyle's "The Adventure of the Blue Carbuncle." They will learn about implications and consequences in the text, as well as how to create an effective summary. They will also examine some of the story's vocabulary words.

MATERIALS

Supplied
- *Summit English Language Arts 5 Expeditions in Reading*
- *Summit English Language Arts 5 Activity Book*
  - Write a Summary of the Story

"The Adventure of the Blue Carbuncle," Parts 2, 3, and 4 Synopsis

Henry Baker comes to the home of Sherlock Holmes. Holmes returns Baker's hat and finds out where Baker bought the goose: the Alpha Inn. Holmes and Watson go to the Alpha Inn, and they learn that the innkeeper bought the goose from a salesman in Covent Garden. At Covent Garden, Holmes learns where the goose was raised and also meets James Ryder, a man who is looking for the goose. Holmes realizes that Ryder is the thief, and he brings Ryder back to Baker Street, letting Ryder believe that he may be able to help him find the goose. Holmes soon reveals that he knows about Ryder's crime and how he stole the gemstone. What Holmes does not know is how the blue carbuncle ended up in the goose. Ryder explains that he hid the stone in the goose, but then the goose was mistakenly sold to Baker. Ryder feels awful for what he has done, and he swears that he will never commit another crime. Holmes takes pity on Ryder and lets him go free, knowing that he has been scared straight and that the case against Horner (the man arrested for the crime) will fall apart once the jewel is returned.

KEYWORDS

consequence – what happens because of an action or event

summary – a short retelling that includes only the most important ideas or events of a text

Lesson Goals

- Take a spelling quiz.
- Finish reading "The Adventure of the Blue Carbuncle."
- Distinguish between implications and consequences in the story.
- Summarize the text.

GET READY

Introduction to Meet Sherlock Holmes (D)

Students will get a glimpse of what they will learn about in the lesson. They will also read the lesson goals and keywords. Have students select each keyword and preview its definition.

Spelling List 27

Students will complete the Spelling List 27 quiz.

Recall "The Adventure of the Blue Carbuncle," Part 1

Students will answer some questions to review the reading that they have already completed.

Before You Read "Blue Carbuncle," Parts 2, 3, and 4

Students will be introduced to some key vocabulary words that they will encounter in the upcoming reading.

"The Adventure of the Blue Carbuncle," Parts 2, 3, and 4

Students will read Parts 2, 3, and 4 of "The Adventure of the Blue Carbuncle" in *Expeditions in Reading*.

Check-In: "Blue Carbuncle," Parts 2, 3, and 4

Students will answer several questions to demonstrate their comprehension of Parts 2, 3, and 4 of "The Adventure of the Blue Carbuncle."

LEARN   Implications, Consequences, and Summaries

Students will learn how to distinguish between consequences and implications in the text, as well as how to recognize which consequences and implications are probable and which are improbable. They will also learn about the characteristics of an effective summary.

TRY IT   Explore Implications, Consequences, and Summaries

Students will answer questions in which they demonstrate their understanding of implications and consequences in "The Adventure of the Blue Carbuncle" and what makes for an effective summary of the text.

TRY IT Apply: Implications, Consequences, and Summaries

Students will apply to a new work what they've learned about distinguishing between implications and consequences before summarizing the text.

TRY IT Write a Summary of the Story

Students will complete Write a Summary of the Story from *Summit English Language Arts 5 Activity Book*. They will write a brief summary of "The Adventure of the Blue Carbuncle," including only key details and themes from the text and describing events in the correct sequence.

LEARNING COACH CHECK-IN This activity page contains an open-ended question, so it's important that you review students' responses. Give students feedback, using the sample answer provided to guide you.

TRY IT Practice Words from "Blue Carbuncle," Parts 2, 3, and 4

Students will answer a question to demonstrate their understanding of the vocabulary words from the reading.

WRAP-UP

Question About "Blue Carbuncle," Parts 2, 3, and 4

Students will answer a question to show that they understand how to recognize and distinguish between implications and consequences in "The Adventure of the Blue Carbuncle."

Meet Sherlock Holmes (E)

Lesson Overview

ACTIVITY	ACTIVITY TITLE	TIME	ONLINE/OFFLINE
GET READY	Introduction to Meet Sherlock Holmes (E)	**1** minute	🖥️
	Spelling List 28 Pretest **LEARNING COACH CHECK-IN**	**10** minutes	🖥️
	Before You Read *The Adventure of the Six Napoleons*	**9** minutes	🖥️
READ	*The Adventure of the Six Napoleons*	**30** minutes	📄
	Check-In: *The Adventure of the Six Napoleons*	**5** minutes	🖥️
LEARN AND TRY IT	Pictures Tell a Thousand Words	**10** minutes	🖥️
	Examine the Influence of Illustrations	**10** minutes	🖥️
	Apply: Graphic Novels	**15** minutes	🖥️
	Plan Your Own Graphic Mystery Story **LEARNING COACH CHECK-IN**	**20** minutes	📄
	Practice Words from *The Adventure of the Six Napoleons*	**8** minutes	🖥️
WRAP-UP	Question About *The Adventure of the Six Napoleons*	**2** minutes	🖥️

Content Background

Students will learn about graphic novels before reading a graphic novel about Sherlock Holmes called *The Adventure of the Six Napoleons*. After reading the story, students will learn about the way in which pictures in graphic novels enrich a reader's understanding of the text.

MATERIALS

Supplied
- *The Adventure of the Six Napoleons* adapted by Vincent Goodwin
- *Summit English Language Arts 5 Activity Book*
  - Spelling List 28 Pretest
  - Plan Your Own Graphic Mystery Story

The Adventure of the Six Napoleons Synopsis

Inspector Lestrade tells Sherlock Holmes of a series of robberies involving busts of Napoleon. Holmes is intrigued, since the busts themselves are worth very little money. Then, when someone is murdered during the robbery of another bust, he begins to seriously investigate the case. Holmes visits the manufacturer of the busts, as well as the two shops that sold them. He learns that a man named Beppo, previously imprisoned, might be trying to track down the busts. Holmes intentionally makes it seem as though the police are struggling with the case as a way to encourage the thief to attempt another heist. This time, Holmes sets up a sting operation, and Beppo is caught in the act. There is just one bust remaining. Holmes buys that from its owner and finds, hidden inside it, the object of Beppo's quest: a valuable black pearl.

Lesson Goals

- Take a spelling pretest.

- Learn about graphic novels.

- Read *The Adventure of the Six Napoleons*.

- Examine how visuals can shape and improve one's understanding of a text.

- Determine the meanings of unfamiliar words.

GET READY

Introduction to Meet Sherlock Holmes (E)

Students will get a glimpse of what they will learn about in the lesson. They will also read the lesson goals.

Spelling List 28 Pretest

Students will take a spelling pretest.

LEARNING COACH CHECK-IN   Have students turn to Spelling List 28 Pretest in *Summit English Language Arts 5 Activity Book* and open the online Spelling Pretest activity. Online, students will listen to the spelling word, type the word in the space indicated, and then check their answer. In the activity book, students will write the correct spelling of the word in the tables provided and indicate with a ✓ or an ✗ if they spelled the word correctly or incorrectly online. Students will repeat this process with the remaining words.

As needed, help students with the interaction between the online activity and the activity book page until they become comfortable with what they need to do. As students practice their spelling words throughout the workshop, they should pay special attention to words they spelled incorrectly on the pretest.

This is the complete list of words students will be tested on.

More Compound Words			Suffix –dom
billboard	foolproof	teammate	boredom
landscape	furthermore	woodpecker	stardom
drawbridge	headquarters	seashore	freedom
bookkeeper	jackknives		wisdom
checkbook	skyscraper		
countdown	suitcase		
driveway	sweetheart		

NOTE Have students keep their completed activity page in a safe place so they can refer to it later.

GET READY
Meet Sherlock Holmes (E)

Spelling List 28 Pretest

1. Open the Spelling Pretest activity online. Listen to the first spelling word. Type the word. Check your answer.

2. Write the correct spelling of the word in the Word column of the Spelling Pretest table on the next page.

Word	✓	✗
1 blindfold		

3. Put a check mark in the ✓ column if you spelled the word correctly online.

Word	✓	✗
1 blindfold	✓	

Put an X in the ✗ column if you spelled the word incorrectly online.

Word	✓	✗
1 blindfold		X

4. Repeat Steps 1–3 for the remaining words in the Spelling Pretest.

MEET SHERLOCK HOLMES (E) **465**

Meet Sherlock Holmes (E)

Spelling List 28 Pretest

Write each spelling word in the Word column, making sure to spell it correctly.

Word	✓	✗		Word	✓	✗
1 billboard				12 skyscraper		
2 landscape				13 suitcase		
3 drawbridge				14 sweetheart		
4 bookkeeper				15 teammate		
5 checkbook				16 woodpecker		
6 countdown				17 seashore		
7 driveway				18 boredom		
8 foolproof				19 stardom		
9 furthermore				20 freedom		
10 headquarters				21 wisdom		
11 jackknives						

Students should use the ✓ and X columns to indicate whether they spelled each word correctly or incorrectly online.

466 MEET SHERLOCK HOLMES (E)

Before You Read *The Adventure of the Six Napoleons*

Students will be introduced to some key vocabulary words that they will encounter in the upcoming reading and learn some important background about the genre of graphic novels.

The Adventure of the Six Napoleons

Students will read Sir Arthur Conan Doyle's *The Adventure of the Six Napoleons* adapted by Vincent Goodwin.

Check-In: *The Adventure of the Six Napoleons*

Students will answer several questions to demonstrate their comprehension of *The Adventure of the Six Napoleons*.

LEARN AND TRY IT

LEARN   Pictures Tell a Thousand Words

Students will learn how graphic novels use images to enhance or enrich readers' experience and help them fully understand the text.

TRY IT   Examine the Influence of Illustrations

Students will answer questions in which they demonstrate their grasp of how the images in *The Adventure of the Six Napoleons* enrich or enhance their understanding of the text.

TRY IT   Apply: Graphic Novels

Students will apply to a new work what they've learned about how pictures enhance or enrich their understanding of a text.

TRY IT   Plan Your Own Graphic Mystery Story

Students will complete Plan Your Own Graphic Mystery Story from *Summit English Language Arts 5 Activity Book*. They will brainstorm ideas for a graphic novel of their own about Sherlock Holmes. They will consider the crime that Holmes will solve in their story, where and when it will take place, which characters will be involved, and how the plot will unfold.

LEARNING COACH CHECK-IN   This activity page contains open-ended questions, so it's important that you review students' responses. Give students feedback, using the sample answers provided to guide you.

NOTE   Once completed, students should keep their planning sheet, as they will use it when they write/illustrate their graphic novel in an upcoming lesson.

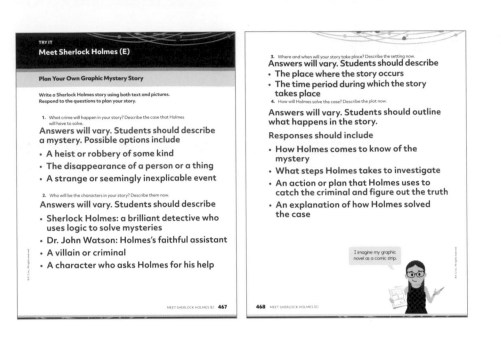

TRY IT   Practice Words from *The Adventure of the Six Napoleons*

Students will answer questions to demonstrate their understanding of the vocabulary words from the reading.

Question About *The Adventure of the Six Napoleons*

Students will answer a question to show that they understand how the images enrich or enhance reader understanding of *The Adventure of the Six Napoleons*.

Meet Sherlock Holmes (F)

Lesson Overview

ACTIVITY	ACTIVITY TITLE	TIME	ONLINE/OFFLINE
GET READY	Introduction to Meet Sherlock Holmes (F)	**1** minute	🖥️
	Spelling List 28 Activity Bank	**10** minutes	📄
	Recall *The Adventure of the Six Napoleons*	**4** minutes	🖥️
LEARN AND **TRY IT**	Images Affect Mood, Appeal, and Purpose	**10** minutes	🖥️
	Examine Mood, Appeal, and Purpose	**10** minutes	🖥️
	Apply: Visuals in Another Text	**15** minutes	🖥️
	Write a Graphic Mystery Story LEARNING COACH CHECK-IN	**68** minutes	📄
WRAP-UP	Question About Mood, Appeal, and Purpose	**2** minutes	🖥️

Content Background

Students will learn about the role of pictures in a graphic novel and how they affect the mood, appeal, and purpose of the text. They will also write a graphic-novel-style Sherlock Holmes story of their own.

Advance Preparation

Gather students' completed Spelling List 28 Pretest activity page from Meet Sherlock Holmes (E). Students will refer to this page during Get Ready: Spelling List 28 Activity Bank.

Gather students' completed Plan Your Own Graphic Mystery Story from Meet Sherlock Holmes (E). Students will refer to this page during Write a Graphic Mystery Story.

Lesson Goals

- Practice all spelling words offline.
- Explore how images can affect the mood, appeal, and purpose of a graphic novel.
- Create a graphic novel-style Sherlock Holmes story.

MATERIALS

Supplied

- *The Adventure of the Six Napoleons* adapted by Vincent Goodwin
- *Summit English Language Arts 5 Activity Book*
  - Spelling List 28 Activity Bank
  - Write a Graphic Mystery Story

Also Needed

- completed Spelling List 28 Pretest activity page from Meet Sherlock Holmes (E)
- students' completed Plan Your Own Graphic Mystery Story from Meet Sherlock Holmes (E)

Introduction to Meet Sherlock Holmes (F)

Students will get a glimpse of what they will learn about in the lesson. They will also read the lesson goals and keywords. Have students select each keyword and preview its definition.

Spelling List 28 Activity Bank

Students will practice all spelling words from the workshop by completing Spelling List 28 Activity Bank from *Summit English Language Arts 5 Activity Book*. Make sure students have their completed Spelling List 28 Pretest activity page from Meet Sherlock Holmes (E) to refer to during this activity.

Remind students to pay special attention to words they spelled incorrectly on the Spelling Pretest.

Recall *The Adventure of the Six Napoleons*

Students will answer some questions to review the reading that they have already completed.

LEARN AND TRY IT

LEARN   Images Affect Mood, Appeal, and Purpose

Students will learn how the images in a graphic novel can shape the mood of the story, its appeal to readers, and whether or not the writer achieves his or her purpose.

TRY IT Examine Mood, Appeal, and Purpose

Students will answer questions in which they demonstrate their understanding of how the images in the story affect its mood, appeal, and purpose.

TRY IT Apply: Visuals in Another Text

Students will apply to a new work what they've learned about how images affect a text's mood, appeal and purpose.

TRY IT Write a Graphic Mystery Story

Students will complete Write a Graphic Mystery Story from *Summit English Language Arts 5 Activity Book*. They will use the plan they created in Meet Sherlock Holmes (E) to guide their writing. For this reason, be sure that students have the activity book page entitled Plan Your Own Graphic Mystery Story from that lesson with them as they work.

LEARNING COACH CHECK-IN   This activity page contains a writing assignment. Students are expected to take more than an hour to complete it. Several pages have been provided for this purpose.

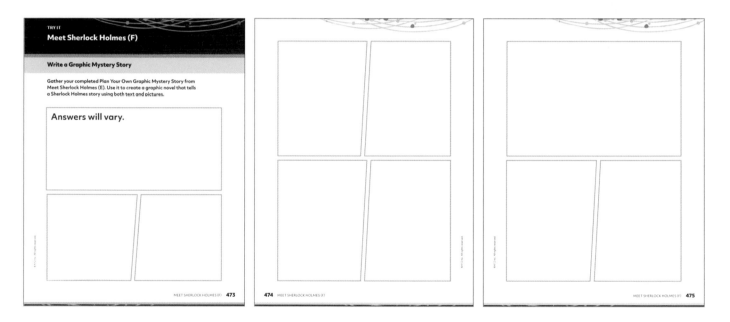

WRAP-UP

Question About Mood, Appeal, and Purpose

Students will answer a question to show that they understand how the images in a graphic novel can affect how readers understand the text.

Meet Sherlock Holmes (G)

Lesson Overview

ACTIVITY	ACTIVITY TITLE	TIME	ONLINE/OFFLINE
GET READY	Introduction to Meet Sherlock Holmes (G)	**1** minute	🖥
	Spelling List 28 Practice	**10** minutes	📶
	Before You Read "The Adventure of the Three Students"	**14** minutes	📶
READ	"The Adventure of the Three Students"	**30** minutes	📄
	Check-In: "The Adventure of the Three Students"	**5** minutes	📶
LEARN AND **TRY IT**	Mystery Stories vs. Mystery Plays	**10** minutes	📶
	Compare Genres	**10** minutes	📶
	Apply: Explore Another Drama	**15** minutes	📶
	Write About Your Reactions **LEARNING COACH CHECK-IN**	**15** minutes	📄
	Practice Words from "The Adventure of the Three Students"	**8** minutes	📶
WRAP-UP	Question About "The Adventure of the Three Students"	**2** minutes	📶

Content Background

Students will read a dramatic adaptation of "The Adventure of the Three Students." They will learn about comparing and contrasting plays and short stories, as well as comparing and contrasting works within the same genre. They will also examine some of the text's vocabulary words.

MATERIALS

Supplied
- *Summit English Language Arts 5 Expeditions in Reading*
- *Summit English Language Arts 5 Activity Book*
  - Write About Your Reactions

"The Adventure of the Three Students" Synopsis

Holmes and Watson are in Oxford when a university professor named Soames comes to them for help. He believes that a student has stolen part of an important exam he is about to give. Holmes agrees to investigate the situation, and he zeroes in on three possible culprits. By gathering clues and using logic, Holmes deduces that the guilty party is a student named Giles Gilchrist. Gilchrist is the only one tall enough to see the exam papers through Soames's window. He is the only one who could have left behind certain clues (lumps of clay from the university's track and a tear caused by his spikes). And he is the only one whom Bannister, Soames's servant, would try to protect. Gilchrist confesses to the deed, and he promises to withdraw from the university.

Lesson Goals

- Practice all spelling words online.
- Read "The Adventure of the Three Students."
- Compare and contrast a play about Sherlock Holmes with short stories about him.
- Use context clues to determine the meanings of unfamiliar words.

GET READY

Introduction to Meet Sherlock Holmes (G)
Students will get a glimpse of what they will learn about in the lesson. They will also read the lesson goals.

Spelling List 28 Practice
Students will practice all spelling words from the workshop.

Before You Read "The Adventure of the Three Students"
Students will be introduced to some key vocabulary words that they will encounter in the upcoming reading and learn some important characteristics of dramas.

READ

"The Adventure of the Three Students"
Students will read "The Adventure of the Three Students" in *Expeditions in Reading*.

Check-In: "The Adventure of the Three Students"

Students will answer several questions to demonstrate their comprehension of "The Adventure of the Three Students."

LEARN   Mystery Stories vs. Mystery Plays

Students will explore how to compare and contrast the short stories about Sherlock Holmes with the play about him.

TRY IT   Compare Genres

Students will answer questions in which they demonstrate their understanding of how to compare and contrast short stories and plays about the same characters and the same types of events.

TRY IT   Apply: Explore Another Drama

Students will apply to a new work what they've learned about comparing and contrasting texts.

TRY IT   Write About Your Reactions

Students will complete Write About Your Reactions from *Summit English Language Arts 5 Activity Book*. They will explain which text they enjoyed most and why, citing the characteristics that they found most appealing.

LEARNING COACH CHECK-IN   This activity page contains an open-ended question, so it's important that you review students' responses. Give students feedback, using the sample answers provided to guide you.

TRY IT
Meet Sherlock Holmes (G)

Write About Your Reactions

Respond in complete sentences.

You have read two short stories, one graphic novel, and one play about Sherlock Holmes. Which of these four works did you like best? What did you like about it? How does the genre (category or type of literature) of the work—short story, graphic novel, play—affect your opinion of it?

Answers will vary. Appropriate answers will

- **Identify the work students most enjoyed.**
- **Provide reasons for selecting this work. Reasons may relate to plot events, character behaviors, setting, or any other element that students enjoyed.**
- **Explain why a particular genre is interesting.For instance, students might enjoy one of the short stories because they like having Watson serve as a narrator.**

MEET SHERLOCK HOLMES (G)   **477**

TRY IT   Practice Words from "The Adventure of the Three Students"

Students will answer questions to demonstrate their understanding of the vocabulary words from the reading.

Question About "The Adventure of the Three Students"

Students will answer a question to show that they understand how to compare and contrast works of drama and prose stories.

Meet Sherlock Holmes (H)

Lesson Overview

ACTIVITY	ACTIVITY TITLE	TIME	ONLINE/OFFLINE
GET READY	Introduction to Meet Sherlock Holmes (H)	**1** minute	🖥
	Spelling List 28 Review Game	**10** minutes	🖥
	Recall "The Adventure of the Three Students"	**5** minutes	🖥
LEARN AND **TRY IT**	Listening vs. Reading	**42** minutes	🖥
	Listen Up	**10** minutes	🖥
	Apply: Hear It Out Loud	**35** minutes	🖥
	Write About Listening to a Text **LEARNING COACH CHECK-IN**	**15** minutes	📄
WRAP-UP	Question About Listening	**2** minutes	🖥

Content Background

Students will listen to several snippets of "The Adventure of the Three Students" being read aloud. They will learn how listening to a text in this way can improve their understanding and appreciation of it.

Lesson Goals

- Practice all spelling words online.

- Compare the text of "The Adventure of the Three Students" with an audio presentation of the play.

MATERIALS

Supplied
- *Summit English Language Arts 5 Expeditions in Reading*
- *Summit English Language Arts 5 Activity Book*
  - Write About Listening to a Text

GET READY

Introduction to Meet Sherlock Holmes (H)

Students will get a glimpse of what they will learn about in the lesson. They will also read the lesson goals.

Spelling List 28 Review Game

Students will practice all spelling words from the workshop.

Recall "The Adventure of the Three Students"

Students will answer some questions to review the reading that they have already completed.

LEARN AND **TRY IT**

LEARN   Listening vs. Reading

Students will explore how hearing a text being read aloud affects and improves their understanding of it.

TRY IT   Listen Up

Students will answer questions in which they demonstrate their understanding of the influence of hearing a text read aloud.

TRY IT   Apply: Hear It Out Loud

Students will apply to a new work what they've learned about reading and listening to a text and the value of doing both when possible.

TRY IT   Write About Listening to a Text

Students will complete Write About Listening to a Text from *Summit English Language Arts 5 Activity Book*. They will describe why listening to a text being read aloud is a valuable experience for readers.

LEARNING COACH CHECK-IN   This activity page contains an open-ended question, so it's important that you review students' responses. Give students feedback, using the sample answers provided to guide you.

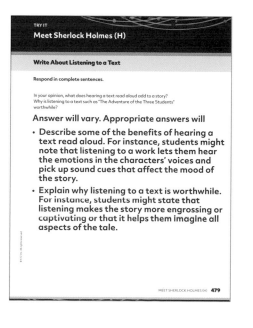

Question About Listening

Students will answer a question to show that they understand the value of listening to a text being read aloud.

Meet Sherlock Holmes Wrap-Up

Lesson Overview

ACTIVITY	ACTIVITY TITLE	TIME	ONLINE/OFFLINE
GET READY	Introduction to Meet Sherlock Holmes Wrap-Up	**1** minute	🖥️
TRY IT	Write About Sherlock Holmes **LEARNING COACH CHECK-IN**	**30** minutes	📄
	Read and Record	**10** minutes	🖥️
	Review Meet Sherlock Holmes	**20** minutes	🖥️
QUIZ	Meet Sherlock Holmes	**30** minutes	🖥️
	Spelling List 28	**10** minutes	🖥️
WRAP-UP	Keyboarding	**10** minutes	🖥️
	More Language Arts Practice	**9** minutes	🖥️

Content Background

Students will write about the character of Sherlock Holmes and his enduring popularity. Students will then have an opportunity to review the texts from this workshop before demonstrating their knowledge of them on a quiz.

Advance Preparation

During the Keyboarding activity, students will practice their keyboarding skills using an external website or program. **You will need to work with students to select an appropriate keyboarding practice website or program; K12 does not specify which resource to use.** A few suggestions are provided in the online activity.

Depending on which program you choose, students may need to set up an account to save their progress. If needed, assist students in setting up and running their chosen keyboarding practice program.

> ### MATERIALS
>
> **Supplied**
> - *The Adventure of the Six Napoleons* by Vincent Goodwin
> - *Summit English Language Arts 5 Expeditions in Reading*
> - *Summit English Language Arts 5 Activity Book*
> - Write About Sherlock Holmes

Lesson Goals

- Take a spelling quiz.

- Write about the character of Sherlock Holmes.

- Read and record text with fluency.

- Demonstrate knowledge, using quotes and evidence to support conclusions.

- Explain how the narrator's perspective influences how events in a text are described.

- Summarize a text, including its theme and relevant details.

- Explain and analyze how visuals enrich a text for readers.

- Compare and contrast how plot is developed among stories in different genres.

- Compare and contrast the way stories are presented in text and aloud.

GET READY

Introduction to Meet Sherlock Holmes Wrap-Up

Students will read the lesson goals.

TRY IT

Write About Meet Sherlock Holmes

Students will complete Write About Sherlock Holmes from *Summit English Language Arts 5 Activity Book*. They will offer their opinion as to why the character of Sherlock Holmes, despite being created more than 130 years ago, remains so interesting and popular with audiences.

LEARNING COACH CHECK-IN   This activity page contains an open-ended question, so it's important that you review students' responses. Give students feedback, using the sample answers provided to guide you.

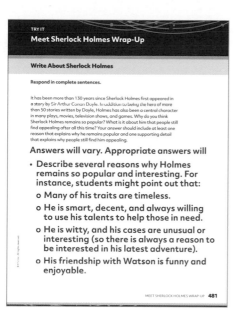

Read and Record

Good readers read quickly, smoothly, and with expression. This is called *fluency*. Students will record themselves reading aloud. They will listen to their recording and think about how quick, smooth, and expressive they sound.

TIP Encourage students to rerecord as needed.

Review Meet Sherlock Holmes

Students will answer questions to review what they have learned in the Meet Sherlock Holmes workshop.

QUIZ

Meet Sherlock Holmes

Students will complete the Meet Sherlock Holmes quiz.

Spelling List 28

Students will complete the Spelling List 28 quiz.

WRAP-UP

Keyboarding

Students will practice their keyboarding skills using an external website or program.

More Language Arts Practice

Students will practice skills according to their individual needs.

Presentation: Revising

Lesson Overview

ACTIVITY	ACTIVITY TITLE	TIME	ONLINE/OFFLINE
GET READY	Introduction to Presentation: Revising	**2** minutes	🖥️
	Look Back at an Informational Presentation	**15** minutes	🖥️
LEARN AND TRY IT	Revising an Informational Presentation	**20** minutes	🖥️
	Revise Your Informational Presentation **LEARNING COACH CHECK-IN**	**60** minutes	📶 and 📄
WRAP-UP	Question About Revising an Informational Presentation	**3** minutes	🖥️
	Go Read!	**20** minutes	📶 or 📄

Content Background

Students will continue working on their **informational presentation about a historical figure**, a presentation that they created in PowerPoint. In this lesson, students will **revise** their presentation in PowerPoint.

Writing Process

| 1 Prewriting | 2 Drafting | **3 Revising** | 4 Proofreading | 5 Publishing |

To revise their presentation, students will use a checklist. The checklist focuses on content (*Do I provide enough facts I found during research to support the main idea of each slide?*) and organization (*Does the order of the body slides make sense?*). Using the checklist, students will revise the content and organization of all aspects of their presentation: the text, the media, and the audio that they recorded.

Students may not understand the difference between revising and proofreading. When revising, writers and speakers focus on large issues, such as the order of ideas. When proofreading, writers and speakers fix errors in grammar, usage, and mechanics, such as spelling or punctuation mistakes.

Encourage students to focus on revision during this lesson. In the next lesson (Presentation: Proofreading), students will proofread. Additionally, students should not focus on the clarity or pace of their recorded audio in this lesson. Those speaking skills are included on the checklist in Presentation: Proofreading.

MATERIALS

Supplied

- *Summit English Language Arts 5 Activity Book*
  - Revise Your Informational Presentation
- Model Presentation (PowerPoint file)
- Presentation Template (PowerPoint file)
- Informational Presentation: Revision Feedback Sheet (printout)
- Presentation Instructions (printout)

Also Needed

- students' presentation draft from Presentation: Drafting (B)
- folder in which students are storing presentation assignment pages
- reading material for Go Read!

Advance Preparation

Help students locate their draft presentation that they saved to the computer in Presentation: Drafting (B).

Gather the folder that students are using to store the activity pages related to their presentation. The folder should contain the following:

- Students' completed Plan for Your Presentation activity page from Presentation: Planning

- Students' completed research notes from Presentation: Research

Prior to the Revise Your Informational Presentation activity in this lesson, review students' draft presentation and complete Informational Presentation: Revision Feedback Sheet.

During the Go Read! activity, students will have the option of using the digital library. Allow extra time for students to make their reading selection, or have students make a selection before beginning the lesson.

KEYWORDS

revising – the stage or step of the writing process in which the writer goes back, rereads the piece, and makes changes in content or organization

Lesson Goals

- Use a checklist to revise your presentation.

- Read for pleasure.

GET READY

Introduction to Presentation: Revising

Students will get a glimpse of what they will learn about in the lesson. They will also read the lesson goals and keywords. Have students select each keyword and preview its definition.

Look Back at an Informational Presentation

Students will review a model informational presentation about a historical figure and explore what makes it successful.

LEARN AND TRY IT

LEARN   Revising an Informational Presentation

Through a guided activity, students will explore how to revise a sample informational presentation about a historical figure.

TRY IT Revise Your Informational Presentation

Students will complete Revise Your Informational Presentation from *Summit English Language Arts 5 Activity Book*. They will need the draft of their informational presentation about a historical figure, which they completed and saved to the computer in Presentation: Drafting (B).

LEARNING COACH CHECK-IN Guide students through the revision process.

1. Gather and use the Informational Presentation: Revision Feedback Sheet that you filled out to guide a discussion with students.

    • Tell students the strengths of their presentation. Provide positive comments about the ideas, language, detail, or other elements of the presentation that you enjoyed.

    • Walk through your feedback with students.

    • As you discuss your feedback, encourage students to actively revise their draft in response. Reassure students that it's okay to remove or move around text, media, and even slides. Students should revise their draft directly in PowerPoint. That includes revising audio as necessary by using the PowerPoint recording tool.

2. Have students review and revise their presentation draft once more, using the Revise Your Presentation activity page to guide them.

    • For students having difficulty recognizing areas they should revise, suggest a revision, and think aloud to model your revising. For example: *The events you describe on Slide 5 happened right after the events on Slide 3. Would it make sense to move Slide 5 right after Slide 3 so that the slides are in time order? Or is there a different way to organize the body slides?*

3. Make sure students save their revised draft in a folder on the computer. Help students give their revised draft a new file name in case they want to revisit their original draft.

TIP Remind students to focus on the checklist questions. Emphasize that they should not worry about spelling, punctuation, grammar, and so on.

NOTE If you or students wish, you can download and print another copy of the Presentation Instructions online. The Model Presentation and Presentation Template are also available online as references.

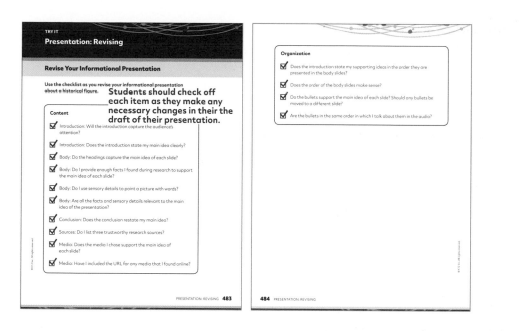

Question About Revising an Informational Presentation

Students will answer a question to show that they understand a key revision skill.

Go Read!

Students will read for pleasure. They should choose a book or a magazine that interests them, or they may choose a selection from the digital library, linked in the online lesson.

Students should read for the entire time. Have students select something to read ahead of time to help them stay focused.

Presentation: Proofreading

Lesson Overview

ACTIVITY	ACTIVITY TITLE	TIME	ONLINE/OFFLINE
GET READY	Introduction to Presentation: Proofreading	**2** minutes	🖥️
	Look Back at Combining, Expanding, and Reducing Sentences	**15** minutes	🖥️
LEARN AND **TRY IT**	Proofreading an Informational Presentation	**20** minutes	🖥️
	Proofread Your Informational Presentation LEARNING COACH CHECK-IN	**60** minutes	🖥️ and 📄
WRAP-UP	Question About Proofreading an Informational Presentation	**3** minutes	🖥️
	Go Read!	**20** minutes	🖥️ or 📄

Content Background

Students will continue working on their **informational presentation about a historical figure**, a presentation that they created in PowerPoint. In this lesson, students will **proofread** their revised presentation in PowerPoint.

Writing Process

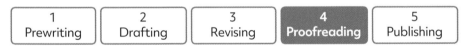

1 Prewriting   2 Drafting   3 Revising   **4 Proofreading**   5 Publishing

To proofread their presentation, students will use a checklist. The checklist focuses on grammar (*Are all sentences complete and correct?*), usage (*Are there sentences that can be reduced to get rid of redundant words?*), and mechanics (*Is every word spelled correctly, including frequently confused words?*).

The checklist also focuses on the speaking skills of pace and clarity. *Pace* refers to how quickly or slowly someone speaks. *Clarity* refers to correct pronunciation of words, as well as appropriate volume.

Proofreading is sometimes called *editing*.

Advance Preparation

Help students locate their revised presentation that they saved to the computer in Presentation: Revising.

MATERIALS

Supplied
- *Summit English Language Arts 5 Activity Book*
  - Proofread Your Informational Presentation
- Model Presentation (PowerPoint file)
- Presentation Template (PowerPoint file)
- Informational Presentation: Proofreading Feedback Sheet (printout)
- Presentation Instructions (printout)

Also Needed
- students' revised presentation from Presentation: Revising
- folder in which students are storing presentation assignment pages
- reading material for Go Read!

Gather the folder that students are using to store the activity pages related to their presentation. The folder should contain the following:

- Students' completed Plan for Your Presentation activity page from Presentation: Planning

- Students' completed research notes from Presentation: Research

Prior to the Proofread Your Informational Presentation activity in this lesson, review students' revised presentation and complete Informational Presentation: Proofreading Feedback Sheet.

During the Go Read! activity, students will have the option of using the digital library. Allow extra time for students to make their reading selection, or have students make a selection before beginning the lesson.

KEYWORDS

pace – the speed, and the change of speeds, of a speaker's delivery

proofreading – the stage or step of the writing process in which the writer checks for errors in grammar, punctuation, capitalization, and spelling

Lesson Goals

- Use a checklist to proofread your presentation.

- Read for pleasure.

GET READY

Introduction to Presentation: Proofreading
Students will get a glimpse of what they will learn about in the lesson. They will also read the lesson goals and keywords. Have students select each keyword and preview its definition.

Look Back at Combining, Expanding, and Reducing Sentences
Students will review how to combine, expand, and reduce sentences for meaning, reader interest, and style.

LEARN AND TRY IT

LEARN   Proofreading an Informational Presentation
Through a guided activity, students will explore how to proofread a sample student informational presentation about a historical figure.

TRY IT   Proofread Your Informational Presentation
Students will complete Proofread Your Informational Presentation from *Summit English Language Arts 5 Activity Book*. They will need their revised informational presentation about a historical figure, which they saved to the computer in Presentation: Revising.

Guide students through the proofreading process.

1. Have students proofread the text in their presentation for grammar, usage, and mechanics.

   • Have students slowly read the text aloud on each slide, listening for errors and opportunities for improvement, such as missing words, incomplete sentences, agreement errors, wordiness, and word choice. As students catch errors, have them fix the errors in PowerPoint.

2. Have students review the audio for pace, clarity, sentence structure, and word choice. Follow this process for each slide.

   • Have students listen to the audio that they recorded. As they listen, they should note any words that they did not pronounce clearly, as well as any issues with pace or volume. Students should also listen for sentences that can be combined, expanded, or reduced to improve meaning, audience interest, and style, as well as for language that is too formal or informal. For example, students may notice that combining sentences can make it clear how two ideas relate.

   • Have students practice their speech before they rerecord it. Give students feedback to help them fix issues related to pronunciation, pace, volume, sentence structure, and word choice.

   • When students are ready, have them rerecord the audio.

SUPPORT   For the audio on the first slide, point out and explain ways that students can make improvements.

3. Have students review their presentation once more, using the Proofread Your Informational Presentation activity page. Note that some of the items on the checklist listed under Grammar and Usage apply to both the text and audio. Students should fix any additional errors that they find.

4. Have students save their presentation in a folder on the computer. Help students give their edited presentation a new file name in case they want to revisit their previous version.

OPTIONAL   Have students exchange presentations with a peer and use the Informational Presentation: Proofreading Feedback Sheet to proofread the other student's presentation.

NOTE   If you or students wish, you can download and print another copy of the Presentation Instructions online. The Model Presentation and Presentation Template are also available online as references.

Students should check off each item as they make necessary changes in the revised draft of their presentation.

WRAP-UP

Question About Proofreading an Informational Presentation

Students will answer a question to show that they understand a key proofreading skill.

Go Read!

Students will read for pleasure. They should choose a book or a magazine that interests them, or they may choose a selection from the digital library, linked in the online lesson.

Students should read for the entire time. Have students select something to read ahead of time to help them stay focused.

Presentation: Publishing

Lesson Overview

ACTIVITY	ACTIVITY TITLE	TIME	ONLINE/OFFLINE
GET READY	Introduction to Presentation: Publishing	**2** minutes	🖥️
LEARN AND **TRY IT**	Reflecting on an Informational Presentation	**20** minutes	🖥️
	Reflect on Your Informational Presentation	**40** minutes	🖥️ and 📄
	Present Your Informational Presentation **LEARNING COACH CHECK-IN**	**25** minutes	🖥️
WRAP-UP	Turn In Your Informational Presentation	**1** minute	🖥️
	Keyboarding	**10** minutes	🖥️
	More Language Arts Practice	**22** minutes	🖥️

Content Background

Students will reflect on and share their **informational presentation about a historical figure**. In this lesson, they will also submit their presentation to their teacher.

Writing Process

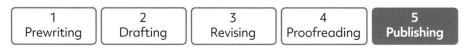

| 1 Prewriting | 2 Drafting | 3 Revising | 4 Proofreading | **5 Publishing** |

NOTE   During the reflection activities, students will think about ways they could share and publish their presentation. Because of potential media copyright issues, however, students should not actually publish their presentations. Publishing includes sharing their presentations online via social media or personal websites.

Advance Preparation

Help students locate their edited presentation that they saved to the computer in Presentation: Proofreading. They will need to refer to their presentation in several of the activities.

During the Keyboarding activity, students will practice their keyboarding skills using an external website or program. **You will need to work with students to select an appropriate keyboarding practice website or**

MATERIALS

Supplied
- *Summit English Language Arts 5 Activity Book*
  - Reflect on Your Informational Presentation

Also Needed
- students' edited presentation from Presentation: Proofreading

program; K12 does not specify which resource to use. A few suggestions are provided in the online activity.

Depending on which program you choose, students may need to set up an account to save their progress. If needed, assist students in setting up and running their chosen keyboarding practice program.

Lesson Goals

- Reflect on audience and purpose in a presentation.
- Learn about publishing a presentation.
- Share your presentation with your Learning Coach.
- Submit your presentation to your teacher.

GET READY

Introduction to Presentation: Publishing
Students will read the lesson goals.

LEARN AND TRY IT

LEARN Reflecting on an Informational Presentation

Students will explore how the author of a presentation reflects on audience and purpose. They will also learn how audience and purpose affect where an author might choose to share or publish a presentation.

TRY IT Reflect on Your Informational Presentation

Students will complete Reflect on Your Presentation from *Summit English Language Arts 5 Activity Book*. As they complete this activity, they will need to refer to their informational presentation about a historical figure, which they saved to the computer in Presentation: Proofreading.

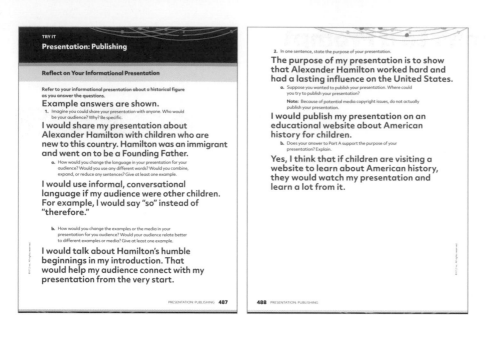

TRY IT   Present Your Informational Presentation

Students will present their informational presentation about a historical figure to their Learning Coach.

LEARNING COACH CHECK-IN   Watch students present their informational presentation. After they finish, give specific praise and ask thoughtful questions. For example:

- *I like how Slides 3 and 4 show contrasting ideas. That made me think about your historical figure in a new way.*

- *That fact surprised me. Where did you learn that? Did anything you learned surprise you?*

WRAP-UP

Turn In Your Informational Presentation

Students will submit their informational presentation about a historical figure to their teacher.

Keyboarding

Students will practice their keyboarding skills using an external website or program.

More Language Arts Practice

Students will practice skills according to their individual needs.

Big Ideas: Respond to a Prompt

Lesson Overview

Big Ideas lessons provide students the opportunity to further apply the knowledge acquired and skills learned throughout the unit workshops. Each Big Ideas lesson consists of these parts:

1. **Cumulative Review:** Students keep their skills fresh by reviewing prior content.

2. **Preview:** Students practice answering the types of questions they will commonly find on standardized tests.

3. **Synthesis:** Students complete an assignment that allows them to connect and apply what they have learned. Synthesis assignments vary throughout the course.

   In the Synthesis portion of this Big Ideas lesson, students will respond to an essay prompt based on reading selections. To respond meaningfully, students will need to use their own ideas as well as examples from the readings. Students' writing will be assessed in four categories: purpose and content; structure and organization; language and word choice; and grammar, usage, and mechanics.

   LEARNING COACH CHECK-IN   This is a graded assessment. Make sure students complete, review, and submit the assignment to their teacher.

All materials needed for this lesson are linked online and not provided in the Activity Book.

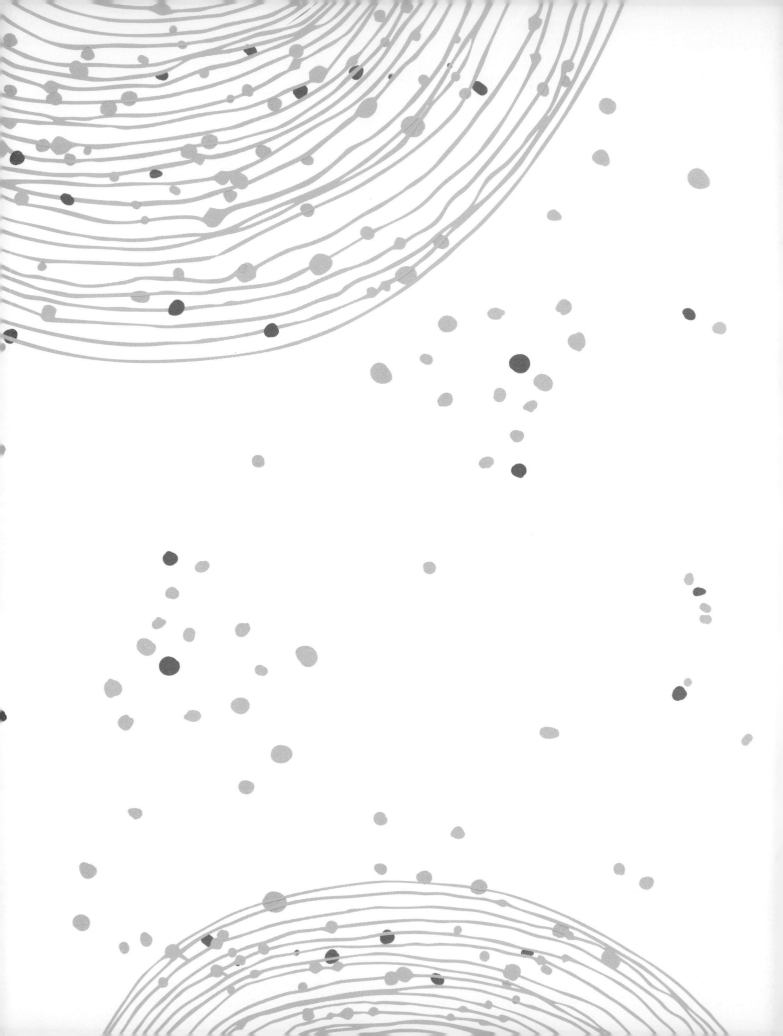